Holding
CHARLESTON
by the Bridle

---※---

Castle Pinckney and the Civil War

W. Clifford Roberts, Jr.
and Matthew A. M. Locke

SB
Savas Beatie
California

© 2024 W. Clifford Roberts, Jr. and Matthew A. M. Locke

All rights reserved. No part of this publication may be reproduced, stored in a retrieval system, or transmitted, in any form or by any means, electronic, mechanical, photocopying, recording, or otherwise, without the prior written permission of the publisher.

First edition, first printing

ISBN-13: 978-1-61121-714-8 (hardcover)
ISBN-13: 978-1-954547-65-0 (ebook)

Library of Congress Cataloging-in-Publication Data

Names: Roberts, William Clifford, Jr., 1958- author. | Locke, Matthew A. M., 1974- author.
Title: Holding Charleston by the Bridle: Castle Pinckney and the Civil War / W. Clifford Roberts, Jr. & Matthew A. M. Locke.
Other titles: Castle Pinckney and the Civil War
Description: El Dorado Hills : Savas Beatie LLC [2024] | Includes bibliographical references and index. | Summary: "This is the first book on the subject, from the fort's innovative design as part of America's "Second System" of coastal fortifications to the modern challenges of preserving its weathered brick walls against rising sea levels. It uses primary research and archaeological evidence to tell the full story of the Castle for the first time. Given its importance to America's history, it is a history long overdue"-- Provided by publisher.
Identifiers: LCCN 2024012292 | ISBN 9781611217148 (hardcover) | ISBN 9781954547650 (ebook)
Subjects: LCSH: Castle Pinckney (Charleston, S.C.) | Fortification--South Carolina--Charleston--Design and construction--History--19th century. | Charleston (S.C.)--Buildings, structures, etc. | Castle Pinckney National Monument (Charleston, S.C.) | Charleston (S.C.)--History, Military.
Classification: LCC F279.C48 C373 2024 | DDC 975.7/915--dc23/eng/20240321
LC record available at https://lccn.loc.gov/2024012292

SB

Savas Beatie
989 Governor Drive, Suite 102
El Dorado Hills, CA 95762
916-941-6896 / sales@savasbeatie.com / www.savasbeatie.com

All of our titles are available at special discount rates for bulk purchases in the United States. Contact us for information.

Printed and bound in the United Kingdom

Jacqueline Locke and Abigail Locke—wife and daughter
for their patience and support.

Vicki Roberts and Trey and Katy Roberts—wife and children
for their benevolence.

Friends and family for their support and encouragement.

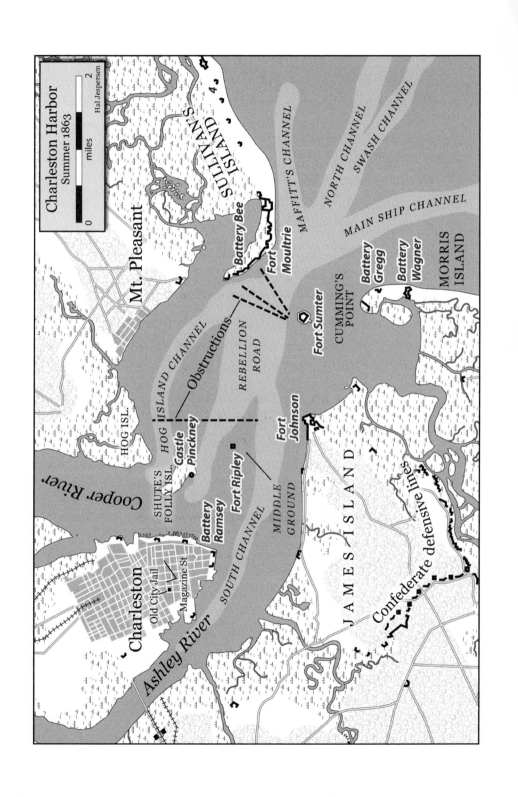

TABLE OF CONTENTS

Foreword   ix

Acknowledgments   xi

A Glossary of Significant Fortification Terms   xiii

Castle Pinckney Biographies   xvii

Chapter 1: Before There Was a Castle on Shute's Folly   1

Chapter 2: Building a Castle (1807–1828)   13

Chapter 3: Lynchpin of the Nullification Crisis (1829-1834)   25

Chapter 4: A Convenient Repository (1835-1859)   37

Chapter 5: Scaling Ladders (1860)   53

Chapter 6: Declaring Southern Independence (1861)   69

Chapter 7: A Prison by the Sea (1861-1862)   89

Chapter 8: A Small Artillery Garrison (1862)   113

Chapter 9: Circles of Fire (1863)   125

Chapter 10: The Middle Ground (1863-1864)   137

Chapter 11: Lowering the Stainless Banner (1864-1865)   149

Chapter 12: American Bastille (1865-1875)   161

Chapter 13: Lighthouse Depot (1876-1916)   175

Chapter 14: Holding the Hot Potato (1916 -2011)   191

Epilogue   201

Appendix 1: Patriotic Toasts Given at the Naming Ceremony   207

Appendix 2: 1814 Resolution Written from Castle Pinckney   207

Appendix 3: Clothing Received at Castle Pinckney   208

Appendix 4: An 1834 "Memorial" Petition   209

Appendix 5: Field & Staff Officers of the 1st Rifles, South Carolina Militia   210

Appendix 6: 1858 Returns of Officers and Privates in the Meagher Guard   210

TABLE OF CONTENTS
(continued)

Appendix 7: Roster of the Washington Light Infantry   211

Appendix 8: A Newpaper Description of Castle Pinckney   215

Appendix 9: Confederate Signal System   215

Appendix 10: Record of the Baltimore Volunteers   216

Appendix 11: 1861 Castle Pinckney Armaments Inventory   219

Appendix 12: List of Union Prisoners of War   220

Appendix 13: Muster Roll of the Charleston Zouave Cadets   222

Appendix 14: Roster of 1st Regiment South Carolina Artillery Officers   223

Appendix 15: 1st South Carolina Artillery Companies   225

Appendix 16: List of Prisoners from the 54th Massachusetts   231

Appendix 17: Record of Prisoners Confined at Military Prison   232

Appendix 18: 1895 Memoir of Jane E. Chichester   234

Bibliography   239

Index   249

About the Authors   260

Photos have been placed throughout the text for the convenience of the reader.

LIST OF ABBREVIATIONS

ARLHB	Annual Report of the Light-House Bureau
ASP	American State Papers, 1789-1819
CSS	Confederate States Ship
CWSR	Civil War Service Records
DFJP	David Flavel Jamison Papers
OAG	Letters Received by the Office of the Adjutant General, 1822-1860
OR	Official Records of the Union and Confederate Armies
RG	Record Group
RMP	Returns from Military Posts, 1806-1916
SCHM	*South Carolina Historical Magazine*
SCHS	South Carolina Historical Society
TBGD	Thomas Butler Gunn Diaries
USLHT	United States Lighthouse Tender
USCI	United States Colored Infantry
USS	United States Ship

Foreword

Charleston Harbor is imbued with history. Its natural features of depth, location and climate have made it instrumental to the founding of Charleston and to the successful economies that have supported the rise of the city and the state. Defending the harbor from foreign invaders has been and continues to be a major consideration. We tend to forget that protecting coastal seaports in the 19th century was instrumental to the success of the United States. Castle Pinckney was a major component of this military strategy to secure this magnificent Southern harbor and provide safety for the inhabitants of Charleston.

It is a truism that we tend to forget those things that are not immediately a factor in our lives. A corollary to that idea is that, for those things that are not immediately apparent, it is a requirement that repetition of presentation or the tie-in to a seminal event will raise the visibility of those things to at least a level of nodding acquaintance. Unfortunately, much that is repeated, either through curriculums or commemoration of historic events, is overly simplified. These accounts lack context, leave off important actors, and do not provide a meaningful framework for integrating the event, place, concept, or people into a richer understanding of one's community or society.

Castle Pinckney is one such place. It is attached to a series of events and personages that has until now fallen through the cracks. Most people are aware of Fort Sumter, but far fewer are aware of Castle Pinckney. This is unfortunate. These two harbor fortifications share a timeline, a series of political landscapes, and many of the same social and economic issues. They weren't produced in isolation but as a tactical and strategic solution to an existential problem.

The chapters of this volume are presented thematically and chronologically. The first chapters cover the founding of Castle Pinckney as the second fortification on the island of Shute's Folly. The next chapters leading to the outbreak of the Civil War firmly cement Castle Pinckney into the economic difficulties and political landscape that defined this antebellum period. Special note should be taken of the use of the Castle as a prisoner of war camp in 1861. It was the creation of the Lieber Code during the American Civil War that eventually led to the Geneva Conventions. Fortunately, Castle Pinckney was a humane prisoner of war camp. This is noteworthy as camps of this form were in short supply on both sides of that terrible conflict. The final chapters deal with Castle Pinckney's new life as a depot for the Lighthouse Service, and, after 1916, its waning importance and its eventual slipping away from the thoughts of the general public.

The preservation of forts such as Castle Pinckney and their connecting threads to both the past and present are essential. They are the physical manifestation of the past decisions, people, and events that underpin our present.

Jonathan Leader, PhD
South Carolina State Archaeologist
South Carolina Institute for Archeology and Anthropology

Acknowledgments

We are indebted to several great people and institutions that have shared their time, expertise, and collections with us. We wish to acknowledge Edward Blessing, South Caroliniana Library, The University of South Carolina, Giles Dawkes, UCL Institute of Archeology, Byron Faildey, Washington and Lee University, John Fisher & Dr. John Leader, South Carolina Institute for Archeology and Anthropology, Lisa Hayes, Charleston Library Society, James M. Holland, Fort Sumter SCV Camp 1269, Joe Long, Confederate Relic Room, Robert D. Mikell, Castle Pinckney Historical Preservation Society, Melissa Murphy, Harvard Business School, Terese M. Murphy and Sara Quashnie, Clements Library, University of Michigan, Jill Hunter Powell, Confederate Museum at Market Hall, MG Henry I. Siegling, Sr., The Washington Light Infantry, Rebecca Schultz, City of Charleston Historical Records, and Karen Stokes and Molly Silliman, South Carolina Historical Society.

Many veteran scholars and professionals also gave us their valuable insights and access to their private collections and research. They include Richard W. Hatcher, III, William "Bill" E. Lockridge, Thomas Pinckney Lowndes, Jr., Jack W. Melton, Jr., & Peter Milne.

Those who helped us refine our manuscript were Thomas P. Lowndes Jr., Danielle C. Elum Smith, Grace V. Foster, Richard Horres, Edward "Ebbie" Jones III, & Alice (Torie) Jones. Katy Roberts was instrumental in enhancing the photographs used in this book.

We would be remiss if we both failed to thank the staff at Savas Beatie for taking this book from rough manuscript to finished product: Richard Holloway for his editing expertise; Veronica Kane for her keen eye in designing the layout and overall incredible support; Hal Jespersen for his cartography services. We both also deeply appreciate the assistance and support of Donna Endacott, Sarah Keeney, and Sarah Closson at Savas Beatie who have helped turn our aspirations into reality. A final word of that thanks must of course be for Ted Savas's commitment to publishing historical works and for recognizing the importance of Castle Pinckney and Shute's Folly Island to the history of not only Charleston but to South Carolina and the nation. Thank you.

Finally, we wish to praise the many Charlestonians who continue to volunteer their time, money, and labor to the ongoing preservation of Castle Pinckney. They include Steven A. Earnhardt, Tharin R. Walker, Michael S. Sarvis, William L. Snow Sr., Yale M. Huett, Samuel W. Howell IV, Esq, Phillip A. Middleton, Esq, Ronald C. Plunkett, Robert M. Baldwin, Richard P. Moore, John J. Mahoney, Robert D. Oswald, Thomas R. Campbell & Thomas C. Salter, and the board members, past and present, of The Castle Pinckney Historic Preservation Society. The Carolina Yacht Club has helped this endeavor by allowing the use of their facilities and their gracious support.

A Glossary of Significant Fortification Terms

Adapted primarily from Frederick Augustus Griffith's 1859 *Artillerist's Manual* and John R. Weaver's *A Legacy in Brick and Stone.*

24-pounder: A heavy smoothbore gun, firing a solid shot weighing just over 24 pounds.

42-pounder: Capable of firing a solid shot weighing 42.5 pounds as well as shells, this smoothbore cannon was among the largest guns employed during the first half of the 19th century.

Banquette: A wooden platform or step a soldier would use to fire over the parapet. The platforms could also be utilized by artillerymen to help with loading and firing of their elevated cannons.

Barbette: The platforms behind the parapet where guns are mounted. Guns mounted on these platforms are mounted en barbette.

Barbette Carriage: A carriage, on which a gun is mounted to fire over a parapet.

Barracks: A permanent structure for the accommodation of soldiers, as distinguished from tents or huts.

Bastion: The Corner of a fort that projects outward, usually in the shape of an arrow, thereby providing defenders with the ability to enfilade besiegers attempting to attack an adjoining wall. The rear bastions of Castle Pinckney are curved, however, and have more in common with the bastion towers of a medieval castle.

Battery: A broad term used to describe any emplacement of guns or mortars under the direction of a single officer.

Bombproof: A portion of a fortification designed to provide overhead protection to the garrison from enemy artillery and mortar fire. Bombproofs were built with heavy timbers and their roofs covered with dirt.

Carriage/Gun Carriage: A supportive base used to carry a cannon barrel so that it may be moved around the battlefield. The carriages for heavy seacoast artillery-pieces had triangular bases made of thick wooden timbers and were not designed to be mobile. They had a single forward-axis for wheels so that the weapon could slide up and down its inclined iron-rails while being loaded, aimed, and fired. The combination of the carriage and the chassis that it sat upon was referred to as a barbette-carriage.

Cascabel: A protrusion of metal extending from the breech of any muzzle-loading cannon. Cascabels were a permanent design-feature that allowed a rope to be wrapped around it to help hoist the barrel onto its carriage.

Casemate: A bombproof vaulted chamber of reinforced masonry generally located under the rampart. Designed to protect a single artillery-piece and crew as they fired the cannon through an embrasure in the scarp wall. Casemates were also used as quarters, magazines, and storage rooms.

Cistern: A masonry, metal, or wood containment area designed to catch and store fresh rainwater. Castle Pinckney had brick cisterns in its two bastions.

Embrasure: An opening made in a scarp wall through which a cannon could be fired. The sides of an embrasure known as cheeks would typically splay outward from the throat. An embrasure gave protection to the artillerymen and their gun, but it had the adverse effect of limiting the field of fire.

En-barbette: A type of artillery emplacement, originating in France, where cannons were raised behind a protective wall so that only their gun-barrels protruded above the parapet. This afforded the gun crew some limited protection from counter fire.

Exterior Slope: A steep slope on the exterior of the parapet, usually of earth or sand, designed to absorb artillery fire.

Fraise: Stakes or palisades placed horizontally along the berm or at the top of the counterscarp to stop or slow a climbing attacker. They prevented the earthworks from being taken by a surprise assault.

Garrison: A collective term for a body of troops stationed in a fort, castle, town, or city.

Guard Room: A room that guards the main sally port and has loopholes facing the sally port.

Hot-Shot Furnace: A free-standing brick structure within a fortification with iron grates and racks where solid cannonballs are heated to red-hot intensity and then fired into wooden ships, sails, & rigging.

Howitzer: A shorter barreled gun with a chamber for smaller powder charges, designed to fire shells at higher elevations over less range than guns of the same caliber.

Limber chest: An artillery box or chest that held ammunition and other artillery implements.

Loophole: A narrow opening in a wall which allowed a rifle to fire through it.

Lunette: A defensive military field work or outwork of half-moon shape without walls on either side.

Machicoulis Gallery/Tower: A protruding enclosure that extended over the edge of a rampart or a wall that was like a balcony. Soldiers in the gallery utilized an opening in the floor to fire downward or to drop explosives on assaulting troops.

Magazine: The place for storage of gunpowder inside a fort. They were designed to produce a dry atmosphere and prevent sparks.

Martello Tower: A round tower of three or more floors with one to three artillery pieces mounted en barbette on the top level.

Moat: Another name for a ditch around a fortress or castle that is often filled with water.

Mortar: An artillery piece, primarily intended for siege work, with a short, thick iron barrel designed to throw hollow projectiles packed with powder at great angles of elevation beyond or behind enemy walls.

Ordnance: A military term used to describe cannon, ammunition, and weaponry, as well as the tools and equipment required to operate, store and repair armaments.

Palisade: A wooden fence of vertical and sharpened stakes that formed a defensive wall. Driven into the ground, the stakes typically stand about ten feet tall.

Parade Ground: An open area in the center of the fort reserved for drilling soldiers.

Parapet: A low sloping wall of masonry and/or earth that formed a protective barrier on top of a rampart. The parapet provided some degree of protection for the en barbette artillery and their artillery crews.

Pintle: The pin around which a gun carriage rotates. Guns mounted en casemate sit on a front-pintle carriage with the pintle at the narrowest part (throat) of the embrasure. Center-pintle carriages are used on barbette emplacements and can allow a full 360-degree traverse of the guns.

Rampart: Designates a stone or earth wall surrounding a castle or fort, erected for defensive purposes. Griffiths' Manual declares that a rampart consists "of an interior slope, terreplein, banquette, parapet, and an exterior slope or escarp."

Sabot: Meaning "wooden shoe" or clog, it was a conical piece of wood or metal attached to the of base of canister- or spherical-case shells, so that they sat snugly in the chamber at the back of a cannon-bore in order to receive the full effect of the powder-cartridge and help guide an explosive shell.

Sally Port: A gate or passage usually under the rampart, with a vaulted ceiling. Elements of a garrison could "sally" forth from this entrance and make a sudden attack on their besiegers.

Scarp: The slope of the ditch next to the walls of the fort. A counterscarp is the slope on the ditch opposite the fort.

Sentry: A soldier standing guard. The term is used interchangeably with picket.

Shell: A projectile fired from a cannon that has a hollow interior that has been filled with explosives and has a timed fuse.

Shot: A solid iron projectile fired from a cannon. A shot has more momentum than a shell, but does not explode upon impact, and does its damage only through momentum.

Terreplein: A French expression meaning "level ground." The term describes the flat area atop the inner portion of a rampart. It is closest to the interior parade ground and is not protected by the raised parapet.

Trunnion: The protrusions on either side of a cannon-barrel, that allows it to be rested evenly and swiveled up and down atop a gun carriage. The trunnion was often stamped with foundry casting information.

Wicket Gate: A small door in the main wooden gate of a fortified place, allowing free passage to and fro, without having to open the main gate.

Castle Pinckney Biographies

Alfred O'Neil Alcock (1823-1864) was a member of the 11th New York Fire Zouaves and a prisoner at Castle Pinckney in Oct. 1861. Born in England, Alcock contributed articles to a New York newspaper about his ten months of captivity in Southern prisons. As a member of the 10th New York Infantry, he was mortally wounded at Laurel Hill in the battle of Spotsylvania Courthouse. He is buried at the Soldier's Home in Washington, D.C.

John Julius Pringle Alston (1836-1863) was transferred to Castle Pinckney for rest after displaying immense courage fighting at Battery Wagner. He grew up in the Edmondson-Alston mansion at 21 East Bay Street and was educated at Cambridge College in Massachusetts. Lt. Alston succumbed to typhoid fever complicated by exhaustion while on leave in Greenville. He is buried in Christ Church Cemetery in Greenville.

Addison Bowles Armistead (1768-1813) was the commander of Castle Pinckney at the beginning of the War of 1812. His brother Walker was a general in the same war and the father of Gen. Lewis Addison Armistead, who was killed leading Confederate troops atop Cemetery Ridge at the battle of Gettysburg.

Pierre Gustave Toutant Beauregard (1818-1893) commanded the Confederate defenses of Charleston Harbor during the April 12-13, 1861 bombardment of Fort Sumter, which formally started the Civil War. After commanding troops at First Manassas and Shiloh, Beauregard returned to Charleston to command the Department of SC, GA and FL. Beauregard finished the war commanding Southern troops in Virginia. After the war, he served as adjutant general of the Louisiana State Militia and Commissioner of Public Works in his native New Orleans.

Ormsby DeSaussure Blanding (1823-1889) was commanding Castle Pinckney when Gen. Beauregard visited the post for the first time in March 1861. Blanding was the Sergeant

Major of the Palmetto Regiment in the Mexican War. He served as captain of Company E, 1st South Carolina Artillery and was severely wounded at the battle of Averasboro. He was a farmer in Sumter County after the war.

Theodore Gaillard Boag (1833-1895) was the Confederate quartermaster with the Charleston Zouaves who supplied the Federal prisoners on Castle Pinckney with rations. He later served in the Gist Guard Artillery. Boag was a cotton broker and city alderman after the war. He is buried in Magnolia Cemetery.

Henry Brown (1828-1907) was the captain of the USLHT *Wisteria* from 1882 until his death. Born in Drobab, Norway, he served in the Civil War under Adm. Farragut and was assigned by the Lighthouse Service to Charleston in 1869. He is the inventor of the Bell Buoy and is buried in Magnolia Cemetery.

Charles Henry Caldwell (1793-1831) was wounded in a duel with Lt. Taylor fought at Castle Pinckney in 1818. A Connecticut native, he perished in the Pacific aboard the brig *George & Henry*.

Ellison Capers (1837-1908) was second in command when three companies of the 1st Rifles of the Charleston Militia captured Castle Pinckney in 1860. He was a professor of Mathematics at his alma mater, the Citadel, at the time. During the war, Capers was colonel of the 24th South Carolina Infantry and was severely wounded at the Battle of Franklin. After the war, Capers became an Episcopal priest and later the Episcopal Bishop of South Carolina. In 1904, he was elected chancellor of the University of the South in Sewanee, Tennessee. The "Soldier Bishop" is buried at Trinity Episcopal Church in Columbia.

Francis Fishburne Carroll (1828-1903) was a South Carolina plantation owner who conducted torpedo experiments at Castle Pinckney. After the war he became postmaster of the hamlet of Midway near Bamberg.

Charles Edward Chichester (1834-1898) was the commander of the Charleston Zouave Cadets that garrisoned Castle Pinckney in the fall of 1861. As captain of the Gist Guard Artillery, Chichester would be a chief of artillery during the siege of Battery Wagner, where he was severely wounded. Chichester became a Presbyterian minister in 1873 and served as chaplain of Charleston's Port Society. He is buried next to the Confederate Monument at Magnolia Cemetery.

Jane Elizabeth Chamberlain Chichester (1833-1914) lived with her husband Capt. Charles Chichester at Castle Pinckney in 1861 and 1862. A native of Philadelphia, Jane married Charles in 1855. The couple moved to Charleston in 1860 where Charles worked as a clerk for Walker & Evans. After the war Jane was president of the Ladies Seamen's Friends Society in Charleston.

Frederick Lynn Childs (1831-1894) commanded Castle Pinckney in March and April 1861. Son of Gen. Thomas Childs, Frederick graduated from West Point in 1855. Childs's Light Artillery became Company C, 15th Battalion, South Carolina Heavy Artillery. Childs finished the war as a lieutenant colonel in charge of the Fayetteville Arsenal. After the war, he lived in Charleston working as a purser of a New York steamship company, and later an Inspector of Customs. Childs is buried next to Joel Roberts Poinsett in Stateburg, South Carolina.

George Louis Choisy (1837-1880) commanded Company D, 40th USCI at Castle Pinckney in 1867 and 1868. A native of South Carolina, Choisy joined the 14th U.S. Infantry as a private in 1861 and rose to major. He died of dropsy at Fort Lee, New Jersey.

George Smith Cook (1819-1902) took photographs of the prisoners and guards at Castle Pinckney in October 1861. Born in Stamford, Connecticut and orphaned at an early age, Cook trained under Mathew Brady before opening his own Charleston studio on King Street. He moved to Richmond in 1880.

Michael Corcoran (1827-1863) was a prisoner at Castle Pinckney in October 1861. He commanded the all-Irish 69th New York Militia Regiment and was a founder of the Fenian Brotherhood. After his exchange in August 1862, he dined with President Lincoln, was promoted to brigadier general, and returned to New York City to form the Corcoran Legion of Irish regiments. Assigned to defend Washington, D.C., he died in a horseback accident near Fairfax, Virginia.

George Washington Cullum (1809-1882) was the superintending engineer for the construction of Fort Sumter and repairs at Castle Pinckney, and Forts Moultrie and Johnson from 1855 to 1859. In 1864 he was appointed superintendent of the West Point Military Academy.

William Holding Echols (1834-1909) was a Confederate engineer assigned to Castle Pinckney in the fall of 1863. Echols was an Alabama native and an 1854 graduate of the U.S. Military Academy. After the war Echols was a civil engineer for the Memphis & Charleston Railroad and president of a Huntsville, Alabama bank.

William Alexander Eliason (1800-1839) was the U.S. Army engineer who designed and supervised the construction of the wooden palisade behind Castle Pinckney. Eliason graduated first in his West Point class of 1819 and oversaw the construction of Fort Macon in North Carolina.

Henry Saxon Farley (1840-1927) was commander of Castle Pinckney from April 1862 to August 1863. He was the son of a Laurens County politician and went, as a young man, to prospect for gold in California. Farley was a cadet at West Point when the war began. As a major, he spent the final 15 months of the war commanding the dismounted cavalry corps of the Army of Northern Virginia. After the war, he farmed near Spartanburg and later worked in the motion picture industry.

Daniel Munroe Forney (1784-1847) was an officer in the Lincolnton, NC militia and commissioned as a major at the start of the War of 1812. Forney was given command of the 6th District, which included Charleston, in May 1813. After the war, Forney was a successful planter and served in the U.S. Congress.

John Gray Foster (1823-1874) was the U.S. Army engineer officer superintending the construction of Fort Sumter and repairing the forts in the Charleston Harbor in 1860. An 1846 graduate of West Point, Foster became a career military officer. In 1862 and 1863 he commanded the Department of North Carolina. As Commander of the Department of the South in 1864 he directed the bombardment of Fort Sumter. Foster was a brevetted major general by war's end. Foster died in his native New Hampshire in 1874.

Robert Cogdell Gilchrist (1829-1902) served as first lieutenant of the Charleston Zouave Cadets. Gilchrist would command Battery Gregg at the northern tip of Morris Island in August 1863 and would reach the rank of major. After the war, he took his family to the Southern Adirondacks where he funded the construction of the first suspension bridge across the Hudson River in 1871. He later practiced law in Charleston and, in 1884, published *The Confederate Defense of Morris Island, Charleston Harbor*.

Robert M. Gill (1787-1828) was the controversial captain in the 2nd U.S. Artillery dismissed in 1813 for conduct unbecoming an officer and a gentleman. He became a planter in Wilkinson County, Mississippi.

John Gordon (1787-1835) along with his older brother, James Gordon (1783-1814), were the principal contractors under Lt. Macomb in the construction of Castle Pinckney. John also helped Robert Mills construct the Fireproof Building on Meeting Street in 1823. In later years, Col. Gordon (He was an officer in the Irish Volunteers militia in Charleston) constructed a giant brickmaking facility at Moreland Plantation, his home on the Cooper River.

Charles Carroll Gray (1838-1884) kept a diary as a prisoner at Castle Pinckney. A native New Yorker, he was an assistant surgeon with the 2nd U.S. Cavalry when he was captured at First Bull Run. Gray remained an Army surgeon until his retirement in 1879.

William Heyward Grimball (1838-1864) was the junior 1st lieutenant of Company E when it garrisoned Castle Pinckney in the summer of 1863. From a distinguished Charleston family, his brother John Grimball was an officer on the raider CSS *Shenandoah*. Grimball died of typhoid fever while on detached service at Fort Johnson.

Henry William Griswold (1795-1834) was commanding Castle Pinckney at the time of his death in 1834. A native of New Milford, Connecticut, Griswold had graduated from West Point in 1815.

David Bullock Harris (1814-1864) was the chief Confederate engineer under Beauregard. An 1833 West Point graduate, Harris was a railroad surveyor in Virginia before the war. Despite clashing with R. S. Ripley over the pace of construction, his defensive fortifications proved too formidable for besieging Union forces. Harris contracted yellow fever in the fall of 1864 and died in Summerville.

Theodore Brevard Hayne (1841-1917) led the Maryland volunteers as a Confederate artillery company commander for most of the war. He was the son of South Carolina's Attorney General Isaac William Hayne. After the war, Hayne was a cotton broker in Charleston and Greenville.

John A. Hennessy (1834-1877) rose, over the course of the Civil War, from 1st lieutenant to lt. colonel of the 52nd Pennsylvania. Hennessy drew fame for being the first Federal soldier to raise the U.S. flag over Forts Sumter, Ripley, and Castle Pinckney. He died in his hometown of Pottsville, Pennsylvania.

Robert Little Holmes (1830-1861) A member of the Carolina Light Infantry, Holmes was killed at the Castle's sally port by a nervous sentinel in January 1861. He was the Republic of South Carolina's first casualty and arguably the first military fatality of the Civil War. Holmes's funeral service was held at the Circular Church in Charleston and his body was buried in Magnolia Cemetery.

William H. Hume, Jr. (1836-1926) was a Charleston civil engineer who oversaw the renovation of Castle Pinckney in the winter of 1863-64. He moved to Asheville after the war.

Jacob Bond I'On (1782-1859) commanded a company at Castle Pinckney from the 2nd Regiment of Artillery during the War of 1812. He would return to state politics in 1816 and serve as president of the South Carolina Senate from 1822 to 1828. Described as a "true Carolina gentleman," I'On died on his Mount Pleasant plantation.

George Izard (1776-1828) was a lieutenant in the U.S. Corps of Artillerists and Engineers when he oversaw the construction of the first Fort Pinckney from 1797 to 1800. In that year, he was promoted to captain and became an aide-de-camp to Gen. Alexander Hamilton in New York. George Izard went on to become a major-general in the War of 1812 and later Arkansas' second territorial governor.

David Flavel Jamison (1810-1864) witnessed the test firing of a "sabot" at Castle Pinckney in his role as South Carolina's first secretary of war. A lawyer, politician, author, and planter, Jamison was chosen president of South Carolina's Secession Convention in 1860. He died of yellow fever at his Orangeburg plantation.

Jonathan Johnson (1828-1864) was a member of Company F, 1st South Carolina Artillery and the only soldier killed at Castle Pinckney from hostile fire. While visiting his wife and four children in the Georgia mountain county of Fannin, he had been taken into Federal custody and was released in Chattanooga on February 19, 1864 after taking an Oath of Allegiance. He then returned to his Confederate artillery unit.

Abraham Charles Kaufman (1839-1918) promoted turning Castle Pinckney into a sanitarium for Union veterans at the end of the 20th century. A prominent Charleston businessman and Republican, he represented South Carolina at President McKinley's funeral. He is buried at St. Philip's Episcopal Church.

James Crawford Keys (1813-1895) was one of four men held at Castle Pinckney in 1866 for their alleged involvement in the 1865 Brown's Ferry Murders. Keys was a prominent planter from Anderson County.

Edna Maud King (1874-1924) was the stepdaughter of Capt. James Whiteley and raised on Shute's Folly. 13-year-old Maud was one of two Whiteley women to save three stranded boatmen in turbulent seas in 1888. Maud was recognized by the city of Charleston as the "Heroine of Castle Pinckney." She was a bookkeeper for the Lighthouse Service as an adult.

John Gadsden King (1831-1906) was the last Confederate commander of Castle Pinckney. In the final weeks of the war, he was promoted to major. Gadsden King moved to Atlanta around 1870 where he became a fire insurance agent. He is buried in the King Crypt in Atlanta's Oakland Cemetery.

Francis Dickinson Lee (1826-1885) was a Confederate officer who conducted submarine experiments in the Charleston Harbor. A prominent architect before the war, he designed both the Citadel Square Baptist Church and Unitarian Church in Charleston. He resumed his architectural practice in St. Louis after the war.

Robert Edward Lee (1807-1870) led the Army of Northern Virginia from 1862 to its final 1865 surrender at Appomattox. Lee was a career U.S. army officer and engineer before the war and served as commandant of West Point from 1852 to 1855. Beginning in November 1861, Lee spent four months directing Confederate operations on the South Atlantic coast. After the war, he served as president of Washington College in Lexington, Virginia.

Stephen Dill Lee (1833-1908) was a native of Charleston and an 1854 West Point graduate. As a member of Beauregard's staff, Lee delivered the final ultimatum to Maj. Anderson at Ft. Sumter before the bombardment on April 12, 1861. Lee received numerous promotions in Confederate service eventually reaching lieutenant general commanding a corps in the Army of Tennessee. After the war, Lee was the first president of the Mississippi Agricultural and Mechanical College. He was commander in chief of the United Confederate Veterans at the time of his death.

Henry Russell Lesesne (1843-1865) commanded Castle Pinckney in the winter of 1864-65. The young captain was killed at the battle of Averasboro in 1865. He is buried at St. Philips Church in Charleston.

Thomas Pinckney Lowndes (1839-1899) was a member of the Washington Light Infantry during their time at Castle Pinckney. He was the grandson of Thomas Lowndes who founded the WLI in 1807. Young Thomas spent the war in the Confederate Signal Corps. After the war he was an insurance and stockbroker and active in the Society of the Cincinnati.

Patrick Neeson Lynch (1817-1882) arrived in Charleston from Ireland in 1840 as a Catholic priest. He was consecrated as Bishop of the Charleston Diocese in 1858. The compassionate and intellectual Lynch made several trips in 1861 to Castle Pinckney to preach to and support the Bull Run prisoners held at the Castle.

Alexander Macomb (1782-1841) was the young engineering officer who oversaw the construction of Castle Pinckney in 1809. In 1828, President John Quincy Adams bypassed Winfield Scott and Edmund Gaines to give command of the U.S. Army to Macomb. Maj. Gen. Macomb died while in office.

Edward McCrady, Jr. (1833-1903) was the captain of the Meagher Guards, the Charleston militia unit that was the first to reach the ramparts of Castle Pinckney. McCrady rose through the ranks of the 1st South Carolina Infantry reaching lieutenant colonel by 1863. He was seriously wounded at Second Manassas and Fredericksburg. After the war he was a staunch conservative who helped re-establish "Home Rule" in 1876 and represented Charleston in the state House of Representatives from 1880 to 1890. He is the author of a four-volume history of South Carolina.

John McCrady (1831-1881) was a mathematics professor at the College of Charleston who accompanied his brother's Meagher Guards on their seizure of Castle Pinckney. As a Confederate engineer, Capt. McCrady designed and supervised the ring of defenses around Savannah including Fort McAllister.

Richard Kidder Meade, Jr. (1835-1862) surrendered Castle Pinckney to the South Carolina militia on December 27, 1860. In April 1861 Meade resigned his commission and pledged his allegiance to his native Virginia. Meade was commissioned a major and served on the staffs of Gen. John B. Magruder and Gen. James Longstreet, respectively. He died of disease in Petersburg, Virginia.

Edward Barnwell Middleton (1842-1910) was posted with Company H, 1st South Carolina Artillery at Castle Pinckney in the fall of 1863 and spring of 1864. Educated at the Citadel, he spent the first 18 months of the war as a private in the 46th Georgia. He was appointed a 2nd lieutenant in the 1st South Carolina Artillery upon the recommendation of W. Porcher Miles. Captured at the battle of Averasboro in March 1865, Middleton was not released from the Johnson's Island prison until June 19, 1865. He is buried at Magnolia Cemetery.

James Monroe (1758-1831) was the only U.S. President to visit Castle Pinckney. The Virginian served from 1817 to 1825 in an "Era of Good Feelings."

Carsten Nohrden (1827-1861) of the German Artillery company commanded Castle Pinckney in February 1861. A native of the Kingdom of Hanover, Nohrden reached Charleston in the 1840s and became a successful businessman. He died of hemorrhagic fever in July 1861 on Morris Island. His engraved sword is on display at the Charleston Museum.

Niles Gardner Parker (1827-1894) commanded Company A, 33rd USCI while they garrisoned Castle Pinckney in 1865. After leaving the army, Parker represented Barnwell County in the 1868 State Constitutional Convention and was subsequently elected state treasurer of South Carolina during a period of graft and mistrust. He is buried in Merrimack Cemetery in West Newberry, Massachusetts.

William Henry Peronneau (1823-1874) commanded Castle Pinckney for five months in 1863 as the captain of Company G, 1st South Carolina Artillery. A descendant of French Huguenots, William suffered from poor eyesight and was forced to resign on November 4, 1864. He is buried in Magnolia Cemetery.

James Johnston Pettigrew (1828-1863) led three companies of the 1st South Carolina Rifles militia regiment over the walls to capture Castle Pinckney for the state of South Carolina. A graduate of the University of North Carolina, Pettigrew was a Charleston lawyer as the war began. At the battle of Gettysburg, he led Heth's Division in Pickett's Charge. He was mortally wounded in West Virginia in the subsequent Confederate retreat.

Francis Wilkinson Pickens (1805-1869) was the governor of South Carolina during the Fort Sumter crisis. The grandson of Revolutionary War hero Gen. Andrew Pickens and a cousin of Senator John C. Calhoun, Pickens was the ambassador to Russia before becoming governor in 1860. In 1865, Pickens called for the repeal of the state's Ordinance of Secession saying, "It doesn't become South Carolina to vapor or swell or strut or brag or bluster or threat or swagger,.... She bids us bind up her wounds and pour on the oil of peace."

Charles Cotesworth Pinckney (1746-1825) was the namesake of Castle Pinckney. From a family of elite Charleston planters, Pinckney was an officer in the American Revolution, a delegate to the Constitutional Convention, and twice nominated as a presidential candidate. He was a cousin of Charles Pinckney who submitted the Pinckney Draft of the U.S. Constitution in 1787.

Thomas Pinckney (1750-1828) oversaw military operations in the Southern states during the War of 1812. The younger brother of Charles C. Pinckney, Thomas was elected governor of South Carolina in 1797 and was the minister to Great Britain from 1792 to 1796.

Joel Roberts Poinsett (1779-1851) headed the Unionist faction in South Carolina during the Nullification Crisis of 1832. He sent detailed reports on the Charleston forts to President Andrew Jackson. The former minister to Mexico would go on to become Martin Van Buren's secretary of war.

Anthony Toomer Porter (1828-1902)) was an Episcopal clergyman who preached to the Washington Light Infantry at Castle Pinckney on Sunday, Dec 30, 1860. Porter was the rector of the Church of the Holy Communion on Ashley Street. After the war he established the Porter Academy for boys orphaned or left destitute by the Civil War. His well-received autobiography *Lead On* was published in 1898.

John B. Porter (1810-1869) was the military surgeon in Charleston during the yellow fever outbreaks in the 1850s. In 1847, Porter assisted Edward Barton in the first use of anesthesia in a military operation, but he became a lifelong opponent of the practice.

James Reid Pringle (1842-1871) was a young 1st lieutenant in the 1st South Carolina Artillery stationed at Castle Pinckney. He came from an aristocratic Charleston family. Pringle was promoted to captain on November 5, 1864 upon the resignation of Capt. Peronneau. After the war he became a member of the San Francisco bar and died at age 29 in Manhattan, New York. He is buried at St. Michael's Church in Charleston.

Alfred Moore Rhett (1829-1889) commanded Fort Sumter during the Union ironclad attack on April 7, 1863 and the first heavy bombardment of the fort by Union forces in August 1863. In September 1863 Rhett was given command of Charleston's inner ring of fortifications. He was the son of U.S. Senator Barnwell Rhett and an 1851 graduate of Harvard. Rhett was captured at the battle of Averasboro in the closing days of the war. He resumed rice planting on his plantation after the war and became chief of police in Charleston under two mayors.

Anthony Wilhelm Riecke (1842-1907) was the son of German immigrants and a young soldier in the Charleston Zouave Cadets in 1861. He went on to serve in the Washington Artillery. In 1879, he completed, but did not publish *Recollections of a Confederate Soldier of the Struggle for the "Lost Cause."*

Roswell Sabine Ripley (1823-1887) was a skilled artillery officer who commanded the coastal defenses of Charleston for much of the war. Born in Worthington, Ohio, Ripley was an 1843 graduate of West Point and a veteran of the Mexican War. He married into a Charleston family and gave his allegiance to the South. Ripley had a volatile temper, was argumentative and stubborn, and accused of excessive consumption of alcohol. After the war, he lived in England for two decades.

Edmund Ruffin (1794-1865) was a leading advocate of states' rights and secession across the South. Ruffin was present on Morris Island for the bombardment of Fort Sumter where he fired one of the first shots of the bombardment. A Virginia native, Ruffin was a noted agriculturalist, writer, and editor of a journal for farmers. Ruffin committed suicide shortly after learning of Robert E. Lee's surrender at Appomattox Court House.

Henry Saunders (1788-1876) commanded Castle Pinckney during the Nullification Crisis. Saunders was a Virginian who served in the U.S. Army from 1813 until 1844. While at Castle Pinckney, he was promoted from captain to major. He farmed near Leesburg, Virginia until his death.

Winfield Scott (1786-1866) provided deft leadership of the military forces in the Charleston Harbor during the Nullification Crisis. In 1847, he led the American military campaign that captured Mexico City. "Old Fuss and Feathers" was the Whig nominee for president in 1852.

Daniel Edgar Sickles (1819-1914) was a controversial Union general who served as the military governor of South Carolina from 1865 to 1869. A New York politician before the war, Sickles was a War Democrat given command of New York's Excelsior Brigade. On the second day of the battle of Gettysburg, Sickles advanced his III Corps into the famous Peach Orchard in defiance of direct orders. The salient he created was overrun by

James Longstreet's assault. Sickles lost his right leg in the fight. President Grant appointed him ambassador to Spain after his service in South Carolina. Sickles is buried in Arlington National Cemetery.

James Skillin (1821-1897) was a career soldier who served as the ordnance sergeant at Castle Pinckney both before and after the Civil War. He and his wife Ruby retired to Lincoln, Maine.

John Caldwell Tidball (1825-1906) was a lieutenant stationed in the Castle in 1852. He was noted for his service in the famed U.S. Horse Artillery Brigade in the Army of the Potomac. After the war, he was made a major in the regular army and served six years as the commander of Alaska. Tidball retired as one of the Army's premier artillerists.

James Heyward Trapier (1815-1865) was the U.S. Army engineer officer who produced the most detailed drawings of Castle Pinckney in the 1840s. A Mexican War veteran, Trapier would become a Confederate brigadier general.

Robert De Treville (1833-1865) was a young lawyer and member of the Washington Light Infantry who took part in the state seizure of Castle Pinckney in 1860. By the end of the war, Treville was lieutenant colonel of the 1st South Carolina Infantry. He was killed at the battle of Averasboro and is buried in nearby Chicora Cemetery.

James Gilmore Tuttle (1839-1906) was a member of Company F, 4th Michigan. As a Bull Run prisoner at the Castle, his stubbornness landed him in solitary confinement. A native of Ontario, Canada, Tuttle moved to Morristown, Tennessee later in life.

Johann Andreas Wagener (1816-1876) was the commander of the Charleston German Artillery and briefly commander of Castle Pinckney in 1861. Born in the Kingdom of Hanover, "John" Wagener reached Charleston in 1833. A prominent immigrant, he founded the first German-language newspaper of the South. In 1871, he was elected mayor of Charleston.

William Waud (1832–1878) was an English-born architect, illustrator, and correspondent during the American Civil War. In the 1850s, he joined his brother, Alfred Waud, in America and was employed as an artist for *Frank Leslie's Illustrated Newspaper* and *Harper's Weekly*. His illustrations of the inauguration of Jefferson Davis and the bombardment of Fort Sumter are widely published.

William Welsh (1835-1912) commanded Castle Pinckney in 1867 as a captain in the 40th USCI and kept a ledger of prisoners kept at the Castle. A career soldier, he retired in 1891 as a brevet brigadier general. Welsh is buried in Mound View Cemetery in his hometown of Mount Vernon, Ohio.

Edward Brickell White (1806-1882) designed and supervised the improvements to Castle Pinckney in January 1861. A Charleston native and 1826 graduate of West Point, White became one of Charleston prominent architects in the 1840s and 1850s. His noted works include Market Hall, the Huguenot Church, Grace Church, and the steeple for St. Philips Church. He is buried at St. Michael's Church.

James Wilfred Whiteley (1858-1907) was the long serving keeper and resident of the Castle Pinckney Lighthouse Depot from 1880 until his death. He is buried in Magnolia Cemetery.

Orlando Bolivar Willcox (1823-1907) was the colonel of the 1st Michigan Infantry when he was captured at Bull Run and later sent to Castle Pinckney as a prisoner. Born in Detroit and an 1847 graduate of West Point, Willcox led a division in Burnside's Corps at the battle of Antietam. A career military officer, he retired in 1887 as a brigadier general. He is buried at Arlington National Cemetery.

William Herbert Withington (1835-1903) was a Union prisoner at Castle Pinckney. As a captain in the 1st Michigan Infantry at the battle of Bull Run, he would be awarded a Congressional Medal of Honor for his bravery that day. After being exchanged, Withington was appointed colonel of the 17th Michigan. After the war he was a manufacturer in his hometown of Jackson, Michigan, and a state politician.

Joseph Atkinson Yates (1829-1888) of Charleston commanded Castle Pinckney from January through April 1862. He commanded the artillery on Morris Island when Federal troops captured its south end in July 1863. Yates was present for the final parole at Greensboro on April 28, 1865. A mining supervisor after the war, he died in Bessemer, Alabama.

Chapter 1

Before There Was a Castle on Shute's Folly

When the United States of America elected George Washington to be its first president in January 1789, the new republic was comprised of 13 coastal states. It was clear to President Washington that the nation's port cities were lightly defended and vulnerable to attack by a European power.

In 1794, the 3rd U.S. Congress, at Washington's request, approved modest funds to begin fortifying 20 harbor towns along the Atlantic Seaboard. The congressional report recommended that Charleston, the most important port in the South, be given sea-facing defenses second in scope only to New York City. Unfortunately, the small war department under Henry Knox lacked the expertise to do little more than establish a handful of inexpensive and half-completed fortifications.[1]

News of the XYZ Affair in 1797 awoke Americans to the possibility of a war with France. Upon their arrival in Paris to negotiate a treaty, South Carolinian Charles Cotesworth Pinckney, along with fellow diplomats John Marshall and Elbridge Gerry, were confronted with demands that bribery money be paid before negotiations could begin. The three Americans indignantly refused as Pinckney was said to have replied, "No! No! Not a sixpence!" Reacting to a possible military threat from the French islands in the West Indies, prominent citizens of Charleston met in St. Michael's Church to raise money to improve their city's defenses. Their

---

1 David Weirick, *Castle Pinckney: Past, Present, Future*, Ph.D. dissertation, Clemson University and the College of Charleston, May 2012, 5-6; Arthur Wade, *Artillerists and Engineers: The Beginnings of American Seacoast Fortifications*, 1794-1815, Ph.D. dissertation, Kansas State University, 1977, 21.

contributions would serve as an important supplement to the $16,212 already appropriated by Congress. Shute's Folly, a small island located in the Charleston Harbor roughly one mile from the city wharves along the Cooper River, was selected as a site for a new fort.[2]

Talk of building a fortification on this marsh island went as far back as 1745 when Capt. Peter Henry Bruce, an experienced military engineer, was dispatched to the Charlestown harbor. Bruce had just completed his work on Fort Nassau in the Bahamas. With the British colony of South Carolina threatened by a Spanish attack from Florida, Bruce recommended that a canal be constructed across the Neck of the peninsula to prevent a surprise attack by land and a battery be built at Rhett's Point (southwest corner of Concord and Pritchard Streets in the Union Pier area) to prevent a surprise landing by sea. Bruce noted that Fort Johnson protected the main harbor channel used by sailing ships to reach the wharves on the Cooper River. Still, he observed that the alternate Hog Island Channel that ran between Mount Pleasant and Shute's Folly was deep and not defended by cannon.

The Scottish engineer recommended building a sizable horseshoe-shaped fort on the part of the marsh island that was "solid and firm, and what is not may be made so by driving piles." Bruce envisioned mounting "thirty pieces of cannon of the largest size, which would not only command Rebellion-road, but also both channels (that of Johnson's Fort and Hog Island)." The defensive plan would, by Bruce's estimates, cost the South Carolina colony £100,000 pounds. This was a tall order indeed and would require a large bank loan from London. Bruce was asked to oversee the construction, but he declined, citing a lack of fortitude among the Governor's Privy Council members. In the end, only modest defensive improvements were made at Rhett's Point and at Anson's House.[3]

In 1746, a Quaker merchant and land speculator named Joseph Shute bought the 244-acre tidal marsh island from the Parris family. Shute called his new acquisition his "delight," but it would be "folly" that would follow his name and that of the island from 1750 forward. The word folly can be interpreted in several directions. An archaic meaning refers to a verdant thicket of plants and trees, and a bit of local lore maintains that, during Shute's time, a grove of orange trees stood on the island. Another definition describes a folly as an eccentric or whimsical structure built on the grounds of a fashionable 18th-century English garden. A

---

2 Weirick, *Castle Pinckney: Past, Present, Future*, 10-11; Edwin C. Bearass, *The First Two Fort Moultries: A Structural History* (Charleston, 1968), 40-41. Charlestown changed its name to Charleston in 1783, shortly after the American Revolution.

3 Henry Bruce, *Memoirs of Peter Henry Bruce Esq.* (Dublin, 1783), 512-514; Nic Butler, "The Hard: Colonial Charleston's Forgotten Maritime Center," Charleston Time Machine, Charleston County Public Library, posted May 5, 2023.

Before There Was a Castle on Shute's Folly 3

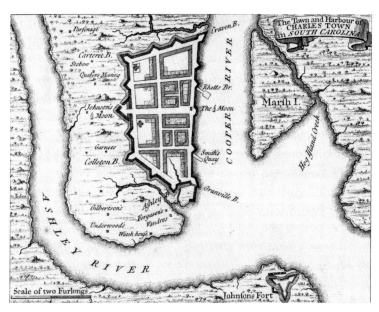

"Town and Harbour of Charles Town in South Carolina," a 1733 map. Marsh Island is directly across the Cooper River from the walled city. *Library of Congress*

---

small tea house reportedly operated on the island during Shute's time, and it is possible that Folly was attached to this enterprise, which was unceremoniously washed away by the Gale of 1752. In the end, though, it may simply be that Shute's purchase of this low-lying tidal marsh island, which had but a sliver of firm ground, was considered a foolish financial investment by the residents of Charlestown. While Shute owned a wharf on the Cooper River, a plantation in Colleton County, and several parcels of land in Charlestown, he was financially overextended by 1750 and forced by Provost Marshall Rawlins Lowndes to sell his slaves, his new city home, and "one half of Shute's Delight (otherwise known as Shute's Folly)" at public vendue. His fellow citizens, it seems, could not help but mock Shute's investment in the marsh island as an ignominious "folly."[4]

Lacking a fort, Shute's Folly was best known in colonial times for "Hangman's Point," which was a piece of higher ground on the southern tip of the island. Criminals and pirates were said to have been hanged here from a gallows tree as a macabre warning to the crews of ships entering and leaving the harbor. In 1788,

---

[4] Turk McCleskey, *The Road to Black Ned's Forge: A Story of Race, Sex, and Trade on the Colonial American Frontier* (Charlottesville, 2014), 33-36; "To be Sold at Public Vendue, at Joseph Shute's New House on the Bay," *The South Carolina* [SC] *Gazette*, May 28, 1750, 3; "Sullivan's Island: No. 3, Castle Pinckney," *The Rose Bud* [SC], Dec. 8, 1832, 57.

Capt. William Rogers of New London, Connecticut, and four seamen from the schooner *Two Friends* were the last to be executed at "Hangman's Point, opposite the city" for murder and piracy on the American Seas.[5]

On January 6, 1773, James Laurens of Charlestown wrote to his brother Henry Laurens, who was across the Atlantic spending the year in London. The 49-year-old Henry Laurens was a wealthy Lowcountry planter, having built a fortune as a partner in the largest slave-trading house in North America. In the coming years, Henry was to become an important Founding Father, succeeding John Hancock as the president of the Continental Congress. In 1773, however, it was the duty of his younger brother James to keep him abreast of his financial affairs and the news from Charlestown. In a postscript to his letter to Henry, James wrote, "I had almost forgot to tell you that I have purchased, a few days since, the North part of Shutes Marsh for you at £795." It seemed to be an expensive price, but Henry approved of the purchase, as the southern part of the marsh island had an even higher price. The northern part of Shute's Folly did produce some amount of revenue as ship owners paid for the privilege of "careening on the Hards," which meant pulling their boat up onto a sandy beach. Once on dry land, the boat or schooner would be turned on its side and the hull cleaned, caulked, and repaired. Henry wrote back that he laughed at himself when he learned of the purchase, writing, "With respect to the Marsh I have often said I would have bought it, if I had not dreaded the sound of Lauren's Folly."[6]

As tensions mounted between the colonists and the government of King George III, British engineers in 1775 studied the Charlestown harbor in case the capital of the South Carolina colony would have to be forcibly seized. Maj. Gen. Frederick George Mulcaster of the Royal Engineers, the half-brother of the King, wrote from St. Augustine a 16-page letter outlining British strategy. Mulcaster recommended the silencing of Fort Johnson followed by the placement of a 13-inch mortar on Shute's Folly that could bombard the nearby city. Mulcaster's letter was intercepted by the Americans, but he was among the first of many subsequent military men who understood that the military force that occupied Shute's Folly also controlled the fate of the city of Charleston.

---

5 Suzannah Smith Miles, "Castle Pinckney: Silent Sentinel in Charleston Harbor," *Moultrie News, Charleston* [SC] *Post and Courier*, Nov. 27, 2012, updated Aug. 20, 2020; "Charleston, June 19," *Norwich* [CT] *Packet*, Jul. 10, 1788, 1; "Charleston, June 17," *Charleston* [SC] *City Gazette*, Jun. 17, 1788, 2.

6 Henry Laurens, *The Papers of Henry Laurens*, 16 vols., George Rogers, David Chesnutt, & Peggy Clark, ed. & trans. (Columbia, SC, 1980) 8:607,613; Henry Laurens, "The Subscriber," *Charleston Courier*, Aug. 22, 1814, 1.

During the Revolutionary War, Charlestown found itself surrounded by British forces in the spring of 1781. After a six-week siege, Gen. Benjamin Lincoln surrendered 2,571 Continental soldiers and about the same number of Patriot militiamen. During the siege, the Americans managed to obstruct the British fleet by sinking eight ships in a long row from the dock by the Exchange Building across the Cooper River to Shute's Folly. Cable chains and spars were lashed and secured to the lower masts of the sunken ships to hold them in place.[7]

In August 1781, America's Southern commander Nathaniel Greene wrote to Gen. George Washington that the British were building a fortification on Shute's Folly that "would have great command of the Town as well as the Rivers." Scottish-born Lt. Col. James Moncrieff, chief engineer to Henry Clinton, had been ordered to put the fortifications of the city and the harbor into "a sufficient state of defense." His labor force was composed primarily of the thousands of runaway slaves who had fled from Lowcountry plantations to Charlestown and were now under the protection of the British Crown. Among Moncrieff's projects was the construction on Shute's Folly of a timber and earth half-moon fort that faced the harbor to the south. "Moncrieff's Battery" was an impressively large structure, roughly twice the size of Charlestown's famous half-moon battery. The north wall alone measured some 231 ft., and there were embrasures for fourteen cannons. The new island fort completed around June 1782 was part of a complex system of forts and defensive works that would, according to Moncrieff, "improve the security of the harbor" against any possible assault by a French or Spanish fleet. After six months of occupation, the British abandoned their new fort with the evacuation of Charlestown on December 14, 1782, more than a year after Cornwallis's surrender at Yorktown.[8]

The new 1798 American fort, to be named for Charleston's favorite son Charles Cotesworth Pinckney, was not built on the abandoned remains of the British fort of 1782 but atop Hangman's Point on the dryer southern extremity of the island. A story survives that President George Washington personally selected the location

---

7 Letter, Intercepted Letter of Major General F.G. Mulcaster, Dec. 30, 1775, *Journals of the Continental Congress*, 34 vols. (Washington, D.C., 1904) 2-538.

8 Henry A. M. Smith, "Hog Island and Shute's Folly," *South Carolina Historical Magazine* (Apr. 1918), 19:91-93. Hereafter cited as SCHM; Kenneth Lewis & William Langhorne, Jr., *Castle Pinckney: An Architectural Assessment with Recommendations*, 1978, Research Manuscript, University of South Carolina, 1978, Series 145, 15; William Roy Smith, *South Carolina as a royal province, 1719-1776* (New York, 1903), 200-201; Letter, Nathaniel Greene to George Washington, Aug. 6, 1781, Washington Papers, Founders Online, National Archives; Moncrieff Letter book, Dec. 31, 1780 to Oct. 7, 1782, James Moncrieff Papers, William Clements Library, University of Michigan; William Gratton to James Mercer, Charleston, Aug. 11, 1781, U.S. Continental Congress Papers, 1774-1789, NARA, RG 360, M247, roll 65, 663.

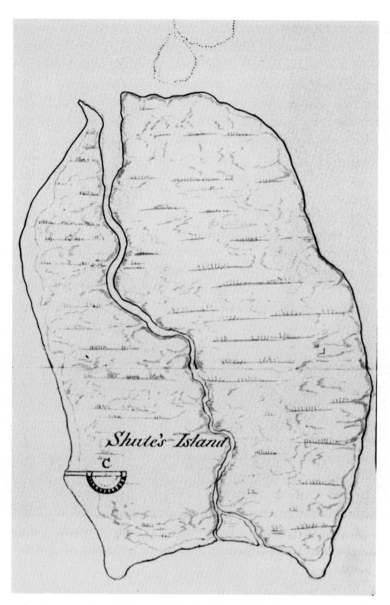

This is a portion of George Taylor's *Plan of Charlestown 1781*, which shows Shute's Folly in detail, including the British fort designed and built by Lt. Col. James Moncrieff in 1781. The island was 244 acres at the time of the American Revolution, and is, today, less than 24 acres.
University of Michigan Library

A 1796 painting of Charles Cotesworth Pinckney done by an unknown artist. Castle Pinckney was named after this Founding Father, diplomat, and South Carolina military figure. *National Portrait Gallery*

for Fort Pinckney on his Southern Tour, which included a visit to Charleston in May 1791. Indeed, there may be an element of truth to this as Washington spent two days viewing Revolutionary War battle sites around Charleston, one on horseback around the Neck, and one day by boat. At dawn on May 5th, Washington sailed from the city past Shute's Folly to inspect Forts Johnson and Moultrie with Gen. William Moultrie as his tour guide. They were joined by "gentlemen of great respectability," which probably included South Carolina's two Senators,

Trained in military engineering in France, Lt. George Izard supervised the construction of Fort Pinckney in 1798. As a major general, he led an American Army protecting Lake Champlain in the War of 1812. *Arkansas Secretary of State's Office and the Old State House Museum*

Pierce Butler and Ralph Izard. Only the ruins of the two Revolutionary War forts remained, which should have crystallized to the delegation Charleston's complete vulnerability to a seaward attack in the early years of the republic. A large late afternoon dinner was then held at the residence of Governor Thomas Pinckney. Two years later, as relations with the French Republic frayed, Gen. Moultrie was writing President Washington requesting funds to mount a handful of cannons at Forts Johnson and Moultrie and he reminded the president of the strategic importance of fortifying Shute's Folly.[9]

French-born engineer Paul Hyacinthe Perrault arrived in Charleston on May 4, 1794, having been appointed by Secretary of War Henry Knox to construct a series of defensive batteries along the South Carolina and Georgia coast. Perrault did work that year rebuilding Forts Johnson and Moultrie with the limited funds at his disposal. He also located a sandbank, 150 fathoms long and 60 fathoms wide, that was largely dry at ebb tide and located off the southeastern tip of Shute's Folly. Perrault took a surprised Governor William Moultrie to the location, and the two military men conceived of building a cannon battery atop the shoal, though Moultrie was weary whether it could withstand "the vehement fury of the waves." Perrault never built the battery, though the Confederates would construct Fort Ripley on this submerged sandbank in 1863.[10]

Fort Pinckney was constructed in 1798 under the direction of 24-year-old Lt. George Izard of the 1st Regiment of Artillerists & Engineers in an irregular

---

9 George Washington, *The Diaries of George Washington*, 6 vol., Donald Jackson and Dorothy Twohig, ed. & trans. (Charlottesville, 1979), 6:126.

10 Bearss, *The First Two Fort Moultries*, 35-37; Letter, Henry Knox to Paul Perrault, Apl. 14, 1794, *Papers of the War Department, 1784-1800*, digital editorial project; Letter, P. H. Perault to Henry Knox, May 31, 1794, Military Affairs, 7 vols., *American State Papers, 1789-1819* (Washington, 1832), 1:102-103. Hereafter cited as *ASP*. A fathom is six feet long.

pentagonal layout with earthen walls stabilized by timbers, which were probably palmetto logs, and the ground covered in sod. Its low profile made it a difficult target to strike and ideal for absorbing cannon shots. Lt. Izard was the son of South Carolina U.S. Senator Ralph Izard and had received military engineering instruction in France. He reported for duty with the secretary of war on November 21, 1797. Fort Moultrie was being completely rebuilt at the same time that Fort Pinckney was being constructed, and both fortresses would share similar layouts and dimensions. Each was built atop a foundation of bricks with further brickwork supporting the ramparts. The construction cost was paid for by a subscription of the local citizens combined with grants from the War Department.

On September 27, 1798, with the fort on Shute's Folly declared completed and several cannons mounted, a naming ceremony was performed with the raising of the 15-star flag of the United States and salutes fired from Forts Johnson and Mechanic and from armed ships in the harbor. Izard had managed that day to gather together an impressive collection of Revolutionary War heroes, which included Christopher Gadsden, Edward Rutledge, and William Washington. The formal ceremony concluded with General William Moultrie proclaiming "Pinckney" to the cheering dignitaries. Sixteen Patriotic toasts followed and uplifted all who were present (see Appendix 1).[11]

During the autumn of 1798, a company of artillerists recruited from Maryland and Delaware under the command of Capt. Francis Huger arrived in Charleston to garrison the newly built Fort Pinckney. The summer of 1799 proved a medical disaster, as Izard would write in his 1825 memoirs, "These poor fellows suffered sadly during the ensuing summer when more than half of them died of the Yellow Fever." Izard nearly died himself from the same "dangerous malady" but was saved by the efforts of Dr. Jean Louis Polony, a French physician and plantation owner from Santo Domingo. Desertion from Fort Pinckney also became a problem for the 2nd Artillery. In April 1799, Lt. J. White posted several ads searching for Pedro Arezano, a native of Seville, Spain, and a private in the 2nd Artillery. White offered a $10 reward for the return of Arezano to Fort Pinckney. Commanding officers at Forts McHenry and Warwick reported to the head of the United States military, Maj. Gen. Alexander Hamilton, that deserters from Fort Pinckney had been returned to their respective posts. Despite these issues, Fort Pinckney had joined Fort Moultrie, Fort Johnson, and Fort Mechanic in a defensive network that

---

11 George Izard and Charlton DeSaussure, Jr., "Memoirs of General George Izard, 1825" SCHM (Jan. 1977), 78:47-48; "Fort Pinckney," *Newport* [RI] *Mercury*, Oct. 30, 1798, 4; William Simmons, Certification of payment for Fort Pinckney; William Simmons to James McHenry, Jun. 25, 1799, *Papers of the War Department, 1784-1800.*

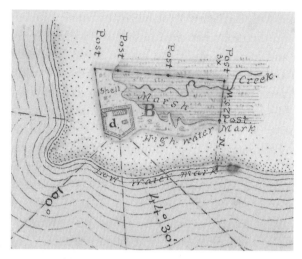

A map of Fort Pinckney drawn in 1840 by Eng. Edward B. White. The details were taken from an 1807 survey done by John Diamond. The outline of the fort is similar to what was constructed at Fort Moultrie during the same timeframe. Both forts were destroyed by an 1804 hurricane. *National Archives Cartography Division*

surrounded the Charleston Harbor and appeared formidable to incoming ships. These four forts were part of the "first system" of coastal defenses constructed along the Eastern Seaboard on land owned by the respective states.[12]

Fort Pinckney drew national attention in February 1799 as five French spies were captured in Charleston and sent to the new island fortress. Alerted by a January letter from the Secretary of State Timothy Pickering, a staunch Federalist who favored close relations with Britain, Governor Edward Rutledge was ready when the brig *Minerva* arrived in Charleston on February 21st after a 119-day voyage from Hamburg. The ship was boarded by Maj. Simons, the port inspector, and William Crafts, an agent for the War Department. Four men and their female accomplice were arrested. Three of the men were mulattoes, including Matthew Salmon, who was a deputy to the French National Convention, and it was alleged that they had come to America under orders from the French Directorate to ferment a slave rebellion on the island of Santo Domingo (Hispaniola). When

---

12 Izard and DeSaussure, "Memoirs of General George Izard, 1825" SCHM (Jan. 1977), 78:47-48; "Fort Pinckney," *The Georgia Chronicle and Gazette of the State*, Oct. 6, 1798, 3; "Deserted," *City* [SC] *Gazette*, Apr. 27, 1799, 3; Letter, Staats Morris to Alexander Hamilton, Jun. 18, 1799, Hamilton Papers, Founders Online.

arrested, the French citizens had been attempting to throw tubs of some sort overboard. The tubs turned out to have false bottoms that held secret diplomatic papers enclosed in wood rollers. Names in the documents were written under a cipher. According to the *Augusta Chronicle*, "The horrors of guilt were depicted strongly on the countenances of the guilty wretches, and their bodies shook with fear and trembling."

Maj. Gen. Thomas Pinckney had the spies confined to Fort Pinckney and their luggage sent to the Customs House for review. In a play on words from the title of a Jonathan Swift satire, the newspaper called the developing incident *Tales of the Tubes*. On February 28th, the Charleston papers reported that the French prisoners had been released from close confinement and were allowed to walk about the fort. Their luggage was also returned to them. Satisfied that the papers found in the tubs were not "hostile to the peace and welfare of the United States," Gen. Pinckney allowed these French agents to board the brig *Romain* bound for Guadeloupe on March 17th.[13]

On March 12, 1799, Maj. Gen. Charles Cotesworth Pinckney wrote to James McHenry, the Secretary of War, lamenting the condition of Fort Johnson and asking for cannon and carriages for Fort Moultrie. He also praised his namesake, Fort Pinckney, on Shute's Folly, noting that it was "well constructed of brick & the foundations laid upon Piles—The cannon are mounted on double garrison carriages, & fire over the parapet which is not cut with embrasures." The new fort possessed a reverberating furnace for heating red hot shot that could set afire wooden ships and their canvas sails. All three forts soon received two ten-inch mortars, "at which Ships are greatly alarm'd notwithstanding this uncertainty of their hitting them."[14]

The nation's third president, Thomas Jefferson, was more sympathetic to the French, and tensions, as well as military appropriations, quickly abated. The Virginian disliked the idea of a large federal government, and he had little interest in establishing permanent coastal fortifications. Thus, the four Charleston forts soon stood virtually abandoned, and a furious hurricane all but destroyed them in September 1804. Charleston lay defenseless until 1808, when Congress appropriated $1,000,000 for a "second system" of coastal defenses. New York,

---

13 "Beware of French Emissaries," *Augusta* [GA] *Chronicle*, Mar. 2, 1799, 3; Letters, Thomas Pickering to Charles Cotesworth Pinckney, 1799, Charles Cotesworth Pinckney letters, University of South Carolina Library; "From a Charleston Paper of February 28," *Centinel* [NJ] *of Freedom*, Mar. 19, 1799, 2.

14 Charles Cotesworth Pinckney to James McHenry, Mar. 12, 1799, *The Papers of the Revolutionary Era Pinckney Statesmen*, digital edition, Constance B. Schultz, ed., Rotunda project, University of Virginia Press, 2016.

Norfolk, Charleston, and New Orleans were designated to receive priority attention. This Congressional action was a direct reaction to growing tension between Jefferson's young nation and the British navy. Great Britain was, at the time, fully engaged in a desperate fight with Napoleonic France and, as such, had little respect for American claims of neutrality on the open seas. This English contempt was highlighted in 1807 when the HMS *Leopold*, seeking to impress seamen for the Royal Navy, forcibly boarded an American navy frigate, the USS *Chesapeake*. Many Americans considered Britain's indifference to maritime law an affront to their national pride. Secretary of the Treasury Albert Gallatin added fuel to the fire by predicting the arrival of a British fleet and landing party somewhere along the coast within months.[15]

---

15 Weirick, *Castle Pinckney: Past, Present, Future*, 14; Wade, *Artillerists and Engineers*, 204; "Fortifications & Gunboats," *ASP*, 1:204.

Chapter 2

Building a Castle
1807–1828

"[Castle Pinckney] was built, in the year 1811, by Mr. John Gordon, now alive, and a resident of Charleston, and was erected in anticipation of a war with Great Britain, which was declared the year after."[1]

America's "second system" of coastal defenses would include more substantial masonry forts and the design expertise of the newly created Corps of Engineers. Under the inspired leadership of Col. Jonathan Williams, the grandnephew of Benjamin Franklin and the first Superintendent of West Point, young engineer graduates from the Academy began construction of several coastal forts, including three circular "castle" forts: Castle Pinckney in Charleston and Castles Clinton and Williams in the New York Harbor.

Jonathan Williams is credited with designing these structures, but he was strongly influenced by the work of a French engineer, Marquis de Montalembert. Williams believed that the principal advantage of these upright castle forts was the ability to place numerous cannons on three separate floors (tiers) in a small circular casemated perimeter, providing both concentrated fire when needed and significant lateral range for the protection of large expanses of water. Large coastal guns would be permanently mounted in casemates, which were massive bombproof brick vaults with arched ceilings. Each cannon would fire at ships through a slit-like embrasure. Only the top level, called a barbette, would have guns mounted on mobile wooden carriages.

Part of the inspiration for circular-style fortresses came from the 103 "Martello" towers the British built along their coastline during the ongoing Napoleonic

1 *The Rose Bud* [SC], Dec. 8, 1832, 1.

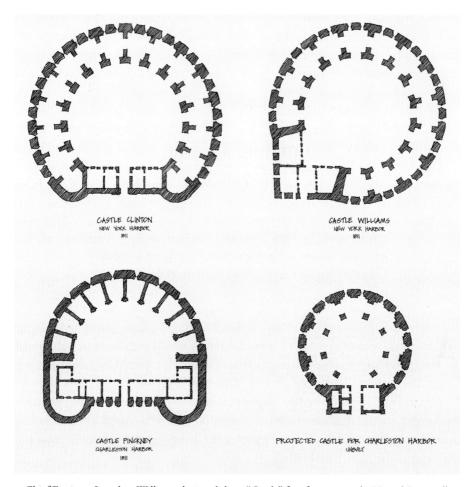

Chief Engineer Jonathan Williams designed three "Castle" fortifications in the United States, all had circular casemate design footprints. *Drawn by David Wierick*

Wars. Looking like a castle piece on a chess board, these circular towers, with their massive stone or brick walls, were three-story structures that featured one-, two-, or three-gun emplacements atop the flat roof. A garrison of 24 men and one officer would live inside the 40-foot tower and, at a moment's notice, provide a formidable defense against invaders coming by sea. Fort Johnson in the Charleston Harbor would be home to a 38-foot martello tower from 1821 to 1859, when it was torn down after a fire. The engineering designs of Williams significantly added complexity to this rudimentary martello tower concept by making his structures much larger and adding tiers of artillery casemates to his "castles." The American design, Williams maintained, rendered the question of combat "A question of floating wooden Walls against impregnable Stone Walls with equal number of guns within the same space." The wooden ships of the line would no longer have the advantage of concentrated firepower. The first known blueprints for Castle Pinckney, now at the National Archives, show a fort that looked much closer to a martello tower than would ultimately be built on Shute's Folly.[2]

In 1807, Williams visited Charleston to assure local authorities that the defenses of their city were not being neglected and that construction of a new federal fort on Shute's Folly was about to begin. The South Carolina Legislature had set the table in December 1805 by deeding the land under the remains of Forts Johnson, Moultrie, and Pinckney to the national government. Brig. Gen. Jacob Read, the Intendant (Mayor) of the City of Charleston, headed a commission that employed John Diamond to survey the abandoned sites. On Shute's Folly, federal authority now extended over "Three Acres of high marsh land, contiguous to, and around the old Work (Now in ruins) of Fort Pinckney." Col. Williams returned to New York to take particular interest in constructing the two circular castles in New York Harbor. His masterpiece would be Castle Williams on Governors Island which mounted 102 guns on four tiers.[3]

Capt. Alexander Macomb, only 25 years old, was the engineer officer sent to Charleston in 1807 to supervise the construction of coastal fortifications in the Carolinas and Georgia. Born in British-held Detroit in 1782, he joined the army at age 16 upon the recommendation of Alexander Hamilton. After serving as the personal secretary of Gen. James Wilkinson, Macomb joined the new engineering corps in 1802.

On May 20, 1807, Secretary of War Henry Dearborn was writing William Linnard, a military agent in Philadelphia, that bricks made in Charleston "ought to be preferred" for Castle Pinckney, but he was also sending Linnard $4,000 to purchase and pay for the transport to Castle Pinckney of three or four hundred "perch" of 2nd or 3rd quality stone. Perch was an old construction term equating to roughly 25 cubic feet of stone, which would have weighed about 4,700 pounds. Connecticut brownstone was procured to decorate the top and base of the four pilaster wall protrusions on the Castle's north side.[4]

---

2 Weirick, *Castle Pinckney: Past, Present, Future*, 15-16; Wade, *Artillerists and Engineers*, 206.

3 John R. Weaver, *A Legacy in Brick and Stone: American Coastal Defense Forts of the Third System, 1816-1867* (McLean, 2018), second edition, viii; On December 19, 1805, the South Carolina Legislature passed an act ceding four sites around the Charleston Harbor to the federal government for the erection of forts.

4 Letter, Dearborn to Linnard, May 28, 1807, Sol Feinstone Collection of the American Revolution, American Philosophical Society, Call Number Mss.B.F327.

16   *Holding Charleston by the Bridle: Castle Pinckney and the Civil War*

Captain of Engineers Alexander Macomb oversaw the construction of Castle Pinckney in 1809. *National Portrait Gallery*

Using the design plans of Williams, Macomb built Castle Pinckney on the site of old Fort Pinckney from the ground up as a state-of-the-art seacoast fortification. His principal contractors were the Scottish-born brothers, John and James Gordon. The brothers, still in their twenties, had been trained by their father as master brick masons and their practical knowledge in the building trades allowed them, in later years, to become architects in their own right. Immediately after completing Castle Pinckney, they would design and build both the Second Presbyterian Church on Meeting Street and the Cathedral of St. Luke and St. Paul on Coming Street.[5]

The Gordon brothers used large teams of leased enslaved labor to build the fort. Long timber pilings had first to be driven into the soft soil to support the masonry structure. Once construction of the fort began in the spring of 1809, Macomb was soon ordered to eliminate one of the planned tiers of casemates as a cost-saving measure. When fully completed in early 1811, this innovative fort featured space for nine cannons in the lower casemates and 11 guns on the upper barbette. The cannons on the top tier fired over a five-foot-high brick protective parapet wall. The semi-circular front of Castle Pinckney allowed the mounted cannons to command the harbor in a broad arc of 180 degrees. In April 1810, the brig *Polly* sailing from Baltimore, delivered ten 18-pounders and sixteen 24-pounders for the new fortress.

The entrance to the fort, a large sally port, was in the back of the fort. A wicket gate was built into the heavy wooden door that permitted a single person to enter or exit the Castle. Two semi-circular turrets protected the two rear corners of the fort. Small openings, called loopholes, allowed small arms fire to help repel a possible land-based assault. Each turret also held a cistern to ensure a sufficient water supply

---

5 Beatrice St. Julien Ravenel, *Architects of Charleston* (Columbia, 1945), 99-103; "Sand Wanted," *City* [SC] *Gazette*, Mar. 23, 1809, 2; "Sullivan's Island: No. 3, Castle Pinckney," *The Rose Bud* [SC], Dec. 8, 1832, 57.

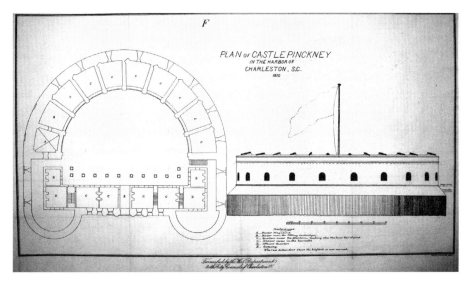

An 1883 drawing showing the 1810 plan for the construction of Castle Pinckney. The original sketch was possibly drawn by Alexander Macomb. *Matthew Locke*

for the garrison. Inside the fort, attached to the back wall, was a handsome two-story brick building that held the soldier's barracks and officer quarters. Each floor had eight rooms with fireplaces and wood-planked floors. A long porch or "piazza" ran the length of the building and looked down on the inside parade ground. Two hundred officers and men could crowd into these barracks in a time of conflict.

In October 1810, the governor of South Carolina, John Drayton, and Maj. Gen. Charles Cotesworth Pinckney, the namesake of the Castle, visited the nearly completed fort on the corvette *John Adams*. Pinckney, who had twice been a presidential candidate under the Federalist banner, was now an elder statesman. They were met with cannon salutes. The engineer Macomb left Charleston a few months later, having completed the construction of Castle Pinckney. At the start of the War of 1812, Macomb was promoted to brigadier general and put in charge of troops along the New York frontier. His clever defensive strategy during the battle of Plattsburg earned him a Congressional Gold Medal. In 1829, he became the commanding general of the U.S. Army and served in that position until he died in 1841.[6]

By the end of 1811, Secretary of War William Eustis could report to Congress that the energetic Macomb had rebuilt Fort Johnson on James Island with

---

6 Weirick, *Castle Pinckney: Past, Present, Future*, 22-23; "Brig Polly," *Charleston* [SC] *Daily Courier*, Apr. 12, 1810, 3; "His Excellency the Governor," *Carolina* [SC] *Gazette*, Oct. 12, 1810, 3.

a "marine battery of irregular form built of brick and wood" that mounted 16 guns and had barracks for 200 men. Fort Moultrie presented "a battery of three sides on the sea front, and the whole is enclosed with ramparts, parapets, and mounting 40 guns." Finally, built with brick and mounting 30 guns across two tiers, Castle Pinckney was "considered the most important in the harbor." It had cost $10,418.12 to construct.[7]

Older Charlestonians still had memories of the British siege and occupation of their city by Redcoats during the American Revolution. A second attack seemed in the cards in 1814 as the British had, that summer, managed to sail up the Chesapeake Bay and burn the nation's capital. The sentiment that Charleston would be next led to the construction of impressive zig-zag brick entrenchments, complete with moats, that crossed the half-mile "Neck" of the Charleston peninsula. The sea approaches were protected by three of Macomb's rebuilt forts— Johnson, Moultrie, and Pinckney—and their 80 coastal guns. Regular U.S. Army artillery soldiers garrisoned these forts, though almost all were 1812 volunteers who had joined newly organized companies that would constitute the 2nd U.S. Regiment of Artillery.

A May 1812 report of troop strength in the Lowcountry under the overall command of Capt. Addison Bowles Armistead has survived. 62 troops under Capt. Armistead were at Fort Moultrie, 68 soldiers under Capt. Wilson were at Fort Johnson, 35 troops under 1st Lt. Francis Stribling were at Castle Pinckney, and a detachment of infantry, 24 men in all, were at Fort Winyah in Georgetown. Capt. John R. Spann should have been in command at the Castle, but he was listed as "under arrest" and would soon be cashiered from the army for misappropriating funds for his personal use.[8]

Capt. Jacob Bond I'On is still widely recognized for defending Charleston in the War of 1812. The only son of a wealthy planter, he graduated from Yale College in 1804 in the same class as the future statesman John C. Calhoun. He resigned from the South Carolina House of Representatives in 1812 to accept a captain's commission in the U.S. 2nd Regiment of Artillery. By the summer of 1812, the 30-year-old I'On was commanding Castle Pinckney. His steady leadership throughout this war has been frequently noted.

---

7 Weirick, *Castle Pinckney: Past, Present, Future*, 328; Wade, *Artillerists and Engineers*, 238; "Statement of Money expended on account of fortifications from the year 1794 to 1824," ASP, 3:249.

8 Nic Butler, "War of 1812 Fortifications in Urban Charleston," Sep. 5, 2014, Walled City Task Force, https://walledcitytaskforce.org/category/fortifications/page/4/; "Monthly Return of Troops of the Harbour of Charleston for May 1812," roll 197, *Returns from Military Posts*, 1800 -1916, NARA, M617. Hereafter cited as RMP.

In May 1813, the army organized the national defenses around nine military districts. The two Carolinas and Georgia made up the sixth district. Maj. Daniel Forney of Lincolnton, North Carolina, was given command of the district's artillery, and he set up his headquarters at Fort Moultrie. Forney had three companies in Charleston—I'On's, Robert Gill's, and the late Addison Armistead—to man the three harbor forts and another two companies of artillery in North Carolina—under Captains Donoho and Hawkins. The 36-year-old Addison Armistead was a Virginian who had served in the army for 18 years, but he died at Fort Moultrie in February 1813 and was buried at Fort Johnson. His nephew, Gen. Lewis Addison Armistead, would, some 50 years later, fall on the last day of the battle of Gettysburg, leading his brigade to the farthest point reached on Cemetery Ridge by Confederate forces during Pickett's ill-fated charge.[9]

Hanging over the soldiers stationed around Charleston Harbor were the affairs of Capt. Robert Gill. The commander of one of the three artillery companies assigned to Charleston, Gill was dismissed from the service on December 9, 1813, following a court martial held at Fort Moultrie under the direction of Maj. Forney. Gill had been charged with conduct unbecoming of an officer and a gentleman relating to a duel held on Sullivan's Island in September. Gill, who was acting as a Second in the duel, had given the combatants two different size pistol balls, leaving Lt. Edwin Sharpe at a severe disadvantage. In February 1814, President James Madison surprised many by remitting Gill's sentence and ordering that the captain be reinstated to his rank and command.

This pardon was not well received by the U.S. Army officers stationed in Charleston. They responded with a proclamation written on February 28th and passed on to Washington by Lt. Jacob Farley from Castle Pinckney. The officers expressed their surprise at Gill's reinstatement and believed they had been impartial judges at the court-martial as "men of honor and unimpeachable integrity." Henceforth they would restrict their communications with Capt. Gill to only that most required in line with their military duties, but they would never "conceive him to be entitled to the privileges and respect due to a Gentleman and a *Man of Honor*." This extraordinary document was signed by the commanders of the 2nd Artillery Regiment and the 18th and 43rd Infantry Regiments, as well as 29 captains and lieutenants (see Appendix 2).

With Charleston's infantry and artillery officers in something just short of open rebellion, it was left to Thomas Pinckney, the major general commanding the Southern Division of the U.S. Army, to calm the waters. The 64-year-old Pinckney,

---

9 Military Districts, *The Army Register of the United States* (Philadelphia, 1813), 82; "Mortuary Notice," *Daily* [DC] *National Intelligencer*, Mar. 23, 1813, 3.

the younger brother of diplomat Charles Cotesworth Pinckney, had in his long career of public service been a Patriot officer, the governor of South Carolina, and the minister to Great Britain. He had now been recalled to military service from his plantation on the Santee River because of the war with Great Britain. Pinckney told the Charleston officers that he did not think President Madison knew all the particulars when he remitted Gill's termination. It was considered best, wrote Pinckney, that Capt. Gill be appointed to a post in another district. Meanwhile, Capt. Gill was writing to the adjutant general from Charleston on March 19th, noting that "by some strange fatality," his reinstatement had not been "published at this place." If he was not to be immediately reinstated, could he be appointed to a Northern position for the upcoming summer campaign? With months passing, Gill took his grievances to James Monroe, the secretary of war.

Ultimately, the war with Britain ended abruptly with the signing of the Treaty of Ghent on December 24, 1814, and Andrew Jackson's surprising victory outside of New Orleans on January 8, 1815. Like most wars, there was a rush by citizen soldiers to return to their former lives. Robert Gill never would command United States troops again. In contrast, Jacob I'On was called upon to command all of Charleston's harbor fortifications. Ready to resume his political career, however, I'On did not stay long in his new military post, leaving the service in June 1815 to run for office in Christ Church Parish. By July 1816, the Charleston Harbor defenses were under the command of Lt. Edwin Sharpe at Fort Moultrie. Sharpe ran an ad in the *City Gazette* offering $10 for the return of any of the 31 soldiers who had abandoned their posts in the last year.[10]

On June 19, 1818, the *Charleston Courier* reported that a duel had recently taken place at Castle Pinckney between two naval officers, Lt. Charles Caldwell of the schooner USS *Lynx* and Lt. James Taylor of the brig USS *Prometheus*. The 24-year-old Caldwell received a flesh wound to his body. The Charleston newspaper lamented that these officers "who have, on all occasions, displayed the utmost bravery when engaged with the enemies of their country, should conceive it necessary so frequently in vindication of their character to resort to this murderous expedient." It was the third or fourth duel between naval officers in the Southern Squadron in less than six months.

From the Revolutionary War to the Civil War, Charleston and New Orleans recommended themselves as notorious hotbeds for dueling among well-heeled

---

10   Robert M. Gill folder, War of 1812, *Letters Received by the Office of the Adjutant General, 1805-1821*, NARA; "Desertions," *City* [SC] *Gazette*, Jul. 16, 1816, 4. The present-day neighborhood community of I'On in Mount Pleasant is named after Jacob Bond I'On, as is a major road on Sullivan's Island.

Southern gentlemen willing to risk their lives over matters of honor, politics, and manners. Complete with pre-negotiated ground rules, special large caliber smoothbore flintlock pistols, and overseen by Seconds and Surgeons, dueling was an accepted way of settling disputes. The U.S. Navy would not forbid the practice of dueling until 1862, and the governor of South Carolina, John Lyde Wilson, took it upon himself in 1838 to publish the definitive dueling manual of its day. Historian Grahame Long notes that these contagionists sought a place that would be private and beyond the city limits, thereby avoiding an audience or an arrest. Castle Pinckney and Fort Johnson were preferred locations as they were both out-of-the-way and not under the jurisdiction of the state.[11]

On April 17, 1819, Col. James Bankhead informed his harbor troops, one or two artillery companies at the most, that President James Monroe would visit Charleston as part of his grand tour of the Southern states. Bankhead informed his fort commanders that each fort would provide a national salute of 21 guns when the president's party crossed from Mount Pleasant to the city. The signal for the commencement was to be given from Castle Pinckney, and the guns would be fired at 12-second intervals. Monroe's visit to Charleston was considered a success, and he was honored with parades and dinner parties. On April 30th, he boarded the steamboat *Charleston* with his family, the governor of South Carolina, the secretary of war, Gen. Edmund Pendleton Gaines, a musical band, and numerous military officers. The day was devoted to touring federal forts in the Charleston Harbor. Upon landing at Castle Pinckney, and Forts Johnson and Moultrie, the president was met, on each occasion, with another 21-gun salute. The day closed with an "eloquent collation" held in Col. James Bankhead's quarters at Fort Johnson.[12]

The federal presence in Charleston was never great at this time. Besides the post office and the collection of tariff revenue, there was a modest federal court system and a small military garrison. Monthly post records for Charleston Harbor in 1820 show that virtually the entire 1st Battalion of Artillery was on detached service to Fernandina on Amelia Island, Florida. Left at Charleston was Lt. John O. Kirk, in charge of recruitment, Lt. J. L. Engle, commanding Fort Moultrie, a paymaster, the post surgeon, and less than a dozen privates. With a lean budget, the U.S.

---

11 "Duel," *Charleston* [SC] *Courier*, Jun. 19, 1818, 2; *Register of the Navy for the year 1818, 15th Congress*, Naval History and Heritage Command; J. Grahame Long, *Dueling in Charleston: Violence Refined in the Holy City* (Charleston, 2012), 20-22, 41-42, 47.

12 ASP, Report of the Secretary of War, Jan. 12, 1819, 1:819; Lt. J. M. Washington, "Harbor Orders, April 17, 1819, Fort Johnson," *The Papers of Captain Thomas J. Baird, Third Regiment of Artillery, 1813 to 1828* (Philadelphia, 1848) Supplemental; "Charleston, April 30th," *Milledgeville Georgia Journal*, May 11, 1819, 6. In 1819, Castle Pinckney had 30 guns, Fort Moultrie, 40 guns, Fort Johnson, 16 guns, and Fort Mechanic, 7 guns.

President James Monroe inspected Castle Pinckney on a trip to Charleston in 1819. This painting of Monroe was done by John Vanderlyn in 1816.
National Portrait Gallery

Army had few troops and little reason to post them in Charleston, where a surprise attack by a naval sea power seemed unlikely. This negligible military presence in Charleston would continue until 1832.[13]

In 1821, the "Third system" of coastal fortifications began with the adoption of a Board of Engineers report outlining a comprehensive plan for the defense of the American coast. Considering the advances in military technology, specifically the increasing range and power of artillery, the commissioners viewed Castle Pinckney, and similar fortifications, as being too close to the ports for which they were designated to defend. A first line of defense needed to be closer to the ocean and away from the civilian population. This report led directly to the construction of Fort Sumter in South Carolina, Fort Pulaski in Georgia, Fort Monroe in Virginia, Fort Macon in North Carolina, and Fort Jackson in Louisiana. In 1821, two of the three engineers on the Board formally toured Castle Pinckney. A detailed survey by Capt. Guillaume Tell Poussin at the time shows that little had been altered from Williams's original 1809 design drawings. What the engineers did take from Pinckney was Williams's innovative casemate design, a concept they would reproduce on a much larger scale at Forts Sumter and Pulaski. In 1822, Castle Clinton, which was on the tip of the Manhattan peninsula and deemed impractical for the defense of the New York City harbor, was de-commissioned as an active military post. It was believed Castle Pinckney would face a similar fate or would be designated for interior defense as a secondary military structure.

While not garrisoned in the 1820s, Castle Pinckney had its share of tragedy. During this time, the fort was home to only an ordnance sergeant and his family. In 1825, Ordnance Sgt. John Gowan was crossing the Cooper River from the city

---

13 RMP, Feb. & Mar. 1820, roll 197.

to the Castle with his wife and child when his small batteau overturned. Gowan drowned, but his wife and child were saved. The waters in Charleston Harbor could be treacherous, and drowning incidents around Castle Pinckney were not uncommon. Black fishermen and oyster collectors were often the victims. The hurricane of September 1822 tore through the harbor wharves, resulting in several sloops being torn from their moorings and run aground on the sand banks of Shute's Folly. Another unfortunate death was that of Isaac Parker, a grocer living at 2 Elliott Street near Kiddell's Wharf. In 1826, Parker and his brother-in-law J. M. Happoldt rowed over to Shute's Folly to enjoy some bird hunting. Parker was killed while in the act of jumping through a barracks window of the empty Castle. Parker's bird gun, which was in one of his hands, went off with the charge passing through his head. Parker had buried his wife only weeks earlier, leaving an infant child deprived of both parents.[14]

14 Weirick, *Castle Pinckney: Past, Present, Future*, 28-29; "Sergeant John Gowan," *Charleston* [SC] *Courier*, Jan. 6, 1825, 2; "Hurricane," *City* [SC] *Gazette*, Sep. 30, 1822, 2; "Fatal Accident," *Charleston* [SC] *Courier*, Jun. 2, 1826, 2; "Melancholy Casualty," *City* [SC] *Gazette*, Jun. 2, 1826, 4.

Chapter 3

Lynchpin of the Nullification Crisis
1829–1834

South Carolina had a difficult time recovering from the Panic of 1819. Cotton planters found that their tired lands had become less productive than the new farms in Alabama and Mississippi. Both people and wealth began moving out of the Palmetto State. By 1820, New Orleans had surpassed Charleston as the principal seaport in the South.

Radical states-rights advocates blamed their woes on the national tariff, especially the 1828 Tariff of Abominations. Feeling pressure from his home state, Vice President John C. Calhoun produced the *South Carolina Exposition* later that year. His treatise asserted that a protective tariff was unconstitutional as it sheltered the industrial sector of the Northeast while penalizing agrarian interests in the South and West. He went on to declare that American states could interpose their sovereignty and nullify unconstitutional federal legislation. Led by Representative John Quincy Adams, Congress reacted to the rising tension by adjusting downward the federal tariff in 1832. This action was well received by most of the nation and led to the re-election of Andrew Jackson as president later that year.[1]

The distinctive nature of South Carolina politics, however, produced a negative response to the compromise tariff of 1832. Led by its planter elites, who were apprehensive about the future federal protection of slavery, South Carolina voted for a State Nullification Convention that promptly declared the tariffs of

---

1 Daniel Walker Howe, *What Hath God Wrought; The Transformation of America, 1815-1848* (New York, 2007), 396-399; Michael D. Thompson, *Working on the Dock of the Bay: Labor and Enterprise in an Antebellum Southern Port* (Columbia, 2015), 6.

South Carolina Senator John C. Calhoun set in motion both the 1833 Nullification Crisis and helped end it in a compromise with Senator Henry Clay of Kentucky. From an 1834 drawing done by James Barton Longacre. *National Portrait Gallery*

1828 and 1832 unconstitutional. Beginning in February 1833, the Palmetto State would, according to the convention delegates, refuse to allow the collection of the national tariff in their state. Their ordinance threatened secession if the federal government attempted to coerce their citizens. The South Carolina legislature backed this position by calling for 25,000 volunteer militiamen to defend their state's rights. Calhoun resigned from the vice presidency and returned to his seat in the U.S. Senate. There he rose from his chair to claim that Castle Pinckney and Fort Moultrie were being used by President Jackson to "keep the people themselves in awe and subjection." A national crisis was at hand.[2]

The year 1832 began with three companies from the 2nd U.S. Artillery Regiment stationed in the Lowcountry under the overall command of Bvt. Maj. Julius Heileman. Company A, under 1st Lt. Allen Lowd, with 53 men, was assigned to Castle Pinckney, while the 45 men of Company B garrisoned Fort Moultrie, and the 55 men of Company F garrisoned the Citadel Armory. In June, Companies A and B departed for Fort Armistead in the Cherokee Territory of Tennessee to assist with Indian removal.

The three companies of the 2nd Artillery were replaced by two companies from the 1st Regiment of Artillery. Company A was ordered to Fort Moultrie, and Company E, 47 men under Capt. Henry Saunders, moved into Castle Pinckney. On July 2, Saunders sent a formal request to Washington asking that he be transferred to the command of Fort Moultrie, "believing it to be a much more important post than this (Castle Pinckney)." Saunders was senior to Lt. M. A. Patrick of Company A, and he and his lieutenant in Company E both had families

---

2 Howe, *What Hath God Wrought*, 404-405; John C. Calhoun, *The Papers of John C. Calhoun*, 28 vol., Robert Lee Meriwether & William Edwin Hemphill, ed. & trans (Columbia, 1959), 12:181.

Lynchpin of the Nullification Crisis: 1829–1834

1831 watercolor sketch of Castle Pinckney from George Lehman to Mary Eliza Bachman Audubon. Lehman was a skilled artist who painted backgrounds for James Audubon's *Birds of America*. The walls of the Castle were no longer exposed red brick but were covered by an off-white lime cement wash. *Winterthur Library: Joseph Downs Collection of Manuscripts and Printed Ephemera*

that would be better accommodated at Fort Moultrie. Lt. Patrick and his officers, on the other hand, were young bachelors.

Saunders's request for a transfer was not acted upon, but instead both Companies A and E were assigned to Castle Pinckney, bringing the garrison strength to about 100 men. Capt. Saunders soon alerted Washington that his post was dangerously overcrowded, "indeed I have had to quarter a family in an open casemate." Most importantly, there was no place to shelter the sick. With most of his men being from the North, he expected an abundance of illness in the humid Lowcountry summer. Saunders requested $400 from the Quartermaster Department to build a hospital. In another letter to the quartermaster general in Washington, Saunders reported that his company was "destitute of music," and asked that a drummer and fifer be sent to him from among the new recruits training in New York. In September, Saunders received 12 new recruits from the New York Depot, but he found that two, John Davis and James Grime, had previously deserted the army and had reenlisted using aliases. He had both arrested.[3]

---

3 "Returns from 2nd Artillery Regiment, 1831-1840," *Returns from Regular Army Non-Infantry Regiments, 1821-1916*, NARA, M727, roll 10; "Returns from 1st Artillery Regiment, 1831-1840," *Returns from Regular Army Non-Infantry Regiments, 1821-1916*, NARA, M727, roll 2; Letters, Request of Henry Saunders, Jul. 2, 1832, Jul. 15, 1832, roll 470, *Letters Received by the Office of the Adjutant General Main Series 1822-1860*, NARA, M567, RG 94, roll 470. Hereafter cited as OAG.

An 1831 view of Castle Pinckney and the Charleston Harbor painted by Samuel Barnard.
Yale University Art Gallery—Mabel Brady Garvan Collection

On October 29, 1832, Maj. Gen. Alexander Macomb, the original builder of Castle Pinckney, ordered Julius Heileman, the popular commander of Federal troops in the harbor, to "call personally on the commanders of Castle Pinckney and Fort Moultrie and instruct them to be vigilant to prevent surprise in the night, or by day, on the part of any set of people whatever, who may approach the forts with a view to seize and occupy them." Sen. Calhoun's accusations had a basis in truth in that Macomb had, as far back as 1826, written to the secretary of war that he viewed Castle Pinckney "as an auxiliary in the defense of the harbor, and as serving as a sort of citadel in case of internal commotion."

That commotion was now at hand. In a follow-up letter to Heileman, Macomb instructed the Charleston commander to release to state authorities, if so demanded, the arms belonging to South Carolina that were held in the Citadel, but, if this happened, Heileman was also to use his command judiciously to evacuate the Citadel and transport federal property held there to Castle Pinckney.[4]

On orders from Secretary of War Lewis Cass, 46-year-old Winfield Scott arrived at Fort Moultrie on Sullivan's Island on November 26, 1832, to direct

---

[4] "Military Orders," *Niles'* [DC] *Weekly Register*, Feb. 23, 1833, 436-437; ASP, 1826 Engineer Board Report, 3:293.

federal operations. News of the arrival of such a high-ranking general brought indignation among the citizenry of nearby Charleston. Scott toured Moultrie and Castle Pinckney and immediately began resupplying the forts with food and ordnance. Taking advantage of the crisis, Saunders ordered for his men at Castle Pinckney coats, shako caps, trousers, gray wool overalls, knapsacks, cockades, pompoms, socks, and leather stocks (see Appendix 3). Perhaps most importantly, Saunders received in November a new garrison national flag. The 24 stars included South Carolina, and this was an overt and visible reminder of the increased presence of federal authority in the harbor.[5]

Meanwhile, South Carolina divided into two camps, the Nullifiers and the Unionists, with both groups procuring arms and enlisting volunteers for their new militias. The *Columbia Times* predicted that Gov. Robert Hayne would have 12,000 men at his disposal by February. Joel Poinsett, a member of the U.S. House of Representatives and the able leader of the 8,000 Unionists, predicted a civil war. He confidentially wrote President Jackson on November 24 with his assessment of the harbor forts. The Charleston diplomat and namesake of the poinsettia plant believed Fort Moultrie to be "in a very dilapidated state," but viewed Pinckney as being "in fine order." This assessment was partly due to a $10,000 renovation of the fort begun in 1829 by Lt. Henry Brewerton and completed in 1831. Poinsett thought the island fortress was formidable and could only be attacked from the rear by a flotilla coming across the Hog Island Channel. The Charlestonian noted that Capt. Saunders had placed two field pieces outside the Castle, but he recommended that a temporary work be thrown up by the entrance that was capable of mounting two heavy guns. He also recommended temporarily moving the Custom House to Shute's Folly.[6]

In December 1832, President Andrew Jackson declared the actions of the South Carolina convention to be an "impractical absurdity" and that "Disunion by armed force is treason." Old Hickory considered the actions of South Carolina to be a threat to both his personal and patriotic authority. More importantly, the president recognized the severe pressure that would be placed on government revenue and credit if South Carolina got away with nullifying the tariff. The commander in chief announced to the nation that reinforcements had been sent

---

5 John Eisenhower, *Agent of Destiny: The Life and Times of General Winfield Scott* (New York, 1997), 136; Henry Saunders, supply requisition form from Nov. 5, 1832, Castle Pinckney, private collection of Cliff Roberts.

6 Eisenhower, *Agent of Destiny*, 137; Letter, Joel Poinsett to Andrew Jackson, Nov. 24, 1832, *Papers of Andrew Jackson*, digital edition, Michael E. Woods, ed., Rotunda project, University of Virginia Press, 2015; Weirick, *Castle Pinckney: Past, Present, Future*, 32; ASP, Annual report of Secretary of War, John Eaton, to Congress, Nov. 21 1831, 4:729.

to Fort Moultrie and Castle Pinckney. The U.S. schooner *Experiment* and the U.S. sloop-of-war *Natchez* were also dispatched from Norfolk to the Charleston Harbor. Castle Pinckney, in particular, had become newsworthy, as its guns commanded the Charleston wharves and much of the city.[7]

Readers of newspapers nationwide soon read a January 1833 description of Moultrie and Pinckney from a recently arrived Virginia officer that was first published in the *Winchester Republican* and then reprinted across the young nation. We speculate that the writer was Dr. Henry Lee Heiskell, a native of Winchester. The unnamed officer spent the night of January 3 at Moultrie before embarking for Castle Pinckney. The officer was emotionally taken by the summer residences of the Charleston elite that dotted Sullivan's Island, writing, "The dwellings, surrounded by piazzas—the palmetto, the boast and pride of the Carolinians—the Spanish bayonet (an evergreen from 10 to 15 ft. high) the soft, elastic atmosphere,—all together produced such an impression upon me that I could very readily imagine myself in some oriental village, so different was everything from what I had been accustomed to." That night, Gen. Winfield Scott dined with the officers, "on which occasion toasts were drank, speeches made, and great loyalty and patriotism avowed."

The Virginian described his new post at Castle Pinckney as "a small, but strong castellated fortification, built upon a marsh, a small portion of which has been reclaimed for that purpose." With eight 24-pounders, two 12-pounders, two 6-pounders, and a 10-inch howitzer, the newly reinforced garrison "completely commands the city." Two artillery companies from Fortress Monroe, under Capt. Saunders, would defend the Castle. The letter writer lamented the lack of space to exercise, noting "the whole space beyond the reach of the tides not being much more than a half-acre." On the other hand, the officer welcomed the ongoing opportunities for a hearty feast, noting an abundance of oyster shells lying along the tidal break.[8]

By the end of January 1833, there were six artillery companies at Fort Moultrie and two at Castle Pinckney. In all, close to 500 men defended the federal forts. New construction began on the outlying defenses of Fort Moultrie, with Scott also demanding that regular officers stationed in the harbor forts renew their oaths of allegiance. Untrustworthy officers were to be replaced. On February 19, 1833, with District Judge Thomas Lee presiding, the six "gentlemen officers in the army of the United States now stationed at Castle Pinckney" retook their oath of allegiance

---

7 Howe, *What Hath God Wrought*, 405-406; Carl Lane, *A Nation Wholly Free: The Elimination of the National Debt in the Age of Jackson* (Yardley, PA, 2014), 29; Eisenhower, *Agent of Destiny*, 137.

8 "Castle Pinckney," *Columbian* [DC] *Register*, Feb. 2, 1833, 2.

Unionist Joel Roberts Poinsett was President Jackson's Charleston confidant during the Nullification Crisis. This is an 1838 engraving taken from a sketch by Charles Fenderich. *National Portrait Gallery*

to the United States of America. On February 20, Gen. Scott wrote Washington that he did not believe that Gov. James Hamilton of South Carolina would be so bold as to order an attack on Castle Pinckney nor Fort Moultrie, but he feared an "unauthorized multitude, under some sudden excitement," might take matters into their own hands. Better he thought to show strength and resolve, thereby dissuading such sentiments.[9]

On January 27, 1833, a more confident Poinsett reported to the president again. "I have visited the forts and carefully examined their situations," he explained. Capt. James W. Ripley, he believed, had done a remarkable job of supervising the extensive repairs to Fort Moultrie. Poinsett was disappointed that Fort Johnson remained abandoned and open to occupation by a hostile militia. "Castle Pinckney is safe, I think," he informed Jackson, "both from the position and nature of the work, and from the character of Capt. Saunders, who commands there." President Jackson responded on December 2, writing that he had ordered "5,000 stand of musket with corresponding equipment" be sent to Castle Pinckney for use by the Unionists under Joel Poinsett's command. "The commanding officer of Castle Pinckney will be instructed by the Secretary of War," wrote the president, "to deliver the arms and their equipment to your order, taking a receipt for them, and should the

---

9 RMP, *Charleston Harbor*, Jan. 1833; OAG, Oath of allegiance of the officers at Castle Pinckney, Feb. 19, 1833, roll 087; OAG, Report from Winfield Scott, Feb. 20, 1833. The six officers from Castle Pinckney who signed the Oath of Allegiance in 1833 were H. Saunders, Capt. 1. Arty; M. A. Patrick, Lt. 1st Arty, G. W. Turner, Lt. 1st U.S. Arty, Jacob Ammen, Brevet 2nd Lt. 1st Arty; H. L. Heiskell, Asst. Surg; E. French, Lt. 1st Arty.

emergency arise he will furnish to your requisition such ordnance and ordnance stores as can be spared from the arsenals."[10]

Winfield Scott also looked over Castle Pinckney and quickly put his trust in Capt. Saunders, the immediate commander of the fortress. Scott ordered Capt. William A. Eliason of the engineers to design and build a tall wooden palisade that would effectively double the size of the fortification and provide protection to the rear side of the Castle. Eliason's irregularly shaped wall was built in 1833 and provided firing positions for 18 cannons. Tons of dirt were brought inside the walls to raise the new parade ground above the marsh, and an elevated platform was built along the timber walls for cannon and rifle positions. A small hospital building, a workshop, and a guardhouse were soon constructed within the palisade perimeter. A stone seawall was also constructed around the walls of Castle Pinckney to strengthen the foundations of the fortress.[11]

President Jackson increased the stakes in the standoff by sending Congress a proposal, quickly called the Force Bill, explicitly authorizing him to use military force to collect the tariff revenue in the harbor of Charleston. Virginia Senator and future President John Tyler rose on the Senate floor to oppose the bill describing Charleston as a "beleaguered city" and accused Jackson of being ready to drive the defenders of South Carolina "into the swamps where Marion found refuge." At the same time, President Jackson sweetened his position by allowing Congressman Gulian Verplanck of New York to offer a bill that would dramatically reduce tariff rates to 1816 levels in two short years.

With politicians in Washington making speeches, Scott used every opportunity over the next two months to keep tempers in check among the residents of Charleston. On the daily supply boats to Charleston, troops were instructed to be especially cordial with merchants and citizens. Scott also invited hundreds of Charlestonians to visit the dock at Fort Moultrie, where he mingled with both Nullifiers and Unionists. On February 16, 1833, a large fire broke out in a Charleston rag and cotton storehouse. The commanding general could see the smoke from Fort Moultrie, and he acted with dispatch by sending 300 unarmed volunteers in rowboats across the harbor to help put out the flames. Capt. Saunders from Castle Pinckney had already sent a detachment of soldiers under Lieutenants George Turner and Jacob Ammen. Upon dousing the fire, the American soldiers were greeted by local women bringing bread, cheese, and cider.

---

10 Letter, Joel Poinsett to Andrew Jackson, Jan. 27, 1833, Papers of Andrew Jackson. Letter, Andrew Jackson to Joel Poinsett, Dec. 2, 1832, Papers of Andrew Jackson.

11 Report of Winfield Scott, Mar. 11, 1833, OAG; Weirick, *Castle Pinckney: Past, Present, Future*, 25-33.

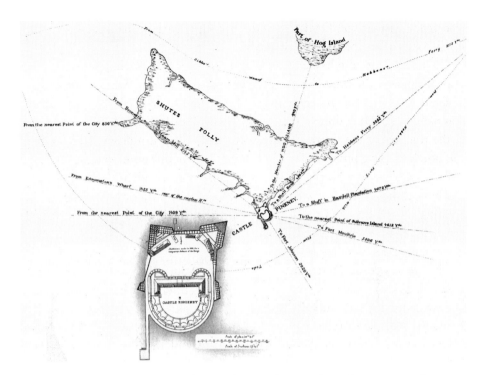

An 1833 sketch by William Ellison showing distances from Castle Pinckney to various locations around the harbor. Superimposed on the sketch is an 1839 engineering diagram showing the extensive palisade walls constructed behind Castle Pinckney during the Nullification Crisis of 1833. *National Archives Cartography Room and the Charleston Library Society*

A soldier in Capt. Samuel Ringgold's company recounted that on their way back to the wharf, a group of Charleston gentlemen "insisted that we should follow them to an adjoining restaurant, where the tables were spread with the best things that could be had."[12]

February 22 was the 101st birthday anniversary of George Washington, the "Father of his Country," and it proved another opportunity to express national unity in Charleston. As the local men in the Washington Light Infantry and the Union Light Infantry paraded down the streets of the city, Federal soldiers under Gen. Scott at both Fort Moultrie and Castle Pinckney, as well as sailors aboard the two Navy ships and two revenue cutters, all fired loud salutes at sunrise and again at sunset. Rockets were also fired at night. At 10:30 a.m. both forts began firing blank cartridges from their heavy guns, field guns and infantry muskets.

12 Lane, *A Nation Wholly Free*, 130; "Charleston Courier," *Philadelphia* [PA] *Inquirer*, Feb. 27, 1833, 2; "Touching Incdent of Nullification Times," *American* [PA] *Presbyterian*, Feb. 14, 1861, 1.

Painting of 1833 Charleston by Robert Lavin. The Revenue cutter *McClane* is sailing in front of Castle Pinckney. *Courtesy of the U.S. Coast Guard Collection*

Scott may well have viewed this celebration as the perfect excuse to get in some needed training and to loudly exhibit to the nearby Nullifers the power of his small army. Commercial ships in the harbor added to the occasion by decorating their masts with various flags and signals. According to historian John S. D. Eisenhower, Winfield Scott's strength of purpose, coupled with his moderation, contributed significantly to the resolution of the Nullification Crisis, which ultimately petered out without violence. A February 12, 1833 editorial written for the *Charleston Courier* and entitled "Corn, Fodder, & Bacon" pointed to the futility of the poorly prepared Nullifiers, who would need the immediate imports of corn, fodder, and bacon from "the very people we are about to defy and fight." John C. Calhoun ultimately sat down with Henry Clay of Kentucky and worked out a new compromise tariff structure. Their bill passed the Senate on March 1, 1833, and President Jackson agreed to accept peace with South Carolina.[13]

On July 23, 1833, Capt. Henry Saunders wrote to Army Commander Alexander Macomb from Castle Pinckney requesting that his two companies be relieved from their present station. Saunders also enclosed a similar petition signed by the eight officers garrisoned at the Castle for the general's consideration (see Appendix 5). In Saunders's letter, the commander of the post closest to Charleston believed that his officers and men had "a claim to some indulgence after serving more than a

---

13 OAG, Report from Winfield Scott, Feb. 23, 1833; "Charleston," *Charleston* [SC] *Courier*, Feb. 23, 1833, 2; Eisenhower, *Agent of Destiny*, 138-139. "Corn, Fodder and Bacon," *Charleston* [SC] *Courier*, Feb. 12, 1833, 2.

year at this confined & uncomfortable post, & through the Nullification War." Now that "the immediate apprehension of violent measures on the part of the state authorities has subsided," Saunders believed his men should be withdrawn "from the vicinity of Charleston where they are looked upon by the citizens with dislike." A new set of soldiers, who had not been present when "excitement was so great," might, in Saunders's estimation, "be received by the inhabitants with some show of respect if not kindness." The following month, Saunders's request was granted, and his command was transferred to Fort Trumbull in Connecticut.

Shortly before the departure of Saunders and his men, a gruesome and violent assault occurred on Castle Pinckney's wharf. On August 13, 1833, a party of soldiers returning to Fort Moultrie from the city stopped at the Castle to visit. Cpl. James Straton and Pvt. Robert Vias remained with the boat, where an altercation soon ensued over Vias's inattention to duty. Straton struck Vias "on the head, and various parts of his body" with the boat's tiller knocking the Maryland native unconscious. Several of the boat's crew, having seen the brutal attack, then conspired with Stratton to conceal the events from the officers at Fort Moultrie where, on August 14, Vias died of supposed alcohol poisoning. Once the story had been recounted, the body of Vias was disinterred from his grave, and a jury of inquest was convened on Sullivan's Island. The coroner of the district, Francis Michel, confirmed that Vias had died "in consequence of a blow or blows inflicted by James Straton." The army corporal was taken to the Moultrieville jail.[14]

Tempers over nullification had cooled by 1834 when Capt. Henry Griswold of the 3rd Artillery dined on the 4th of July with the Washington Society of Charleston. He recorded in his army account book that the dinner toast to the Union, "Our glorious Union—There is nothing like it—It shall be preserved," brought forth six loud cheers. In a Fall 1834 Ordnance Report, Griswold's Castle held 12 artillery pieces, with most being howitzers and field artillery designed to thwart a possible infantry attack. Unfortunately, the 39-year-old commander of Castle Pinckney passed away in October 1834, probably from yellow fever. His body was brought to the Charleston wharves, where it was met by two companies of Charleston militia, the Cadet Riflemen and the Sumter Guard. In a sign of respect, the colors of the various ships anchored at the wharves were brought to half-mast. Officers of the army and navy served as pallbearers, and the slow-moving procession made its way up Broad and Meeting Streets to the Circular

---

14 OAG, Letter from H. Saunders to Col. R. Jones, Jul. 23, 1833; "Death by Violence and Disinterment," *Washington* [DC] *National Intelligencer*, Sep. 4, 1833, 3.

Church, where a service was held. Griswold's body was temporarily placed in a cemetery vault until it could be sent to Boston for final burial.[15]

15 1834 Army Accounts Logbook, Castle Pinckney, Henry W. Griswold Papers, Box 1, v. B-3, Baker Library Special Collections, Harvard Business School, Cambridge; "Funeral of Captain Griswold," *Charleston* [SC] *Mercury*, Oct. 27, 1834, 2; ASP, 1834 Ordnance Report, 853.

Chapter 4

A Convenient Repository
1835–1859

The construction of Fort Sumter, which began in 1829, would occupy the attention of Congress and the United States military for the next thirty years. As part of the Third System of coastal fortifications, Sumter was one of forty-two forts constructed between 1816 and 1867.

When the Civil War broke out in 1861, the masonry fort was still unfinished. Seventy thousand tons of New England granite had been shipped to Charleston to build a foundation atop a shallow shoal that was across the harbor entrance from Fort Moultrie. Built atop this newly created 2.4-acre island was a new three-tiered, five-sided coastal fortification designed to hold a garrison of 650 men and 135 artillery pieces. It took some four million "Carolina grey" bricks to construct this fortress which featured five to twelve ft. thick walls that rose 44 ft. above the foundation. Fort Johnson, which served as a staging area for the giant project, was closed during Sumter's construction.[1]

Until Fort Sumter was completed, Fort Moultrie and Castle Pinckney would together be responsible for the defense of the harbor from an attack by a foreign foe. Companies A and H, 1st Artillery Regiment garrisoned the harbor forts from March 1833 through 1835. Each company spent half the year at Castle Pinckney, while the other was stationed at Fort Moultrie. Overall command of the harbor transferred among military officers: Maj. William Gates to Capt. Giles Porter to

---

[1] Richard Hatcher, *Thunder in the Harbor* (El Dorado Hills, 2024) 3-5; John R. Weaver, II, *A Legacy of Brick and Stone: American Coastal Defense Forts of the Third System, 1816-1867* (McLean, VA, 2018), 2nd edition, 54.

Col. Abraham Eustis. Gates was charged with applying a second coat of off-white lime cement wash to both Castle Pinckney and Fort Moultrie. The first coat, which was applied in 1831, had in only three short years become dirty and was peeling in places. At a cost of $200, Engineer Easton oversaw the application of the second coat. An ordnance report from the fourth quarter of 1834 listed Castle Pinckney with a dozen cannons of various sizes, over 650 pounds of gunpowder, 100 muskets, plus nearly 1,000 rounds of artillery ordnance. In January 1836, both artillery companies stationed in Charleston were ordered to St. Augustine, leaving Col. Eustis and his small field staff to run the entire regiment from Charleston.[2]

The Second Seminole War, which began in late 1835 and lasted six dreary years, emptied most of the coastal forts of regular soldiers. Their place on the ramparts of Fort Moultrie and Castle Pinckney was taken, at times, by detachments of state militia soldiers. The forts in Charleston Harbor also provided a secure place to hold captured Seminoles until the war mercifully ended in 1842. The famous warrior Osceola, accompanied by a party of 230 captured chiefs, warriors, women, and children, was brought to Fort Moultrie in December 1837. The renowned painter George Catlin was there to capture the likeness of Osceola, Micanopy, Cloud, Coahajo, and other Seminole chiefs. Suffering from a severe throat infection, the 34-year-old Osceola died within a month of his arrival in South Carolina. The famous chief is buried near the sally port of the Sullivan's Island fortress.

In 1838, Capt. Alexander Hamilton Bowman arrived in Charleston to supervise the ongoing construction of Fort Sumter. The 35-year-old engineering officer also submitted numerous proposals to the War Department to improve Castle Pinckney's defenses. His assistant in 1841, Lt. James H. Trapier, a South Carolinian, West Point graduate, and future Confederate general, produced the most detailed drawings of Castle Pinckney ever published. While few of Bowman's recommended improvements were adopted, his assistant engineers designed and built a substantial timber dock for Castle Pinckney that was reinforced and held in place by stone rubble. The outbreak of the Mexican War in 1846 prompted more proposals to increase Pinckney's firepower. Under consideration, but never adopted, was a series of connected batteries to either side of the Castle that would bolster the firepower of the island of Shute's Folly to over seventy guns.[3]

On a humid August morning in 1839, the steamboat *Charleston* pulled up to the Castle Pinckney pier to unload 23-year-old Lt. Weightman Kay Hanson with his 49 Seminole Indian prisoners. The junior officer from the 7th Infantry had been

2 ASP, 5:853-854; OAG, Report from Maj. Gates, Sep. 18, 1834.

3 "The Army," *The Savannah* [GA] *Georgian*, Sep. 20, 1836, 1; Weirick, *Castle Pinckney: Past, Present, Future*, 36-40.

A Convenient Repository: 1835–1859   39

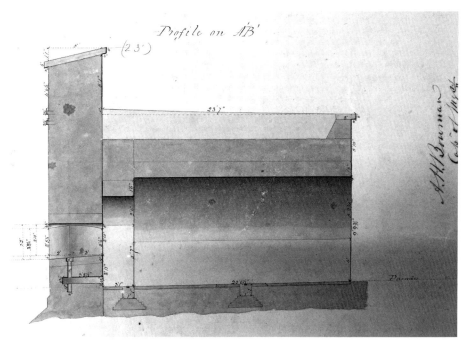

1841 drawing by Lieutenant Trapier of a 20'6" long casemate. The casemates at Castle Pinckney were poorly ventilated and became filled with smoke when a cannon was fired.
National Archives Cartography Room

---

stationed at Fort Mellon, north of present-day Orlando, when he learned that Col. William Harney's command had been massacred near Cape Coral. Not waiting for orders, Hanson and his small detachment captured the men, women, and children camped outside his wooden stockade. He was soon ordered to take his prisoners to the virtually unoccupied Castle Pinckney. While guarding these prisoners, five soldiers from Company B, 7th Infantry died of yellow fever at Castle Pinckney and Lt. Hanson nearly perished from the disease as well. With an epidemic of yellow fever sweeping through Charleston, Hanson wrote the adjutant general of the War Department on September 13 that he had been, "compelled to send the Troops and Indians from Castle Pinckney to St. Augustine, as they suffered much from sickness." Hanson never fully recovered from his bout of yellow fever and died in Washington, D.C. in 1844.[4]

---

    4 "Capture of Forty-Six Indians," *The Tri-Weekly* [GA] *Chronicle*, Aug. 15, 1839; George Catlin, "Osceola," *The Cross and Baptist* [OH] *Journal*, Feb. 16, 1838, 4; George M. Brown, *Ponce de Leon and Florida War Record* (St. Augustine, 1902), 6th Edition, 171-175; OAG, Hanson to Jones, Sep. 13, 1839.

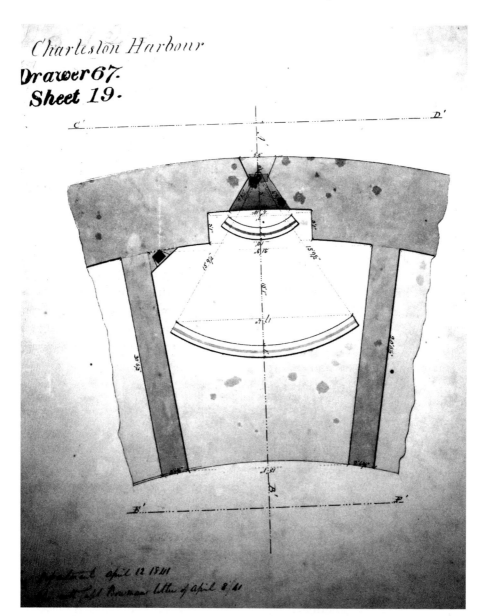

A view looking down into Casemate #4. The cannon fired through an hour-glass shaped embrasure. The gun carriage moved back and forth on the chassis, which allowed the cannon space to recoil after being fired. Gunners rolled the heavy gun left or right along metal traverse half-circles. *National Archives Cartography Room*

This was not the first time that the almost idle Castle Pinckney had been put to good use in an emergency. In 1824, the fishing smack *Tickler* of Groton, Connecticut, arrived in Charleston from Havana. Several crew members were sick with yellow fever, and Capt. Packard soon died from the infectious disease. Newspapers reported that the harbor's commanding officer, "has given up Castle Pinckney to be used as a Hospital, there being no Lazaretto in the harbour." A lazaretto is a quarantine hospital placed in an isolated location. Where to establish a permanent lazaretto in the Charleston Harbor would become a source of contention for the next two decades.

Charleston suffered from two dangerous maladies every summer. Cholera, an infectious bacterial disease, swept through the Cooper River wharves in 1836. It spread rapidly from contaminated water or food and disproportionately impacted black Charlestonians, who were more exposed to filthy conditions, poverty, and poor diets. Four years earlier, the brig *Amelia*, sailing from New York to New Orleans with 108 aboard, wrecked off Folly Island with many of the crew and passengers seized with cholera. Capt. Dickinson was brought before the Charleston City Council where he reported that more than twenty people had died on his ship, mainly among the laborers and mechanics kept in the overcrowded steerage section of the brig. A terrified council, in conjuncture with the governor, ordered two patrol boats, under Lieutenants Knight and Elmo, to block any communication between the city and Folly Island. One six-person skiff would ply between Castle Pinckney and Fort Johnson while the other patrolled the cuts between Wappoo Creek and James Island. The destitute survivors left on Folly Island were provided provisions and medical attention, but they were not allowed to enter the city until the disease had passed. All ships entering the Charleston Harbor were ordered to first stop at Castle Pinckney and be inspected by the port physician and people authorized by the governor or city council.[5]

Yellow fever was the second malady that Charlestonians had to contend with, though the disease overwhelmingly struck down newly arrived whites, particularly the "unacclimated" German and Irish immigrants. Yellow fever season stretched each year for nearly six months, from late May through early November. In time, Charleston medical authorities correctly deduced that the fever, which is spread by a species of South American mosquitos, was not native to the Carolina Lowcountry, but originated elsewhere, namely the West Indies. According to Dr. Robert Lebby of Charleston, this knowledge only came with trial and error. The outbreak of 1832 was incorrectly attributed by medical members of the Board of Health to

---

5 "The smack Tickler," *Charleston* [SC] *Courier*, 21 July 1824, 1; "A Distressing Case," *American* [CT] *Mercury*, Nov. 19, 1832, 3; "Charleston," *Charleston* [SC] *Mercury*, Nov. 2, 1832, 2.

Irish laborers working at the Castle. They ascribed its cause to the men digging up and disturbing an oyster bed for the purpose of filling up the parade ground. Dr. Lebby, on the other hand, believed the cause of the current yellow fever outbreak was the opening of two privies in the north wall, which had been bricked up since the Castle had been used as a lazaretto.

The yellow fever epidemic of 1839 spurred the Charleston City Council to pass an ordinance the following year requiring all ships coming from infectious ports to report to a quarantine zone located two miles from the city near Fort Johnson. Inbound ships were to remain in this quarantine ground for five days or 20 days if any of their crew had symptoms of the malady. This ordinance was necessary as those infected with yellow fever often showed no outward symptoms for several days. However, these maritime rules were never strictly enforced, and several Caribbean ships managed to bypass quarantine and sail directly to berths on the Cooper River wharves. Black "lightermen" took small boats to vessels anchored in the quarantine zone and ferried the cargo to the docks. Outbreaks of yellow fever in Charleston were inevitable under these circumstances, and the epidemics seemed particularly bad in the 1850s, with significant outbreaks in 1850, 1852, 1854, and 1858.[6]

In 1852, a special committee of three city councilmen was organized to sort out where to best place a lazaretto for the Charleston Harbor. The current dilapidated hospital on Morris Island was difficult "to reach from the quarantine grounds and almost an act of cruelty to convey a sick seaman from a ship to this island in an open small boat," which was necessary to navigate the small creek leading to the facility. The committee's first choice was Fort Johnson, but the U.S. government required it as an appendage for the completion of Fort Sumter. This left Castle Pinckney, which had been used as a lazaretto as early as 1820. It had advantages and disadvantages. The insular and isolated fortress on Shute's Folly had the necessary buildings to become an effective hospital for yellow fever. On the other hand, many citizens believed it too near the city for certain safety. In their report to the mayor, the committee recommended that the Castle be selected as the new harbor lazaretto. The barracks inside the masonry fort would house the staff and probationary, while the outwardly sick seamen would be placed in the former officer quarters that were in the two buildings located on the outside parade ground. While the committee knew that the contagion could overleap a wharf and

---

6 John B. Porter, M.D., Surgeon, U. S. Army, "On the Climate and Salubrity of Fort Moultrie and Sullivan's Island, Charleston Harbour, S. C., with Incidental Remarks on the Yellow Fever of the City of Charleston" *The American Journal of the Medical Sciences* (Philadelphia, Blanchard & Lea, Jul. 1854), 28:26-27; Michael D. Thompson, *Working on the Dock of the Bay: Labor and Enterprise in an Antebellum Southern Port* (Columbia, 2015), 126-128, 133, 136.

infect a neighboring vessel, they did not believe the malady could travel the 4,620 ft. separating Castle Pinckney from the Market Street Wharf.[7]

If he ever tried, Mayor Thomas L. Hutchinson did not get far in his negotiations with the U.S. government, since Castle Pinckney did not become a lazaretto for yellow fever victims. The old fort on Shute's Folly had, in fact, become a pawn in the growing sectional tension that continued to fester after the Compromise of 1850. In late November of that year, with loose talk of secession in the air and Southern Rights Associations forming in all sections of South Carolina, President Millard Fillmore decided to reinforce Fort Moultrie and garrison the half-built Fort Sumter and the long-neglected Castle Pinckney. Four companies of artillery were brought up from Florida to reinforce the two companies stationed at Fort Moultrie. Company H, 56 men under 1st Lt. William Hays, arrived at Castle Pinckney on November 27, 1850, arriving from Fort Capron on the Indian River in East Florida. Hays was a brevet-major because of his bravery in the Mexican War and an 1840 West Point graduate in the same class as William T. Sherman and George H. Thomas. Charleston's citizenry was justifiably curious about these reinforcements in blue. Three days after their arrival, Maj. Charles Parker, the surveyor for the city of Charleston, wrote in his field journal that he had taken the spyglass from Webb's supply room to watch the soldiers unloading wood at the Castle's wharf. By all appearances, the artillerymen were settling in for the winter.[8]

South Carolina Governor Whitemarsh Seabrooks submitted his Message to the Legislature a few days after the Federal troops arrived. The previous year he had appealed to the national government to release an empty Castle Pinckney back to the state, for a possible lazaretto. In May 1849, the governor had visited the Castle and found "but one man in it and he be not a soldier." Now a skeptical Seabrooks had to report that, "As Castle Pinckney, with the three acres around it, is deemed by the General Government essential to the safety of Charleston, in the event of a foreign war, my application for its retro-cession to the State has been unsuccessful." The governor's message lamented the renewed presence of Federal troops "stationed on the coast to overawe or coerce" the people of South Carolina and "that guns upon Pinckney Castle and Fort Moultrie are frowning upon Charleston."[9]

---

7 "Proceedings of Council," *Charleston* [SC] *Courier*, Jan. 6, 1855, 1. The special committee was made up of William Hume, Benjamin F. Scott, and William Kirkwood.

8 Philip May Hamer, *The Secession Movement in South Carolina, 1847-1852* (Allentown, 1918), 72; MPR, November 1850; Notation, Field notebook of Charles Parker, Nov. 30, 1850, *Records of the Surveyors of the City of Charleston, 1817-1916*, City of Charleston Archives, box 2, file 27, 12.

9 "South Carolina Legislature—Message of the Governor," *The New York Times*, Nov. 27, 1851, 2; N.W. Stephenson, "Southern Nationalism in South Carolina in 1851," *The American Historical Review* (Jan 1931), 36:321.

The editors of the *Charleston Mercury* felt the same way, editorializing on December 3 that the governor understood the true feelings of South Carolina voters. Castle Pinckney was not needed for national defense, but "in reality its guns can be brought to bear on the city." The editorial repeated a rumor that the U.S. Arsenal near the intersection of Ashley Avenue and Mill Street had been emptied of weapons. The writer doubted claims that the newly arrived troops would soon be dispatched to Texas. Bids by the Commissary General of Subsistence for 1851 showed that the troops were not going anywhere. Castle Pinckney, now garrisoned with about 50 soldiers from Company H, 2nd Artillery under Capt. Henry Swartwout, required only a third of what was requisitioned for Fort Moultrie, namely 85 barrels of pork, 125 of fresh flour, 290 bushels of field beans, 14 of salt, 876 pounds of hard soap, and 290 of hard sperm candles. The Castle was armed with eight 42-pounders, ten 24-pounders, four 8-inch howitzers, and three seacoast mortars. By December 1851, there were four artillery companies at Fort Moultrie, two at Fort Sumter, and one, Company H, 3rd Artillery, at Castle Pinckney.[10]

Ohioan 2nd Lt. John Tidball, an 1848 West Point graduate, was stationed at Castle Pinckney with Company M in 1852. In 1890, he wrote of his posting, "The people of South Carolina were then very noisy upon the subject of secession, and were having their war dance all around, to work themselves up to the scalping pitch." Tensions were still evident in June 1851 when Lt. Col. John Erving, a Boston native, refused to allow the customary celebration of the 1776 battle of Sullivan's Island to be held inside Fort Moultrie. Senator Robert Barnwell Rhett addressed the gathering from a tent erected outside the walls. Months later, in the U.S. capitol, Senator Henry Foote of Mississippi would accuse Rhett of attempting, on that occasion, to stir up the people to commit violence against the Federal troops stationed there.

The U.S. Army had four regiments of artillery by 1850. Each regiment's staff included a colonel, a lieutenant-colonel, and a major. There were nine to twelve companies, each designated by a letter, in each regiment. At full strength, a company comprised a captain, two first lieutenants, two second lieutenants, and fifty-seven enlisted men. A company handled four to six cannons, with the lieutenants directing a section of two guns or serving as the chief of caissons. The 2nd Artillery Regiment was under the overall command of Col. James Bankhead, whose headquarters were at Fort Monroe in Hampton, Virginia. Five of his

---

10 Stephenson, "Southern Nationalism in South Carolina in 1851," 321; "South Carolina," *The Daily* [DC] *Union*, Dec. 1, 1850, 2; "Office of Commissary General of Subsistence," *The Daily* [DC] *Union*, Sep. 25, 1851, 4; MPR, Dec. 1851; Joseph Totten, *Report of General J. G. Totten on the Subject of National Defenses* (Washington, 1851), 95.

German sketch of Castle Pinckney about 1850. Published in Hildburghausen. *Matthew Locke*

companies were in Charleston, with the other seven scattered about in Florida, Virginia, and New Mexico Territory. The regiment was habitually understaffed, suffering from desertion, disease, and poor recruitment levels. A Pvt. Evans, for example, deserted his post at Castle Pinckney on September 7, 1851, and was last seen boarding a schooner for Baltimore with a fresh loaf of bread under his arm.[11]

Capt. Henry Swartwout's Company H garrisoned Castle Pinckney for all of 1851. An 1832 West Point graduate, Swartwout had fought against Seminole Indians, and he had been at Vera Cruz in the Mexican War. On April 29, his three officers and 38 men paraded in the tight confines of the fort before Inspector General Sylvester Churchill. They displayed both maneuvers of infantry and exercised their 12-pounder field pieces. Churchill, a veteran of both the War of 1812 and the Mexican War, viewed the undersized company as "rather below middling—some mistakes were made by the officers in words of command, and by them and sergeants in their positions." This company, he noted, had served more than a year "in the wilderness of Florida" before coming to Charleston and that Capt. Swartwout told him that their "labor has been severe since." About January

---

11 Eugene C. Tidball, *"No Disgrace to My Country:" The Life of John C. Tidball* (Kent, 2002) 119; Stephenson, "Southern Nationalism in South Carolina in 1851," p. 322; Returns from Regular Army Artillery Regiments, 1851-1860, NARA, M727, roll 11; OAG, Captain Swartwood to Adjutant General, Oct 7, 1851, roll 0453.

1852, after a year's service at Castle Pinckney, Company H returned to Fort Moultrie and was replaced by Company M under Capt. John Frederick Roland.[12]

From their arrival in 1850, the artillerists stationed in the Charleston Harbor became regrettable and regular victims of the yellow fever scourge. This was particularly true in the late summers of 1850 and 1852. Surgeon John B. Porter reported a streak of 42 days beginning on August 20, 1850, when 81 of the 97 officers, men, women, children, and servants living at Fort Moultrie came down with Southern bilious fevers of one sort or another. As he had done at a hospital in Veracruz in 1847, the surgeon treated the sick with quinine and calomel (blue mercury pills that induced vomiting), and depending on the severity of the fever, also with prescribed laxatives, capsicum (cayenne pepper), brandy, and morphine. The 40-year-old Porter was responsible for all the military personnel garrisoned in the harbor forts. The erudite doctor conducted a series of studies, built meteorological tables, and tried to determine the cause of yellow fever outbreaks. His soldiers seemed to be taken with fever in late summer when rain "fell in torrents," and there was excessive dampness across the garrisons. The disease was not contagious, but Porter thought people were more susceptible to catching the fever in the humid night air. In his 1856 paper published in the prestigious *American Journal of the Medical Sciences*, Porter asserted that "intemperance is a strong predisposing cause of fever in hot climates."[13]

1852 proved a grim year for the artillerymen at Castle Pinckney. During the July 4th national celebration, a 24-pounder prematurely discharged as the Castle guns fired a series of salutes. Pvt. James Murphy, who was ramming home the cartridge, was "blown to atoms," while Pvt. Michael Shanaghy was described as mortally wounded. In August, Roland reported that part of the southeast seawall protecting the Castle collapsed for a length of 15 feet. During a September week in 1852, in which 43 Charlestonians died from yellow fever, the death of Capt. John Frederick Roland, commander of Company M at Pinckney, brought national attention to the epidemic. The 36-year-old West Point graduate and Mexican War hero caught the fever while visiting the city and died four days later on September 28 in the officer's quarters of Castle Pinckney. With no medical officer on duty at the island fortress, Dr. John L. Dawson had been hired from the city at $45 a month to make occasional visits to the fortress. 2nd Lt. John Tidball, who would serve in the army for 40 years and eventually reach the rank of brigadier general, reported that "Roland took the fever and died in a few days, and so did several

---

12 OAG, Report of S. Churchill, 1851, 16; MPR, Jan. 1851, Jul. 1851.

13 Porter, "On the Climate and Salubrity of Fort Moultrie and Sullivan's Island," 26-27, 73.

of the company." 1st Lt. Samuel S. Anderson abandoned his post rather than stay in the tightly confined Castle. This left 27-year-old Tidball commanding the beleaguered garrison. "Being refused repeated requests to remove the healthy part of the company to some more suitable place," he wrote, "I finally called a boat and removed them to Fort Moultrie." A small detachment remained "for the protection of public property," but the Castle was not an active Federal base again until 1865.[14]

The men of Company M perplexed surgeon John Porter. They seemed to arrive at Sullivan's Island reasonably healthy, only to develop fevers a few days or weeks later. Porter began focusing on the soldier's alcohol consumption. He determined that 18 of the company's 43 men were sober, 11 were drinkers, and 14 drunkards. Nine drunkards caught yellow fever, and the disease proved fatal for four of them. The doctor described Case 58 in his records, 1st Sgt. Charles Platt, as "sober as regards spirituous liquors, but an habitual opium-taker." On the morning of October 5, Platt was admitted to the hospital with yellow clammy skin and eyes, and a slow feeble pulse. Black vomit came on the 6th, and he died on the morning of the 8th. Fort Moultrie's commanding officer noted that Platt had been sick two or three days before reporting to the surgeon. He warned his command that, "In yellow fever, more than in any other disease, three, four, five, or six hours at the outset are of immense consequence; and no man with yellow fever can expect to recover after 24 hours' delay."[15]

In October 1852, Lt. Tidball reported to the harbor commander, Maj. John Munro, about the extent of the damage to the stone seawall standing between the harbor water and the southeast side of Castle Pinckney. The 11-foot-thick stone wall stood seven feet above the low tide mark since its construction in 1809, but Tidball now reported that "the force of the water from beneath." had compromised 74 feet of protective wall. Twenty-three feet had entirely given way and the stones were loose on the wall's other 51 feet. The West Point graduate feared that without quick repairs the still sound portion of the seawall would soon give way as well. More importantly, the foundation of the main wall of Castle Pinckney where the breach had occurred was now exposed. On September 9, 1854, Mother Nature dealt Castle Pinckney a further blow. The gale storm, known

---

14 "Fatal Accident," *New York Tribune*, Jul. 10, 1852, 5; "Deaths," *Lancaster* [PA] *Daily Intelligencer*, Oct. 12, 1852, 21-75; OAG, J. F. Roland to J. F. Robinson, Aug. 9, 1852, roll 470; Tidball, "No Disgrace to My Country," 119; OAG, John Munroe to S. Cooper, Oct. 2, 1852, roll 470. The 24-year-old Shanaghy turned out to have survived the Jul. 4 cannon misshape. A native of County Kildare, Ireland, he was working at the U.S. Arsenal in Charleston according to an 1859 city directory and at the same arsenal, now under Confederate control, in 1863. The promising Capt. Roland was buried in his hometown of New Holland, Pennsylvania.

15 Porter, "On the Climate and Salubrity of Fort Moultrie and Sullivan's Island," 56-58, 71.

as the "Great Carolina" Hurricane, made first landfall near St. Catherine's Island before sweeping over Charleston. Water breached the already damaged southeast protective sea wall of Castle Pinckney, damaged the wharf, broke the flagpole, and shattered five "penthouses," which were wooden structures protecting the cannons on the parapet from severe weather. President Franklin Pierce found himself asking the 34th Congress for $10,000 to effect repairs and construct a new shot furnace and two cisterns at the Castle. George Washington Cullum of the U.S. Engineers would oversee the construction project. A veteran of the Mexican War, Cullum had been an instructor at West Point before he was assigned to Charleston to complete Fort Sumter and repair Castle Pinckney.[16]

In the 1850s Charleston remained a busy seaport chiefly exporting cotton and rice, but its commercial importance had fallen considerably behind New York in the east and New Orleans and Mobile in the west. Now servicing faster and larger steamships, Charleston labored under the hindrance of a natural sand bar extending one to three miles offshore at the entrance of its harbor. Ships needing more than an 11-ft. draft could not reach the Charleston wharves. Even worse, the situation seemed only to deteriorate as soundings indicated a steady and continued shoaling of the main shipping channel. Other ships avoided the port because of the Negro Seaman Law, a South Carolina statute that allowed free black seamen from Northern states to be arrested if they left their docked ship and entered the city. All deep draft vessels entering Charleston were forced to approach from the south with Morris Island on their port side. Lights, beacons, and buoys were all needed to help pilots keep ships in the narrow passage prone to shifting in a storm. Hoping to improve navigation in the harbor, the U.S. Corps of Engineers installed a channel light at Fort Sumter and Castle Pinckney in 1856. The new red beacon, lit for the first time on May 15, 1856, consisted of a French-built fifth order Fresnel lens placed atop a yellow-painted, open wood frame tower, 18 feet square at the bottom and ten at the top. The light, about 100 ft. northwest of the actual Castle, stood 50 ft. above the low water mark with a beacon producing an arc of illumination of 350 degrees.

No dredging of the harbor had succeeded until the arrival of the *General Moultrie* from New York in 1857. Financed by James M. Eason, who owned a foundry on the Neck above Charleston, the two-masted dredger was 153 ft. long. The secret to this ship's success was its first-ever use of a hydraulic steam-driven suction pump designed by a local inventor named Nathan Lebby. Previously, Lebby

---

16 OAR, Tidball to Munro, Oct. 19, 1852; Franklin Pierce, *Message from the President of the United States to the Two Houses of Congress at the Commencement of the First Session of the 34th Congress, Part Two* (Washington, D.C., 1855), 200.

had built steam-powered pumps to pull river water up to flood rice plantation fields. By June 1857, the suction pump on the *General Moultrie* was pulling 350 cubic ft. of sand into its spoil hold each day. Maffitt's Channel was deepened and widened through 1859 when the State ran out of funds.[17]

In January 1855, Congressman William Aiken relayed a request from the Charleston mayor and city council to Secretary of War Jefferson Davis to use Castle Pinckney as a temporary lazaretto. The local military engineers objected, arguing that the Castle was important to the port's defense. In December, Mayor Thomas Leger Hutchinson again asked Davis's permission to use the Castle but was refused because of the high cost of removing the powder from the fort's magazine. An arrangement was soon finalized whereby the city assumed the cost of removing the powder, and for most of 1856 the Castle served as a lazaretto for sailors afflicted with yellow fever.

Capt. Cullum's renovations of Castle Pinckney, which began in 1857 and continued under Capt. Foster in 1858, brought the fortress into a state of military readiness. Under Cullum, the wharf was rebuilt with an abutment of heavy granite blocks and a substantial boat house erected. The entire sea wall was thoroughly repaired and coped with large flagging stones, a new 15-ft. shot furnace built on the inside parade ground, the floors and roofs of the officers' quarters and soldiers barracks repaired, and the chimney tops rebuilt. Under Foster's direction, the walls received two coats of cement wash, casemates repaired, a new granite flood sill installed at the outer gates, bricks repointed with fresh mortar, and walls plastered among the officer quarters, barracks, and hospital, and the addition of new piazzas to the same.[18]

Castle Pinckney briefly returned to the front pages of American newspapers a few days after the August 21, 1858 capture of the slave trading ship *Echo* by the man-of-war USS *Dolphin* along the northern coast of Cuba. Importing enslaved people from across the Atlantic had been illegal since 1808, but the financial returns of a successful operation were such that Capt. Edward Townsend of the *Echo* was willing to chance it. Townsend bought 455 Africans at Cabinda at the mouth of the Congo River, but, after 35 days at sea, 144 of his charges had died

---

17 John B. Bonds, "Opening the Bar: First Dredging at Charleston, 1853-1859," *SCHM* (Jul. 1997) 98:230-250; Paul Strarobin, *Madness Rules the Hour* (New York, 2017), 61; "Castle Pinckney Beacon," *The Merchants' Magazine* [NY] and *Commercial Review*, Jun. 1, 1856, 34. The General Moultrie made one successful blockade run in 1864 and was sold in Nassau.

18 Jefferson Davis, *The Papers of Jefferson Davis, 1853-1855*, 14 vol., Lynda L. Crist and Mary S. Dix, ed. & trans. (Baton Rouge, 1985), 5:293; Weirick, *Castle Pinckney: Past, Present, Future*, 46; G.W. Cullum, "Annual Report," Sep. 30, 1857, Records of the Office of the Quartermaster General, RG95; NARA; J.G. Foster, "Annual Report," Jun. 30, 1858. Records of the Office of the Quartermaster General, RG 95.

from malnutrition or dysentery. Sent to Charleston for trial, 16 of Townsend's crew walked to the city jail in irons facing death-penalty charges of piracy. The Africans, reduced by death to 246 males and 60 females, were off-loaded to the steamer *General Clinch*, which took them to Castle Pinckney for quarantine. A reporter for the *Charleston Courier* described them as "walking skeletons" who presented "a sad and affecting sight." Most of the children, ages 8 to 16, were completely naked except for a small strip of rag tied around their waists. A guard of federal soldiers from Fort Moultrie was immediately dispatched to Pinckney to watch over the unfortunate Africans.

The secretary of navy ordered Lt. Bradford, who had brought the *Echo* to Charleston, to hand responsibility for care and supervision of the Africans to U.S. Marshal Daniel Heyward Hamilton, a 40-year-old from an old Charleston family. Hamilton brought blankets, bacon, rice, and tobacco to the Africans. Castle Pinckney was deemed too small for the housing of the Africans, and they were transferred to the empty parade ground of the nearly completed Fort Sumter. They stayed here for several weeks, a curiosity for many of the citizens of Charleston. On September 1, the *Charleston Mercury* reported that the *General Clinch* brought a delegation of politicians, merchants, and planters to view the Africans, who treated their visitors to a spirited song and dance performance. Their athletic dancing "resembled in great degree the popular burlesque of the Shaking Quakers."[19]

The sudden arrival of the *Echo*'s human cargo at Castle Pinckney presented a host of unexpected questions. Many Southerners, led by the editors of the *Charleston Mercury*, believed that the Africans should be handed over to the jurisdiction of the State of South Carolina and retained as slaves. A handful of wealthy planters offered the state government large sums to purchase these people. The Palmetto State had an 1835 law prohibiting the importation of free people of color into their state, and the presence of Africans in the federal forts seemed in violation of state law. In fact, the *Echo* affair had again brought the entire question of re-opening the trans-Atlantic slave trade into the national conversation. This proposition created an uproar in the North, but there was also no general call for the *Echo* survivors to be bought above the Mason-Dixon Line and given their freedom. President James Buchanan found the solution in an 1819 act granting him the authority to remove the cargo of captured slavers from U.S. territory. On September 19, 1858, the surviving Africans, now down to 271 people, were loaded onto the steamer *Niagara* and taken back across the Atlantic Ocean to Liberia. The

---

19 "The Captured Africans," *Charleston* [SC] *Courier*, Aug. 30, 1858, 1; "The Slave Ship at Charleston," *Cincinnati* [OH] *Daily Commercial*, Sep. 6, 1858, 1; "The Slave Ship and Slave Cargo at Charleston," *New York Times*, Sep. 6, 1858, 3.

Colonization Society received $45,000 to shelter and protect the *Echo* prisoners for a year after their return to Africa. Finally, the trial of the *Echo*'s crew was held in Columbia, South Carolina, before a grand jury of the U.S. Circuit Court for South Carolina. The charges were soon dropped, with a retrial set for Charleston, which, not unexpectedly, promptly reached a not guilty verdict.[20]

---

20 "President's Message," *Cleveland* [OH] *Plain Dealer*, Dec. 10, 1858, 1.

Chapter 5

Scaling Ladders
1860

"The battalions of South Carolina, duly provided with scaling ladders, battle-axes, and pontoons, march in grim array to the assault of these fortifications [Castle Pinckney & Fort Moultrie]—the clear and indisputable property and domain of the United States ....
These are seditious proceedings."[1]

By 1860, Castle Pinckney was a 50-year-old masonry structure and a familiar sight to the thousands of draymen, porters, and stevedores who worked on the wharves along East Bay Street. The antiquated fort had not been garrisoned with a company of Federal troops since 1852. The place was not empty as an experienced ordnance sergeant was assigned to the Castle.

Besides shooing away the curious, his principal responsibility was maintaining the channel light and keeping the fort ready for military service at short notice. This would include ongoing cleaning and maintenance, polishing the artillery, applying protective grease on the piled cannonballs, oiling and inspecting the elevating screws, eccentric wheels, and traversing gears of the gun carriages, and accounting for the ammunition and gunpowder held in the storeroom. Two men served as ordnance sergeants at Castle Pinckney between 1851 and 1860. Sgt. John Collins, a native of Genese, New York, served at Castle Pinckney until he was relieved from duty in 1855. It is not clear why Collins lost his job, but it was at this time that the old brick fortress was temporarily designated a lazarette for use by the city of Charleston. Collins had requested money to refurbish a building inside the palisades to be living quarters for himself while the Castle served as a hospital. He

---

1 "The Republic is Imperishable," Speech of the Honorable Daniel Sickles of New York on the State of the Union, January 16, 1861.

was succeeded by James Skillin, an Irishman from Company E of the 1st Artillery. In 1860, the 42-year-old Skillin lived in the Castle with his wife and daughter.[2]

When Abraham Lincoln was elected president in November 1860, the federal military presence in the Charleston Harbor was negligible. Companies E and H, 1st Artillery, a contingent of seven officers, 61 enlisted men, as well as the 13 musicians of the regimental band, were stationed together behind the cracked 12-foot-high walls of Fort Moultrie. Neither Castle Pinckney nor Fort Sumter were garrisoned with soldiers. Across the harbor, the white citizens of Charleston were wearing blue cockades in their lapels and marching in torchlight parades behind banners demanding immediate secession. "Resistance" was their slogan. Citizen militia, both well established—The Washington Light Infantry, the Palmetto Guards, the Meagher Guards, the Montgomery Guards and the Charleston Light Dragoons—and new—the German Fusiliers, the Jasper Greens, the Vigilant Rifles, the Charleston Riflemen, and the Charleston Zouave Cadets—were drilling in various city parks in the afternoons. All of these militia companies were part of the First Regiment of Rifles of South Carolina and served under the capable leadership of a prominent local lawyer, James Johnston Pettigrew.

Fearing the worst, the War Department in Washington rushed Maj. Robert Anderson to Charleston to take command of Fort Moultrie. A native of Kentucky, the 55-year-old Anderson was a career soldier with experience fighting Black Hawk Indians, Mexican soldiers, and Seminoles. It was anticipated that this level-headed and discreet artillery officer could maintain the peace until the new Republican administration took office in March 1861. His orders from Secretary of War John Floyd were to do nothing that might "light a spark" and start a civil war.[3]

Radicalized in part by Robert Barnwell Rhett, Jr.'s *Mercury* newspaper, most of the white population of Charleston had been advocates for secession since the 1860 Democratic Convention - the most raucous political convention in American history. That gathering had fallen apart under the chandeliers at Institute Hall on Meeting Street. Irrevocably split, the Democratic party fielded two regional candidates while the new Republican party coalesced behind Abraham Lincoln of Illinois. The November election of Lincoln was "the red rag to the bull so far as South Carolina was concerned," wrote Thomas Pinckney Lowndes. The entire nation focused on both the new president and how Charleston, the epicenter of

---

2 David Detzer, *Allegiance: Fort Sumter, Charleston, and the Beginning of the Civil War* (New York, 2001), 102; Re-enlistment of James Skillin, Jul. 5, 1854, Fort Monroe, VA, Register of Enlistments in the US Army, 1798-1914, NARA, vol. 49 & 50; OAG, Orders & letters regarding John Collins, Mar. 17, 1855.

3 Starobin, *Madness Rules the Hour*, 67, 127, 138; Clyde Wilson, *Carolina Cavalier: The Life and Mind of James Johnston Pettigrew* (Athens, 1990), 135; Detzer, *Allegiance*, 56.

Engraving from an 1850s daguerreotype of James Johnston Pettigrew. The colonel of the 1st Rifles, Pettigrew captured Castle Pinckney, a Federal installation, with three companies of Charleston militia on December 27, 1860. *First printed in the University of North Carolina's* University Magazine *in October 1886*

revolution, would deal with one another in the coming weeks.

Closely watching these political events was 41-year-old Abner Doubleday, the second ranking officer at Fort Moultrie on Sullivan's Island. A New Yorker with strong abolitionist leanings, the captain wrote detailed letters to his brother that were then passed forward to President-elect Abraham Lincoln, who was eager for any reliable information from Charleston. Doubleday was the captain of Company E and, as such, a frequent visitor to the city to secure supplies and payroll for the men inside Fort Moultrie. "Every public assemblage," he noted, "was tinctured with treasonable sentiment, and toasts against the flag were always warmly applauded." Doubleday also lamented that large work crews of masons from Baltimore under a captain named John G. Foster, an engineer officer who was independent of his control, had arrived on Sullivan's Island and were quickly turning the fort's grounds into a giant construction zone. Repairing these forts at such a late date would not help the American cause. "Forts constructed in an enemy's country, and left unguarded, are built for the enemy," thought Doubleday.[4]

On November 23, 1860, Maj. Anderson filed his first report to Washington. He deemed Fort Moultrie untenable for his small garrison force. Though empty of troops, Fort Sumter had some guns mounted in its lower tier and others stored on its parade ground, along with 40,000 pounds of cannon powder in its four magazines, and, most importantly, the ability to command Fort Moultrie, which was only one mile directly across the harbor channel. After touring Castle

---

4 Thomas Pinckney Lowndes, "Reminiscences of Thomas Pinckney Lowndes, 1896," *William Lowndes papers*, 1754-1941, 8 vol., Southern Historical Collection, Wilson Library, University of North Carolina, 4:12.; Abner Doubleday, *Reminiscences of Fort Sumter and Fort Moultrie in 1860-61* (New York, 1876), 13-14, 44.

Pinckney, Anderson deemed it "in excellent condition, with the exception of a few repairs." The new commander saw Castle Pinckney as the key to any Federal defense of Fort Moultrie. Holding this small caseated work on Shute's Folly, he wrote, would have more of an impact than would quadrupling his present force. In short, "The Charlestonians would not venture to attack this place [Fort Moultrie] when they knew that their city was at the mercy of the commander of Castle Pinckney." Anderson asked for two companies of troops for Fort Sumter and half a company "under a judicious commander," be sent to Castle Pinckney. If reinforcements were not forthcoming, Maj. Anderson asked permission to send "one officer, two masons, two carpenters, and twenty-six laborers" to the Castle to make general repairs. He believed their arrival would not arouse suspicion, and it might even be possible to instruct the workers in the use of the cannons if it came to armed conflict.[5]

Adjutant General Samuel Cooper could only reply that Anderson's proposals for reinforcements were under consideration by Secretary of War John B. Floyd and President Buchanan. Permission was granted to Capt. Foster to send one officer, four mechanics, and 30 laborers to Castle Pinckney "for purposes of repairs." As Abner Doubleday remembered in 1876, "the brave ordnance-sergeant Skillen" at Castle Pinckney "begged hard that we would send him a few artillerists." The Castle was so close to Charleston that it "could easily control the city by means of its mortars and heavy guns." Anderson and Doubleday believed they were too short-handed to send soldiers from Fort Moultrie to Castle Pinckney. However, after a lengthy discussion, "Captain Foster thought he could re-enforce Skillen by selecting a few reliable men from his masons to assist in defending the place." Doubleday wrote that Lt. Richard Kidder Meade, Jr. was dispatched with 20-odd workmen to the Castle to make some general repairs. The moment that Meade attempted to give the contracted workmen some general instructions on how to operate the heavy guns, however, "they drew back in great alarm, and it was soon seen that no dependence could be placed on them."

Anderson wrote Washington again from Fort Moultrie on November 28. Adding Federal troops to Castle Pinckney and Fort Sumter would do more "than by anything that can be done in strengthening the defenses of this work." The South Carolinians, he believed, had some kind of "romantic desire" to seize Fort Moultrie, as it had been "so nobly defended by their ancestors in 1776." If

---

5 *The War of the Rebellion: A Compilation of the Official Records of the Union and Confederate Armies*, 128 vol., (Washington, DC, 1880-1901) Series 1, vol. 1, Part 1, 74-76. Hereafter cited as *OR*. All references are to Series 1 unless otherwise noted.

Washington did not intend to reinforce his position, Anderson was "inclined" to withdraw to Fort Sumter, "which so perfectly commands the harbor and this fort."

Capt. John Foster of the Engineers reported on the 30th that he was sending a contingent of 30 workmen to Castle Pinckney on December 3 with one month's supply of provisions. Maj. Anderson had loaned him a veteran officer, Jefferson C. Davis, the second-in command to Doubleday in Company E, to oversee the workers until another engineering officer, Richard Meade, could reach Charleston. On December 6th, Anderson reported that the 115 workmen at Fort Sumter had refused to bear arms to defend the fort, and he expected the same from the 30 masons assigned to Castle Pinckney. On the 11th, Anderson requested permission to destroy the powder and armaments at Fort Sumter and Castle Pinckney so that they would not fall into the hands of the secessionists. This was enough for Washington to dispatch Don Carlos Buell, an assistant adjutant-general to visit the major with strong verbal instructions on how to proceed. The artillery officer was to "carefully avoid every act which would needlessly tend to provoke aggression," but if attacked, he was to defend his position "to the last extremity." Buell acknowledged that Anderson's force was only large enough to occupy one of the three forts but noted that "an attack on or attempt to take possession of any one of them will be regarded as an act of hostility." Anderson would be free to place his command in the fort "you may deem most proper to increase its power of resistance." Upon his return to Washington, Buell put his instructions to Anderson in the form of a memorandum that both Floyd and Buchanan read and approved, with neither fully grasping that they had given Anderson the discretion to abandon Fort Moultrie and occupy Fort Sumter.[6]

On December 13, Capt. Foster of the Engineers reported to his superior, Lt. Col. De Russy, that Lt. Meade had relieved Davis at Castle Pinckney two days earlier. He added that repairs to the main gate, rebuilding the two cisterns, and replacing decayed banquettes were proceeding at the Castle. The gun carriages had been oiled and now moved "with perfect facility." Foster found it necessary to maintain a strict night watch and to post a man at the gate to keep "interested parties" from entering the post. His confidence in his handpicked workmen had increased over the last few days, and he now believed they would be "reliable" against a disorderly mob attempting to attack the Castle.[7]

On December 17, Francis Pickens, the son of a notable South Carolina family, was elected governor of South Carolina. Portly, opinionated, and overbearing,

---

6 *OR* 1/1-79-81, 87-88; 89-90; Detzer, *Allegiance*, 82.

7 *OR* 1/1-90-91; Samuel W. Crawford, *The History of Fort Sumter: An Inside History of the Affairs of 1860 and 1861, and the Events which brought on the Rebellion* (New York, 1896), 96.

the 55-year-old politician was determined to free South Carolina from federal authority. As commander of the state militia, he would decide if the forts in Charleston Harbor were to be forcibly taken. Pickens initially relied on the talented and accomplished James Johnson Pettigrew for military advice. Three civilian commissioners—Robert W. Barnwell, James H. Adams, and James L. Orr— were immediately sent to Washington to be ready to officially inform President Buchanan that the Palmetto State had left the Union and to open negotiations for the peaceful transfer of federal properties in the state.

On December 20, 1860, the five established militia companies of Charleston, under the command of Col. Pettigrew, marched together for the first time as the 1st Regiment of Rifles. The Charlestonians marched up to the Magnolia Parade Ground on the outskirts of Charleston for drill and instruction. As the sun set that evening, the delegates to the South Carolina Constitutional Convention lined up outside St. Andrew's Hall on Broad Street and walked under gas lamps in formation to Institute Hall on Meeting Street. In front of a raucous collection of 2,000 Charlestonians standing in the upper galleries, the leaders of South Carolina stepped forward to sign the Ordinance of Secession. South Carolina was now an independent commonwealth. A copy of the ordinance was sent to the soldiers and read to the assembled command by Maj. Ellison Capers, where it was "received with the greatest enthusiasm."[8]

That evening Capt. Foster observed a steamer, which showed no lights, patrolling between Fort Moultrie and Fort Sumter. The next night there were two steamers. These were the steamboats *Nina* and *General Clinch* on orders from the new governor to prevent any attempt by Anderson to move Federal soldiers to Fort Sumter. One of the small steamboats sailed up to Castle Pinckney, where the night watch called out to it, asking what she wanted. The reply was, "You'll know in a week."

By Christmas 1860, events were escalating quickly toward a crisis. Unionists had informed an apprehensive Maj. Anderson that militia units in Charleston were constructing scaling ladders and State engineering officers were openly studying the land approaches to Fort Moultrie. In the early evening of December 26, hours before Governor Pickens' watch boats would be in place, Anderson, acting on his own initiative, moved his small garrison from Moultrie to Sumter in the small work schooners belonging to the Engineering Corps. It was a well-planned and executed operation that was completed under the cover of darkness. Staying behind at Fort Moultrie for another day was Capt. Foster, who, according to Doubleday, was "one

---

8 Detzer, *Allegiance*, 94-95; Wilson, *Carolina Cavalier*, 135-136; Walter B. Capers, *The Soldier-Bishop Ellison Capers* (New York, 1912), 44.

of the most fearless and reliable men in the service," and six of Anderson's soldiers. Foster's squad spiked the cannons by hammering musket ramrods into the vents of the big guns and then burned the wooden carriages underneath them. By the time they had finished and loaded their boat, the old War of 1812 fortification looked looted and abandoned.[9]

The citizens of Charleston awoke on December 27 to see smoke pouring from the ramparts of Fort Moultrie, and they could make out, with the help of a spyglass, gangs of men unloading cargo from schooners at Fort Sumter. Rev. Toomer Porter would recollect in 1898, "I do not think that anyone can portray the scenes of that day. There was no more shouting, but men and women were hurrying to and fro, with an excitement words cannot express at all." Everyone, it appears, was convinced that artillery shells would soon rain down on the city from Fort Sumter.[10]

At noon, Maj. Anderson ordered out his troops and the 100 or more workers present to witness the raising of a large American "garrison" flag—36 ft. by 20 ft.—over Fort Sumter. The federal soldiers on the parade ground presented arms while the band on the ramparts played the "Star-Spangled Banner." The soldiers in blue shouted their huzzahs as the large flag was raised. Since most of the soldiers had been born in Ireland, they finished by giving three load cheers for their Old Sod (Ireland). It was a moving ceremony that was depicted weeks later in both the *Harper's Weekly* and *Frank Leslie's Illustrated Newspaper* and helped to spark a patriotic reaction among readers in the Northern states. The *Charleston Courier*, on the other hand, saw the raising of Old Glory as proof that the imposing fortress had "become a stronghold of defiance and insult to the State for whose defense it was commenced and designed."

Governor Pickens was in town as the South Carolina Convention was still officially in session. Earlier in the day, Pickens had sent two military representatives, Col. Johnston Pettigrew and Maj. Ellison Capers, to Sumter to demand that Anderson return his soldiers to Fort Moultrie. Dressed in their full militia uniforms, Pettigrew and Capers returned to town and informed the governor that Anderson had declined to "accede to his request." Anderson had emphasized his stance by raising the garrison flag over Fort Sumter. Pickens then ordered Pettigrew to assemble a military force that afternoon and seize Castle Pinckney. The agitated governor was acting in a bold fashion and crossing something of a Rubicon: Never

---

9 *OR* 1/1-106-107; Detzer, *Allegiance*, 100-101, 109, 120; Doubleday, *Reminiscences of Fort Sumter*, 22.

10 Anthony Toomer Porter, *Led on! Step by step, scenes from clerical, military, educational, and plantation life in the South, 1828-1898* (New York, 1898), 120.

had a state militia, under the orders of a governor no less, undertaken a course of military aggression against the national government of the United States. Pickens was unwilling to wait for the state legislature to set a course of action. Bloodshed might well be expected as it was unknown at the time whether Anderson had also sent federal soldiers to Castle Pinckney.[11]

Since 1853, most of the militia companies in Charleston had been organized into either a rifle regiment or an artillery regiment that were part of the Fourth Brigade of the South Carolina militia. These two regiments of state militia would be tasked with carrying out the orders of Governor Pickens. The 23-year-old Ellison Capers, an 1857 graduate of the Citadel and from a distinguished Lowcountry family, had been elected, in the autumn of 1860, the major of the 1st Regiment of Rifles. The 32-year-old Pettigrew was from North Carolina, but since 1852, he had worked in Charleston as the junior law partner of his uncle James Louis Petigru. As colonel of the regiment, Pettigrew called on three of his better-trained infantry companies to immediately assemble on the Citadel Green, the parade ground of the Citadel. Messengers were soon racing about the city, finding the men at their homes or places of business.[12]

By 2:00 in the afternoon, elements of the Washington Light Infantry under Capt. Charles Simonton, the Carolina Light Infantry under Capt. B. G. Pinckney, and the Meagher Guards under Capt. Edward McCrady, Jr., were in formation on the Citadel Green. Many men came in their winter uniforms, equipped with blankets, knapsacks, and revolvers. According to McCrady, their "holiday arms" were exchanged for old smoothbore muskets and bayonet. Buck and ball ammunition was issued to each soldier and rammed home, and "we felt that the war had indeed nearly commenced." In all, Pettigrew and Capers had roughly 150 men under their command.[13]

Observing all this firsthand was James Skillin, the ordnance sergeant of Castle Pinckney, who had been sent into the city by Lt. Meade to reconnoiter what he could. The veteran Skillin was a native of Westbrook, Maine who had joined the army at age 21 in 1839, served in the Mexican War, and voluntarily re-enlisted five times. Most citizens of Charleston assumed that the local militia was being assembled to storm Fort Sumter, and many of the wives of the volunteer soldiers

---

11 "Major Anderson," *Charleston* [SC] *Courier*, Dec. 28, 1860, 2; Detzer, *Allegiance*, 125-126, 129-130.

12 Donald M. Williams, *Shamrocks and Pluff Mudd: A Glimpse of the Irish in the Southern City of Charleston, South Carolina* (Charleston, 2005), 98-100.

13 Edward McCrady, "Speech of the Hon. A. G. Magrath," *The Irish Volunteers: Memorial Meeting and Military Ball, Oct-Nov 1877* (Charleston, 1878).

became emotional as the uniformed men shouldered arms and began marching at double quick time for several blocks to the Railroad Accommodation Wharf on the Cooper River. While Pettigrew's men boarded the steamboat *Nina* at about 4:00 p.m., Skillin slipped back to Castle Pinckney in his small craft. Once underway, the crowded *Nina* headed straight for Castle Pinckney, only 30 minutes away.[14]

Under a gray wintry sky and a disappearing sunset, the South Carolinians disembarked onto Castle Pinckney's stone wharf with bayonets fixed. First to leave the *Nina* was a storming party that moved around to the backside of the bricked Castle, where they found the sally port gate closed and barred. There was no response as they pounded on the gate and demanded entrance. Col. Pettigrew ordered ladders stored on the boat to be brought up. The handsome officer was among the first dozen to scale the walls. The volunteers quickly worked their way down to the inner parade ground and opened the gate for their fellow militia soldiers.[15]

According to a speech given at Hibernian Hall in 1877 by Col. Edward McCrady, Jr., the first men over the wall of the Castle that evening were members of his Meagher Guard. They were splendidly dressed in new uniforms made by Hugo Koppel, a German tailor on King Street. This all-Irish militia unit had been organized in 1853 shortly after Irish patriot Thomas Francis Meagher had given a rousing speech to the Society of United Irishmen at their meeting hall at 90 Meeting Street. McCrady was a 27-year-old lawyer in 1860 and the recently elected captain of the Meagher Guards. In his postwar speech, he noted, "The feet of the Irish Volunteers were the first to tread the forbidden ground of United States territory."[16]

One civilian accompanied the Meagher Guards. 29-year-old John McCrady, the older brother of Capt. McCrady, had been swept up in the excitement of the moment and had boarded the *Nina*. Out for winter break, John was teaching mathematics at his alma mater, the College of Charleston. After the war, in which he served as a Confederate engineer, Professor McCrady became a pioneer in

---

14 William A. Courteney, *The Centennial of Incorporation, 1883* (Charleston, 1884), 163; "Events of Yesterday," *Charleston* [SC] *Mercury*, Dec. 28, 1860, 2; Military files of James Skillin, National Park Service, Fort Moultrie Visitor Center, Sullivan's Island, SC; Detzer, *Allegiance*, 133; Williams, *Shamrocks and Pluff Mudd*, 99. The Accommodation Wharf was behind 178 East Bay Street.

15 Detzer, *Allegiance*, 134; "The Events of Yesterday," *Charleston* [SC] *Mercury*, Dec. 28, 1860, 2; Letter, J. J. Pettigrew to D.F. Jamison, Jan. 17, 1861, David Flavel Jamison Papers, Washington and Lee University Special Collections and Archives. Hereafter cited as DFJP.

16 Williams, *Shamrocks and Pluff Mudd*, 98; "Commendable Enterprise," *Charleston* [SC] *Courier*, Dec. 21, 1860, 1; McCrady, "Speech of the Hon. A. G. Magrath"; There were three Irish companies in Charleston in 1860: The longstanding Irish Volunteers under Edward McGrath, Sr., the Montgomery Guards under James Conner, and the Meagher Guards under Edward McGrath, Jr.

This lithograph of the seizure of Castle Pinckney by three companies of Charleston militia appeared in *Harper's Weekly* on January 12, 1861. Union officer Meade is shown with his arms folded on the stone wharf. *Matthew Locke*

hydrozoan zoology, and he went on to head the biology department at Harvard College in Boston before joining the faculty of the University of the South in Sewanee, Tennessee in 1877.

Standing on the ramparts of Castle Pinckney was 25-year-old Lt. Richard Meade. The son of a Virginia planter, politician, ambassador to Brazil, and grandson of an aide-de-camp to George Washington, Meade was an 1857 graduate of West Point. Like his fellow Southerner Robert Anderson, Meade felt his responsibilities and loyalties as an American Army officer trumped his own political sympathies towards states' rights. Col. Pettigrew spotted the young engineer, strode towards him, and began reading the governor's orders aloud. A blunt Meade interrupted him, stating that he refused to recognize the authority of the South Carolina governor on a federal military post. Rather than watch the flag-raising ceremony, Meade returned to his room to write his report. Skillin, the only other federal soldier then at Castle Pinckney, was furious with these uninvited intruders, declaring, "This is a pretty thing to happen to a U.S. fort."[17]

The formal seizure of Castle Pinckney by South Carolina authorities on December 27, 1860, was, by some accounting, the first military action of the Civil

---

17 Jack Leland, "Prof. McCrady and the Spirit of Secession," *Charleston* [SC] *News and Courier*, Jan. 1, 1861, 17; Detzer, *Allegiance*, 134.

War. Pettigrew had his men form upon the parade ground. The American flag was pulled down and replaced with the flag of the *Nina*, a red flag emblazoned with a single white star. Why was this red ship's flag raised over the Castle? In truth because no one had thought to bring a flag with them in their hurry to seize the harbor fort. The ceremony took place in front of cheering state militiamen and a crying Katie Skillin. According to Abner Doubleday's account, a Southern officer attempted to comfort the pretty 16-year-old and assured her that she and her family were safe. That was not what she was worried about. "I am crying because you have put that miserable rag up there," she told him. Capt. Doubleday would also call Foster's handpicked masons at Castle Pinckney a "bad investment," as they did not attempt to defend the post. They remained in the barracks and were sent to Fort Sumter the following day. After receiving assurances from Col. Pettigrew that the old ordnance sergeant and his family would be treated kindly, Lt. Meade, with four masons, rowed to Fort Sumter that night in a small boat. A few days later, Col. Pettigrew would write James Simons, "I sent to town [U.S.] Ordnance Sergeant Skilling & his family. He was the light-keeper. I have treated him as kindly as was in my power, because I thought it unworthy of the cause to war upon isolated individuals."

Two hours after Pettigrew had marched his men off the Citadel Green, Lt. Col. Wilmot DeSaussure of the First Regiment of South Carolina Artillery began assembling his regiment—Marion Artillery, the Lafayette Artillery, the German Artillery, and the Washington Artillery and 30 riflemen—on the same parade ground. DeSaussure was a Huguenot, and had similar instructions from Pickens, but his mission was to take possession of Sullivan's Island. Crossing the harbor in the *Nina* and *General Clinch*, his force of 225 men took control of the emptied Fort Moultrie by 8:00 p.m. South Carolina soldiers occupied the federal customs house and post office the following day. A three-day standoff ensued at the Federal Arsenal near the Ashley River between its 15 defenders and elements of the Cadet Riflemen and the Palmetto Guard. Military storekeeper Frederick Humphries ultimately surrendered his post without shots being fired.[18]

President Buchanan and Secretary of War Floyd, a former Virginia governor, were caught off guard by Anderson's bold action to protect his garrison. John Floyd telegraphed Anderson, "Intelligence has reached here this morning that you have abandoned Fort Moultrie, spiked your guns, burned the carriages, and gone to Fort Sumter. It is not believed because there is no order for any such movement. Explain the meaning of this report." The South Carolina politicians, from the

18 Doubleday, *Reminiscences of Fort Sumter*, 72-76; DFJP, Letter, Pettigrew to Simons, Jan. 2, 1861; "The Events of Yesterday," *Charleston* [SC] *Mercury*, Dec. 28, 1860, 2.

governor to their congressional delegation, were also surprised by Anderson's action, as they had assurances from President Buchanan that any hostile or provocative actions concerning the forts would be avoided. Now in Washington, the South Carolina Secession Commissioners wrote the president that Anderson "not only without but against your orders, has dismantled one fort and occupied another." Buchanan answered the next day, "My first promptings were to command him [Anderson] to return to his former position," but before any steps could be taken in that direction, the "Palmetto flag floated out to the breeze at Castle Pinckney." Buchanan rebuked the Carolinians for not giving him the time to sort out the situation. With the political chessboard materially changed, the commissioners withdrew from the negotiations.[19]

Capt. Foster reported to Adj. Gen. Samuel Cooper in his final report that Castle Pinckney was "generally in excellent condition" at the time of its capture. The cannons of the fort were all mounted, except for two or three guns on the barbette tier and one 42-pounder in the casemate tier. The carriages were in good order, and the magazine was well furnished with implements and powder. Six days before the Castle changed hands, Capt. William Maynadier reported to Washington that Castle Pinckney held 22 cannons—14 iron 24-pounders, four iron 42-pounders, and four iron 8-inch seacoast howitzers. Other early reports mention two mortars, possibly one 10-inch and one 8-inch mortar, as well other unspecified pieces of artillery. On December 29, the *Charleston Courier* reported that ten 24-pounders were mounted on the ramparts with other guns in the casemates. It would later be proven that the reporter was incorrect in his assumption that the Castle was "beyond the reach of the largest guns of Fort Sumter."

Thomas P. Lowndes recalled that he had been out of town celebrating Christmas with his family when he received news that South Carolina state forces had seized Castle Pinckney and Fort Moultrie. As a 21-year-old member of the Washington Light Infantry, he rushed back to Charleston to join his militia company. With other "belated soldiers," Thomas took a small and "miserable" steamer to the Castle, which was almost swamped in the crossing due to high winds. The novice soldier found his new post crowded with men, and he incorrectly estimated there were 300 or 400 men confined in the small fortress. It was "very pretentious in armament, mounting guns en-barbette and in Casemate, about 24 in number." The guns in the casemate, he was told, "could not be fired more than once owing to defective ventilation." Pvt. Lowndes also recounted a humorous tale he had heard of an obese militiaman who needed the point of a bayonet "dexterously placed by

---

19 OR 1/3, 109-110; Robert Livingston Stanton, *The Church and the Rebellion Against the Government of the United States* (New York, 1864), 122.

a comrade in the seat of his breeches" to prod this would-be hero up the scaling ladder and over the brick wall.[20]

The *Charleston Mercury* on December 29 reported that Castle Pinckney was the new home of 160 men—60 from the Washington Light Infantry, 35 from the Carolina Light Infantry, 35 from the Meagher Guards, and some artillerymen. A strong guard had been detailed on the ramparts, the wharf, and the breakwater. Working under a fluttering Palmetto flag, two former West Point Military Academy cadets, Wade Hampton Gibbes and Frank Reynolds, began instructing the garrison on how to use the big guns. Dr. Robert Wilcot Gibbes, the surgeon general of South Carolina, visited Fort Moultrie and Castle Pinckney to inspect and report on the hospital accommodations. There was also a swapping of forces on the afternoon of the 28th, with a detachment of the Marion Artillery under Capt. Gadsden King coming to Castle Pinckney, while a detachment of 30 men from the Washington Light Infantry left the Castle and reported to Fort Moultrie. The reporter for the *Charleston Courier* felt that Castle Pinckney was "far from being an insignificant position" and would, under Col. Pettigrew and Maj. Capers, "make itself felt, if need be."[21]

Sunday fell on December 28. Reverend Toomer Porter, the rector of the Church of the Holy Communion on Ashley Avenue, was rowed to Castle Pinckney to preach to the Washington Light Infantry. Porter had been elected chaplain of the company in 1858, and he would proudly hold the office for the next 38 years. Choosing his text from Second Timothy, the 32-year-old Episcopal minister entitled his sermon "As a Good soldier of Jesus Christ." Porter would note in his autobiography that "I had the honor of preaching the first sermon to the troops in the civil war." Two days later, on January 1, 1861, Patrick Lynch, the Roman Catholic Bishop of the Diocese of Charleston, was rowed out to the Castle. Lynch had come to preside over the Feast of the Circumcision with the Irish Meagher Guards. Mass was held, and Lynch preached a sermon "suitable to the occasion."[22]

The cerebral James Johnston Pettigrew had been a firsthand participant in the Southern reaction to Robert Anderson's decision to move his small garrison

---

20 OR 1/3, 130; "Affairs at Fort Moultrie, Sumter and Castle Pinckney," *Charleston* [SC] *Courier*, Dec. 29, 1860, 1; Lowndes, *Reminiscences of Thomas Pinckney Lowndes*, 4:12-13.

21 "General Orders to Major-General Schnierly. Issued Dec 30, 1860," *Charleston* [SC] *Daily Courier*, Jan. 16, 1861, 1; "Dr. Gibbes," *Charleston* [SC] *Courier*, Dec. 29, 1860, 2; "Affairs at Fort Moultrie, Sumter and Castle Pinckney," *Charleston* [SC] *Courier*, Dec. 29, 1860, 1; W. A. Harris, *The Record of Fort Sumter from Its Occupation by Major Anderson, to Its Reduction by South Carolina Troops, During the Administration of Governor Pickens* (Columbia, 1862), 13.

22 Porter, *Led on!*, 121; David Heisser & Stephen White, *Patrick N. Lynch 1817-1882: Third Catholic Bishop of Charleston* (Columbia, 2015), 77.

from Fort Moultrie to Fort Sumter. Now commanding Castle Pinckney, Pettigrew devised a system of signals for the various militias in the Charleston Harbor to alert one another to an impending attack. During daylight hours, Castle Pinckney and the city would communicate through signal flags. Three flags on the Castle's flagstaff, descending from red to black to white, signified that a large enemy force was approaching and that reinforcements were needed. A single red flag indicated that an enemy force was threatening an attack, and the addition of a black flag indicated that the militia in the Castle believed they could meet the threat by themselves. At night, three white lanterns in a triangular form signaled the approach of an overwhelming enemy force. Two white lanterns perpendicular to one another indicated an attack was in the making. Two horizontal white lights alerted the military command in the city that Castle Pinckney would meet the impending threat bearing down on them.

Over the broader harbor, Pettigrew wanted large signal rockets that would burst into balls of various colors at their highest trajectory point. Three rockets fired in rapid succession, roughly at ten-second intervals, would indicate the approach of a large enemy force and the immediate request for assistance. One rocket meant approaching enemy forces and the threat of an attack. If a reply rocket acknowledging receipt of the message was not fired, the fort in question should fire its message again. The South Carolina command officially instituted Pettigrew's warning system on January 1, 1861.

Among the Washington Light Infantry was Capt. William Ashmead Courtenay, a bookseller, and the business manager of the *Charleston Mercury*. Courteney was destitute after the war, but he recovered to build a shipping business and become mayor of Charleston in 1879. A 1908 newspaper chronicler recorded his memory of Courteney going to the sentinels on the ramparts of Castle Pinckney, "who were shivering in the winter wind," and offering each a sip of fine French brandy from his canteen. The story goes that Courteney did not drink, which brought no objection from his fellow Irish-born soldiers as one remarked, "More power and long life to you, and may you remain a teetotaler as long as we are stationed together."[23]

It was a surprisingly small number of combatants whose deeds were covered on the front pages of every major newspaper and hurtled the nation toward disunion. The evacuation of Fort Moultrie and the investiture of Fort Sumter by the small federal garrison, followed by the state militia's occupation of Castle Pinckney, Fort Moultrie, and the Federal Arsenal involved less than 500 armed soldiers in total

---

23 DFJP, Pettigrew to Jamison, Jan. 17, 1861; "Joyous Trip to Jacksonville," *Charleston* [SC] *Courier*, Apr. 17, 1908, 10.

Scaling Ladders: 1860   67

Members of the Washington Light Infantry in early 1861 on James Island, SC. The W.L.I. participated in the seizure of Castle Pinckney on December 27, 1860. William Courtenay, a future mayor of Charleston, is on the far left of the back row. *Charleston Library Society*

—hardly more than a regiment in the coming Civil War. Whether these military maneuvers in December 1860 were preliminary steps towards sustained Southern independence or the immediate need to forcefully put down a Southern rebellion was about to be determined.

Chapter 6

Declaring Southern Independence
1861

AFTER THE RESTORATION OF STATE SOVERIENTY FOR SOUTH CAROLINA THE CAROLINA LIGHT INFANTRY WAS DETAILED TO ACT AS A PORTION OF THE GARRISON OF CASTLE PINCKNEY AND IN THE PERFORMANCE OF THAT DUTY HIS WAS THE FIRST SACRIFICE OF LIFE IN THE SERVICE OF THE STATE.[1]

Both militaries continued to overestimate the capabilities of their opponent. On January 1, 1861, Brig. Gen. James Simons, commander of the 4th Brigade of Charleston Militia, wrote to Gov. Pickens, giving a frank and forthright assessment, albeit slightly inaccurate, of the state's current military position. The report stated that Fort Sumter, currently in Union hands, commanded the harbor and that the state's forces were ill-prepared, ill-equipped, and disorganized. In the event of open hostility, communication between the militia-held harbor forts, with perhaps the exception of Castle Pinckney, would be cut by Fort Sumter's "first return fire."

The governor's rebuttal to the militia general was equally as frank, stating whilst he knew the disposition of the state's forces was not perfect, he entirely rejected the conclusion of Simons' report, which, if the governor accepted, suggested that "we should withdraw our troops from our positions, abandon our efforts and yield without a struggle on every point" which would cover "our cause with imbecility and probable ruin."

The first day of 1861 also saw James Johnston Pettigrew at Castle Pinckney writing his friend and fellow Charleston lawyer Nelson Mitchell. Pettigrew thanked

---

1 Tombstone inscription of 30-year-old Robert Little Holmes at Magnolia Cemetery.

Mitchell for the use of his powerful binoculars, allowing him to view the Federal soldiers in Fort Sumter "as if I was there." His small garrison force at the Castle, he told Mitchell, was "absolutely 'Spoiling for a fight.'" A Unionist in sentiment, Mitchell saw in Pettigrew a moderate in temperament and political outlook. Col. Pettigrew explained in his New Year's letter to Mitchell that, while standing watch on the parapet the night before, he had decided that "the machinations of a few unformidable office seekers" and an unscrupulous press were to blame for creating "the gulf of civil war between my garrison and that of Fort Sumter and destroyed the only government which had secured liberty to the world."[2]

Gov. Pickens January 2 letter to Brig. Gen. Simons expanded on his reasoning behind ordering state militia companies to seize the two federal outposts of Castle Pinckney and Fort Moultrie. The South Carolina chief executive had been operating under a "distinct pledge of faith" between the national government in Washington and representatives of South Carolina that the harbor forts were to remain "precisely <u>as they</u>, <u>then were</u>," until the commissioners could present themselves in Washington. Maj. Anderson had not only moved his troops to Fort Sumter, but had spiked the cannons at Fort Moultrie, which was "in open violation of the faith of the [National] Government." Simons noted that Col. Pettigrew, his military advisor, believed that "if I had not occupied Castle Pinckney when I did, it too, in like manner, would have been destroyed" by the federal soldiers.

The next day Col. Edward B. White, a local architect and now a newly designated state engineering officer, wrote Gov. Pickens that Pettigrew at Castle Pinckney had submitted a plan to defend the Castle against an attack and detailed its current defensive condition. Col. Pettigrew believed that Castle Pinckney's ability to engage the enemy "is limited" and that little could be done to protect its walls against a prolonged bombardment from Fort Sumter or any Federal vessel that managed to enter the harbor. That said, the able lawyer's chief concern was not from any potential artillery bombardment but from its vulnerability to "assault by troops from Fort Sumter." Pettigrew feared Federal troops could be landed on the open beach areas on either side of the Castle. Faced with the dilapidated condition of the wooden palisade walls at the rear of the Castle, Pettigrew requested between $3,000 and $4,000, a significant sum of money at the time, to repair the stockade (palisade) fence, and to construct a wooden frieze around the parapet, which would prevent federal soldiers from scaling the walls with ladders. In addition, Pettigrew asked that 1,000 sandbags and 1,000 hand grenades be sent to the Castle. The governor responded by authorizing White to draw no more than $2,000 for repairs

---

2 W. A. Harris, *The Record of Fort Sumter*, 14-18; Letter, Pettigrew to Mitchell, Jan. 1, 1861, Archives of the Charleston Museum, box 3, folder 40, 1983.1.

and defensive improvements and added the instructions that "no expenditure is to be made except with a view to present necessity and the present emergency."³

On January 3, Col. Pettigrew alerted the citizens of Charleston that "No boat shall be allowed to approach the Castle, except by the head of the wharf." Every boat was to halt instantly and not advance until "express permission is given" by the sentinel. Most people and supplies arrived at the Castle on the Steamer *Osiris*, which ran twice daily shuttles between the pier at Market Street (adjacent to the unfinished Customs House) and Sullivan's Island, while touching at Castle Pinckney each way.

In the first few days of January, two English reporters, Thomas Butler Gunn and William Carlyle, with whiskey flasks in their coat pockets, took the *Osiris* to Sullivan's Island. Gunn saw a lively scene at Castle Pinckney, "for the Zouave troops garrisoning it ran around the fort to the wharf in a brisk trot peculiar to their corps, while others formed in free and easy style, musket in hand and talked with acquaintances on the *Osiris*." Allen Hanckel, the quartermaster of the First Regiment of Rifles, announced that any articles intended for the soldiers on duty at the Castle were to be left at the State Cotton Press, at the corner of East Bay and Pinckney Streets. Pettigrew described his first Southern command in a January 2 letter. His 181 officers and men included 64 militiamen from the Washington Light Infantry, 48 from the Carolina Light Infantry, 42 from the Meagher Guards, and 27 from the Marion Artillery.⁴

Tragedy struck the Castle on January 7 when a nighttime sentinel mortally wounded a militia soldier. Pvt. Robert Little Holmes of the Carolina Light Infantry was, according to Thomas Lowndes of the Washington Light Infantry, quartered in the house outside the fort's walls. After the bugle played "Retreat," Holmes ran from his quarters to report to the guard room for his shift as a sentry. It was 10:00 p.m., and the sally port entrance was about to close. A 15-year-old member of the Meagher Guards, who was posted at the sally port, "halted him with musket cocked probably with hand on trigger; nervous and excited by the approach of one from the outside." In the darkness, the young lad's musket discharged. The "buck and ball"—three small buck shot and one single large round ball—entered the militiaman on his left side under the shoulder, while the smaller balls punctured both lungs. The 31-year-old Holmes died from his mortal wounds in 20 minutes,

---

3 DFJP, Pickens to Simons, Jan. 2, 1861; *OR* 53/1-115-116.

4 "Quartermaster's Department," *Charleston* [SC] *Courier*, Jan. 5, 1861, 2; "Castle Pinckney," *Charleston* [SC] *Mercury*, Jan. 16, 1861, 2; DFJP, Pettigrew to Simons, Jan. 2, 1861; Thomas Butler Gunn Diary, 22 vol., Missouri Historical Society, 15:21. Hereafter cited as TBGD.

making him the Republic of South Carolina's first military casualty and arguably the first military fatality of the war.[5]

Sammy W. Dibble wrote that the incident caused intense excitement among the soldiers stationed at the Castle, and it was "only the discipline here that prevented lynch law being carried into affect." Col. Pettigrew kept a lid on the rising tension by sleeping between the two militia companies at night. The next day was "more cool and calm but still there is a damper on the spirits of the whole garrison." Gunn, who posed as an artist for the *London Illustrated News,* but was actually a clandestine Charleston correspondent for the *New York Evening Post,* wrote that Holmes' death was testimony to the spirit and desire of the South Carolina troops. "The young Pole [Holmes] who was accidentally shot the other day, and who died regretting that his comrades would attack Fort Sumter without him," wrote Gunn, "may be considered the sample exponent of the popular feeling—there are hundreds like him."[6]

At dawn on January 9, the *Star of the West,* carrying supplies and 200 reinforcements for Fort Sumter, approached the entrance to the Charleston Harbor from the south. The beacons and buoys that would normally guide the large two-decked steamer into port were missing. Citadel cadets assigned to a newly constructed masked battery on Morris Island spotted the merchant ship in the main channel. Without hesitation, they began firing on the steamer, hitting her twice but doing no real damage. As the *Star* rounded Cumming's Point, Fort Moultrie started to fire warning shots at the relief ship. The steamer turned to starboard and, pushed by the ebb tide, headed out of the harbor. Some historians have viewed this 45-minute confrontation as the first military action of the Civil War. It certainly raised the stakes for both sides. At Castle Pinckney, according to the *Charleston Courier,* the men sprang to the heavy guns without the orders of their officers. They hoped for a shot at the "stranger," intending to " bring out the fire of Fort Sumter." Col. Pettigrew issued peremptory orders not to fire unless ordered to do so.[7]

---

5 Thomas Lowndes, *Reminiscences of Thomas Pinckney Lowndes,* 4:18-19.

6 Tribute of Respect," *Charleston* [SC] *Mercury,* Jan. 28, 1861, 2; SCHS, letter, Samuel Dibble to Harriet Williams, Jan. 8, 1861; "Terrible Accident at Castle Pinckney," *Charleston* [SC] *Mercury,* Jan. 9, 1861, 2; Clyde Wilson, *Carolina Cavalier,* 139; TBGD, 15:97. On Jan. 26, 1861, the Washington Light Infantry gathered at their post on Morris Island and formally paid their respects to their comrade Robert L. Holmes, who had been killed at Castle Pinckney on the 7th. They resolved that in his death, Carolina had lost a "faithful and devoted citizen and soldier—society an honest man, a courteous gentleman, and an industrious member."

7 David Detzer, *Allegiance,* 156-159; "The Feeling at Castle Pinckney," *Charleston* [SC] *Courier,* Jan. 10, 1861, 1.

On the same day that the *Star of the West* was fired upon, Gov. Pickens created an ordnance board to direct military operations in the harbor to eventually reduce and compel the surrender of Anderson's small garrison at Fort Sumter. Under the active command of Lt. Col. Roswell Sabine Ripley, Fort Moultrie was being restored into fighting shape with defensive merlons added to protect artillerymen on the parapet. Large crews of enslaved people also constructed three batteries—Bee, Beauregard, & Marshall—on Sullivan's Island and built platforms for batteries at Cummings Point (the northern extremity of Morris Island) and Fort Johnson.

On January 13, Edmund Ruffin, the staunch advocate of States' Rights and the protection of slavery, was among a delegation that included South Carolina Secretary of War David Jamison, which stopped to inspect Castle Pinckney and Fort Moultrie. Ruffin complimented "the patriotism & liberality of private planters" who had sent hundreds of their slaves without charge to the state to work on the fortifications. According to Wylie Crawford, the surgeon at Fort Sumter, all his fellow federal officers could do was use their spyglasses to watch "the gradual construction of works intended to close the harbor to all relief to them and to be used in their destruction."[8]

The directives issued by Gov. Pickens on January 9 included dispatching local architect Edward B. White to Castle Pinckney to direct "only such work as immediately necessary for securing that post." The 55-year-old White graduated West Point in 1826. By the 1840s, he had become a noted Charleston architect. In 1853, White became the superintending architect of the U.S. Customs House under construction on East Bay Street. He held that position until federal funding ran out in 1859.[9]

The talented and energetic White made a series of immediate repairs to Castle Pinckney in ten short days. According to his January 19 report, which was hand-delivered to South Carolina Secretary of War Jamison by Capt. Gadsden King, White's enslaved work force had dug a 15-foot-wide moat completely around the stockade. Any infantry force landing on the marsh and shoal would have to first wade through the moat's water and soft pluff mud to reach the wooden enclosure

---

8 Samuel W. Crawford, *The History of Fort Sumter: An Inside History of the Affairs of 1860 and 1861, and the Events which brought on the Rebellion* (New York, 1896), 208-209; Edmund Ruffin, *The Diary of Edmund Ruffin*, 3 vol., ed. William Kauffman Scarborough (Baton Rouge, 1972), 1:531. The South Carolina Ordnance Board was made up of Gen. James Jones, Gen. Gab. Manigault, Gen. Jamison, Maj. Walter Gwynn, & Thomas F. Dayton.

9 Ravenel, *Architects of Charleston*, 181-200; DFJP, Pickens to Simons, Jan. 2, 1861. Edward White was one of the first Americans to popularize the Gothic Revival style, designing, along medieval lines, the Huguenot Church in 1844 and Grace Episcopal in 1847. White was also comfortable with classical Greek and Roman designs evident in his Market Hall, Johannes Lutheran Church, the United States Arsenal, and the steeple of St. Philips Church.

at the back of the Castle. A large gap in the old wooden stockade was also closed with new fencing. The architect then focused his attention on strengthening the defenses around the sally port entrance to the brick fort. A crescent-shaped outer work, called a lunette, was constructed from squared timber in front of the fort's entrance, complete with loopholes for musketry. Above the wooden door, White's men built an impressive "Machicoulis" gallery using plank timbers. The box-like structure extended about four feet out from the parapet and had musket loopholes that fired into the stockade yard and a trap door in the floor so that primitive hand grenades could be dropped on hostile infantry attempting to force their way through the sally port entrance. Carpenters charred or "fire hazed" the new structures so that the new wood would be difficult to set on fire. In all, White had kept his expenditures to a modest $1,100. Observing all this from Fort Sumter was Capt. Foster, who identified changes at Castle Pinckney, noting that sandbags were present on the parapet to possibly protect the heads of "sharpshooters."

Col. White used the second half of his report to the secretary of war to comment on the "character of this post." White ventured that with a few large pieces of artillery, the Castle could fire on Fort Sumter, which was 2 ½ miles distant and might even be a launching point for an amphibious assault on Anderson's men. More realistically, its intrinsic value was defensive, protecting the city and commanding the inner harbor. He wrote, "Under the existing circumstances, Castle Pinckney requires to be carefully protected; for should it come into the hands of an Enemy it would Hold the City in check." White then pointed out that the entire stockade wall, built "in the times of nullification," should be wholly replaced. He estimated it would take 122,500 ft. (over 23 miles) of lumber and many barrels of nails at a total cost of $4,259.

Thomas Lowndes recalled in his 1896 memoir that most of the volunteer soldiers stationed at Castle Pinckney, and especially the elected officers, had little to no practical experience in their new military roles. This affliction would hamper both sides during the first year of the Civil War. "The ignorance of our officers, of heavy artillery drill is lamentably displayed at these early drills," he reported, "in fact, none of our officers from Col. Pettigrew the Commander of the 1st Rifles.... to the so-called artillery officers—But they worked with the manual with eye fixed steadily on its pages and gave the order to 'take implements, limber, heave, form battery.'" Thomas recalled that one unfortunate officer, having skipped several pages in the artillery manual, managed to dismount one of the 24-pounder guns at the Castle.[10]

10 D. F. JP, E. B. White to D. F. Jamison, Charleston, Jan. 19, 1861; Hatcher, *Thunder in the Harbor* (El Dorado Hills, CA, 2023), 29; Lownes, *Reminiscences of Thomas Pinckney Lowndes*, 4:18.

Declaring Southern Independence: 1861

Sketch of Castle Pinckney done by William Waud in January 1861. The subsequent etching was published in *Frank Leslie's Illustrated Newspaper*. Behind the lighthouse is the wooden palisade that was constructed during the Nullification Crisis. *Matthew Locke*

A state militia in an open stand-off with the national army created unexpected ramifications even for the civilian citizens of Charleston. 24-year-old Jacob Frederick Mintzing spent 14 days at Castle Pinckney as a member of the Carolina Light Infantry, before returning to his job as a clerk at Walter Hovey's paint, oil, and glass store at 137 East Bay Street. Mintzing, the son of a former mayor of Charleston, soon discovered that Hovey had deducted from his pay the 14 days that he had served at the Castle. When the young clerk objected, Hovey dismissed the employee. An agitated *Charleston Mercury* demanded on January 28 that Walter Hovey "shut up his store forthwith," warning that "It behooves men of northern birth to be very careful as to their behavior right now." The provocative newspaper speculated that Hovey would "probably be waited upon by a committee of gentlemen with a requisition to leave Charleston within a limited time."

In the middle of January, the ordnance board transferred the Washington Light Infantry and the Meagher Guards from Castle Pinckney to Morris Island. Col. Pettigrew was replaced by 45-year-old Maj. John Andreas Wagener, who commanded the German Artillery militia of Charleston. Since emigrating from Germany as a teenager, Wagener had become an inveterate organizer in the city's large ethnic German community. Possessing boundless energy and intelligence, he was president of the German Fire Company, founded the first German-language newspaper in the South, started three German ethnic organizations, and was instrumental in establishing St. Matthew's Lutheran Church.

A statue of John Andreas Wagener in his Confederate uniform stands atop this monument in Bethany Cemetery. Wagener is buried below the granite monument, but the markers pay tribute to the devotion to the Confederate Cause made by Charleston's German community. *Cliff Roberts*

On January 15, Wagener reported to Secretary of War Jamison that his new command consisted of a detachment from the Marion Artillery under Capt. Gadsden King, Company A, the Columbia Battery of the German Artillery, under Capt. Carsten Nohrden, and a detachment from Company B under an unnamed sergeant. In all, Wagener had 76 men at Castle Pinckney, a force that he viewed "as being smaller than I expected to have." He respectfully asked that he be reinforced by King's whole command of Marion Artillery, and the rest of Company B of the German Artillery, which was currently stationed on Morris Island. Wagener also requested two 8-inch Columbiads so that "We might put them to very effective use in assisting an attack on Fort Sumter." He also encouraged South Carolina's new secretary of war to inspect Castle Pinckney writing, "I think I can fully satisfy you of the great value of the position in our present crisis of affairs."[11]

On January 29, an innovative test of technology by the South Carolina military took place at Castle Pinckney. In front of the state's new secretary of war, David F. Jamison, and his staff, a "sabot" designed by Wagener was successfully tested using a 24-pounder cannon. A wooden sabot for a smoothbore spherical ball projectile was made of poplar, basswood, or other close-grained wood and was banded around the projectile with the fuse pointed forward and in the center of the bore. The purpose of Maj. Wagener's experimental sabot was to extend the gun's range, probably by sealing the subcaliber projectile thereby improving muzzle velocity.

---

11 TBGD, 15:117; Robert Alston Jones, *Charleston's Germans* (Milwaukee, 2021), 9-10; DFJP, Maj. Wagener to Gen. Jamison, Jan. 18, 1861. In 1849, Wagener's German Colonization Society of Charleston purchased a large tract of land in the foothills of the Blue Ridge Mountains which became the town of Walhalla, South Carolina.

According to the *Charleston Mercury* the successful trial increased the range of the gun by more than half a mile from 1,900 to 3,520 yards, thus serving to highlight the "ingenuity" of the German experimenter. A month later, the *Charleston Daily Courier* reported on Wagoner's new "Patent Sight for cannon of any calibre." The major had placed a spirit leveler attached to a small screw for the front sight of the gun. This allowed the sight itself to slide back and forth on the screw.[12]

On February 1, a beautiful new flag "with a unique and showy design" was run up the staff at Castle Pinckney. Purchased by the German-born officers of the garrison under Maj. Wagener, it featured two white palmettos blazoned on a red field, with a crescent between them. Fifteen stars were in an arch above the trees, with alternate stripes of blue and white instead of red and white, as in the federal flag. The two palmetto trees on the large 11' by 20' flag may have reflected the thinking of many South Carolinians that they were embarked on a second war of independence. A few months later, Wagener would take the flag on to Hilton Head, where it became known as the "Fort Walker Flag."[13]

On February 3, 1861, a New York bound steamer collected the 42 women and children who had been dependents of the Federal artillery garrison. Four days later, delegates from seven independent republics met in Montgomery, Alabama, to form a republican government of Confederate States. Within weeks, a provisional constitution had been written, and the delegates elected Jefferson Davis of Mississippi as the first president of the Confederate States of America. Commissioners were appointed to seek peace with the United States and their president-elect Abraham Lincoln. Leroy Pope Walker was selected as the secretary of war, and he ordered Capt. W. H. C. Whiting, a former officer of engineers in the U.S. Army, to Charleston. On March 1, Gen. Pierre Gustave Toutant Beauregard was also sent to Charleston to assume military command of the harbor. The Louisiana native and distinguished engineering officer had recently assumed the superintendency of the Military Academy at West Point, but he had been relieved when the Pelican State withdrew from the Union. The dashing and diminutive 43-year-old Beauregard was, by Shelby Foote's narrative, "as flamboyant by nature as by name." He was also a wise choice as he was diplomatic in his dealings and

---

12 Jack W. Melton, Jr., *The Half-Shell Book: Civil War Artillery Projectiles* (Charleston, 2018), 364; "Trial at Castle Pinckney," *Charleston* [SC] *Mercury*, Jan. 31, 1861, 2; "Important to the Military," *Charleston* [SC] *Daily Courier*, Feb. 27, 1861, 2. John Wagener had tinkered with cannons in the past, having gained a federal patent in 1853 for an improved cannon-sight for correcting tilt or cant.

13 "Matters at Castle Pinckney," *Charleston Mercury*, Feb 1, 1861, 2; Tom Elmore, *The Flags That Flew Over Castle Pinckney: Research, Analysis, Findings, and Recommendations*, 2013, essay posted on https://www.castlepinckney.org/, 14; Robert Behre, "143-Year-Old Flag Returns to Charleston," *Charleston* [SC] *Post & Courier*, Mar. 24, 2004, A1.

The unique "Fort Walker Flag," originally 11 ft. by 20 ft., first flew over Castle Pinckney on February 1, 1861. Major John Wagener took the flag with him when his German Artillery company was transferred to Fort Walker on Hilton Head Island. Captured by U.S. Naval forces, the flag was displayed in the Capitol on George Washington's birthday. In 2003, the Massachusetts Historical Society gifted the flag to the South Carolina Historical Society.
South Carolina Historical Society

---

a Creole gentleman from Louisiana's first families. In short, his background was in congruence with that of the planter elites who controlled affairs in Charleston.

On Sunday morning, February 10, 1861, the 55 members of the Marion Artillery under Capt. Gadsden King were transferred to Fort Johnson. An artillery officer present at the morning departure of the Marion Artillery penned a piece in the *Charleston Daily Courier* under the pen name HOWITZER. He noted that an hour before the departure of the "Marions" from Castle Pinckney, the artillery militia company was drawn up in a line, with the Germans ready to escort them to the boat. Stepping from the boat, brought over from the city, was 3rd Lt. J. McPherson Washington, who had been serving admirably under Maj. Wagener as the acting adjutant at Castle Pinckney. The 24-year-old officer was a direct descendant of American Revolutionary War cavalry commander William Washington, and he had just earned a commission as a 1st lieutenant of the 1st Artillery of the new South Carolina army. Washington had impressed everyone who had served with him at the Castle, and here was an opportunity to recognize his diligent service. The young adjutant was requested to step to the center of the line and was caught entirely by surprise when Lt. Johann Diedrich Lesemann of the German Artillery came forward and made a few appropriate remarks. Officers and men had all donated money for handsome gifts—a dressing case and an elegant sword and sash—to Washington for his service to South Carolina. Wagener added a beautiful pair of epaulets. This show of genuine affection was a special moment at Castle Pinckney, and the emotional McPherson Washington would momentarily be deprived of his "coolness of equanimity." Unfortunately, he would also be deprived of his young life in Virginia six months later.[14]

On February 15, the Meagher Guards were returned to Charleston from Morris Island and dismissed after seven weeks of duty. The 55 men were congratulated by their captain, Edward McCrady, "for their exemplary behavior and for their willingness to endure hardships in the cause of the State." The Washington Light Infantry, under Capt. Charles Simonton, returned home from Morris Island three days later. They were escorted from their boat to their military hall by members of the Washington Light Infantry home detachment, and soldiers from the Citadel and the Meagher Guards.

With the departure of the Marion Artillery, Castle Pinckney was left briefly to Company A, German Artillery, some 60 men, under the 34-year-old Capt. Carsten Nohrden. According to the 1860 census, the tall German owned a saloon and grocery store near Laurens Street on the Charleston waterfront. On February 19, the German militiamen left the Castle by boat to be replaced by 135 "regulars" of the South Carolina army. Company A was met at the Ferry Wharf at the foot of Market Street by Company B, German Artillery, the German Riflemen, the German Fusiliers, and the Palmetto Riflemen. The companies formed into a battalion and preceded by the German band, marched along Broad Street and up Meeting Street to the Citadel Green. The battalion then formed a hollow square and was formally welcomed home by Capt. S. Lord, Jr. of the German Fusiliers, with an appropriate response made by Wagener. After a six-gun salute, the soldiers were dismissed. Three drill sergeants from the German Light Artillery remained at the Castle to instruct the newly constituted Confederate soldiers in using the guns. Respite for these local militiamen, however, turned out to be a short-lived as the First Rifles were called back into service in March and sent to Sullivan's Island to handle various mortar batteries.[15]

---

14 Samuel Crawford, *The History of Fort Sumter*, 206; "Lt. J. McPherson Washington," *Charleston [SC] Daily Courier*, Feb. 14, 1861, 1.

15 Neil F. Nohrden, "Captain Carsten Nohrden's Sword," 2013, Charleston Museum website, https://www.charlestonmuseum.org/news-events/captain-carsten-nohrdens-sword/; "Military Movements,"

On the morning of February 22, the tranquility of the harbor was shattered when cannon fire ripped through the air as the guns of Castle Pinckney roared into life. This thunder of cannon was not an act of aggression, but one of celebration, as it was the birthday of George Washington, a universal day of celebration across America, both North and South. In Montgomery, Alabama, the day was also marked by the inauguration of Jefferson Davis as the first Confederate States of America president. Thirteen times the guns of Castle Pinckney thundered, with each shot representing one of the thirteen original colonies. At noon, Maj. Anderson responded from Fort Sumter with, depending on the account, either 13 or 34-gun salute, with each shot representing one of the states in the Union, including South Carolina.[16]

On March 4, the untested Abraham Lincoln was inaugurated as the 16th American president, while on the same day, Gen. Beauregard formally assumed command of the Charleston Harbor. The Creole general had 8,027 men under his command, which included almost 2,000 men on Sullivan's Island and 1,400 on Morris Island. Lt. Ormsby Blanding commanded the 81 enlisted men at Castle Pinckney. Changes were undertaken immediately, with mortar batteries on Morris and Sullivan's Island relocated beyond the range of the guns of Fort Sumter. At the same time, the batteries at Cummings Point were reoriented to fire on Sumter and ships that might attempt to enter the harbor. On March 5, Beauregard and Gov. Pickens visited Castle Pinckney and Fort Moultrie.

The following day, Beauregard received a detailed report concerning the construction and deployment of guns at the batteries being built on Morris Island from Maj. Whiting. The engineering officer requested that two seacoast howitzers and five 24-pounders, currently at Castle Pinckney, be sent to these island batteries. On March 8, Edmund Ruffin wrote in his diary, "This day, the dismantling of Castle Pinckney was begun." By the 16th, Anderson was reporting to Washington that "they [the Confederates] are removing the armament from the parapet of Castle Pinckney" and went on to surmise that these were the same guns he had observed being unloaded at Cummings Point on Morris Island. "Nearly the whole of the upper tier of which [Castle Pinckney] is being removed for this purpose." Two days later, Capt. Foster reported that seven barbette carriages,

---

Charleston [SC] *Mercury*, Feb. 11, 1861, 2; "The Meagher Guards," *Charleston* [SC] *Mercury*, Feb. 15, 1861, 2; "Washington Light Infantry," *Charleston* [SC] *Courier*, Feb. 18, 1861, 1; "The Military Yesterday," *Charleston* [SC] *Mercury*, Feb. 20, 1861, 2.

16 Samuel Crawford, *The History of Fort Sumter*, 271.

which he stated had come from Castle Pinckney, were now lying on the beach at Cummings Point.[17]

In early spring, Confederate workmen constructed an unwieldy "floating battery" on one of the Cooper River wharves. This primitive ironclad was a military innovation about a hundred feet long, twenty-five feet wide, and built from massive pine timbers. It was protected by six layers of iron that were bolted together. Embrasures for four heavy cannons, all reportedly taken from Castle Pinckney, were assigned to the floating battery. Too heavy to be powered by a steam engine, the vessel was towed to a protected cove off Sullivan's Island and pinned against four large wedges to hold her in place. The Federals in Fort Sumter now had one more battery to contend with.

Meanwhile, the new Confederate government forming in Montgomery, Alabama, faced a cacophony of pressing organizational issues. Building a military to defend the new nation may have been the most urgent in character. After consulting with William J. Hardee and P. G. T. Beauregard, the new secretary of war created a military structure for the Confederacy. The act of March 6, 1861, authorized a modest-sized Southern "regular" army of 15,000 men that would, in the time of war, be supplemented by 100,000 volunteers serving in a "provisional" force from various state militias. A quarter of the officers serving in the United States Army would soon resign, and most of these trained soldiers would accept commissions in the "regular" army of the Confederacy. Robert E. Lee, Albert Sidney Johnston, Braxton Bragg, and Beauregard are all examples of officers who served in the regular Confederate military instead of a specific state's provisional force.[18]

Recruitment stations were also established to fill the enlisted ranks of the regular Southern army. With few exceptions, one being the Baton Rouge Barracks, this effort failed as Southern men preferred instead to enlist in local companies composed of friends, family, and neighbors. Castle Pinckney, interestingly enough, was chosen as a training ground for the first group of volunteers who had enlisted in the new Confederate regular army. These were men from Baltimore, Maryland, who held Southern sentiments and had been recruited by the colorful and imaginative Texas U.S. Senator Louis T. Wigfall. Only 40 miles south of the Mason and Dixon line, Baltimore was, in the spring of 1861, a divided and volatile place. After securing permission from Secretary of War Walker on March

---

17 *Reports and Selections of the General Assembly of the State of South Carolina at the Regular Session Commencing January 9, 1900* (Columbia, 1900), 18; Samuel Crawford, *The History of Fort Sumter*, 278-279; "Report of Robert Anderson," *The Diary of Edmund Ruffin*, 1:563.

18 David Detzer, *Allegiance*, 199-200; "Map of the Fortifications in the Harbor," *Charleston* [SC] *Courier*, Apr. 15, 1861, 5; Richard P. Weinhart, *The Confederate Regular Army* (Shippensburg, PA, 1991), 4-11.

6, Senator Wigfall went to Baltimore for this secret endeavor. Twelve days later, Walker was telegraphing Beauregard in Charleston to dispatch Robert E. Haslett, a native of Baltimore, to his hometown. Haslett was to find Wigfall at the brokerage house of William T. Walters and arrange steerage to Charleston for the volunteers that Wigfall had recruited. Haslett was slow to leave Charleston, which prompted Walker to order Capt. William Dorsey Pender of the newly formed Corps of Artillery from Montgomery to Baltimore to oversee the operation.

On March 25, Gen. Beauregard informed Gen. Samuel Cooper, the new adjutant-general of the Confederate Army, that 64 Baltimore recruits had arrived in Charleston under the charge of Haslett. The men had been sent to Castle Pinckney and put under the command of Capt. Frederick Childs and Lieutenants O'Brien and Robertson. The South Carolina quartermaster volunteered to provide the recruits with rations and clothing. Beauregard was compelled to ask Cooper "to prescribe the uniform for the Regular Army as early as practicable." Capt. Childs was an 1855 West Point graduate who resigned on March 1st from frontier duty at Fort Duncan, Texas.

Capt. Pender arrived in Baltimore on March 24. The North Carolinian had been a lieutenant in the 1st U.S. Dragoons only months earlier. After two days in Baltimore, he wrote his young wife Fanny to reassure her that "in the first place I shall be prudent and in the second I am well backed." Pender believed that Baltimore was "strong for secession, and I am backed up by the sympathy of the first men here." On April 3, Pender wrote home that another 61 recruits had been sent south. Called back to Montgomery, the 27-year-old Confederate officer slipped out of Baltimore the day before Fort Sumter was fired upon. Over the next two years, William Dorsey Pender would rise to the rank of major-general in the Army of Northern Virginia before being killed on the second day of the battle of Gettysburg.[19]

The *Charleston Daily Courier* reported on April 6 that another 28 volunteers arrived from Baltimore on the steamship *Thomas Swan* and had been brought directly to Castle Pinckney. Child's newly arrived Maryland volunteers were not men of wealth and leisure. His soldiers included 45-year-old George Moog, a French baker, Edward Kelly, a 20-year-old carpenter, New Yorker Samuel Hart, a 35-year-old butcher, and Henry O. Wills, a 25-year-old bookkeeper from the District of Columbia. According to an unsigned letter in *The Baltimore American*, not all these recruits embraced their new military life. "We arrived on Sunday morning at nine o'clock and were immediately taken to Castle Pinckney, where we were set to work transporting two heavy 48-pounders to the wharf," wrote the

---

19 OR 1/1:276-278; OR 1/1:279-284; Richard Weinhart, *The Confederate Regular Army*, 78.

Maryland volunteer, "We are treated worse than negroes here. We don't get enough to eat, and what we do get is of the coarsest and most common description."[20]

By the beginning of April, rumors were swirling in the North and in Charleston that Winfield Scott, "Old Fuss and Feathers" himself, was organizing a large flotilla to relieve the siege of Fort Sumter. A New York newspaper speculated that Navy Capt. Gustavus Fox would use steam-powered tugboats from New York Harbor to rush a small force of marines to Castle Pinckney. "There is only a small force in Castle Pinckney, but from this position, which is near Charleston," speculated the *New York Express*, "the city could be easily bombarded and set on fire." Capt. Childs, at Castle Pinckney, was given orders by one of Beauregard's aide-de-camp on April 9 to have his small command in "readiness to embark this evening, about 7 p.m., on board three steamboats." Each man was to have his musket with him and 40 rounds of ammunition. They would be posted with 25 soldiers on each steamboat "in the outer harbor" and ready to respond to any challenge. According to Capt. S. W. Ferguson, "These detachments will be returned in the morning and will hold themselves in readiness for similar duty every night until further orders."[21]

It was a strange time as volunteer units poured into Charleston from adjoining states. Louis Wigfall arrived in the city on April 1 and gave a series of well-received public speeches. Swept up in the excitement, he briefly enrolled as a private and, according to the *Charleston Courier*, served at Castle Pinckney with his Baltimore volunteers. It would be a brief assignment, as Beauregard, on April 10, made the political fire-eater an honorary member of his military staff. The apex of Southern social prominence came with wearing the sword and red sash of a Confederate staff officer.

At precisely 4:30 a.m. on Friday, April 12, 1861, a mortar from the beach battery next to Fort Johnston fired on Fort Sumter. Alert spectators could follow the red burning fuse swing over the harbor in a wide arc and then burst into flames over the federal position. Fort Moultrie fired next, followed by batteries at Morris Island. The roar of the cannons brought an estimated 5,000 Charlestonians through the narrow passageways between the grand mansions and onto the High Battery for a splendid view of the cannonading. Soon a dozen Rebel batteries, and even the floating battery, were fully engaged in reducing the thick walls of Sumter. Novelist Dubose Heyward thought the people on the upper stories of

---

20 South Carolina Service Records of Samuel Hart, Civil War Service Records, M267, group 109. Hereafter cited as CWSR; *OR* 1/1:281; *Supplement* [CT] *to the Courant*, Apr. 6, 1861, 55; "Recruits," *Charleston* [SC] *Courier*, Apr. 6, 1861, 1; Caroline E. Janney, *Ends of War: The Unfinished Fight of Lee's Army after Appomattox* (Chapel Hill, 2021), 95.

21 *OR* 1/1-296; "Daily Dispatch," *New York Express*, reprinted in the *Wheeling* [VA] *Daily Intelligencer*, Apr. 13, 1861, 4.

the homes could see "in the gray half-light a world in flux, pouring out over the White Point Gardens and massing solidly along the sea wall." Caught between the low ceiling of cloud and the floor of the harbor, the sounds of guns firing were deafening, to be soon followed by smoke, that smelled of burning sulfur and saltpeter, that "commenced to drift across the town." Anderson's Federals waited for daylight and did not join the engagement until 7:00 a.m. With the Stars and Strips flying above them on a 100-ft. flagpole, they fired their guns principally at Fort Moultrie from both the embrasures and the barbette of the fort. At 8:00 a.m., using furnace-heated solid shot, Confederate artillery at Fort Moultrie managed to set the officer's quarters at Sumter on fire. Aided by the wind, the fire threatened to reach the magazine. Early in the evening of the second day, Anderson accepted Beauregard's terms of surrender.[22]

The official records of the war make no mention of Castle Pinckney participating in the two-day bombardment of Fort Sumter. Nor is there any mention of Federal artillery at Fort Sumter directing any of their shots at the Castle. With most of the large cannons removed from the outdated fort in March, it seems likely that the Marylanders stationed in the Castle could do little more than enjoy their front row seat to the cannonading in the harbor. That said, there are some clues perhaps pointing to Castle Pinckney making a token contribution to the Confederate attack. In mid-March, Beauregard, who was surrounding Sumter with artillery positions, secured mortar guns from Pensacola and Savannah. He wrote that three mortars were placed at Fort Johnson, three on Sullivan's Island, two in Christ Church Parish, and one at Castle Pinckney. If the gun assigned to the Castle was a 10-inch seacoast mortar, then it had the range, albeit at extreme range, to reach Sumter, some 2.5 miles away. Another source was William Merrick Bristoll, a Yankee school teacher and 1860 Yale graduate who was visiting his father in Charleston at the time of the bombardment. In his account of what he witnessed from the High Battery, he wrote, "Boom, boom go the cannon. Now the puff of white smoke comes from Fort Johnson. There goes one from Castle Pinckney." Given the wherewithal to participate in the bombardment, the men stationed at Castle Pinckney would have eagerly participated.[23]

The hard-drinking English reporters in Charleston made the most of the bombardment of Fort Sumter. Their precarious position as reporters for Northern newspapers required them to send their stories to New York using elaborate codes and displaying Southern sympathies by wearing blue secession cockades on their

---

22 Alvy L. King, *Louis T. Wigfall: Southern Fire-eater* (Baton Rouge, 1970), 118-119; Heyward, Dubose, *Peter Ashley* (New York, 1932), 276-277.

23 William Merrick Bristoll, "Escape from Charleston," *American Heritage* (Apr. 1975), 26:3.

lapels. Thomas Butler Gunn of Horace Greeley's Republican-aligned *New York Tribune* kept a daily diary of the late-night carrying-on of this talented bunch of newspapermen. One of Gunn's favorite English running mates was Will Waud, a "special artist" for *Frank Leslie's Illustrated Newspaper* and brother of the *Harper's Weekly* illustrator Alfred Waud. Leslie had instructed the 30-year-old Will Waud to use his discretion in finding ways to draw his sketches, and the Englishman had decided that his best course was to throw himself in with the Charleston elite by attending meetings, rallies, and regimental reviews. He, therefore, had little trouble gaining permission from Confederate authorities to sketch the numerous Rebel installations around the Charleston Harbor. His illustration of Castle Pinckney, which appeared in *Leslie's* January 26, 1861 edition, is one of the best early-war views of this Southern military post.[24]

Thomas Gunn and Will Waud were fellow Bohemians of pre-war New York. Gunn described Waud as "A good-looking little chap, of good address, capable of singing a good song," and, in short, "decidedly popular among his acquaintances in Charleston." While Gunn thought Waud's ability with a pencil was unmatched, "his stint of work is, really, about one day of labour to six of loafing." Gunn recounted in his diary the antics of Waud before the Sumter bombardment. On February 7, 1861, Gunn had written in his diary that Waud "had been carried off by the two Murdochs to Castle Pinckney to spend a day and a night." 1st Lt. Robert Murdoch was in the Marion Artillery at the time. Will evidently became an honorary member of sorts in this local artillery regiment which "spent no end of dollars on wines and spirits." Waud was again with the Marion Artillery on Morris Island for the bombardment of Sumter, going "hither and tither from one battery to the other, making sketches." Will Waud's first-hand observations became quite the scoop for his newspaper, and Gunn noted that he now sported a "military cap, with a gilded Palmetto on it."

With Fort Sumter in their pocket, the Confederate high command set about organizing the defenses of greater Charleston. Ripley, now a Southern hero for his leadership of Fort Moultrie, was sent to Fort Sumter to repair the extensive damage to the seacoast fortress. Castle Pinckney, during this time, became an important warehouse for the Confederate military. Special Order no. 99, issued on April 26 by Beauregard, directed that the Morris Island guns aimed at Fort Sumter were to be dismantled and sent to Fort Sumter, with the balance to be

---

24 Gary McQuarrie, "William Waud: 'Special Artist' for Leslie's and Harper's," *Civil War Navy* (Winter 2020), vol. 7, 3:51-58; Louis Morris Starr, *Bohemian Brigade; Civil War Newsmen in Action* (New York, 1954), 21.

sent to Castle Pinckney. "At Castle Pinckney the guns, shot, and shell will be left in the depot outside the walls; the chassis, carriages, pintle blocks, traverse circles and other appurtenances will be put away carefully in the casemates." On April 22 the *Charleston Courier* reported that the Rifle Regiment under Pettigrew had been relieved of duty guarding positions on Sullivan's Island.[25]

On May 11, 1861, at Beauregard's request, the Baltimore regulars were organized into two companies of the Corps of Artillery. One company of 78 men would be under the command of Capt. Stephen Dill Lee, who had been serving as Beauregard's quartermaster in Charleston, and the other company of 60 men was assigned to Charles S. Winder, a former captain in the 9th United States Infantry and a Marylander by birth. The 28-year-old Lee, a Charlestonian by birth, was not released from his desk duties by Beauregard and thus never took the field with these Maryland regulars. Lt. William Barnwell would instead command Lee's company. Stephen Lee would, in time, be steadily promoted and ultimately reached the rank of lieutenant general in 1864 and serve as a corps commander in the Army of Tennessee. Winder's company left first for the Charleston Arsenal, and Lee's company left Castle Pinckney on May 30 for Fort Palmetto on Cole's Island, a strategic location that guarded the entrance to the Stono River. Winder did not stay long with the Maryland men either, eventually becoming a brigadier general commanding the Stonewall Brigade. On November 15, 1861, with both companies reduced in numbers, the War Department ordered the Maryland men consolidated into one company, which became Company C, 15th Battalion, South Carolina Heavy Artillery (The Lucas Battalion) under Capt. Theodore Hayne. They spent most of the remainder of the war manning the Confederate fortifications on James and Johns Island, where it served with some distinction guarding "the back door" to Charleston.

In August, representatives of both the state of South Carolina and the Confederate States of America produced a full inventory of "*Ordnance and Ordnance stores*" at Castle Pinckney (see Appendix 11). The detailed inventory lists the number of gun barrels at the Castle, the types of gun carriages on hand, their number and condition but also the parts of gun carriages that were available, an exact count of the various types of artillery implements such as fuse mallets, priming wires, pass boxes etc. as well as a precise inventory of more than two dozen

---

25 TBGD, 15:134, 148, 16:217-218; *OR* 65/1-157-158: "The Rifle Regiment," *The Charleston* [SC] *Courier*, Apr. 22, 1861, 2.

types of cannon balls and shells that were on hand for more than a dozen different types of guns.[26]

The battle of Fort Sumter led directly to Abraham Lincoln's call for 75,000 volunteers to put down the rebellion of seven states. Unable to support a war against their fellow Southerners, four more states—Arkansas, North Carolina, Tennessee, and Virginia—joined the Confederacy. The local militia units in Charleston did not hold together after Fort Sumter but rather split into various companies that would subsequently join South Carolina regiments. Having learned "with infinite disappointment" that Irish patriot Thomas Francis Meagher had pledged his allegiance to the North and "joined the oppressors of this their adopted land," the Meagher Guards of Charleston voted on May 6 to become the "Emerald Light Infantry." For the remainder of 1861, they served as a militia unit guarding the South Carolina coast. In February 1862, efforts were made to raise an Irish Volunteer Battalion. That initiative fell short, but the Meagher Guards merged with the Jasper Greens and, with a contingent from the Montgomery Guards, went to Virginia to be a company in Maxey Gregg's 1st South Carolina Infantry.[27]

---

26 Richard Weinhart, *The Confederate Regular Army*, 83-86; "Ordnance Bureau Records, 1860-61," South Carolina Historical Society, Manuscript 43/0418.

27 Donald Williams, *Shamrocks and Pluff Mudd*, 98-101; W. Chris Phelps, *Charlestonians in War: The Charleston Battalion* (Gretna, 2004), 39.

Chapter 7

A Prison by the Sea
1861–1862

"Dull" you find it comrade? Rather. Like two lizards on a wall,

Here we lie and bask together – watch the tides that rise and fall;

Watch the sun – it travels slowly, dropping brilliants in the sea;

Count the crests of dark palmettos. Nay, you should not curse the tree![1]

The battle of First Bull Run was fought for control of Manassas Junction in northern Virginia on July 21, 1861. With timely reinforcements from the Shenandoah Valley, Brig. Gen. P. G. T. Beauregard was able to drive Irvin McDowell's unseasoned army back to Washington, D.C.

A small brigade of South Carolinians, Louisianans and Virginians under Col. Nathan "Shanks" Evans played an important role in the early fighting near the Stone Bridge. The Confederate victory was enthusiastically received across the South, while the devastating news tested the determination of the North to hold the Union together. An immediate question was what to do with the federal prisoners captured in the war's first major battle.

David Silkenat, in his 2019 book *Raising the White Flag: How Surrender Defined the American Civil War*, estimates that one out of every four Civil War soldiers surrendered at some point during the four-year war. He calculates that more than 673,000 men laid down their arms rather than continue to fight, roughly the equivalent of the number of soldiers who perished. Some prisoners were exchanged or paroled, while others ended up in notorious prison camps such as Andersonville, Georgia, or Elmira, New York. None of this was foreseeable in

---

[1] First stanza of a poem by Alice Bradley Neal entitled "Castle Pinckney" published in *Harper's Monthly*, Dec. 1, 1861.

the summer of 1861 when the Rebels captured some 1,000 green federal soldiers at Bull Run, or as the Southerners called the battle: 1st Manassas. While these new volunteer soldiers understood that enlistment meant the possibility of being wounded, becoming seriously ill, or even dying, few foresaw the possibility of being made a prisoner of war.[2]

Fearing that any formal exchange of prisoners would be seen as recognition of the nascent Confederate government, Abraham Lincoln refused to negotiate over the Bull Run prisoners. He would maintain throughout the war that Jefferson Davis was leading an illegal insurrection and that this struggle was never a war between two nation-states. This left Confederate officials with a decision about what to do with their new prisoners of war. On September 11, the *Richmond Examiner* announced that 156 Yankee prisoners would be shipped by railroad to Charleston and kept at Castle Pinckney. They were selected mainly from the 11th, 79th, and 69th New York regiments, with a large contingent from the 1st Michigan. They were considered to have the most "insolent and insubordinate" dispositions of the Bull Run prisoners. In double files, they were marched from Edward's Tobacco Warehouse, where they had been held under guard, to the Richmond depot of the Petersburg Railroad. A large and curious crowd followed the procession. A detachment of 25 Louisiana soldiers from the Madison Guard led the prisoners, and 25 Mississippi men from the Natchez Rifles brought up the rear. The Federal prisoners were loaded into three box cars. Security for the journey would be provided by a detachment of 50 men from the Jeff Davis Louisiana Battalion and a contingent from the Mississippi Rifles under the overall command of Capt. George Gibbs.[3]

Just before 6:00 a.m. on the morning of September 13, the train with the prisoners—34 officers and 120 enlisted men—arrived at the Charleston station after a three-day journey. They were, according to Alfred O. Alcock of the 11th New York Fire Zouaves, "tired—almost exhausted—having obtained but little rest since leaving Richmond." Waiting at the Northeastern Railroad Station on Chapel Street for their arrival were companies of the First Rifles under Col. John L. Branch. The prisoners disembarked and were marched into a hollow square formed by the Zouave Cadets, the Washington Light Infantry, the German Riflemen, the Palmetto Riflemen, the Carolina Light Infantry, the Jamison Rifles, the Beauregard Light Infantry, and the Moultrie Guards. With everyone in place,

---

2 David Silkenat, *Raising the White Flag: How Surrender Defined the American Civil War* (Chapel Hill, 2019), 2.

3 Silkenat, *Raising the White Flag*, 88-89; "National Prisoners sent to Castle Pinckney," *New York Times*, Sep. 15, 1861, 1.

they began a slow precession down Washington Street as the sun ascended above the Charleston rooftops. Castle Pinckney was not yet ready to accept prisoners, so their destination was the city jail on Magazine Street, a mile and a half from the train station. Cavalry—the Charleston Light Dragoons in the front and the German Hussars in the rear—bookended the marchers. Upon reaching the jail, the militia companies were dismissed except for Capt. Charles Chichester's company, the Charleston Zouave Cadets, who would guard the prison, and the Washington Light Infantry, who guided the Louisiana and Mississippi escort troops to the Charleston Hotel for some much-needed rest before they returned to Virginia.

Capt. Theodore Gaillard Boag, a 28-year-old local cotton merchant, had been specifically detailed to prepare the old jail for military prisoners. Boag assigned the officers and their trunks to three "airy rooms" on the second floor. Col. Orlando Willcox of the 1st Michigan Infantry remembered it being more like "cattle in a pen" as he shared his 10' X 12' room with a dozen other officers. The *Charleston Mercury* reporter thought the federal officers were "abundantly provided with money," and they were pleased to have the freedom to buy sweet potatoes and bread from outside street vendors. The 120 enlisted men, who each had nothing more than a blanket and their dilapidated summer uniforms from the day of the battle, were placed in the unfurnished twelve rooms on the uppermost story of the jail. The prisoner Alcock, who had been the fire brigade editor for the *New York Atlas* before the war, wrote home that Boag supplied them sufficiently "with soldiers rations of good pork, bread, coffee, sugar, and rice, with knives, forks, spoons, plates, and cooking utensils." Capt. Giles Shurtleff of the 7th Ohio Infantry saw it differently, writing that the officers were given raw coffee, sea biscuit, and "salt pork full of maggots."[4]

The *New York Herald* announced that Castle Pinckney was to become the "Fort Lafayette of the South." Built in the same time frame as Castle Pinckney, Lafayette was a coastal fortification in the narrows of New York Harbor and was used as a Civil War prison for Southern sympathizers and political opponents of the administration who were opposed to the war. President Lincoln had gone so far as suspending any privileges of the writ of habeas corpus on April 27, 1861. The prisoners, in this cold stone New York fortress, made do living in the casemates of this "American Bastille." The friends and family of the prisoners were often denied visiting rights or permission to exchange letters. Southerners viewed Pinckney,

---

4 "The Prisoners at Charleston," *Charleston* [SC] *Mercury*, Sep. 14, 1861, 1; "Letter From Our Fire editor, Now in Prison at Castle Pinckney," *New York Atlas*, Nov. 24, 1861, 1. Hereafter cited as NYA; Robert Garth Scott, *Forgotten Valor; The Memoirs, Journals, & Civil War Letters of Orlando B. Willcox* (Kent, 1999), 311; G. W. Shurtleff, "A Year with the Rebels," Lawrence Wilson, ed. *Itinerary of the Seventh Ohio volunteer infantry, 1861-1864* (New York, 1907), 319.

complete with casemates that could house prisoners, as the retaliatory equivalent of Lafayette. Northern newspapers barked that putting prisoners in Charleston during the fever season was patent cruelty.

On September 18, the Yankee prisoners were transported to Castle Pinckney under the guard of the Zouaves and a detachment of city police. A crowd watched the procession of raggedly dressed Union soldiers whose poor appearance, according to Alcock, "fully equaled that of the famous band with whom Falstaff was ashamed to march through Coventry." As rain fell steadily, the prisoners boarded the steamer *Cecile* for the one-mile trip to Shute's Folly. James Tuttle of the 4th Michigan Infantry described Pinckney as "an old dismounted fort on a marshy island" shaped like a horseshoe. The toe caulk of the horseshoe "looked out to sea," and the two heel caulks pointed "towards the city." According to John Ennis, a private in the 79th New York Highlanders, a written description of each prisoner was recorded by the Rebels and a photograph taken of each Yankee. Each prisoner was also issued a new prison shirt that Ennis thought was "very acceptable, indeed."[5]

The prisoner's new island home for the next six weeks had been reconstituted as a prison by refurbishing the casemates into prison cells. Atop a new wooden floor were two rows of wooden bunks, described by Alcock as similar in arrangement "as those in an emigrant ship." The men slept atop beds of pulverized rice straw. According to Tuttle, the men shook the rice to one end of their bunk and thereby "made a respectable pillow." Bricks sealed in each of the rooms, except for a sturdy entrance door with a barred window, and the embrasures were reduced in size to leave only a loophole for ventilation. The federal enlisted men were assigned to eight of the ten casemates of Castle Pinckney. The captured officers were assigned to the traditional officer quarters on the second floor of the eastern barracks, with the western side barracks occupied by the prison guards. Four Confederate officers shared a single room, with the privates and N.C.O.'s using the remaining free rooms. The Southern privates divided themselves into messes for cooking purposes, adopting names such as the "Beauregard Mess," the "Ripley Mess," the "Rebels Cave Mess," and the "Dutchman's Mess." The rooms on the first floor housed the garrison's kitchen, dining room, offices, and guard room.

The sentries who would guard the prisoners were the 55 members of the Charleston Zouave Cadets under Capt. Charles Edward Chichester and 1st Lt. Robert Gilchrist. At least two uniformed African American musicians were attached to the unit. The Cadets had been formed by Chichester and his friend Gilchrist in

---

5 James Gilmore Tuttle, *Reminiscences*, 1901, Bentley Historical Library, University of Michigan, 16-17; John W. Ennis, *Adventures in Rebeldom: or, Ten Months of Prison Life* (New York, 1863), 12.

early 1860 and were the eighth and last company of the Charleston Rifles Regiment. The cadets tended to be young and hailed from respectable Charleston families. There was also a large contingent of German immigrants listed on the muster roll. The company had established an armory, gymnasium, and library for their members on Queen Street, and only young men of a high moral character were accepted for membership. The Zouave Cadets had been serving as infantry support on Morris Island in January when the Citadel cadets fired the first hostile shots of the war with their two 24-pounders at the *Star of the West*. According to Cadet Anthony Riecke, as guards at Castle Pinckney, they "were never allowed outside their quarters without their side arms (Bayonets carried in a leather frog that was attached to their belts)." Being close to home, the Zouave Cadets received a steady stream of packages left with Sgt. E. C. Green at the corner of Hasell and Meeting Streets. On September 25th, Lt. Gilchrist, the son of the former district judge of the United States for South Carolina, sent a letter to the local Relief Association thanking them for the mosquito nets they had sent to Castle Pinckney.[6]

The 27-year-old Chichester was a competent officer and earned the respect of his men and their prisoners. Alcock viewed him as a strict disciplinarian but also a "humane man" who knew "how to treat fellow-men while in difficulties." Capt. John Drew of the 2nd Vermont Infantry believed the Zouaves were courteous towards the Northerners, writing, "at the North we think them the very firebrands of Secession; the truth is they are the coolest and most courteous men we have met. They believe in Secession and enter into it with all the ardor of patriots." Drew hoped he would be exchanged "for a South Carolina Captain, that we might fight away just as we think we ought."[7]

One Zouave Cadet who left a descriptive account of his time at Castle Pinckney was Felix Calcius, a 20-year-old bookkeeper for a German cotton buying firm. Around 1859, he had arrived in America from Hanover, Germany with his older brother Clemens Calcius. They boarded together at the Carolina House on Broad Street and worked to master the English language. By 1878, Felix had returned to Hanover, where he published his account of the American war in his native language and under the pen name August Conrad. The title translates to

---

6 "The U.S. Prisoners in Charleston Jail," *Burlington* [VT] *Free Press*, Dec. 13, 1861, 1; "Charleston Zouaves," *Charleston Courier*, Sep. 30, 1861, 1; "Soldiers' Relief Association, *Charleston Mercury*, 5; NYA, Nov. 24, 1861, 1; Anthony M. Riecke, "Personal Recollections of a Confederate Soldier," 1904, Anthony W. Riecke papers, 1879-1899, South Carolina Historical Society. Hereafter cited as SCHS; CWSR, Bill for Computation of Rations, Oct. 18, 1861, Captain C. E. Chichester, M267, roll 097, 106.

7 NYA, Nov. 24, 1861, 1; "The U.S. Prisoners in Charleston Jail," *Burlington* [VT] *Free Press*, Dec. 13, 1861, 1; "From Castle Pinckney, S.C.," *Burlington* [VT] *Free Press*, Nov. 22, 1861, 1.

Light and Shadows of American Life During the War of Secession. Felix wrote that the Federal officers under the Zouaves' custody were American in background and well-educated. On the other hand, the privates and non-commissioned officers were from all possible lands and had a raw and imprudent temperament. The strictest discipline would be necessary to keep order in the casemates.[8]

The Charleston Zouave Cadets had two uniforms – a comfortable summer uniform of gray cloth with white cross belts and a full-dress Zouave uniform reserved for the winter months. The Cadets were in their summer uniform on October 11 when George Cook took a series of photographs at Castle Pinckney. Many volunteer units during the first year of the Civil War, both North and South, adopted Zouave uniforms, which featured a French-themed jacket, vest, sash, baggy trousers, and kepis. The French military, considered one of the best in 1860, had adopted this distinctive style of uniform and dress from their colonial occupation of Algeria in the 1830s. Introduced to America in Chicago in 1859, the romanticized adaptations of Zouave fashion and characteristic light infantry drill were all the rage among early war units. Thomas Wiley, a tailor at 154 East Bay Street, sewed the Zouave uniforms for the Charleston Cadets. The elaborate design included a gray, nine-button chasseur jacket with a red collar and cuff facing, red shoulder straps, and gray chasseur-style trousers with red stripes. Below the trousers, at calf level, white canvas gaiters were worn under russet leather *jambieres* that were buckled at the top and laced down the outside. A black cap with a light colored band and a golden palmetto tree badge rested atop their heads.[9]

Zouave Cadet 1st Lt. Gilchrist was a long lanky lawyer with mutton chop whiskers who had clerked before the war under the Unionist James Louis Petigru. He was better known at the time as one of Charleston's more talented landscape artists. By 1859, Gilchrist was a 30-year-old widower living on East Bay Street with a law office at 13 Chalmers Street. Despite his binding obligations as a military officer, Gilchrist found time in 1861 to court young Mary Augusta Gibbes with carriage rides about Charleston. On October 15, before 400 guests, they were wed at the 2nd Presbyterian Church, a block from Marion Square. It would be one of the largest weddings in wartime Charleston. Robert was now 32, and his bride "Gussie" would turn 17 a week before the wedding ceremony, a celebrated union of two prominent Charleston families. Robert Gilchrist returned to his

---

8 August Conrad, *Schatten Und Lichtblicke Aus Dem Amerikanischen Leben Wahrend Des Secessions-Krieges* (Hannover, Germany, 1879). Reprinted in 2011 by the British Library, Historical Print Editions.

9 Shaun Grenan, *We Have Them On Our Own Ground: Zouaves at Gettysburg* (Gettysburg, 2021); Ron Field, *American Civil War Confederate Army* (London, 1998), 8.

responsibilities at Castle Pinckney and fortunately survived the war, rising to the rank of major. After the war, he would inherit property from his mother in the Adirondack region of upstate New York and, in 1871, build the first suspension bridge across the Hudson River.[10]

Security on Castle Pinckney was lax, especially compared to future Civil War prisoner-of-war camps with their brutal conditions and "dead lines" that, if crossed, meant almost certain death. Col. Michael Corcoran of the 69th New York wrote a Northern friend that the officers held at Castle Pinckney "have the liberty of the island" from "reveille to retreat" and had permission to stroll on the ramparts after supper. The rank and file had the liberty of the interior courtyard throughout the day. Alcock reported that each day started with the drums of the Charleston Zouaves. The sergeant of the guard would open each casemate door, and the men would form up on the parade ground, and roll was called by the Officer of the Day. The prisoners were then free to pass the day as they pleased until "tattoo" was played at 9:00 p.m., and the casemate doors were again locked for the night. During the day, the prisoners smoked and read, played games of whist or chess (the black pieces were the Rebels and the white pieces were the Yankees), exercised, rolled cannon-shot, carved trinkets, played practical jokes on the unwary, and, in the evenings, sang together. The outhouse was outside the palisade, and three prisoners were allowed to be past the sally port at any one time.

Providing substance for the more than 200 men in the Castle fell to Commissary Capt. Theodore Boag. "Let all my descendants bless his memory," wrote Col. Willcox of the genial and big-hearted Boag, as rice often supplanted hardtack on the menu. Boag and Willcox seemed to have had a good relationship, as one day Boag asked the Union officer if he wanted to inspect the rice. Upon opening the top of the barrel, Willcox found, to his delight, a copy of the morning newspaper. Water for the post came from the cistern and, in dry spells, from barrels and tar buckets brought over from the city. John Ennis of the 79th Highlanders wrote that squads of prisoners had to pass through the barracks' supply room to get water. On occasion, "when our bacon ran short or bread was scarce," a bit of thievery supplemented their limited rations. His squad's treasure was hidden under the floorboards of their casemate cell.[11]

Prisoners and guards alike received 2/3 of ordinary soldier rations, consisting of ship's bread, pork or beef, coffee, sugar, and rice. Each casemate, which had

---

10 Rosemary Miner Pelkey, *Adirondack Bridgebuilder From Charleston: The Life and Times of Robert Codgell Gilchrist* (Utica, 1993), 25-28, 86-87.

11 "Letters from Col. Cochran, Castle Pinckney, Oct. 21, 1861," *New York Times*, Nov. 20, 1861, 3; NYA, Nov. 24, 1861, 1; Robert Scott, *Forgotten Valor*, 311; John Ennis, *Adventures in Rebeldom*, 11.

Colonel Michael Corcoran of the all-Irish 69th New York was the most renowned of the Bull Run Prisoners sent to Castle Pinckney. From an 1862 photograph taken by Mathew Brady.
National Portrait Gallery

as many as 17 men assigned to it, had an orderly, two permanent cooks, and two men on fatigue duty who kept everything clean and tidy. Long tables with stools ran down the middle of each casemate. Food, candles, vinegar, and soap were issued to each casemate "mess" every five days. Prisoners could supplement their meals by buying food from outside hawkers. A bushel of sweet potatoes fetched $2.50. Cooking was done on outdoor stoves in sheds placed against the hot-shot furnace in the middle of the post. Bathing was permitted outside the palisade in a wide ditch that ebbed and flowed with the harbor tide.[12]

Col. Corcoran thought the out-of-the-way Castle to be "a hundred times more preferable" than the Richmond tobacco warehouses, where idle visitors had thronged the jail daily to view the prisoners. The warm autumn weather in the Charleston Harbor also agreed with most federal prisoners. Chaplain Hiram Eddy of the 2nd Connecticut Infantry wrote his wife, "We have plenty of air, & go out upon the island when we please." Alcock informed the readers of the *New York Atlas*, "The climate here is delightful, and reminds us most of Cadiz (Spain)." Col. Willcox wrote his brother on October 14 that, after five days in the city jail, "we emerged into a new life, in every sense, at this Castle in the harbor of Charleston. The sea breeze, release from close confinement, etc., have brought me up as well as the 150 who share my lot." The health of the prisoners and guards on Castle Pinckney was generally good, with only two fatalities being reported. 23-year-old Noah Porter of the 1st Michigan died of typhoid fever on October 2, and Henry Brink, also from the 1st Michigan, died on November 1. Willcox wrote in his diary

---

12 "Interesting from Richmond: Condition of the Prisoners at Richmond," *New York Times*, Dec. 4, 1861, 8; James Tuttle, *Reminiscences*, 18.

that, through the "courtesy" of Capt. Boag, he was permitted to attend Brink's funeral at Magnolia Cemetery.[13]

The Hospital Department at Castle Pinckney was organized under the direction of a local physician, William Pettigrew, who visited daily. Pettigrew worked closely with Surgeon S. Griswold of the Scott's Life Guards (38th New York) and the clever Harry Perrin, the hospital steward. Nighttime was the least pleasant time for the enlisted prisoners in the casemates. With limited ventilation, the locked casemates proved to be damp, stuffy, and crowded. At other times, reported Pvt. Tuttle, "the wind was cold and raw from the ocean," and "we sometimes got more than we desired." Capt. Shurtleff, who slept in one of the casemates (probably no. 8) taken over by the officers, wrote that the solid masonry of the Castle "was full of water that had been gathering for generations, and soon we began to have coughs and rheumatism and fevers." Alcock thought that jaundice was the most prevalent complaint. Willcox wrote, "With here and there an exception, diarrhea is the only form of disease we have known."[14]

Two of the prisoners, who were roommates at the Castle, received national attention. Col. Orlando Bolivar Willcox of the 1st Michigan had received a shell wound in the right forearm at Bull Run and would, in 1890, receive a Medal of Honor for valor on that occasion. A Mexican War veteran, the 38-year-old former lawyer would eventually be exchanged in time to lead a division in Burnside's Corps at Antietam and Fredericksburg. Willcox's letters and memoirs were found in a trunk 150 years after the war and became the focus of Robert Scott's 1999 book *Forgotten Valor*. Orlando's October 1861 letter to his brother, E. N. Willcox of Detroit, was published in the *New York Times*. The burley Michigan colonel with his muttonchop whiskers begged for clothes for his 50 Michigan men. "Some of the gallant fellows are out of their britches, some bare footed, &c."

Perhaps the most famous of the federal prisoners was the lean six-foot, two-inch tall Col. Michael Corcoran of the all-Irish 69th New York Regiment. The 34-year-old commander of the regiment was captured with many of his troops at the battle of First Bull Run. A native of County Sligo, Corcoran had been an Irish nationalist in New York City while also rising through the ranks of the 69th State Militia. He drew national attention in August 1860 for refusing to turn

---

13 Michael Corcoran, *The Captivity of General Corcoran* (Philadelphia, 1862), 46; Hiram Eddy, letter to his wife, Oct. 20, 1861, Eddy Papers, Connecticut Historical Society; NYA, Nov. 24, 1861, 1; "The Prisoners at Castle Pinckney: A Letter from Col. Willcox," *New York Times*, Nov. 24, 1861, 3; Robert Scott, *Forgotten Valor*, 313.

14 NYA, Nov. 24, 1861, 1; G. W. Shurleff, "A Year with the Rebels," 321; "The Prisoners at Castle Pinckney: A Letter from Col. Willcox," *New York Times*, Nov. 24, 1861, 3; James Tuttle, *Reminiscences*, 17.

out his regiment to march in the city parade honoring the 19-year-old Prince of Wales. Corcoran's second-in-command was none other than his fellow 1848 Irish revolutionary Thomas Francis Meagher. The two Union officers and fast friends were, in short, the two best-known Irishmen in America. The 69th had crossed Bull Run Creek and bravely charged up Henry's Hill only to be knocked back by Confederate reinforcements under Stonewall Jackson. At the end of the day's battle, 38 of the regiment were dead, 59 were seriously wounded, and 200, including Corcoran, were missing. Despite the humiliating defeat of the Federal army at Bull Run, the bravery of the Irish soldiers had been noted by a grateful nation.[15]

"In the quiet of my ocean-bound prison, my thoughts often wandered back to Richmond," recorded Corcoran in his book written shortly after his August 1862 prisoner exchange. In particular, the Irish patriot missed the "mirth-inspiring proceedings of the 'Richmond Prison Association,'" a group organized and led by U.S. Congressman Alfred Ely. Corcoran had been appointed treasurer of the merry band. Ely was a Republican from Rochester, New York, who had ventured from the District of Columbia to witness the battle of Bull Run only to find himself swept up as a prisoner in the subsequent rout. The 45-year-old Ely was a "capital companion, being continually full of merriment, and overflowing with good humor." With an objective of killing time, this association of Federal officers debated, played games, told stories, and sang patriotic songs. Ely was financially better off than the men in uniform whom he shared a mess with, and the politician procured a cot and two white blankets. "We thought his extravagance was passing all bounds," wrote an amused Corcoran, "and threatened to expel him, as an aristocrat, from the 'Prison Association.'" Ely's mild punishment, which was written into the minutes of the said association, was to keep his new possessions in "apple-pie order."

On October 17, 1861, Michael Corcoran scribbled in his diary that his fellow officers had, that day formed the Castle Pinckney Brotherhood. The colonel declared that it would be "similar, in all respects, to that of which we were members in the old Tobacco Warehouse, in Richmond." This hearty group of officers would be the precursor of the Union Prisoners Association, first organized in the Charleston City Jail on December 31, 1861. Its membership included all officers captured in 1861 and held at the tobacco factories of Richmond, then Castle Pinckney, and later Columbia, South Carolina, Salisbury, North Carolina, and New Orleans.

Both prisoners and guards made the best of their seven weeks together at Castle Pinckney. A true highlight for the prisoners was the arrival of the mail,

---

15 "The Prisoners at Castle Pinckney: A Letter from Col. Willcox," *New York Times*, Nov. 24, 1861, 3; Timothy Egan, *The Immortal Irishman: The Irish Revolutionary Who Became an American Hero* (Boston, 2016), 184-185, 258.

A Prison by the Sea: 1861–1862

A close-up of Castle Pinckney taken from an 1863 broadside of the Union War Prisoners Association. Federal officers held at the Castle organized the Castle Pinckney Brotherhood in October 1861. Two months later the group became the Union War Prisoner Association. *Huntington Library, San Marino, California*

with letters from home containing news and needed money. Corcoran thought the sight of his men closely packed together to watch the distribution of a packet of mail as worthy of "a scene for the pencil of a Hogarth." Religious services were held each Sunday. Most of the services were led by Chaplains Hiram Eddy and G. W. Dodge. Willcox described Eddy as "a big, noble-hearted specimen of 'muscular Christianity.'" J. T. Drew, a captain in the 2nd Vermont Infantry, wrote a friend in Washington, D.C., that the "Lord's Supper" was commemorated before 20 of the soldiers. "It was a solemn, sacred time," he observed. Capt. Shurtleff, who had been a tutor at Oberlin College when the war started, remembered that Archbishop Patrick Lynch of the Charleston Diocese, an Irish immigrant from County Fermanagh, called several times on the Federal prisoners, and "though he endorsed the doctrine of secession, he always manifested a genuine Christian spirit and kindly disposition." Corcoran wrote in a letter that Lynch spoke in a "mild, gentlemanly, and Christian spirit" and "handed me all the funds in his possession." The Irishman believed that Lynch's kind words had "driven the gloom and despondency from the hearts of the captives immured within these frowning walls." Bishop Lynch went on to become an advisor to President Jefferson Davis and, in February 1864, ran the blockade to visit Pope Pius IX in Rome to secure Rebel recognition from the Holy See. The artist Conrad Wise Chapman, who spoke fluent Italian, was his secretary. Though politely received, Lynch could not secure the Pope's blessing for the Confederate States of America.[16]

The most belligerent of the Yankee prisoners proved to be a 22-year-old Canadian named James Gilmore Tuttle. Ordered to police the Zouaves' parade and drill grounds outside the walls of the Castle, Tuttle, a member of the 4th

---

16 Michael Cochran, *The Captivity of General Corcoran*, 29,46, 63, 66; G. W. Shurtleff, "A Year with the Rebels," 320; "Letters from Col. Cochran, Castle Pinckney, Oct. 21, 1861," *New York Times*, Nov. 20, 1861, 3; Robert Scott, *Forgotten Valor*, 311.

Catholic Bishop Patrick Lynch frequently preached to the Irish prisoners at Castle Pinckney. A Mathew Brady photograph. *National Portrait Gallery*

Michigan Infantry, refused, believing he was giving aid and comfort to the enemy. Capt. Chichester placed the obstinate prisoner "in an old bomb-proof magazine utterly devoid of light and almost of air until, as he expressed it, 'I came to my senses.'" For the next three days, Tuttle survived in the "dungeon" on a daily ration of a pint of cold water and a hardtack. The stench of the bomb-proof ultimately prostrated young Tuttle. Taken to see Chichester again, the prisoner needed physical support from two guards to reach the commanding officer's quarters. Asked again if he would perform the duty assigned to him, Tuttle replied that he was willing to do his duty as he saw it, but he would not clean up the drill ground of the enemy of his country. An exasperated Chichester turned to the sergeant beside him and exclaimed, "He is the most stubborn man I have ever seen. Take him to his quarters and tell his comrade not to bother him with questions."

"We made five or six plans to escape," wrote Capt. Withington in 1862 to his hometown newspaper in Jackson, Michigan. Withington, who would later be awarded a Congressional Medal of Honor for his bravery at the battle of Bull Run, stated that the prisoners negotiated "with the negroes to bring down a fishing boat," but the Cadet guards proved to be too vigilant. Now released from his solitary confinement, Tuttle had his own plan to escape. He recalled in his 1901 narrative that he managed to secure two old wood palisade posts, each about ten feet long, and "spiked them together." On this primitive paddleboard, he would lay down and, using two paddles strapped to his wrists, "propel his ship" past Fort Sumter and out to the Union fleet. Unfortunately, or perhaps fortunately for Tuttle, the night before his planned escape, "another man belonging to another mess" had made his own set of paddles and took off with Tuttle's improvised craft. 21-year-old James Haig of the 79th New York Highlanders had pleaded illness and persuaded the officer of the guard to allow him outside the castle walls for a few minutes. According to Ennis of the 79th, Haig departed immediately after the evening roll call and used a piece of a gun carriage as his flotation device. His disappearance was discovered three hours later, and rockets were fired into the night sky from Castle Pinckney. A thorough search of Shute's Folly came to naught.

The *Charleston Mercury* wrote that Haig "quietly took to the marsh, and having secured a log of wood, worked his way across the channel to Sullivan's Island." This is not entirely correct as Haig was trying to reach the federal blockading squadron some 14 miles away. Ennis writes that the escapee succeeded in passing Fort Sumter, but as he tried to cross the harbor bar, the tide began to turn against him. Only three miles from the Yankee ships, Haig was swept back to Sullivan's Island. His bout of freedom lasted three days but he found little to eat on Sullivan's Island. A sentinel arrested him when he was unable to return a countersign, and Haig was returned to the prison population. James Tuttle was "terribly disappointed" that his means of escape had been usurped by Haig, "but wished the poor fellow success."[17]

A day after the disappearance of James Haig from Castle Pinckney, the prisoners were told they were being transferred to the city jail in Charleston. John Ennis believed the order came "for fear some more of us would try the same experiment." This may well have been the case, but it was not the reason given by Confederate authorities. The departure of the prisoners from Castle Pinckney came only a few days before the arrival off the Carolina coast of Samuel Du Pont's immense federal naval invasion fleet—17 warships escorting 33 transports carrying nearly 12,000 troops under Gen. Thomas Sherman. The *Charleston Mercury* believed the removal of the prisoners was to put the Castle to "better use" as part of the harbor defense system. With a panoramic view of the Confederate fortifications and the enemy blockading fleet at the harbor entrance, there was also concern that the prisoners might exchange signals with the blockading fleet. The discovery of a pair of powerful opera glasses in a box sent to one of the Union officers only increased the anxiety. Chichester had the glasses seized, and they are now on display at the Confederate Museum at Market Hall.[18]

On the late afternoon of October 30, the Federal prisoners were removed from Castle Pinckney aboard the steamer *John A. Moore* and deposited at the Central Wharf of Charleston. It took time to unload the officer's baggage from the steamer and load the bags onto wagons. Guarded by the Zouave Cadets and two platoons

---

17 James Tuttle, *Reminiscences*, 19-24; "From Castle Pinckney, S.C.," *Burlington* [VT] *Free Press*, Nov. 22, 1861, 1; John Ennis, *Adventures in Rebeldom*, 12-13; "Attempted Escape," *Charleston* [SC] *Mercury*, Nov. 4, 1861, 2.

18 John Ennis, *Adventures in Rebeldom*, 12; Chet Bennett, *Resolute Rebel: General Roswell S. Ripley* (Columbia, 2017), 81, 85.

These opera glasses were sent by mail to a federal officer imprisoned at Castle Pinckney. Fearing that they would be used to send information to the blockading squadron, Captain Chichester seized the glasses and, after the war, had them inscribed with the names of the forts he defended, including Castle Pinckney. *Confederate Museum at Market Hall*

of the City Guards, the procession moved down East Bay, Cumberland, Meeting, and Queen Streets as they worked their way to the city jail. Large crowds came out to watch the spectacle, hoping they would glimpse Col. Corcoran. The privates, marching five abreast, were down to torn rags for a uniform, but they seemed in good spirits and carried on their shoulders chairs, chessboards, and other conveniences that they had "extemporized during their stay at Castle Pinckney."[19]

Conditions for the enemy prisoners took a decided turn for the worse once they left Castle Pinckney for the imposing city jail. "The prison was very filthy, and well stocked with vermin," thought Dr. John McGregor of the 3rd Connecticut Infantry. Capt. John Drew had one of his letters smuggled out of the jail by a sailor from the ship *Grenada*, which had been captured by the Rebel ship *Sallie* and sailed into Charleston. The northern crew spent ten days in the Charleston jail before being released. Drew wrote in his clandestine letter home, "While in Castle Pinckney we were courteously treated; the guards being native born Carolinians were generally gentlemanly." Now everything was different as they were under the scornful watch of the jail turnkeys. The crowded rooms had no furniture, and the

---

19 "The Union Prisoners of War," *Charleston* [SC] *Mercury*, Nov. 2, 1861, 2; "The Yankee Prisoners," *Southern* [GA] *Confederacy*, Nov. 2, 1861, 3; "A Slippery Subject," *The Autauga* [AL] *Citizen*, Nov. 14, 1861, 1.

prisoners slept on the floor using their shoes as a pillow. Letters, clothing, and money from the North no longer reached the P.O.W.s, and communication with the local inhabitants was prohibited. They were now on half rations—three cakes of pilot bread, a piece of maggoty bacon, and coffee. "We are made to stand and answer to our names twice a day," reported Drew, "and were ordered around at the point of a bayonet." Drew's secret letter soon appeared in Northern newspapers and was reprinted in Charleston. Confederate authorities were not amused and placed the lieutenant in "a close cell, heavily ironed, and kept him on short rations for ten days." Many of the Northern prisoners became weak and sick. Dr. Griswold, the surgeon of the 38th New York Infantry, died from typhus fever at the end of November.[20]

The officers were confined in an upper room, and the windows were barred and closed with iron shutters. Now in dire straits, they chose to dispose of anything of value to procure food and medicine. Complicating matters was the news that five officers had now become unwilling participants in the *Enchantress* Affair. The *Enchantress* was a Confederate privateer captured near Hatteras, North Carolina, one day after the Union debacle at Bull Run. On October 22, a federal court convicted 14 Southern seamen of piracy and sentenced the sailors to be hanged. The Confederate government immediately reacted to this rigid interpretation of justice by declaring that 14 Union officers, currently in their prisons, would be hanged in reprisal if the death sentences were carried out. Drawn from a hat by Congressman Ely in the Richmond prison on November 10, several of the Charleston prisoners—Corcoran, Willcox, Woodruff, Neff, and Potter—were selected and designated for the same treatment and fate as that of the Confederate privateers. "If any privateersmen are hung they will hardly be able to keep the mob from us," wrote Capt. Drew. The men watched from their window as gallows were constructed in the prison yard.

On November 19, Col. Willcox wrote in his diary that Richmond authorities had issued orders to place the five Charleston prisoners into solitary confinement. The Union officers were to be treated as pirates and condemned felons, with rations reduced to bread and water. Willcox believed Gen. Ripley, the Confederate commander of the harbor, had "given stringent orders for our fare and keep." An Ohio native who had married a Charlestonian, Ripley, in the eyes of Willcox, had become over-zealous in his attachment to the Southern Cause and wished to show everyone concerned that he "could out-Herod Herod." Capt. William

---

20 Jeremiah S. McGregor, *Life and Deeds of Dr. John McGregor* (Foster, RI, 1886), 52-53; "The U.S. Prisoners in Charleston Jail," *Burlington* [VT] *Free Press*, Dec. 13, 1861, 1; John Ennis, *Adventures in Rebeldom*, 15; "Death of a Prisoner of War," *Charleston* [SC] *Mercury*, Dec. 2, 1861, 2.

Herbert Withington, of the 1st Michigan thought of Ripley as "a renegade of the worst kind," observing that "I wouldn't give six pence for his soul." A sympathetic Capt. Boag bent his orders as much as possible by furnishing the brick-walled cells of each condemned prisoner with a small table and cot. He brought Willcox a bible and a pack of playing cards. By December, cooler heads had prevailed, and President Lincoln suspended the sentence to hang the Confederate sailors. Boag had the five condemned federal officers returned to the shared upper room of the city jail.[21]

During the evening of December 11, 1861, an uncontrolled fire engulfed Charleston in flames. Under a persistent wind, the inferno spread from Hasell Street near East Bay Street across the entire peninsula, destroying a quarter of the city, some 540 acres of homes and businesses. Treasured landmarks, such as the Circular Church and Institute Hall on Meeting Street, and St. Andrew's Hall and Saint Finbar Cathedral on Broad Street, were reduced to smoking ruins. The Charleston Zouaves at Castle Pinckney were disconsolate as they witnessed the sparks and cinders moving from house to house in their home city. The gale-force winds produced waves that crashed high against the walls of the Castle. Capt. Chichester "made a detail of as many men as the post boat could possibly carry and sent them over to the city to render what assistance they could." A second boat soon followed, and Chichester, fearing a possible Federal assault on the distracted harbor defenses, spent the night pacing the ramparts under the glow of the giant fire.[22]

The Northern prisoners in the city jail had an equally frightful night. One of the better accounts appeared in the *New York Times* on Christmas Eve 1861. Lt. Samuel D. Hurd of the 2nd Regiment of Maine Volunteers had been shot through both legs at Bull Run and was subsequently released from Charleston on December 12. With a wooden leg, he was heading home to Banger, Maine, by way of New York City. Hurd told the newspaper that flames from the Great Charleston Fire reached the roof of the city jail, and the guards had vanished. The Federal officers were on the third floor with only one small window that did not have bars. Col. Michael Corcoran, sick with typhoid fever but determined to seize the opportunity and escape, was the first prisoner to leap from the window,

---

21 "Letter from M.A.P., Nov. 11, 1861, Richmond, Virginia," Special Correspondent of the Detroit Free Press, *Ohio Statesman*, Nov. 22, 1861, 2; Robert Scott, *Forgotten Valor*, 312-316; "Life Among the Rebels: Narration of the Experiences of Captain W. H. Withington," *Jackson* [MI] *Citizen*, Feb. 19, 1862, 3.

22 Robert N. Rosen, *Confederate Charleston: An Illustrated History of the City and the People During the Civil War* (Columbia, 1994), 86; SCHS, Mrs. Jane Chichester, "A Lady's Experience Inside the Forts of Charleston Harbor During the War," 1895, U.D.C. pamphlet, 3.

exclaiming, "Beaufort or the North!" Eventually, all the officers made the leap into the street. In the unfolding conflagration, they stayed together, walking the streets and drinking liquor they had found in some abandoned cellars. Eventually rounded up by the City Guards in the late morning, they were taken to Castle Pinckney and left that day and the following night in the open parade ground. Hurd complained that no effort was made to feed or keep them warm. Ten prisoners took an oath of allegiance promising not to take up arms against the Confederacy. They were transported to Fortress Monroe and exchanged. Corcoran was not among the rounded-up prisoners. In his account, the first dozen to make it down the rope and into the street were almost instantly surrounded by Confederate soldiers "ready to transfix us with their charged bayonets." His small group was taken to a nearby building and held until the "dark volumes of smoke" had passed.

Dr. John McGregor, a surgeon in the 3rd Connecticut Infantry, was among a group of prisoners unable to escape the jail on the night of the fire. McGregor wrote that the fire fully illuminated his prison cell for the first time, and as the room filled with smoke, "we formed ourselves into a circle and commenced marching around, and as we passed by the window we would take a breath and then pass on. The heat was becoming intense; but at last the fire was subdued and we were saved, for what purpose we knew not."[23]

The return of the prisoners to Castle Pinckney proved to be a brief one. Sent back to the Charleston jail, the captured officers observed Christmas with a turkey dinner, eggnog made by Dr. Charles Gray, and an abundant supply of whiskey. Boag was the guest of honor at the celebration. Tuttle's section of eight enlisted men had "the grandest supper I ever helped eat," which consisted of a camp kettle filled with sweet potatoes, salted cabbage, and thickened with hardtack. On January 1, 1862, the enemy prisoners were placed in boxcars and sent to the city jail in Columbia. A few months later, they found themselves in the infamous Libby Prison in Richmond. On May 15, to their utter consternation, they were shipped south to Salisbury, North Carolina. It was not until August 16, 1862, that they were formally exchanged and entered Fortress Monroe "under the old stars."[24]

---

23 "Late From Charleston: Interesting Statements of a Returned Prisoner," *New York Times*, Dec. 24, 1861, 4; Michael Corcoran, *The Captivity of General Corcoran*, 74, 85; Jeremiah McGregor, *Life and Deeds of Dr. John McGregor*, 54.

24 1861-1862 Diary of Dr. Charles Carroll Gray, Wilson Library at the University of North Carolina; James Tuttle, *Reminiscences*, 26; Roger Pickenpaugh, *Captives in Blue: The Civil War Prisons of the Confederacy* (Tuscaloosa, 2013), 17-19; Robert Scott, *Forgotten Valor*, 345.

Cook's Extraordinary 1861 Photographs

In 1861, George Smith Cook ran a successful photography studio on King Street opposite Hasell Street. The 43-year-old Connecticut-born businessman had, before the war, established a daguerreotype studio in New Orleans and had previously worked for America's most famous photographer Mathew Brady in Washington, D.C. The shrewd and talented Cook managed in 1860 to gain permission from the governor of South Carolina to visit the besieged Fort Sumter and photograph its commander, Maj. Anderson, and the officers of the beleaguered outpost. Under the clever title "ANDERSON TAKEN" the photographs were bestsellers. During the war, Cook left his King Street studio on three occasions to visit the field—Fort Sumter following its occupation by Confederate forces in 1861, Castle Pinckney in the fall of 1861, and Fort Sumter in 1863, where he photographed an ironclad shelling Fort Moultrie, the first known combat photograph in existence.[25]

According to Cook's studio logbook, he visited Castle Pinckney on October 11, 1861, probably at the invitation of its commander, Captain Charles Chichester. The original photographic plates are held today at the Valentine Museum in Richmond, Virginia.

---

25 Tom Chaffin, "The Southern Mathew Brady," *New York Times*, Archives, Feb. 11, 2011.

A Prison by the Sea: 1861–1862   107

Photographer George Cook is standing behind two friends in this daguerreotype taken around 1862. *The Collection of George S. Whiteley IV, Atlanta, Georgia*

Taken from the second-floor veranda of the east barracks. From right to left are casemates 6,7,8 and 9, each with their heavy wooden doors. Casemate 7 has a sign above the door reading "Music Hall 444 Broadway." Rudimentary porches have been built in front of casemates 8 and 9. Union officers bunked in the barracks and in Casemate 9 while enlisted men and NCO'S occupied casemates 1 through 8. Most of the Union soldiers are in long sleeve shirts, with only a few in army field jackets.

On the parapet above the prisoners are members of the Charleston Zouave Cadets. They are in a relaxed state, and like their Union prisoners are in various stages of undress. One sentry carrying a musket walks along the parapet wall. A dismounted cannon remains on the parapet. Many cadets sit on the raised semi-circular traverse circles, which allowed the barbette carriage, on which a cannon would be mounted, to pivot right or left.

Sitting to the left of the cannon are two the company's four corporals, each holding their NCO swords. Both are in full uniform with inverted stripes on their left arms and their white (buff) leather cross belts extending from their right shoulder to their left hip. A decorative breast plate is affixed to their belts. To the right of the cannon and sitting on a chair in a gray frock coat and wearing a kepi is Capt. Chichester. Sitting on the traverse in front of the captain, with hands clasped and wearing a distinctive white vest is 2nd Lt. E. John White. *The Valentine Museum*

A Prison by the Sea: 1861–1862

A photograph taken on the parapet above casemate 10, which was used as the garrison's dungeon. Behind the tall brick chimneys is the skyline of Charleston. A number of cadets and Union officers stand on the second-floor veranda. Zouave privates occupied a single large room that ran almost the length of the western side, with separate smaller rooms reserved for NCO'S and officers. Federal officers lived in rooms on the eastern side of the barracks.

The first floor of the barracks held storage rooms, offices, the garrison mess hall, a guard room, and kitchen. "Ripleys Mess" is written above the mess hall entrance. In the yard is a dismounted 24-pounder cannon partly covered in blankets, and next to it looks to be another dismounted 24-pounder. A prisoner wearing a kepi leans against the muzzle of the 24-pounder, a pipe firmly clenched between his teeth. Behind him stand three cadets. The one holding a musket with fixed bayonet is at guard post #1 watching over the sally port passage. The guard room is behind him.

To the right of the three cadets are two black musicians lounging on the porch using a drum as a seat. The younger of the two musicians is holding a drummer's mallet in his right hand. He is wearing corduroy trousers and shirt, while the older man is wearing military-style trousers with a single-colored stripe running down the outside seam, and a white shirt with a necktie. Both men are wearing civilian hats. Behind them is a young boy with his shirt sleeve rolled up to the elbow and wearing an apron.

The Castle's large brick hot shot furnace stands in the center of the parade ground across from the sally port entrance. On the roof of the furnace building is a mattress likely put out to dry. At the rear of the furnace is an extended roof added to provide cover for the prisoners who used the converted hot shot furnace as an oven for cooking their own meals. *The Valentine Museum*

A formation of Cadets presents arms in front of the eastern bastion of the Castle. Directly behind the militia soldiers is a wooden palisade fence originally constructed in 1832. The palisade of vertical beams and planks consisted of three connecting walls that created an enclosed secondary parade ground behind the Castle. A firing step along the walls allowed the defenders to fire down on an approaching enemy. The upper section of the eastern bastion walls shows the remains of a coat of wash paint, while the lower section shows the exposed brick walls. The bottom embrasures have been partially bricked up to leave only a vertical firing loophole for a musket. Note the granite lintel above the loophole which indicates the size of the original embrasure.

On the far left of the photograph are two black musicians, a drummer and fifer. Both are in military uniforms and wearing kepis. The fifer appears to have colored cuff trim and colored epaulettes on his shell jacket. Next to the musicians is Capt. Charles Chichester, wearing a plain nine-button dark blue frock coat with his rank identified by tabs on his shoulders. He has a plain dark blue bummer-style kepi, dark pants with one vertical stripe, a plain black officers' belt with an ornate spoon-style buckle that is different from the white uniform waist belt of the Zouave Cadets.

To the left of Capt. Chichester are the men of the Zouave Cadets and the respective company lieutenants. The cadets are almost uniformly dressed in their summer, or "undress uniform," of grey pants with a vertical stripe down the outside seam, a grey shell jacket with an exterior pocket under the left breast, red cuffs, collar and epaulettes. Most of the privates are wearing their white cross belt over the left shoulder decorated with a circular brass plate adorned with a palmetto tree, with a black cartridge box resting on their right hip. Their white waist belts have a rectangular buckle, with a black cap pouch, a bayonet frog worn on their left hip, and white gloves. Subtle differences exist in some uniforms, which include the addition of a patriotic SC Palmetto Tree on several kepi's. Other caps feature unique badges including stars, a cross and semi-circle. The significance of these badges is unknown. Several of the uniforms appear darker in color, with several jackets having a visible exterior left breast pocket. The rifles are model 1842 Springfield smoothbore muskets with fixed socket bayonet. *The Valentine Museum*

A Prison by the Sea: 1861–1862

Taken outside the Castle's walls between the sally port and the western bastion. The four cadet officers in the forefront are from left to right: C. E. Chichester, R. C. Gilchrist, E. J. White, & B. M. Walpole. Lt. Gilchrist is holding an ornately designed curved scimitar-shaped sword often associated with fraternal organizations. The other three officers carry matching straight bladed military style swords, each decorated with a lion's head pommel fitting. As with the cadets, the officers are not uniformly dressed. Capt. Chichester's uniform frock coat differs slightly from his lieutenants as his coat does not have the ornate cuff trim and whose cuff sports three buttons not two. Chichester is wearing a red sash over his right shoulder designating him as the "officer of the day." It is also interesting to note that Walpole is the only man wearing a holster and that his belt, like Chichester's, is different from his fellow officers. Behind the officers, the cadets are at ease with muskets stacked. They are posing for the picture, with one man even sitting in one of the Castle's second floor embrasures. *The Valentine Museum*

Chapter 8

A Small Artillery Garrison
1862

The capture of Port Royal on the South Carolina coast, some 50 miles south of Charleston, was the first significant Union victory since the capture of Hatteras Island in North Carolina. Two days earlier, a concerned Jefferson Davis had dispatched Gen. Robert E. Lee from Richmond to head the new Department of South Carolina, Georgia, and East Florida.

Lee arrived in Charleston on November 7, 1861, the day Port Royal fell, and immediately began reorganizing the entire coastal defense system. With a large Federal force now entrenched at Hilton Head and in the Beaufort area, Lee's strategy was to concede the immediate coast, except for the forts protecting Charleston, Georgetown, and Savannah, and keep a mobile force at the village of Coosawhatchie on the Charleston and Savannah Railroad. The Virginia general would use the railroad to move and concentrate his outnumbered forces wherever the Federal threat was most manifest. As military historian Kevin Dougherty observed, "The situation required an enemy-based rather than a terrain-based defense." The 54-year-old career army officer grew out his white beard for the first time while stationed in South Carolina. He also acquired the handsome horse "Traveller" to transport him on inspections of Confederate troops and fortifications.[1]

The Charleston District, by order of Gen. Lee, was under the command of Gen. Ripley, the hero of Fort Moultrie. The rotund and bombastic Ohio-born Ripley was sometimes controversial, but he also possessed a sharp mind and was a

---

1 Robert Rosen, *Confederate Charleston*, 83-85; Kevin Dougherty, *Military Leadership Lessons of the Charleston Campaign, 1861-1865* (Jefferson, NC, 2014), 79.

superior artillerist. Ripley's district ran from the South Santee River to the Stono River. Ripley and Lee were concerned that the Federals would force their way up the Stono River, cross James Island on foot, and approach Charleston by way of the "backdoor."

In April 1862, the noted Southern author William Gilmore Simms wrote his friend and "Fire-Eater" politician William Porcher Miles, the chairman of the military affairs committee of the Confederate States of America. Simms advocated that Castle Pinckney be "completely roofed & casemated, her barbette being really her most valuable battery," and proposed that an additional battery be constructed on the island, given its strategic location in the center of the harbor. On November 13, 1861, the *Charleston Mercury* printed his extended essay, "Our Coastal Defenses." Among the many arguments made by Simms was his belief that "in full tide, wind and weather permitting, Forts Moultrie and Sumter would be inadequate to the defense of Charleston, and that the sooner we make Castle Pinckney formidable, in heavy guns, the better." Simms understood the military objections to the casemates at the Castle, noting that "the reverberation will hurt the tympanum, and there is no sufficient outlet, we are told, for the smoke." That said, the writer believed a good supply of rifled cannons sitting atop the barbette of Castle Pinckney could effectively join the fight once a Yankee steamer had pushed her way past Fort Sumter and entered the harbor.[2]

August Conrad of the Charleston Zouaves reported that restoring Castle Pinckney to a military post began almost immediately after the prisoners were removed. The Zouaves were assisted in this task by men from the Emerald Light Infantry, under the overall direction of Charles Scanlan, a military engineer. The Irishmen in the Emerald company were, for the most part, former members of the Meagher Guards and they were generally older men, many of them craftsmen. Their expertise was indispensable in repairing the barracks and restoring the casemates to a fighting condition. Ten 24-pounder smoothbore cannons were procured for the Castle, with five mounted on the parapet and five in the casemates. Zouave Cadet Anthony Riecke wrote, "after considerable trouble and hard work the object was accomplished and the Castle was in a condition to take part in any demonstration."[3]

Capt. Charles Chichester took this opportunity to move his 29-year-old wife, Jane Chamberlain Chichester, to Shute's Folly. Like her husband, "Jennie" was

---

[2] William Gilmore Simms, *The Pen as Sword: Simms and the Beginning of the War—Rediscovered Writings from 1861*, vol. 15 of the *Simms Review*, 22 vol. (Columbia, 2007), 15:24; William Gilmore Simms, *The Letters of William Gilmore Simms*, 6 vol. (Columbia, 1955), 4:357.

[3] August Conrad, *Schatten Und Lichtblicke Aus Dem Amerikanischen Leben Wahrend Des Secessions-Krieges*; SCHS, Anthony Riecke, "Personal Recollections of a Confederate Soldier," 1904, Anthony Riecke papers, 1879-1899.

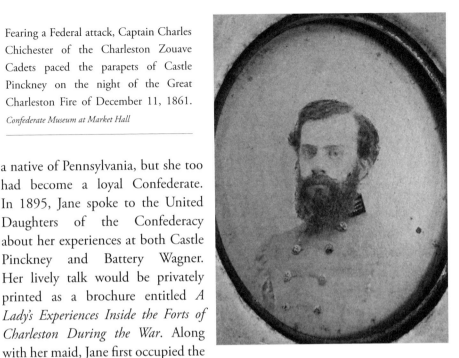

Fearing a Federal attack, Captain Charles Chichester of the Charleston Zouave Cadets paced the parapets of Castle Pinckney on the night of the Great Charleston Fire of December 11, 1861.
Confederate Museum at Market Hall

a native of Pennsylvania, but she too had become a loyal Confederate. In 1895, Jane spoke to the United Daughters of the Confederacy about her experiences at both Castle Pinckney and Battery Wagner. Her lively talk would be privately printed as a brochure entitled *A Lady's Experiences Inside the Forts of Charleston During the War*. Along with her maid, Jane first occupied the small-framed hospital house outside the fort's walls until the officer's quarters had been renovated. She later moved to the Commandant's Quarters on the second floor of the east barracks. The Chichester suite had three rooms—a headquarters office, a dining room for commissioned officers, and a bedroom. Non-commissioned officers and privates occupied the second floor of the western barracks. Mrs. Chichester spoke fluent German, and she established a special connection with the handful of German immigrants in her husband's company.[4]

According to Riecke, who was a son of German immigrants, Castle Pinckney was part of Gen. Lee's tour of Confederate installations in the Charleston Harbor. Jane Chichester, who was not present at the time of his visit, recorded that the Castle was Robert E. Lee's last visit in the harbor that day. After a detailed examination of the military post, he declared the Castle "in better condition in every respect, than any of the other forts, and complimented the garrison on its fine military appearance." Another unexpected visitor to the Castle was Gen. Ripley. Riecke remembered that the Cadets were "sufficiently advanced in the handling of the guns" to fire some heated shots at targets in the harbor. Ripley was impressed, "complementing the officers and men for their skill at the guns." Jennie Chichester

---

4 SCHS, Mrs. Jane Chichester, *A Lady's Experience Inside the Forts of Charleston Harbor During the War*, 1895, U.D.C. pamphlet, 3-8.

Jane Chichester lived at Castle Pinckney with her husband, Captain Charles Chichester, when he commanded the Charleston Zouave Cadets. She wrote an account of her war-time experiences in the 1890s. *Confederate Museum at Market Hall*

recalled that Gen. Ripley and his aide joined the officer's table for a dinner of fresh oysters, "which we had both raw and stewed," with hot biscuits and coffee. Ripley and his aide "lingered around the table in pleasant conversation, seeming loth to tear themselves away."

The arrival of a new gun, an 8-inch Columbiad, brought excitement to the garrison at Castle Pinckney. Capt. Chichester supervised the loading of the gun and sighted it on a buoy in the direction of Fort Johnson. Charles had his young wife pull the lanyard for the first shot of the cannon's life, a round that skipped across the water and splashed water over the buoy. "The men set up a cheer," wrote Jane, "waving their hats, and at once gave my name—Jennie—to the gun." Her name was stenciled in red paint on the cascabel of the Columbiad. Jane Chichester may have been the only lady to pull the lanyard on a loaded artillery piece in the Civil War, even it was only a test fire.[5]

Garrison duty for the Charleston Cadets began each day with "Reveille" played on the drums and fife. The sleepy men fell in to answer roll call. As the sun rose, a cannon was fired, and the fort's flag ran up the wooden pole. Breakfast consisted of fried bacon, cornbread and molasses, and a steaming hot tin cup filled with coffee. Drilling the men in artillery and infantry tactics, both proceeded and followed the early afternoon dinner. Jane Chichester thought the evening dress parade was the highlight of the day. Orders were read at this time, and names for the next day's garrison guards were announced. At sunset, the flag was lowered, and another cannon was fired. The soldiers had liberty in the evenings until "Tattoo" was played, and they were expected to be retired in their bunks at the sound of "Taps." Many of the soldiers gathered in the evening to sing religious hymns.

---

5 Jane Chichester, *A Lady's Experiences Inside the Forts of Charleston During the War*, 3-8; Anthony Riecke, "Personal Recollections of a Confederate Soldier."

A Small Artillery Garrison: 1862

Zouave Cadet Anthony Riecke wrote about his time at Castle Pinckney in his 1879 memoir. This photograph was taken in 1865 at the end of the war. *South Carolina Historical Society*

Sentry duty across the fort was divided into 24-hour shifts. Each day after breakfast, a change of command occurred with a new detail of guards assuming responsibility for the Castle. The officer of the day, who wore a red sash across his shoulders and chest, commanded a detail of men who stood as sentinels at the various assigned posts. After several hours of duty, each man was relieved from his post and allowed to rest in the guard house until it was time to renew their sentry duty. The final task of the soldiers coming off their long 24-hour shift was to take their loaded muskets to the marsh to be cleared with a collective volley. The reward for completing their assignment was a day off to rest and relax. Some men would gain a written leave of absence and hop on the daily supply boat for a day in the city.[6]

While the monotony of garrison duty marked the daily life for the Charleston Cadets at Castle Pinckney, they did have a front row seat to witness Union attempts to close one of the few deepwater ports in the Confederacy. Winfield Scott's "Anaconda Plan" was now beginning to squeeze the South as cotton exports plummeted, which in turn reduced the flow of hard currency into the new Rebel nation. The supply of coffee beans in Charleston had dried up by Thanksgiving 1861. Riecke reported that the men on the parapet "watched the almost nightly illumination of the horizon" as planters on the undefended barrier islands began burning their cotton bales rather than letting them fall into enemy hands. On December 20, sixteen retired New England whaling ships, each filled with heavy stones, were sunk in the main channel of the harbor entrance. Historian Robert

---

6 Jane Chichester, *A Lady's Experiences Inside the Forts of Charleston During the War*, 6.

Rosen notes that "nature had other ideas," and within four months, the spring moon tides had pushed the wrecks out to sea. Robert E. Lee shrewdly interpreted the sinking of the boats as a sign that the Federals were content to bottle up Charleston and would not attempt to capture the port anytime soon.

From the beginning of the war, Charleston was the center for blockade running under the leadership of George Alfred Trenholm, the senior partner of John Fraser & Company. Charleston was one of less than a dozen Southern seaports with rail or water connections into the interior of the new nation. Sailing from England or the Caribbean with war supplies and lucrative luxury goods, these fast, shallow-drafted vessels would maneuver parallel to Sullivan's Island. They would often be successful in eluding the Federal squadron stationed outside the harbor entrance. Riecke recalled the excitement of a "daring intruder" entering the harbor early one morning. As the long roll was hastily beaten, the Cadets at Castle Pinckney raced to their guns and loaded them for battle. When opposite Fort Sumter, the 1,115-ton steamship ran up the Stars and Bars and fired a salute from its gun. "This dispelled the anxiety and caused instead great enthusiasm," wrote Riecke. Soon each fort and shore battery answered the salute given by the large Charleston-based *Isabel*, which was returning with cargo for the Confederacy.[7]

On January 6, 1862, Confederate officials from the Department of Engineers approached the board of directors of Institute Hall (Secession Hall), which had, just weeks before, been destroyed in the Great Charleston. The engineers proposed purchasing the burnt bricks from the building for the "fortification of Fort Sumter and Castle Pinckney," as no other source of bricks was available. Engineer Edwin J. White scribbled at the bottom of the letter that he requested 100,000 bricks at market value. There is no proof whether White's offer was accepted, but in the heady days of early 1862, it is hard to believe that such a request would have been declined.[8]

Near the end of January 1862, the militia companies in South Carolina were under orders to raise the requisite number of men to form a full company for Confederate service or be disbanded so that their members could join one of the newly formed regiments. The Meagher Guards, which had renamed themselves the Emerald Light Infantry, was one of several Charleston-based units that attempted, but ultimately failed to form an all-Irish battalion for Confederate service. At

---

7 Robert Rosen, *Confederate Charleston*, 86; Kevin Dougherty, *Military Leadership Lessons of the Charleston Campaign, 1861-1865*, 21,75; Anthony Reinke, "Personal Recollections of a Confederate Soldier."

8 Letter, Edwin White to President & Directors of South Carolina Institute Hall, Jan. 6, 1862, "Records of Confederate States of America, Army, Corps of Engineers," South Caroliniana Library, University of South Carolina.

Castle Pinckney, Capt. Chichester hoped to transform enough of his company into a coastal artillery unit, but there was a sizeable contingent within the Charleston Zouave Cadets who, according to Riecke, "longed for more achievements in the field." Many of the young men seeking infantry duty would soon join Company H of the Hampton Legion and serve in the Army of Northern Virginia.

In January 1862, Charles Chichester went to Richmond by passenger train seeking authority to form a new artillery regiment. In a letter to Jane, he wrote of his return trip in a railcar filled with Confederate officers, with some being "from Georgia; some from Kentucky and some from Virginia." A minister recognized him as Capt. Chichester of Charleston. Upon arriving in Charleston, he sent his bags to the Mills House and walked to Gilchrist's home on East Bay Street, where "we had so much to talk about all the evening." Both men were optimistic that the ranks of a new regiment would fill up with volunteers. A recruiting station had been set up in a small office "in Mr. Frazer's house, underneath the staircase and piazza, and have a flag flying and everything looks quite busy." Paper signs were posted around the city headed in large type "Capt. C. E. Chichester; Volunteer Company for the War, in Confederate Service."[9]

There was still the matter of Chichester's old Zouave command at the Castle. In his letter to Jane, he noted that on his return to the post, the company "was getting low in numbers," and the officers seemed distant. With half the men wanting to change their branch of service, the Cadets were relieved from duty at the Castle in February and brought back to Charleston, where they were formally dissolved. Chichester and Gilchrist took the remnants of their militia company and formed the Gist Guard South Carolina Artillery Battery, which saw rugged action defending Battery Wagner in 1863.

On the last day of 1860, the South Carolina Secession Convention passed a resolution authorizing the creation of a regular army for the "Palmetto Republic." A month later, the General Assembly decided that the new army should consist of one infantry regiment, one artillery battalion, and one squadron of cavalry. Replacing the Cadets at Castle Pinckney was a company of state "regulars," Company E, 1st Battalion, South Carolina Artillery, under Capt. Joseph Atkinson Yates. Company E was one of the seven companies that comprised the state's artillery battalion. In February 1862, while Company E began its garrison duty at Castle Pinckney, the battalion was enlarged to nine companies, mustered into Confederate service, and redesignated as the 1st South Carolina Artillery Regiment. This decorated artillery

---

9 Letter, Charles Chichester to his wife, Jan. 1862, Archives of the Confederate Museum at Market Hall, Charleston. This was probably the home of the artist Charles Fraser who lived at what is now 55 King Street.

regiment spent almost the entire war in and around Charleston, with its nine companies divided among the various forts and batteries that defended the harbor.[10]

The 33-year-old Yates of Company E would soon make a name for himself by inventing a contraption of cranks and cogwheels that allowed coastal gun crews to traverse their heavy cannons so that their aim could be kept on a moving object. With old-fashioned handspikes no longer needed, gun crews could be reduced in size while accuracy improved. Yate's invention earned a Confederate patent on December 30, 1862, and was installed on guns in the various forts in the Charleston Harbor, including Castle Pinckney.[11]

In March 1862, Lee was called back to Richmond by President Davis. His replacement was Maj. Gen. John C. Pemberton, a Northerner by birth, who relieved the competent Ripley from his command and then quarreled with Gov. Francis Pickens. An uncertain Pemberton wavered on whether Charleston or Savannah could be held, upsetting local officials in both ports. Lee wrote Pemberton from Richmond on May 29 advising him to hold the coastal cities, noting, "If the harbors are taken the cities are to be fought street by street house by house as long as we have a foot of ground to stand upon."

On March 26, 1862, South Carolina formally transferred control of Castle Pinckney to Confederate military authorities. A week later, 1st Lt. Charles Inglesby of Company E tallied up the provisions in the garrison. His entries included 1,600 pounds of salted beef, 300 of rice, 240 of sugar, and 88 of lard. The officers had 245 pounds of ham reserved for themselves. In early June, Company E was replaced at the Castle by Company H. The new company's captain, 22-year-old Henry Saxon Farley, had been a West Point cadet when the war started. A year earlier, Capt. Farley had been instrumental in preparing the harbor fortifications for the bombardment of Fort Sumter. He is generally credited with firing the war's first shot at 4:30 a.m. on April 12, 1861. Farley's mortar shot had arched high across the harbor and exploded almost directly above the three-story Fort Sumter. Company H would garrison the Castle for the next ten months until May 1863. Capt. Farley ordered a new flag for Castle Pinckney, blacksmith and carpenter tools, and wood

---

10 Anthony Riecke, "Personal Recollections of a Confederate Soldier."; Donald Williams, *Shamrocks and Pluff Mud*, 101; Robert S. Seigler, *South Carolina's Military Organizations During the War Between the States*, 4 vol. (Charleston, 2008) 4:24, 135-137, 227-228. The 1st South Carolina Artillery Regiment was assigned to large coastal guns and is often referred to as the 1st South Carolina Heavy Artillery. Other sources have referred to the unit as Rhett's Regiment after its commander, Colonel Alfred Moore Rhett, the son of the arch-secessionist Robert Barnwell Rhett.

11 John Johnson, *The Defense of Charleston Harbor Including Fort Sumter and the Adjacent Islands* (Charleston, 1890), 20; William A. Courtenay, "Fragments of War History Relating to the Coast Defense of South Carolina, 1861-'65," *Southern Historical Society Papers*, 52 vol., ed. by Rev. J. William Jones, 26:67.

planking. At least two new buildings were added to the post during this period as Farley attempted to make Castle Pinckney as self-sufficient as possible.[12]

Halfway between Castle Pinckney and Fort Johnson was the "Middle Ground," a shallow sandbar shoal located about 3/4 of a mile southeast from Shute's Folly. At the beginning of 1862, Confederate engineers began building a wooden fortress in eight feet of water. Using the debris from the December 1861 Charleston fire as a foundation to provide ballast to upright pine logs, they constructed, throughout 1862, a wooden fort that could support a half dozen heavy guns. Once in place, the coastal guns would be 1,100 yards closer to Fort Sumter than were the guns of Castle Pinckney. In short, Fort Ripley would command the center of the harbor and could concentrate its fire on any Federal ship that might make it past Forts Moultrie and Sumter. At Lee's suggestion, the fixed battery was named Fort Ripley, in honor of Gen. Ripley.

On May 12, 1862, the steamship *Planter* collected four heavy guns from one of the seven batteries at Cole's Island for installation at Fort Ripley. In March, Pemberton had made the controversial decision to abandon the fortifications on Cole's Island, a marshy plot of land between Folly and Kiawah Islands, which effectively commanded the Stono Inlet. Pemberton believed the isolated fort was exposed to fire from Yankee gunboats and would likely fall in a concerted amphibious assault. Losing the coastal fort, however, also meant the U.S. forces could seize the opportunity to sail up the Stono River and land soldiers on James Island at the very doorsteps of Charleston.

The side-wheel steamer *Planter* was a familiar sight in Charleston Harbor as it moved ordnance to and from Confederate batteries and was the flagship boat for Gen. Ripley. Its crew consisted of three white officers under Capt. C. J. Relyea and eight enslaved sailors. They were returning to Charleston from Cole's Island but arrived too late in the evening to go directly to Fort Ripley. The steamship tied up at the Southern Wharf. What happened later that night became a historic event in the Civil War. With the white crew members of the *Planter* at home in their Charleston beds, engineer Robert Smalls and his fellow black crew members built up steam at 3:00 a.m. and backed the *Planter* away from her berth. Smalls's audacious plan was to steam past the Confederate forts and surrender his prize to the Union blockading squadron. Pulling up at the North Atlantic Wharf, directly across the Cooper River from the northern tip of Shute's Folly, two men in a rowboat were sent to the Confederate ship *Etowah*. The two black stewards on board that cargo ship were part of the plot, and they had managed to hide several

---

12 OR 14/1-523-524; *Charleston* [SC] *Mercury*, Mar. 26, 1862; CWSR, Lt. Charles Inglesby, 1st SC Artillery, "Receipt for Subsistence Stores," Castle Pinckney, Apr. 2, 1862, M267, roll 61, 57.

family members and friends on the *Etowah*. In all, Smalls's contingent would grow to 16 people. They steamed past Castle Pinckney to Fort Sumter, where Smalls sounded the ship's whistle and donned the white captain's familiar straw hat and jacket. Once by the fort, the *Planter* was surrendered to the Union ship *Onward*. Fort Ripley would never receive the guns from Cole's Island, but more importantly, Smalls was able to inform Adm. Du Pont that Cole's Island had been evacuated. His brazen plan and perfect execution also gave the North a legitimate hero of African descent.

In March 1862, Maj. Gen. David Hunter assumed command of the Army of the South based in Hilton Head. Taking advantage of the intelligence supplied by Smalls, Hunter had Du Pont transport nearly 7,500 Federal troops to the southwestern end of James Island. Here the Union advance bogged down, and the Confederates were given the time needed to reinforce the Tower Battery (later christened Fort Lamar) near the hamlet of Secessionville. In the subsequent battle on June 16, the outnumbered Rebels threw back repeated Federal assaults. Capably led that day by Col.'s Thomas Lamar and Johnson Hagood, the Southerners managed to decisively win the battle of Secessionville and thereby close the "backdoor" to Charleston. Hunter reluctantly withdrew his army back to Hilton Head.[13]

It didn't look like it would be any easier for the United States Navy to capture Charleston. On May 31, 1862, Samuel Francis Du Pont, now a rear admiral, confidentially wrote Gustavus V. Fox, the assistant secretary of the Navy, that this undertaking would be much more complex than the recent capture of New Orleans. The commander of the South Atlantic Blockading Squadron wrote Fox that the defenders of Charleston had been working day and night for 13 months to prepare Charleston's defenses. He warned Fox of a tough fight, "if the enemy do their duty as we expect to do ours." Even if Du Pont's ironclads could somehow punch their way past Forts Sumter and Moultrie into the Middle Ground, there were shore batteries, Fort Johnson, and Castle Pinckney to contend with, "All this mind ye in a 'cul de sac' or bog."[14]

On June 30, 1862, Gen. Pemberton received a telegram from Confederate Secretary of War George W. Randolph informing him that, after two days of hard fighting near Richmond, Lee's Confederate army had driven McClellan's Army of the Potomac across the Chickahominy River. Randolph reported that "the enemy

---

13 Kevin Dougherty, *Military Leadership Lessons of the Charleston Campaign, 1861-1865*, 87-88, 96-100; Report of Lt. F. G. Ravenel, Charleston, May 13, 1862, *Union & Confederate Navies in the War of the Rebellion*, ser. 1, vol. 12, 825-826.

14 Gustavus Fox, *Confidential Correspondence of Gustavus Vasa Fox, Assistant Secretary of the Navy, 1861-1865*, ed. by Robert Means Thompson & Richard Wainwright, 2 vol. (New York, 1918), 1:121-124.

have abandoned their camps, and are in full retreat, closely pursued by our army." On July 1, Pemberton ordered a sunrise salute from each of his fortifications around the Charleston Harbor to celebrate this great Virginia victory. Beginning with a signal gun at Fort Pemberton on James Island, each cannon, some two hundred guns in all, began firing in succession. It took at least ten minutes to complete this military salute. To the many citizens of Charleston who were still in deep slumber, however, this impressive artillery display caught them by surprise with many jumping from their beds convinced that a great pitched battle for control of the Cradle of Secession had finally begun.

Facing pressure from Pickens of South Carolina, President Davis issued Special Order No. 202 on August 29, 1862, replacing the unpopular Pemberton with the popular P. G. T. Beauregard for command of the Department of South Carolina and Georgia. Pemberton was reassigned to Mississippi and would be in command of the citadel of Vicksburg when it surrendered on July 4, 1863.

Before leaving, Pemberton accompanied Beauregard on a tour of the Charleston defenses. The new commander passed by Castle Pinkney but did not stop, "as I am acquainted already with this work, and considered it nearly worthless, capable of exerting but little influence on the defenses of Charleston." He did note that the fortification had nine 24-pounders and one rifled 24-pounder. Gen. Ripley, recovering from a severe neck wound he had received at the battle of Antietam, was ordered back to Charleston in October 1862 to assume his old command of District One. Though contentious with one another, Beauregard and Ripley would be responsible for the successful defense of Charleston Harbor into the spring of 1865.

On September 10, 1862, Lt. Ephriam A. S. Erwin was found guilty of being intoxicated "whilst on duty" as Castle Pinckney's officer of the day on June 13, 1862. The court's sentence was that he be cashiered out of the Southern army. However, a defense was offered, and upon review by the secretary of war and the president of the Confederate States, the sentence was ordered remitted. Lt. Erwin went on to serve with Company H until he was killed on September 7, 1863, at Battery Beauregard in a duel with five monitors. Col. William Butler, who commanded the artillery on Sullivan's Island, considered the 25-year-old Erwin one of his best officers and described him as "more than ordinarily intelligent, brave, and conscientious."[15]

The work to complete Fort Ripley a half-mile in front of Castle Pinckney moved slowly. On October 4, 1862, an engineer report showed that the 17 men

---

15 "The Great Battle," *Charleston* [SC] *Daily Courier*, Jul. 1, 1862, 2; Chet Bennett, *Resolute Rebel*, 138-139; *OR* 14/1-610; *OR* 28/1-716.

working on the 70' by 70' structure were still six weeks away from completing their assignment. The outside and inside walls of the new battery were made from palmetto logs and filled with 10 to 15 ft. of bricks and stone. Beauregard had visited the uncompleted fort in September and wrote that it was "intended for five guns en barbette." The commanding general wanted the stone foundation that supported the structure to rise at least one foot over the tidal high-water mark. Around December, two ten-inch Columbiads were mounted in Fort Ripley. Fuel requisitions show that a detachment of one lieutenant and 25 non-commissioned officers and men from Company H, 1st South Carolina Artillery were stationed at the newly commissioned Fort Ripley in the spring of 1863. An out-of-commission harbor boat was anchored behind the battery, and tents were pitched on the boat's deck for the men to live in. For the remainder of the war, Castle Pinckney and Fort Ripley would be considered the responsibility of one artillery company.[16]

16 *OR* 13/1-447; *OR* 40/1-393; *OR* 14/1-610, 617; "Report of Lt. Commander William Gibson, Memoranda of Information Received from deserters received from Battery Pringle, Apr. 2, 1864," *Union & Confederate Navies in the War of the Rebellion*, ser. 1, 15:393.

Chapter 9

Circles of Fire
1863

Weeping, sad and lonely,

Oh, how bad I feel!

Down in Charleston, South Carolina,

Praying for a good, square meal.[1]

Less than two weeks after returning to his old command in Charleston, Ripley submitted a thorough report on October 25, 1862, describing the state of defenses in the Charleston Harbor. He had an effective force of only 4,169 defenders, which would, he believed, collapse in the face of a combined land and sea attack by Federal forces.

Fortunately for the Southern cause, Ripley did not see a possibility of such an attack in the near future. "Our greatest danger," he thought, "lies in a naval attack by his iron-clad fleet." Wooden warships would not make it past Fort Moultrie and Fort Sumter, but a fleet of Union ironclads might well be able to run past the forts and begin shelling the city. As such, the fortifications around the harbor would need to be strengthened, and more heavy coastal guns and artillerists added. Among Ripley's many requests for guns, manpower, and powder, was the construction of permanent obstructions in the inner harbor, running from Fort Johnson to the Middle Ground and then from the Middle Ground across the Hog Island Channel.

On the day after Christmas 1862, Gen. Ripley sent a detailed circular to the commanders of the various harbor forts and batteries. Here were his instructions

---

1 The chorus of a song written by Sergeant Robert Johnson of the 54th Massachusetts and sung by the prisoners in the Charleston jail.

on how to best fight a battle against a fleet of enemy ironclads. A shotted (pre-loaded) gun, a dipped flag, or a night rocket from the forward positions was to alert all fortifications to the coming naval attack. Gunners would use the marked stationary buoys to estimate distances accurately, and they should discharge their cannons "just as the prows of the vessels come across the line of sight." Wooden ships were to be struck at or near the water-line, while ironclads were to be hit where the turret intersects with the deck. Confederate artillerists would later learn that a well-placed shot might impair the revolution of the turret or disable the machinery for opening and closing the gun ports.[2]

Ripley designated three intersecting "circles of fire" where his artillerists were to concentrate their fire. The first circle would include the guns on Sullivan's Island (Battery Beauregard, Fort Moultrie, and Battery Bee) and those of Fort Sumter. The cannons were to concentrate their fire on the lead vessel, while the mortar batteries in Moultrie and Sumter were to aim at the center of the circle. The barbette guns atop Fort Sumter had the advantage of plunging fire onto the vulnerable rooftops of the turrets, and heated shot would be used to rain down on the ironclads. The second circle would be in the shipping channel in front of Fort Ripley and would have the attention of the heavy guns at Fort Johnson, Fort Ripley, Castle Pinckney, Battery Bee, and the western face of Fort Sumter. Again, the artillerists, using solid shot and heated bolts, were to focus on the lead vessel. The third circle of fire included Battery Glover, the Ramsey Battery, and every gun at Fort Ripley and Castle Pinckney still in the fight. Commanding officers were to make every effort to drive the enemy ships into the lines of obstructions and contact torpedoes. Ripley closed with the admonition that success in battle would come with "careful attention, coolness, and skillful gunnery."[3]

The Union attack came on the early afternoon of April 7, 1863. Adm. Samuel Du Pont's imposing squadron included the twin turret ironclad *Keokuk*, the ironclad frigate *New Ironsides* (Du Pont's flagship), and seven newly constructed *Passaic*-class monitors. Du Pont planned to steam past Morris Island and then duel the guns of Fort Sumter at close range. Each monitor, apart from the *Patapsco*, held two mighty guns in their turret—one a 15-inch and the other an 11-inch smoothbore Dahlgren gun. Fired together, the two Navy cannons sent two round balls—one weighing 400 pounds and the other 200—hurtling toward their enemy. Unfortunately for the Yankees, it was a slow and tedious process as each monitor had to load their guns, turn their turret into firing position, open the shutters,

---

2 OR 14/1-651-655, 732-735; CWSR, W. H. Grimball, M267, group 109, roll 060; Chet Bennett, *Resolute Rebel*, 148.

3 Chet Bennett, *Resolute Rebel*, 148-150; OR 14/1-732-735.

Volatile and obstinate, but also brilliant, Northern-born Roswell Ripley commanded the defenses of Charleston Harbor for much of the war. A photograph attributed to the Mathew Brady Studio.
Library of Congress

fire the guns, close the shutters, turn the turret away from the enemy, and then blow out the smoke from the enclosed firing chamber.

The Confederates, in contrast, had a much faster rate of fire, and their artillerists proved to be unusually accurate. In the two-hour lopsided fight, which never got past Ripley's first circle of fire, the ironclads managed 154 shots to the 2,209 shots fired from 100 well-placed Confederate guns and mortars. The lead monitor, the *Weehawken*, was hit repeatedly and veered into a line of obstructions—a tangled mass of ropes, logs, and floating kegs of powder—that ran from Fort Sumter to Sullivan's Island. Three of Du Pont's ships were forced to abandon the fight and another five monitors were heavily damaged by 400 or so direct hits. The twin turret *Keokuk* took on so much water that she sank off Morris Island the next day.[4]

Three miles away at Castle Pinckney, the 70 Confederate artillery soldiers stood by their guns, ready to join the fight, but the opportunity never presented itself. Thomas Lowndes recalled in his 1890 memoirs that in one of the many subsequent duels between the ironclads and the Charleston forts, the concussion effects from the large Dahlgren guns contained inside the ironclad's turrets not only rattled windows in Charleston but split the exterior reinforcing wall of the Castle's brick magazine from top to bottom and separated it from the main wall of the Castle.

Charleston was proving to be a tough nut to crack for the Union invaders. Adm. Du Pont was replaced by Adm. John Dahlgren and the army commander,

---

4 Stephen Wise, *Gate of Hell: Campaign for Charleston Harbor, 1863* (Columbia, 1994), 26-31; Kevin Dougherty, *Military Leadership Lessons of the Charleston Campaign, 1861-1865*, 119-120.

Gen. David Hunter, was replaced by Maj. Gen. Quincy Gillmore. Federal strategy soon focused on moving Gillmore's army northward along Folly Island, crossing the Lighthouse Inlet, and capturing Morris Island. This barrier island shielded Fort Sumter from the Atlantic Ocean. If they proved capable of capturing the two Confederate forts on the island, the Federal army could then place heavy artillery behind reinforced sand dunes and decimate Fort Sumter, just as Gillmore had done to Fort Pulaski outside of Savannah in 1861. The U.S. Navy, in turn, would then steam past the destroyed fort and enter Charleston Harbor. Instituting this grand plan throughout 1863 would be a bloody and difficult undertaking.[5]

In May 1863, Capt. Farley's Company H was sent to Fort Sumter and replaced at Castle Pinckney by Company G under Capt. William Henry Peronneau. On May 7, 1st Lt. James Reid Pringle ordered white, blue, and red bunting to sew a new garrison flag along the lines of the newly adopted Confederate 2nd National Flag. The 75 men in Company G would garrison Castle Pinckney and Fort Ripley through the summer and fall of 1863. It was considered light duty to serve under Peronneau at Castle Pinckney, certainly compared to the men in the five artillery companies posted at Fort Sumter under Col. Alfred Rhett. The 40-year-old Peronneau came from a distinguished French Huguenot family in Charleston, but his curse was the progressive worsening of his eyesight. He would ultimately be forced to resign his commission in November 1864. A handful of men from Company G did find themselves sick enough to be sent to the Louisiana Wayside Hospital at 564 King Street opposite Cannon Street in Charleston.[6]

The presence of Yankee prisoners of war from the celebrated 54th Massachusetts Volunteer Infantry marked Capt. Peronneau's time at the Castle. As part of a diversion to the planned amphibious assault aimed at the southern tip of Morris Island, a large Federal division under Gen. Alfred Terry landed on the Stono River side of James Island. Part of his force consisted of the 54th, a regiment of free Northern blacks under Col. Robert Gould Shaw. On July 16, 1863, the 54th fought a fierce hand-to-hand struggle with Gen. Alfred Colquitt's Confederates for control of Sol Legare Island, a piece of marshland attached to the southwestern end of James Island. Shaw's men took the brunt of the Confederate attack and would later receive praise for their stubborn stand at this battle of Grimball's Landing, but they had also taken 43 casualties, with 14 of their number becoming new

---

5 Kevin Dougherty, *Military Leadership Lessons of the Charleston Campaign, 1861-1865*, 131-132; Thomas Lowndes, *Reminiscences of Thomas Pinckney Lowndes*, 4:11.

6 Robert Seigler, *South Carolina's Military Organizations During the War Between the States*, 4:141; Stephen Wise, *Gate of Hell*, 26-31, 227; OR 6/2-131; CWSR, Charles Inglesby, 1st SC Artillery, "Request for Leave of Absence, Castle Pinckney," Aug. 8, 1863, M267, roll 61, 97; CWSR, James R. Pringle, 1st SC Artillery, M267, roll 63, 22.

A portrait of General P. G. T. Beauregard with Fort Sumter and the city of Charleston in the background. Beauregard's successful defense of Charleston and its harbor was one of the few Confederate successes in 1863. *City of Charleston and the Confederate Museum at Market Hall*

prisoners of war. Johnson Hagood, the Confederate commander of James Island, had the prisoners stripped of their uniforms and then tied together in a gang, as would be done for a group of runaway slaves. Capturing free black enemy soldiers was a new dimension to the Civil War, and Beauregard immediately telegraphed Richmond for instructions on the proper disposition of these POWs. Placing them in Castle Pinckney until this matter could be sorted out seemed appropriate.[7]

According to the *Charleston Tri-Weekly Courier*, the black soldiers of the 54th, who were captured on James Island, believed that they would most certainly be hung if captured. They had fought as well as they had under the belief that it was better to "die of bullet than rope." On the evening of July 19, Capt. Peronneau sent a telegram from Castle Pinckney to the Charleston adjutant-general reporting that his "negro prisoners" were willing to submit to state law and join a work crew improving Battery Bee on Sullivan's Island. This inquiry was not followed up on, and six days later, Peronneau requested that Capt. William Nance, the A.A.G. of the 1st Military District, remove "the twenty-five negro prisoners now confined at this post." Ultimately, these prisoners would remain at Castle Pinckney for the next month.[8]

---

7 Stephen Wise, *Gate of Hell*, 87-90; "Charleston: Favorable Progress of our Operations," *New Haven* [CT] *Palladium*, Aug. 27, 1863, 1; Luis F. Emilio, *History of the Fifty-Fourth Regiment of Massachusetts Volunteer Infantry*, 1863-1865 (Boston, 1894), 397; Lorien Foote, "A Confederate Concession," *The Civil War Monitor* (Winter 2021), vol. 11, 4:41.

8 "Our War Correspondence," *Charleston Tri-Weekly Courier*, Jul. 18, 1863, 2; Signal from Capt. Peronneau, Military Departments—Telegraphic Dispatches, Charleston, SC, 1863, NARA, RG 109, chap. 2, vol. 189, 97; Thomas J. Ward, "The Plight of the Black P.O.W.," *New York Times*, Opinionator, Aug. 27, 2013; "The Retaliatory Act, Confederate Congress, May 1, 1863," House

Peronneau's July 19 telegram also requested the immediate dispatch of Surgeon Frost, as "I absolutely need his services." The 68-year-old Henry Rutledge Frost was a Professor of Materia Medica (remedial substances used in medicine) at the Medical College of South Carolina. Frost was given the Confederate rank of assistant surgeon and served as the medical officer at the Castle and on Sullivan's Island for much of the war.[9]

Gen. Ripley ordered William Henry Trescot from his staff to Castle Pinckney to inspect and interview the 14 new prisoners (see Appendix 17) from the 54th Massachusetts. The 41-year-old Trescot, who was small in stature and sported a prominent mustache, was a Harvard-trained lawyer who had been the assistant secretary of state during the Secession Crisis and had been an important advisor to President Buchanan. Col. Trescot found a receptive prisoner in 38-year-old Alvis Jeffries. Born free in North Carolina, Jeffries was living in Cleveland, Ohio when he was compelled to enlist as a volunteer "or be drafted by the leading men of the neighborhood." He had been a member of the 54th since May 1863 but had not received his $100 bounty nor his $13 a month pay. Sgt. Jeffries provided Trescot with intelligence on the disposition of the ten Federal regiments (eight were white and two were black) occupying the southern side of James Island and the status of a bridge being constructed between James Island and Morris Island. Trescot would hear similar laments of forced enlistment, mistreatment, and lack of pay from the other members of the 54th. The Confederate interviewer also had a particular interest in determining the status of each black prisoner, whether they had been free or an escaped slave at the time of their enlistment, with Jeffries believing "about six are freeman and that he has heard the others say that they were originally slaves."[10]

On the same day that Trescot was at Castle Pinckney interviewing the prisoners, the courage of the 54th Massachusetts was more famously displayed on Morris Island. On the evening of July 18, some two weeks after impressive Union victories at Gettysburg and Vicksburg, the tired and hungry 54th was, at the request of their commander, Shaw, placed at the front of a division-level frontal assault on Battery Wagner. Described by historian Stephen Wise as "a formidable obstacle," Battery Wagner, which was called Fort Wagner by U.S. forces, spanned

---

Divided: The Civil War Research Engine at Dickinson College; Luis Emilio, *History of the Fifty-Fourth Regiment of Massachusetts Volunteer Infantry, 1863-1865*, 397; OR 6/2-132.

9 Presidential Pardon application of Henry Frost, Confederate Applications for Presidential Pardons, 1865-1867, NARA, RG 94, M1003. Frost applied for a presidential pardon from President Andrew Johnson shortly before his death in 1866.

10 Bonham file, *Letters Received by the Confederate Adjutant and Inspector General*, 1861-1865, M474, Catalog ID: 652418.

the middle of Morris Island, about 250 yards from the waves breaking on the eastern beach to an impassable swamp to the west. Behind a water-filled moat were sloping earthen walls 30 feet above the beach. Confederate artillery and infantry standing in the parapets and looking southward could sweep the sandy approaches of any advancing intruders. To the soldier's left was a sea wall that extended northward with sheltered guns to duel approaching warships. Gillmore and Dahlgren had pounded Wagner all day with a massive land and sea cannonade to the point where it seemed that few of the defenders could muster any form of resistance. Fortunately for the Southerners, their 1,700 soldiers had, for the most part, withstood this onslaught sheltered in an underground bombproof and were prepared, when the time came, to stand behind razor-sharp palmetto stakes and ably defend their fort.[11]

As vividly portrayed in the 1989 movie "Glory," the men of the 54th Massachusetts followed by the 6th and 7th Connecticut Infantry Regiments were the first to charge into a hail of cannister and minie balls. The infantry assault commenced at dusk and proved an outright disaster for the Federals, with the 5,000-man division of Gen. George C. Strong sustaining 1,515 casualties. Col. Shaw, a Harvard graduate, fell as he crested the parapet with a handful of survivors. In all, the 54th took 281 casualties, or roughly 42% of their men who had started forward into the vortex of Rebel guns. Fourteen of their 22 officers become casualties. 116 enlisted men were listed on the regiment's November 7th muster roll as missing, with at least 73 black soldiers subsequently turning up as prisoners of war. The morning after the nighttime attack revealed a scene of carnage in front of the fort. "I have never seen so many dead in the same space." wrote William Booth Taliaferro, the fort's commanding general. The Federals who had surrendered during the assault were marched up the island to Battery Gregg and taken by boat to Charleston.[12]

Accounts vary as to what happened next to these blue-clad prisoners. By Confederate numbers, 237 of the captured Yankees were brought to the provost Marshal in downtown Charleston the day after the battle. 73 of the prisoners were members of the 54th Massachusetts. The uninjured white prisoners were taken to a large warehouse or the Charleston jail, while the "negro" prisoners were escorted to Castle Pinckney. Col. Trescot would return to the Castle on the 20th and

---

11 Brian C. Pohanka, "Fort Wagner and the 54th Massachusetts Volunteer Infantry," *American Civil War Magazine* (Sep. 1991), 4:15-17.

12 Stephen Wise, *Gate of Hell*, 116-117; "List of Names of the Enlisted men of the 54th Massachusetts Infantry Regiment Missing after the Assault on Fort Wagner, South Carolina, July 16-18, 1863," Records of the Adjutant General's Office, 1780's-1917, NARA; Lorien Foote, "A Confederate Concession," 11:41.

personally interview six of these soldiers. The wounded men from the unsuccessful assault on Battery Wagner, of which there were many, were taken to a makeshift hospital in a former Mart on Queen Street. The white and black wounded were separated but given the same medical attention. While their care was no worse than that provided to the Southern wounded, the Yankees were in a blockaded city "sadly deficient" in medicine. The *Charleston Courier* reported on July 23 that "The operations were performed in the rear of the hospital, where half a dozen or more tables were constantly occupied throughout the day with the mutilated subjects." Amputations were the preferred procedure for almost any type of wound to a limb. 51 of the grievously wounded would perish within the week. Exchanged Yankee prisoners complained about the competency of Confederate surgeons, but an August 7 inspector-general's report described a "well managed" hospital under Surgeon John Dawson. The report noted that there were 39 wounded prisoners still in the hospital, of whom 26 were members of the 54th Massachusetts.

An exchange of wounded prisoners was quickly worked out. Sailing from Hilton Head on July 23 was the hospital steamer *Cosmopolitan* with a white flag on her fore and a yellow flag on her main. Under the command of the Provost Marshall James Hall and Dr. John Craven, the chief medical officer, the steamship brought 38 wounded Rebels and four of their surgeons. After crossing the bar and approaching Battery Wagner, she pulled up next to the anchored Confederate blockade runner *Alice*, and a plank was thrown across. The *Alice* held 105 Union prisoners, soon to be paroled, under the overall command of Col. Edward Clifford Anderson of the Confederate artillery. A contingent of Charleston firemen began to transfer the wounded.[13]

Bishop Patrick Lynch had accompanied the wounded Yankees and was "unremitting in his attention to them." According to the reporter from Horace Greeley's *New York Tribune*, the Catholic Bishop of South Carolina "repeatedly expressed the hope that this unnatural and cruel war would soon be over, and that the whole country might again be united and prosperous." Col. Hall of the Department of the South soon noticed that there were no black wounded among the paroled soldiers. He confronted Anderson only to be told that the fate of the black prisoners was to be determined "after consideration."[146]

13 "Further From Charleston: The Killed and Wounded in the Assault on Fort Wagner," *Age* [PA], Aug. 1, 1863, 2; Luis Emilio, *History of the Fifty-Fourth Regiment of Massachusetts Volunteer Infantry, 1863-1865*, 401; OR 6/2-187-188; "From South Carolina," *Lowell* [CT] *Daily Citizen and News*, Aug. 1, 1863, 2.

14 "Exchange of Wounded Prisoners from Morris Island Fights," *The Port Royal* [SC] *New South*, Aug. 1, 1863, 1.

What was to be considered? It turned out to be an immensely significant issue for both sides. In his two-year campaign to allow men of African American descent to wear the blue national uniform with its brass eagle buttons, Frederick Douglas knew that honorable military service would lead directly to American citizenship. President Jefferson Davis also understood that treating captured black soldiers the same as white prisoners legitimized both races as soldiers and men. To do so would be, in essence, to accept the tenets of the Emancipation Proclamation. White Confederate soldiers also questioned whether "being exchanged for a negro" diminished their status as free white men. Months earlier, on May 1, 1863, the Congress of the Confederate States had resolved that those white commissioned officers, who had "commanded negroes or mulattos in arms" were, if captured, "to be put to death or otherwise punished." Black enlisted men captured in war were to be turned over to the state authorities in the state they were captured in.

There was enough concern in the North over the fate of the white officers and black enlisted men of the 54th Massachusetts that Lincoln issued a proclamation on July 30, 1863, declaring that "for every soldier of the United States killed in violation of the laws of war, a Rebel soldier shall be executed, and for every one enslaved by the enemy or sold into slavery, a Rebel soldier shall be placed at hard labor on the public works." Five days later, Secretary of War Edwin Stanton assured Massachusetts Senator Charles Sumner that every effort was being made to secure the release of the "gallant officers and soldiers, black and white, who fell into the hands of the enemy at Fort Wagner." Lincoln's retaliation proclamation seemed to have its desired salutary effect on the South as Davis's government never did move to specifically punish black Union soldiers.

Beauregard received instructions in Charleston on July 22 to turn over his black prisoners to South Carolina authorities. A week later, South Carolina Gov. Milledge Bonham requested that the prisoners be retained in military custody until the state was ready to accept responsibility. The *Charleston Mercury* reported on August 19 that the black prisoners were finally removed from the Castle and taken to the Charleston jail, where they were placed in the custody of the state. Unlike the Bull Run prisoners of 1861, little has been found regarding the 1863 prison conditions and routines for the members of the 54th while they were at Castle Pinckney. Like the experience of the Bull Run men, however, their physical well-being would deteriorate markedly once they were permanently imprisoned in the city jail.[15]

---

15 Abraham Lincoln, *The Collected Works of Abraham Lincoln*, 9 vol., ed. Roy P. Basler (New Brunswick, 1953–55), 6:357; Luis Emilio, *History of the Fifty-Fourth Regiment of Massachusetts*

Gov. Bonham did move quicker on the legal front. On August 10, he ordered the five-person provost-marshal's court for the Charleston district to be convened for the trial of two soldiers from the 54th, who had once been slaves—Sgt. Walter Jeffries of Company H and Corpl. Charles Hardy of Company B. Bonham appointed Attorney General J. W. Hayne to represent the state, while Charleston lawyers Nelson Mitchell and Edward McCrady ably defended the prisoners. Nelson, in particular, was well prepared and eloquent in his argument that free negroes from Northern states should be treated as United States soldiers. After hearing whispers from Beauregard's headquarters that retaliation against Southern troops would follow, the tribunal heard the evidence and then ruled that they had no jurisdiction in the case. Left with few options, Bonham suspended further action related to the negro prisoners until Richmond clarified its position. For the next year, the three dozen or so black prisoners from the 54th Massachusetts lived on the third floor of the Charleston jail in atrocious conditions before they were taken to the Florence stockade and then released in the spring of 1865 at a railroad crossing on the Northeast Cape Fear River. Some survivors rejoined the regiment, while others were discharged from parole camps or hospitals.[16]

This internment of the captured Federal prisoners took place against a backdrop of violent war across the Charleston Harbor. On July 27, 1863, an editorial in the *New York Herald* expounded, "It now appears that upon the success or failure of our efforts to take Fort Wagner the fate of Charleston hangs." After the complete failure of the July 18 frontal assault on Battery Wagner, Gen. Gillmore resorted to a traditional siege operation, pounding the sand fort with heavy artillery that was progressively moved closer to the Confederate citadel. Even heavier Union ordnance was landed on Morris Island, and beginning on August 17, an intensive seven-day shelling of Fort Sumter commenced. By the 24th, Gillmore could report to Washington that Sumter had been reduced to "a shapeless and harmless mass of ruin." Beauregard responded by removing his coastal guns and artillerymen from the fort and trusting in the Charleston Battalion, an infantry unit, to defend the fort from amphibious assault. The passageway through the harbor obstructions was moved next to Fort Moultrie, where it could be better defended.

On August 29, on orders from Lincoln, Gillmore started shelling the city of Charleston. Beauregard called this shelling of a civilian city, from a distance of four and a half miles, "an act of inexcusable barbarity." After 58 days of unrelenting

---

Volunteer Infantry, 1863-1865, 397, 404-405; "The Negro Prisoners," *Charleston* [SC] *Mercury*, Aug. 20, 1863, 2.

16 Luis Emilio, *History of the Fifty-Fourth Regiment of Massachusetts Volunteer Infantry, 1863-1865*, 96-98; Lorien Foote, "A Confederate Concession," 11:45.

bombardment, Battery Wagner's tenacious defenders recognized their position was untenable. On September 7, the Rebels fell back to Battery Gregg and then, by boat, to fortifications in the inner harbor. The U.S. forces now had complete control of Morris Island, the barrier island closest to Fort Sumter.[17]

If there was an oasis in this storm of chaos, it might have been on Shute's Folly and the relatively quiet garrison at Castle Pinckney. On August 19, the same day that the black prisoners were removed from the Castle, a detachment of 15 artillerymen from Company E, under the command of a former Harvard legal student, 1st Lt. John Julius Pringle Alston, was transferred from Battery Wagner to the Castle. Having distinguished themselves two days earlier in an artillery duel with Union ironclads, the detachment had been sent to Pinckney to gain some much-needed rest. The reports state that Alston "fought his gun" through two hours of unrelenting action even though the protective parapet in front of his position had been destroyed.[18]

Lt. William Heyward Grimball had been a young Charleston lawyer at the start of the Civil War. Upon the recommendation of the noted "Fire-Eater" and politician W. Porcher Miles, he had been given an officer's commission in the 1st South Carolina Artillery. By September 1863, he was a 1st lieutenant in Company E, commanding the two-gun battery at Fort Ripley. In a letter home to his mother in Spartanburg, the 25-year-old Grimball marveled at the Federals' progress on Morris Island. "Everything is still and looks as if we are enjoying peace, but about two miles from us, you see our old Battery at Cumming's Point being rapidly transformed into a powerful work with heavy guns already mounted there, and on the upper end of Morris Island, an immense number of tents covering the sandhills." Grimball knew that his reprieve and that of his garrison would not last long, and he was realistic about the prospects for the Confederate nation. "Things look very blue for us right now, but a just God will not allow us to be subdued and trampled upon by our enemies, we who ask but to govern ourselves."[19]

---

17 "Important From Charleston: The Duty of Government," *New York Herald*, Jul. 27, 1863, 4; Robert Rosen, *Confederate Charleston*, 114-119; Stephen Wise, *Gate of Hell*, 161; *OR* 28/2-471, 598, 612; *OR* 28/1-3.

18 "Important From Charleston: The Duty of Government," *New York Herald*, Jul. 27, 1863, 4; Robert Rosen, *Confederate Charleston*, 114-119; Stephen Wise, *Gate of Hell*, 161; *OR* 28/2-471, 598, 612; *OR* 28/1-3.

19 Letter home from Lt. W. H. Grimball, Fort Ripley, Sep. 14, 1863, Schuyler Rumsey Philatelic Auctions.

Chapter 10

The Middle Ground
1863–1864

On September 5, 1863, the *New York Herald* published a letter from the wordsmith Alfred O. Alcock, who had, as a member of the New York Firemen Zouaves, been a prisoner at Castle Pinckney after the battle of First Bull Run. With the recent demolition of Fort Sumter by Federal artillery, Alcock, now a newspaperman in New York, thought that the Castle on Shute's Folly would soon "come in for its share" of Northern attention.

While the old fort was capable of mounting 24 guns—ten in the casemates and 14 on the barbettes—it would be no match for the pounding it would receive from a "two hundred pounder rifle bolt, laden with liquid fire, simulating in velocity, precision, and destructiveness the lightening of heaven." In short, now that the Yankees had planted batteries of 200-pounder Parrott guns on Morris Island that were in range of a besieged Charleston, "it matters but very little how many intermediate batteries of comparatively light guns may be found in the way of the besiegers."

On August 19, orders went out to Confederate Chief Engineer David Harris directing him to put Castle Pinckney in a condition to be "an effective part of the interior lines." All sandbags and material intended for Fort Sumter were redirected to the Castle to construct traverses on the ramparts to protect the gunners from enfilade fire. Firewood and sandbag requisitions show that Engineer William Echols directed large gangs of enslaved laborers, sometimes as many as 200 men, to refurbish the post. Robert Hains of Company G was placed on detached service as an overseer at the Castle. Company G, 1st South Carolina Artillery under Capt.

Peronneau continued to garrison the post, with Peronneau reporting that he had two subalterns and 70 non-commissioned soldiers and musicians.[1]

In late August, Confederate engineers successfully laid two rows of torpedoes (contact mines) in the channel between Castle Pinckney and Fort Ripley. On September 10, 1863, the small garrison at Fort Ripley under Charles Inglesby received 40 haversacks, 40 knapsacks, 45 canteens, 22 Austrian rifles, and other miscellaneous military supplies. These were all clear indications that the Confederate high command believed that the inner harbor defenses of Charleston, especially those near the Middle Ground, were about to be tested. By the middle of September, the correspondent of the *New York Herald* attached to Gen. Gillmore's command reported that the Confederates had been furiously reinforcing their harbor defenses for the last two weeks. "Around Castle Pinckney," he wrote, "they have built up huge barricades of sand extending to the very parapet and have thus rendered that work capable of a strong defense." On September 20, Federal guns on Morris Island opened fire on the Castle for the first time. Castle Pinckney was no longer a secondary fortification in the defense of Charleston.[2]

The fall of 1863 was marked by large-caliber artillery exchanges between Confederate batteries on James Island and Sullivan's Island and the Union positions on Morris Island. The city itself was continually pummeled with incendiary shells, but Fort Sumter remained the central target for Yankee gunners. Frederic Denison of the 3rd Rhode Island Artillery wrote that "Sumter now looked more like a rude bluff or volcanic pile than like a fortification." More than 100 black and white Southerners were killed or wounded while stationed in the ruined brick fort from October through December. During these fall months, both defenders and aggressors were losing the capability to perform anything beyond basic operations around Charleston as orders arrived, calling units away to other theaters of war. Gen. Gillmore was convinced that even if his diminished Union forces managed to capture Fort Sumter outright, that demolished position could not be held as Confederate artillery would bear down on the post from three different directions.[3]

In the shadows of this slow-moving military stalemate was the desperate attempt by Confederate authorities to break the ever-tightening Union naval blockade of Charleston. As part of this effort, the waters around Castle Pinckney were used

---

1 A. O. Alcock, "The Harbor Defenses of Charleston," *New York Herald*, Sep. 5, 1863, 3; *OR* 28/2-295; CWSR, W.H. Echols, "Sandbag requisition," M258, roll 105, 37-38.

2 CWSR, Charles Inglesby, 1st SC Artillery, M267, roll 61, 51; "Castle Pinckney," *New York Herald*, Sep. 11, 1863, 10.

3 *OR* 28/2-604-605; Frederic Denison, *"Shot and Shell:" The Third Rhode Island Heavy Artillery Regiment in the Rebellion, 1861-1865* (Providence, 1879), 199.

as testing grounds for experimental military weapons. In 1862, a spring-powered wooden semi-submersible rocket/torpedo was tested at the Castle. Designed and built by Dr. Francis Carroll of Bamberg, South Carolina, the torpedo weapon was made from a hollowed-out single piece of oak, seven or eight feet long with an inside aperture six inches in diameter. With the assistance of his slave Louis Carroll, Dr. Carroll had previously used the weapon to target and destroy a "tree stump" on the waters of Clear Pond, located on his large plantation six miles south of Bamberg. Following the successful pond testing, Confederate authorities had the Carroll men demonstrate the weapon at Castle Pinckney, where it successfully destroyed its intended target. Yet, despite this achievement, the relatively slow speed with which the torpedo moved across the surface of the water made it vulnerable to small-arms fire in the eyes of the observers. According to a post-war account by Louis Carroll, Dr. Carroll redesigned the weapon to move while fully submerged. In a second test at Castle Pinckney, however, the torpedo reportedly "dived too much" and did not travel at a uniform depth.

In 1863, Capt. Francis D. Lee, a prominent former architect on Beauregard's staff, designed a small torpedo boat named the *Torch*. Complete with an 8-ft. spar attached to the bow of the small craft, Lee's design was a forerunner of what would be employed by the Confederate submarine *H. L. Hunley*. Lee was also instrumental in the *David*-class submarine program. Beauregard's senior aide-de-camp, Col. Alexander Robert Chisholm, would recall in 1907 a day in March 1863 when he accompanied Capt. Lee on a test of the torpedo, which was "cylindrical, made of thin cooper, charged with powder, and was capped with several sensitive fuses on its conical end." Their target was a decked flatboat anchored by Castle Pinckney. The *Torch* struck the flatboat about midship, and the explosion swamped the experimenters under a large wave of water. The sinking of the flatboat was considered a success, and Beauregard soon ordered some large torpedoes along Lee's design.[4]

In the summer of 1863, a smattering of reports indicates that the Southerners employed a hot air balloon to make reconnaissance observations of Federal troop movements on Morris Island and the disposition of the Union blockading fleet outside the harbor entrance. The naval correspondent for the *Boston Herald* reported on July 21 that the Rebels sent up a balloon from Castle Pinckney that was "secured by a strong cord and ascended about three hundred yards." According to the reporter, two individuals were clearly visible in the balloon. Maj. Thomas

---

4 "Aided in Building Torpedo of 60s," *Charleston* [SC] *News & Courier*," Oct. 30, 1933, 3; "The Blowing Up of the Maine: Why an Ex-Confederate Believes the Explosions Were Internal," *New York Sun*, Dec. 29, 1907, 6.

Benton Brooks of New York also spotted the reconnaissance balloon that day but he believed it was flown from Fort Johnson. This fort on James Island seems a more practicable spot to make an ascension given that Johnson was closer to the Federal positions and the large amount of equipment and gas canisters necessary to fly the balloon could be transported there in wagons. An invoice from the Charleston Gas Light Company showed that the July 21 flight consumed 21,000 cubic feet of gas at a cost of $168.[5]

Both militaries had small aeronautic departments in the Civil War. Capt. Charles C. Cevor, an amateur balloonist from Savannah, directed the balloon in Charleston. In April 1862, Cevor was ordered to build a balloon and train Pvt. Adolphus E. Morse as his trustworthy assistant, along with six ground volunteers, all soldiers from Savannah's famed Chatham Artillery. Ordered to Virginia, their multi-colored "Gazelle" balloon did admirable service in the Seven Days Battle, with Col. Edward Porter Alexander serving as the signal officer high above the battlefield. Unfortunately for Cevor and his team, their balloon and equipment were captured while being transported on a tugboat along the James River. Forced to start again, they built a second balloon after buying every yard of silk they could find in Richmond, Savannah, and Charleston. By July 1863, they were in Charleston, making military observation ascents. Beauregard seemed not to have been impressed by the quality of their reconnaissance as his chief-of-staff Thomas Jordan was informing Chief Engineer D. B. Harris on the 23rd, "Whenever another balloon reconnaissance is made, the commanding general desires that some officer shall make the ascension who also knows the country to be reconnoitered." By November 1863, the volunteers had been returned to their artillery unit, and the balloonist department disbanded.[6]

Castle Pinckney was the backdrop for the second sinking of the Confederate submarine *H. L. Hunley*, which happened during trial runs on the overcast morning of October 15, 1863. In front of a small group of spectators assembled on Adger's Wharf, across East Bay Street from Tradd Street, the iron 40-foot submarine pulled away from the pier and headed into the harbor. For the past few weeks, the craft had been practicing approaching and submerging under a Union blockader. Behind the *H. L. Hunley* was a 100-foot tow line with a floating mine at the end of the rope. As the *Hunley* surfaced on the other side of the enemy ship, the mine would strike the side of the anchored ship and detonate the explosive. After the experimental submarine sank on August 29 in an accident near the dock at Fort

---

5 "The Movement on Charleston," *Boston* [MA] *Herald*, Jul. 29, 1863, 2; *OR* 28/2-246.

6 C. Robert Keathley, "The Last Confederate Airman was a Texan," *Corsicana* [TX] *Daily Sun*, May 30, 2010, website; *OR* 28/2-221.

Johnson, a new volunteer crew had been assembled from men who had worked with the craft in Mobile Bay. This second set of trials had gone well with 26-year-old Lt. George E. Dixon at the controls in the forward conning tower. For this day's dress rehearsal, however, Dixon was away from Charleston, and the inventor Horace Hunley himself would steer the craft. Unfortunately, Hunley had virtually no experience inside the secret weapon and probably none at its controls.

Ten minutes after leaving Adger's Wharf and gliding along the surface of the Cooper River, the black submarine slipped under the surface. The mock target was the CSS *Indian Chief*, a three-masted schooner anchored behind Castle Pinckney, near the northern tip of Shute's Folly. Many observers, whether standing on Adger's Wharf, the parapets of Castle Pinckney, or the deck of the *Indian Chief*, had seen these exercises where the long craft disappeared under the waves, only this time, something was different. The water was bubbling from ascending air pockets where the *Hunley* had submerged, and after an agonizing wait, it was evident that the craft was lost. Weeks later, when the submarine and its dead crew were salvaged in 56 feet of water, rescuers found the forward ballast tank valve open, which allowed the sub to fill with water. On the floor was the wrench used to operate the seacock. This fact has led some to speculate that Horace Hunley forgot to close the valve and subsequently failed to find the lost wrench in the dark confusion of a sinking ship. Dixon would return to Charleston and persuade Beauregard to try one more time. With volunteers from the CSS *Indian Chief* among the third crew and a new strategy of using a torpedo attached at the end of a 16-foot spar, the *Hunley* would, months later, with Dixon back at the helm, successfully sink a state-of-the-art Union sloop-of-war USS *Housatonic*. This small crew had executed the first successful combat submarine attack in world history. This was the *Hunley*'s only mission as the submarine never returned to Sullivan's Island, leaving generations of historians to ponder what happened to the doomed craft and its eight-person crew. It was not until 1995 before the sunken craft was located in 30 feet of water some four miles from Sullivan's Island. In August 2000 the *Hunley* was carefully salvaged and brought to the Warren Lasch Conservation Center in North Charleston.[7]

Relations between Confederate Generals Beauregard and Ripley deteriorated rapidly over the fall of 1863, largely over Ripley's frustration with the slow pace of construction overseen by Beauregard's engineers. Beauregard provocatively chose to create a 5th Military District within, what had been, Ripley's 1st Military District. On October 26, it was announced that Col. Alfred Rhett, the former

---

7 Tom Chaffin, *The H. L. Hunley: The Secret Hope of the Confederacy* (New York, 2008), 149-150; Brian Hicks & Schuyler Kropf, *Raising the* Hunley (New York, 2002), 48-50; "The Search for the Hunley," The Friends of the Hunley website, www.hunley.org/the-search-and-recovery/.

commander of Fort Sumter, would head the new district, which embraced the city of Charleston, Castle Pinckney, and Fort Ripley. On November 22, Beauregard was writing Gen. William S. Walker that he only had 12,695 infantrymen of various levels of reliability to defend Charleston, Savannah, and the 110 miles of coastline between the two port cities. Two days later, Gen. Clingman's Brigade, some 1,810 soldiers, was ordered to North Carolina.[8]

Castle Pinckney began having structural issues from the overwhelming weight of the sandbags stacked inside and on the parapets of the brick structure. Observing the fort from the deck of the ironclad ram CSS *Palmetto State* was Augustine Smythe. "The berm of Castle Pinckney, that is the rim round the lower part of the Fort, the edge as it were," he wrote on October 11, "on which were piled the sandbags has given way under the weight & and they have taken them all away & left the fort as before." The Castle, at this point, was likely armed with at least one 8-inch Columbiad and one 42-pounder on its parapet while its casemates remained filled with sandbags. Confederate engineers immediately went to work stabilizing the foundation of the Castle. Working day and night, laborers used a hand-cranked pile driver to sink 43 pilings in and around the brick structure. At the end of October, James Henry Gooding, a member of the 54th Massachusetts, wrote a letter home soon reprinted in the *New Bedford Mercury*. Gooding reported that a 300-pounder Parrott on Morris Island was firing at various Confederate forts around the harbor, including Castle Pinckney. Gooding observed, "Still feeling a little more ambitious she right obliqued and sent a message to Castle Pinckney, which must have caused some commotion in the city, as Pinckney is not a great way from the town."[9]

The Confederates made every effort in the fall of 1863 and spring of 1864 to transform Castle Pinckney into a modern defensive structure capable of withstanding long-range bombardment by large caliber, rifled coastal guns. After stabilizing the fort's foundation, thousands of pounds of sand and dirt were brought inside the Castle and stacked against the circular brick walls creating something of a Roman amphitheater as the new sandhill descended from the ramparts to the base of the barrack buildings. By April 1864, Union Col. W. W. H. Davis of the 104th Pennsylvania reported from Morris Island, "A great amount of work has been done at Castle Pinckney in the past month, but it is not yet possible to tell

---

8 "General Orders No. 1, 5th Military District," *Charleston* [SC] *Mercury*, Oct. 30, 1863, 3; *OR* 28/1-112-113.

9 Letter from James Henry Gooding, *New Bedford* [MA] *Mercury*, Nov. 11, 1863; *OR* 28/2-381-382; Eric Emerson & Karen Stokes, *Days of Destruction: Augustine Thomas Smythe* (Columbia, 2017), 70. James H. Gooding was killed six months later at the Battle of Olustee, FL.

The Middle Ground: 1863–1864   143

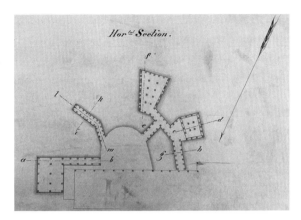

Diagram of the tunnels leading to the bombproofs that were constructed between late 1863 and the final surrender in 1865. *National Archives Cartography Room*

the object of it. There has been a large amount of sand and turf carried inside the fort, and from present appearances they have commenced a wall of sand and turf within the original wall of the fort."

A 1st quarter payroll sheet for enslaved labor at Castle Pinckney shows that 36 slaveowners contributed 66 of their enslaved men to work at Castle Pinckney and at the Marsh Battery. Owners received $11 a month for use of their enslaved men, who were listed on the payroll sheet by their first name—Peter, Friday, Ned, Smart, Chester, Bacchus, Neptune, etc. Five free men of color are also listed. Working conditions must have been harsh as Echols reported that 27 of these enslaved men ran away at some point during the first three months of 1864.[10]

Postwar U.S. engineer records show that three tunnels were dug deep into this giant earthen mound to reach newly constructed magazines and bombproofs. The first tunnel ran in a rough semi-circle from the inside parade ground to the west end of the barracks. Two rooms branched off this tunnel, one roughly 400 square ft. and the other over 250 square ft. This second room was partitioned roughly in half by a wall with a door. In all likelihood, these rooms were used as the Castle's magazine and ordnance storeroom. A second tunnel, some 50 ft. in length, led from the front of the east side of the barrack block to a large room roughly 400 square ft. in size. This room occupied part of the Castle's east wing and was probably designated as the fortification's bombproof for the garrison. Finally, the

---

10 *OR* 35/2-41; "Confederate Army Payrolls for Enslaved Labor, 1840-1883," NARA, RG:109, War Department Collection of Confederate Records, 1825-1927.

third tunnel, roughly 55 ft. long and five ft. wide, led from the parade ground to the former ordnance storeroom in casemate 9.[11]

On October 3, 1863, Capt. Peronneau's Company G was replaced at Castle Pinckney by Company H under Capt. Henry Russell Lesesne. From a prominent Huguenot family in Charleston, Lesesne, who was only 20 years old at the time, had been promoted to captain in July to replace Henry Farley. His company had fought well that summer at Battery Wagner and Battery Gregg and welcomed the October posting to the Castle. At this point in the war, Company H was small in numbers, with Lesesne reporting in December that he had present for duty two lieutenants, an assistant surgeon, and 47 non-commissioned soldiers. Lesesne's company would garrison Castle Pinckney through May 1864, when they were ordered to Battery Bee.[12]

November saw continual tinkering with the gun placements that made up the inner ring of the Southern three-layered defensive system that protected the Charleston Harbor. At the beginning of the month, Beauregard ordered the 8-inch Columbiad at the Castle to be exchanged for a 10-inch Columbiad at nearby Fort Ripley. This may have been because Fort Ripley, like Castle Pinckney, suffered structural issues and flooding in its northwest corner, and the 8-inch gun was some 5,000 pounds lighter. Just as important, the exchange also gave the gunners at the Castle more range while still keeping Ripley, which sat on the edge of the main channel, still very much in the fight should Federal naval forces reach the Rebel's second circle of fire. Lt. Inglesby, a 25-year-old local attorney, had 5,000 pounds of gunpowder and 126 solid shots for his two guns at Fort Ripley. On November 18, Augustine Smythe wrote his mother about Castle Pinckney, "They have built up a wall of sand inside the fort ten feet from the outer brick one. On this are mounted the guns & all the space between is packed with sand forming a pretty good wall." On the last day of November 1863, Battery Gregg, renamed Fort Putnam by federal officers, took aim at Castle Pinckney, firing two shells at the fort with both attempts falling short.[13]

Lt. William Hume, Jr., a 27-year-old civil engineer from Charleston, directed the refurbishment of Castle Pinckney in the winter of 1863-64. Days before Christmas of 1863, he requested that his mechanics and overseers be detailed to

11 Detailed drawing of tunnels at Castle Pinckney, drawn Dec. 12, 1865. National Archives II, Cartographic and Architectural Records, RG 77, Dr. 67, Sheet 42.75

12 Herbert O. Chambers, *And Were the Glory of Their Times: The Men Who Died for South Carolina in the War for Southern Independence. Artillery* (Wilmington, 2014), 3 vols., 3:70-71; CWSR, H. R. Lesesne, 1st SC Artillery, "Requisition for Fuel, Dec. 3, 1863," M267, roll 62, 82.

13 *OR* 28/2-381-382, 466; *OR* 28/1-173; Emerson & Stokes, *Days of Destruction*, 75.

work at the Castle for another 60 days. Vital to Hume's efforts was Pvt. W. S. Coates of the 27th South Carolina Infantry, as an assistant engineer, Pvt. R. H. Barrineau of the 25th South Carolina Infantry, as an overseer, and Pvt. William H. Gruver of the 5th South Carolina Cavalry, as the foreman of carpenters. By April 1864, Col. Davis of the 104th Pennsylvania Infantry could report from Morris Island that a great deal of work had been done at Castle Pinckney, "and from present appearances they have commenced a wall of sand and turf within the wall of the fort."[14]

Lesesne's 2nd lieutenant was 22-year-old Edward B. Middleton of Charleston. Middleton had spent three years as a cadet at the Citadel and 18 months as a private in the Marion Artillery before transferring to the 1st South Carolina Artillery. Today, the South Carolina Historical Society holds Middleton's papers, which include an 1859 *Mills Almanac* that the young lieutenant carried in the war. Middleton had carefully woven blank blue pages into the book and had inscribed, among other items, his duties as an officer of the day, detailed instructions for loading and firing a 10-inch Columbiad, and the correct ranges for a Brooke Rifle. Writing from Castle Pinckney on January 24, 1864, Edward Middleton noted that the duties of the officer of the day included being present for all roll calls, inspecting the living quarters of the garrison, visiting the wharf, and checking that all boats were securely tied up, and ensuring that the inner gate of the sally port was closed at Retreat and opened at Reveille. As darkness set in, he was to speak to his night guard so that each sentinel was "minutely instructed." This was to be followed by a personal visit to each of the Castle's guard posts. The corporal of the guard was to be alerted when a boat approached the fortress, and he was to be present on the pier as the ship drew close. All arrivals and departures would ultimately have to gain the "ascent or refusal" of the officer of the day. Thus, even on the relatively quiet posting at Castle Pinckney, military order was always kept.

Middleton also wrote that the officers at the Castle could visit the city of Charleston twice a week. Furloughs for the garrison, in general, were granted on the condition that no more than two men were absent at any one time. Should anyone overstay their time away, the next person in the line of secession was to be detained for five days for each day his predecessor had not returned. A desertion from Company H meant that all upcoming furloughs were canceled.[15]

---

14 CWSR, W. H. Gruver, M267, roll 34, 18; CWSR, W. S. Coates, M267, roll 357, 2; CWSR, William Hume, Jr., Confederate Engineers, M258, roll 107, 16, 19.

15 Middleton, Edward Barnewall, Handwritten notes in 1859 Mills Almanac, Edward B. Middleton Papers, 1842-1913, South Carolina Historical Society, Manuscript 1168.02.04.

With the number of Charleston defenders steadily diminishing with transfers and desertion, it was important that the artillerists around the bay also be prepared to fight, if needed, as infantrymen. At the beginning of April 1864, Capt. Lesesne received 70 sets of infantry accouterments for his men, together with 1,000 rounds of .57 caliber cartridges and 1,000 percussion caps. The *Philadelphia Press* was soon reporting the arrival into Federal lines of twelve "contraband," with one being H. R. Lesesne's personal servant, who carried a pass dated May 1. "Tony" told the Northern officers that few Southern troops were left to defend the largely deserted city of Charleston, as many had been sent to Lee's army in Virginia. He counted only 45 men as part of the Castle Pinckney garrison.[16]

The Castle had three heavy guns on its ramparts about this time—one rifled and double-banded 42-pounder and two cast-iron 10-inch Columbiads. Smoothbore cannons prior to the Civil War were differentiated by the weight of the cannon balls that they fired, i.e. the gun was a 24-pounder. Beginning with the large Dahlgren cannons placed on the *Monitor* ironclads, the newer guns used in the Civil War were differentiated not by projectile weight but by bore size. The 10-inch Columbiads, for example, were giant guns, each weighing more than 13,500 pounds, and capable of firing, using 18 pounds of black powder, a 100-pound shell, or a 128-pound solid-shot ball towards an approaching ship. The 10-inch guns at the Castle were manufactured at the Tredegar Iron Works located beside the James River in Richmond, Virginia. The Southern version of the Columbiad had a shorter barrel length, which saved valuable iron and reduced the gun's weight. The trunnions on the Tredegar guns were also longer so that they could be mounted on Southern-manufactured wooden barbette carriages. Finally, the exterior finishing on the weapon was much rougher.[17]

The smoothbore seacoast Columbiad had been a mainstay of American heavy artillery since the 1840s, with primitive gun prototypes going as far back as the War of 1812. Many of the 250 or so Confederate cannons that protected Charleston's harbor in 1864 were either 8-inch or 10-inch caliber Columbiads. It was a versatile cannon, capable of firing at high and low trajectories. While lacking the punch of rifled guns, projectiles fired from these smoothbores, at a range of less than 2,000 yards, could skip along the water's surface and hit opposing ships at their vulnerable waterline. By adjusting the gun's elevation, the 10-inch Columbiad had

---

16 CWSR, H. R. Lesesne, "Receipts for Issues to the Army," Mar. 31, 1864, M267, roll 62, 89-90; "Twelve Contrabands," *Philadelphia* [PA] *Press*, May 23, 1864, 1.

17 Michael G. Laramie, *Gunboats, Muskets and Torpedoes: Coastal South Carolina, 1861-1865* (Yardley, PA, 2022) 332. Under the direction of Joseph Anderson, Tredegar manufactured over 1,100 cannons for the Confederacy.

an effective range of 5,500 yards, which meant that any ironclads that managed to breach the harbor obstructions would fall under the guns of Castle Pinckney.

On January 9, 1864, Gen. Beauregard wrote to Col. Josiah Gorgas, the chief of ordnance in Richmond, that one of the most effective and durable guns at Fort Moultrie was an 8-inch Columbiad that had been rifled and double-banded at a Charleston foundry. Gen. Ripley had conveyed to Beauregard that the gun had been fired more than 100 times, "and in action has an immediate effect upon the enemy's iron-clads, which always try to avoid it." While the two Columbiads mounted at the Castle were smoothbore guns, the 42-pounder had been given a second life by being rifled and double-banded in Charleston. Banding meant applying a heavy wrought iron band, that reinforced the breech of the large gun. According to Beauregard, the great advantage to rifling grooves into the bore so that the projectile spun as it left the muzzle was that the modified gun had "a greater range with the same charges and less elevation than the smoothbore." Solid shot fired from a rifled gun also hit their target with a higher velocity.[18]

The 42-pounder at Castle Pinckney had a muzzle diameter of 7-inches and weighed 8,465 pounds. The cannon, called a "James Gun" by the Federals, was considered outdated at the beginning of the war, but the banding and rifling enabled the piece to fire a heavier projectile with more force, range, and accuracy. The Charleston foundry of Eason & Brothers charged the Confederate government $125 in January 1863 to double-band and rifle a 42-pounder cannon. At a top elevation of 5 degrees, this gun, with 14 pounds of black powder, could accurately send a shell some 1,900 yards.[19]

Loading, aiming, and firing a large-caliber coastal gun was complicated. The 1863 Army of the United States *Instruction for Heavy Artillery* manual included four chapters devoted to the Columbiad. One gunner and six cannoneers were needed for each gun. Using wooden and iron handspikes, a rammer, a sponge, a tompion, chocks, various pouches with friction tubes, lanyard, breech-sight, fingerstall, priming-wire, gunner's gimlet, and vent-punch, and, behind the gun, a budge-barrel containing cartridges, the men worked through more than 50 orders to bring the cannon into action.

In his almanac, Lt. Middleton wrote the verbal instructions he would give a cannon crew for handling one of the Columbiads at Castle Pinckney. By way of example, it took seven orders to bring his artillerymen from behind the cannon

---

18 Craig Swain, "The Charleston Theater (1861-1865)," *To the Sounds of the Guns*, Civil War blog, markerhunter.wordpress.com; Jack Bell, "Robert P. Parrott's Checkered History," *The Artilleryman Magazine* (Winter 2022), 44:1-16; *OR* 35/1-513-514.

19 Craig Swain, "The Charleston Theater (1861-1865)."

to their assigned places to begin loading the gun. As he commands, "Detachment to your posts," the gunner sergeant gives the command "right face," followed by "by file left." The gunner places himself to the left of the first artilleryman, and the small column proceeds, at Middleton's command of "march," to the gun. Once by the cannon, the detachment will be in line with numbers 1 & 2 opposite the front truck wheel, 3 & 4 opposite the rear truck wheels, and 5 & 6 near the end of the chassis. The three remaining cannoneers will dress behind numbers 1,2 & 4, respectively. Middleton's following command is "Detachment rear" when the line breaks in two on either side of the cannon, and the gunner commands "Outward face."[20]

20 *Instruction for Heavy Artillery; Prepared by a Board of Officers* (Washington, D.C., 1863), 73-77; SCHS, Edward Barnewall Middleton, Handwritten notes in 1859 *Mills Almanac*, Edward B. Middleton Papers, 1842-1913.

Chapter 11

Lowering the Stainless Banner
1864–1865

"Should you capture Charleston, I hope that by some accident the place may be destroyed, and if a little salt should be sown upon its site it may prevent the growth of future crops of nullification and secession."[1]

On May 18, 1864, Lt. Edward Middleton wrote his mother that his Company H, under Capt. Lesesne, had left the Castle and been redeployed to the city of Charleston. Replacing Company H was Company F under Capt. Gadsden King.

According to Middleton, Lesesne liked his relatively quiet posting at Castle Pinckney and was "loathe" to make the change. King, on the other hand, had been campaigning for weeks to have his company placed at the Castle, arguing to Capt. H. W. Feilden, an assistant adjutant-general on Beauregard's staff, that his was the only company in the 1st South Carolina Artillery Regiment never to have been relieved from the front lines. He wrote that a transfer to Castle Pinckney would "materially add to the efficiency" of his men. A son of Scottish parents, the 32-year-old King had been in the war from the beginning, serving as captain of the Marion Artillery during the firing on Fort Sumter and continuing as captain of Company F through postings at Fort Sumter, Battery Wagner, Battery Gregg, and Fort Johnson.[2]

King's new posting on the island of Shute's Folly was not as quiet as he had hoped. The *Charleston Mercury* reported that on June 29 seven shells were fired

---

1 Gen. Henry W. Halleck to General William T. Sherman, December 1864

2 SCHS, Edward Middleton, letter to his mother, May 18, 1864, Edward B. Middleton Papers; Herbert Chambers, *And Were the Glory of Their Times*, 3:114-115; CWSR, John Gadsden King, 1st SC Artillery, letter, King to Feilden, May 7, 1864, M267, roll 61, 92.

at Castle Pinckney, with at least one exploding inside the parade ground and wounding five men. Signalman Thomas Lowndes, who was present at the Castle, wrote, "three [shells] fell in the parade killed one and wound three or four more men." The *Charleston Courier* described the casualties, all men from Company F, as "Private J. Johnson, mortally; DeHart, severely; Littlefield, painfully; McKenny, slightly. A negro was also slightly wounded." Pvt. Jonathan Johnson, age 36, died from his wounds at the Louisiana Wayside Hospital, which was located on King Street. Hospital records list his cause of death as "Vilnus Sclopeticum," which roughly translates to a gunshot wound. His body was taken to Magnolia Cemetery and buried in the Confederate section.

The shelling had come from Fort Putnam on Morris Island, specifically from the 3rd Rhode Island Heavy Artillery. The New Englanders had been a part of the Department of the South since the capture of Port Royal in 1861. By this point in the war, these artillerists were trained gunners and understood every aspect of their 10" Columbiads, as well as their 100-pounder and 200-pounder rifled Parrotts. "In the rifled guns the drift was to the right," explained Chaplain Denison, "modified by the amount and direction of the wind." The 100-pounder, which had a propensity to burst with heavy usage, took ten pounds of No. 7 powder to send a 101-pound long shot, a 99 ½-pound solid shot, or an 80-pound hollow shot to a target that fell within a range of 1,475 yards to 8,453 yards.[3]

On June 29, 1864, Lt. John Burroughs of Company B trained a 200-pounder Parrott on Castle Pinckney. This was a challenge to his Rhode Island gunners as it was one thing to drop shells indiscriminately upon Charleston, the famous city of the "insurgents," and quite another to hit such a precise target at 5,510 yards. Sgt. William Spooner set the elevation, determined the length of the fuse, and directed the crew to load the cannon with 16 pounds of powder and a 150-pound shell. According to Denison, a look through their telescopic sights showed the Castle's occupants "feeling that they were exempt from our regards, and safe, were sitting and strolling about on the work." Denison recorded that three of their five shots "smote the castle," producing "indescribable excitement" around Shute's Folly. "From that hour," he wrote, "the work began to undergo a change, and soon, by sand-bags and timbers, it became transformed into quite a solid earthwork."[4]

The desultory shelling of the Castle, along with the other Confederate fortifications around the harbor picked up in frequency during the summer of 1864, with the intent of harassing and disrupting the Southern troops. In August,

---

3 "Siege of Charleston," Jul. 3, 1864, *Augusta* [GA] *Daily Constitutionalist*, 1; Frederic Denison, *Shot & Shell*, 238.

4 Frederic Denison, *Shot & Shell*, 238, 251-252.

King's company comprised two captains, a lieutenant, and 81 non-commissioned soldiers. We know more than usual about the affairs of Castle Pinckney during these last six months of the war, as Company F's 400-page guard book has survived and is now in the Rubenstein Library at Duke University. From the guard book, we learn that each 24-hour day was assigned to a 13-man detail that included an officer of the day, a sergeant of the guard, a corporal of the guard, one musician, and nine privates. Three sentry posts—one on the wharf, one at the sally port, and one on the ramparts—always had a soldier on duty. The privates stood watch four times over a 24-hour period, with each shift being two hours long. The responsibilities of officer of the day were rotated between Capt. King and his lieutenants Thomas Middleton and James Reid Pringle.

The guard book pages hold an array of interesting tidbits. One to three members of Company F were listed each day as prisoners, usually for desertion or being absent without leave. Noted, under remarks, were the times the Castle or Fort Ripley was shelled by Federal artillery, times when the entire garrison was called to stations, the arrest of Sgt. W. P. Turner by the commanding officer, the arrest of 1st Corpl. John Stegall, and an inspection visit to the Castle on December 15 by the district commander, Col. Alfred Rhett. Historian Robert Rosen has written that Rhett was "as tough a soldier as the Confederacy ever produced." He commanded Fort Sumter in 1863, successfully repelling the Union ironclad attack on April 7 and holding his garrison together during two concentrated federal bombardments that pummeled the brick fort with 6,878 shells.[5]

Beginning in November 1864, the guard book notes the daily arrival of sloops, schooners, and flats carrying rock, workers, and construction material to the Castle. An intercepted Confederate telegraph from early November 1864 reports, "There are 200 negroes at work on Castle Pinckney." On January 13, 1865, Federal observers on Morris Island reported that heavy working parties were constantly at work on the old fort and that "The Castle at present presents from the outside all the appearances of an earthwork." Indeed, the Confederates had filled the casemates of the Castle with sand and built an exterior wall of earth that ran down from the parapet to the sea—all designed to absorb shelling from large coastal guns. Between January 10 and January 20 over 40 schooners unloaded their cargo on the Castle's wharf. On January 25, the Union commander on Morris Island, the German Alexander Schimmelfennig, reported that fatigue parties continued to work "day and night between low and half tides spreading earth and laying

---

5 CWSR, Gadsden King, Requisition for Fuel, Aug. 1864, M267, roll 61, 34; "Guard Report, 1864, Castle Pinckney, Charleston," Confederate States of America Collection, 1850-1876, Rubenstein Library, Duke University; Robert Rosen, *Confederate Charleston*, 104.

stone." Three days later, Gen. Foster, commander of the Department of the South headquartered in Hilton Head, wrote Gen. William T. Sherman in Pocotaligo that the only observable work the Southerners were still performing around the harbor of Charleston was at Castle Pinckney. In short, the Confederates were, even at this late date, transforming Castle Pinckney into a modern and dangerous earthen barbette battery.

Schimmelfennig's January 25 dispatch from Morris Island also reported the presence of a garrison gin on the ramparts of Castle Pinckney for the last seven days, believing it was "probably changing the carriage of a gun." The gin was a large wooden tripod device, roughly 25 ft. tall, with a block and tackle arrangement in its center that was used to raise and lower the gun tube into and off a gun carriage. The 42-pounder at the Castle was exchanged at about this time for a more powerful cannon. Fort Ripley, in contrast, was being downgraded as its two guns were replaced by "Quaker" decoy weapons. A Federal officer in August 1864 had speculated that the Castle was about to mount a 25-ton British-built Blakely rifled gun capable of firing a 470-pound shell more than a mile. The Confederates had two such guns, which had arrived onboard a blockade runner at Wilmington, then shipped by rail to Charleston. Both would be mounted on the Charleston peninsula, one near White Point Garden and the other near Frazer's Wharf.[6]

What Castle Pinckney did receive was a Seacoast Brooke, a modern rifled cannon named after its designer John Mercer Brooke of the Confederate Navy. Seen as the equivalent of the Parrott rifled gun in the Federal arsenal, Brooke model guns were produced for the Confederacy at both the Tredegar Iron Works in Richmond, and the Confederate Naval Ordnance Works at Selma, Alabama. The 7" double-banded Brooke mounted at Castle Pinckney came from the Selma foundry and weighed 14,800 pounds. A year earlier, in January 1864, Gen. Beauregard had passed on Gen. Ripley's report about a Brooke gun mounted at Fort Sumter. Ripley recounted that by using a ten-pound mixture of coarse grained and common cannon gunpowder, his Brooke gun had sent shells weighing 100 pounds four miles into the enemy camps on Morris Island. Now, in January 1865, Castle Pinckney, with a new Brooke and three giant 10" Columbiads, possessed a serious degree of firepower if Union warships ever managed to push their way into the Charleston Harbor.[7]

Gen. Beauregard had been gone from Charleston since April 1864, having been transferred to Petersburg, Virginia. On October 28, 1864, Lt. Gen. William

6 *OR*, series II, 7:1-1120-1121; *OR* 47/1-151-152, 1011.

7 Warren Ripley, *Artillery and Ammunition of the Civil War* (New York, 1970), 127-129; *OR* 35/1-513-514.

J. Hardee took command of the Department of South Carolina, Georgia, and Florida. Known as "Old Reliable," Hardee was one of the Southern military's most experienced and respected Corps commanders. By this point in the war, however, he had few resources to confront Gen. William T. Sherman's large veteran army of 60,000 men as it swept across a wide swath of Georgia from Atlanta to Savannah. After refitting his army in Savannah in January 1865, Sherman began an audacious winter campaign rampaging along a 40-mile-wide front through the interior of South Carolina. The Bluecoats were eager to wreak vengeance upon South Carolina, prompting Sherman to write Gen. Halleck in Washington that, as for the Palmetto State, "I almost tremble at her fate, but feel that she deserves all that seems in store for her."

In December 1864, the planter and noted botanist Henry William Ravenel wrote about a return trip to a desolate Charleston in his private journal. The 18 months of enemy shelling had put large holes in the buildings, and the concussions had shattered the glass windows. Grass and weeds grew in the empty streets. "Lower down King St & through Broad street we scarcely saw any person," he wrote, "except a party of laboring negroes taking up the stones in Broad St to be sent to Castle Pinckney."[8]

Hardee had been given orders as early as December 27, 1864, to "make silently and cautiously all necessary preparations for the evacuation of Charleston should it become necessary." Unclear at this time was where exactly Sherman was headed, as speculation ranged from Augusta to Charleston. South Carolina Gov. Andrew McGrath took the opportunity to call on Jefferson Davis to abandon Richmond and reestablish his government in Charleston, writing, "Richmond may fall and Charleston be saved, but Richmond cannot be saved if Charleston falls." The reality was that both Southern cities were doomed with Charleston, by the first months of 1865, a lawless and nearly abandoned city. Sherman never marched on Charleston, considering it of little strategic importance and fearful that his army might become bogged down in the marshy swamps of the Lowcountry. Instead, he moved inland, capturing the state capital of Columbia on February 17, 1865. On the same day, the Confederate military evacuated the city of Charleston and nearby fortifications.

Likely made at the Charleston Depot, the last Confederate flag to fly above Castle Pinckney was a second national flag that resides today in storage at the Confederate Relic Room and Military Museum in Columbia, South Carolina. After raising the "Stainless Banner" for the last time, Capt. King and his men

---

8 Robert Rosen, *Confederate Charleston*, 134; Henry David Ravenel, *Private Journal 1863-1865*, digital collections, University of South Carolina Libraries, 66.

This 2nd National Flag is the last Confederate flag to fly over Castle Pinckney. It is 9 ft. by 14 ft. and was taken down by Federal troops on February 18, 1865. The War Department returned the flag to South Carolina in 1905, and it is now in the care of the Confederate Relic Room in Columbia, South Carolina. *Dennis E. Todd*

boarded a small river steamer and departed the Castle at about 9:00 p.m. on the 17th. Signalman Thomas Lowndes recalled that he and Lt. Middleton were the last to leave, having first set fire to the sponge heads in the magazine and the framed pictures in the barracks. If they attempted to burn down the barracks, this failed. King wrote that his company, less than one hundred men in all, sailed up the Cooper River to Sisters Ferry "from where we marched across the country about ten miles, and joined the rest of the regiment." Company F was joining the other nine companies of the 1st South Carolina Artillery, now part of a South Carolina infantry battalion under Col. Rhett. Their orders were to join a hastily assembled Confederate force defending North Carolina from Sherman's advancing army.[9]

Lt. Col. Augustus G. Bennett of the 21st USCI was the commander of U.S. forces on the north end of Morris Island on the morning of February 18, 1865. His suspicions that the city's defenses had been abandoned the previous night were confirmed after an early morning reconnaissance by Capt. Samuel Cuskaden of the 52nd Pennsylvania Infantry. Bennett did not hesitate but took what soldiers he had around him, only 22 men in all, in two small boats and rowed for Fort Sumter.

9 *OR* 44/1-994; J. Gadsden King, "Civil War Remanences," J. Gadsden King Papers, Georgia Department of Archives & History, drawer 283, box 30; Thomas Lowndes, *Reminiscences of Thomas Pinckney Lowndes*, 1896, 4:10.

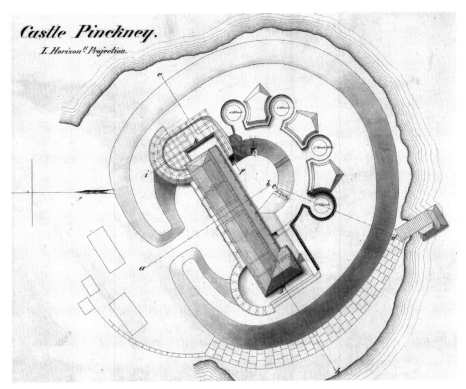

In the summer of 1864, Southern engineers transformed Castle Pinckney into a modern and dangerous earthen barbette battery with a rifled Brooke gun and three giant 10-inch Columbiads. Federal engineers drew this diagram of the captured Confederate fortification in December 1865. *National Archives Cartography Room*

The "Ripley boat" was the faster of the two and reached Fort Sumter first. 35-year-old Maj. John Hennessy of the 52nd Pennsylvania Volunteers scaled the parapet and vigorously waved his regimental flag "over the torn and battered walls of Fort Sumter." It was now a little after 9:00 a.m. The boats headed next for Fort Ripley, with the Ripley boat again out front. Hennessy was again the first to disembark and he successfully replaced the Rebel flag with the 35-star "Old Glory."[10]

Cuskaden was commanding the second boat, and he decided not to wait for Hennessy but to order his men to row for all they were worth toward Castle Pinckney. It was soon a race between the two Yankee boats, with Cuskaden's boat reaching the wharf first. Three soldiers from the 3rd Rhode Island Artillery sprang out and raced for the pole. By the time Lt. Haviland had lowered the large Confederate flag,

10 *OR* 47/1-1018-1019; *OR* 53/1-60-61.

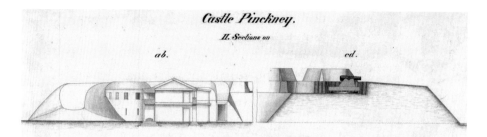

Cross-section of Castle Pinckney in 1865 shows the built-up sand ramparts (or escarp) that sloped down on the outside and inside of the original walls. The sand berms rose as high as the top of the barracks. A 10-inch Columbiad is on the right. *National Archives Cartography Room*

Hennessy's men had also reached the flagpole. According to Cuskaden, "a struggle ensued between the two parties as to which flag should be raised. The major's flag being smaller and easily handled his men succeeded in carrying their point." By 10:00 a.m., both boats had reached Mill's Wharf in Charleston. It was a scene of complete chaos as multiple fires were burning throughout the city. Minutes later, the Confederate Commissary Depot exploded, killing scores of civilians, and the Rebel ram CSS *Charleston* exploded by Mount Pleasant. Col. Bennett accepted the city's surrender from Mayor Charles MacBeth, while Cuskaden's flag was finally put to use, rising above the Citadel barracks. At 5:00 p.m., the 21st USCI arrived in the city to assume provost duties. Bennett reported that his troops, on February 18, 1865, had captured the "flags from Fort Moultrie, Castle Pinckney, and Fort Ripley, and seventeen signal pennants found in the city."

Confusion and rumors abounded. On March 2, 1865, *The Statesman* newspaper from Yonkers, New York, incorrectly reported the total destruction of Castle Pinckney on February 18. Their source was a Yonkers sailor on the USS *Mahopac*, who wrote home under the moniker SHERB. "The rebels blew up Castle Pinckney this morning." he proclaimed, "It was a splendid sight. The smoke rose into the air and then spread out like a large tree." SHERB added that there was great rejoicing among the "navy boys," as "we thought [we were] to have a hard time at this place; but it was not to be."[11]

Meanwhile, the men of Alfred Rhett's Brigade, made up of the 1st South Carolina Artillery, the 1st South Carolina Infantry, and Lucas's South Carolina Battalion, found themselves moving, primarily by foot, some 250 miles in a steady retreat from Sherman's advancing Union army. As garrison troops for most of the

---

11 Smith B. Mott, *The campaigns of the Fifty-second regiment, Pennsylvania volunteer infantry, first known as "The Luzerne regiment"* (Philadelphia, 1911), 171; "Charleston," *The* [NY] *Statesmen*, Mar. 2, 1865, 1.

war, the artillerists, in particular, were unaccustomed to long marches. By March 15, Hardee had lost to desertion half of the soldiers he had left Charleston with a month earlier. The 1st South Carolina Artillery was now fighting as an infantry regiment and as a combined force, something they had never done when their ten companies were dispersed to the various forts around the Charleston Harbor. Companies E, F, G, & H had all spent time as independent commands assigned to Castle Pinckney.

Hardee made his stand five miles south of Averasboro, North Carolina, where the Cape Fear River and the Black River converge. On the afternoon of March 15, Hardee's 6,500 men, assisted by Joseph Wheeler's cavalry, began skirmishing with Sherman's advancing right wing, some 20,000 Federals, under Gen. Henry Slocum. As darkness fell, Col. Rhett was captured by Yankee scouts after riding out to reconnoiter what was in front of his main line. The Harvard-educated rice planter unexpectedly found himself dining with Union Generals Sherman, Slocum, and Davis that evening. Rhett spent several months in 1865 as a prisoner of war at Fort Delaware.

On March 16, 1865, the 1st South Carolina Artillery, 458 in number, held the far-right side of Hardee's first line of defense. The artillerymen proved to be tenacious infantry fighters holding back Kilpatrick's cavalry and then four U.S. infantry regiments for six hours. It was not until the brigade of Henry Case slammed into their undefended right flank that the Charleston men gave way and ran in retreat through muddy farm fields. Capt. King reminisced that Rhett's Brigade, 2,800 in number, withstood eleven frontal assaults over an eight-hour timeframe, leaving "3,300 dead men in front of us." While King's arithmetic was completely inaccurate, there is no doubt that the fighting around the 1st South Carolina Artillery at the battle of Averasboro proved to be the fiercest of the day, with 215 of the Carolinians killed, wounded, or captured. The brave Henry Lesesne, the 22-year-old captain of Company H, was among the dead. As the sun set in the evening, Hardee's third line of defense managed to hold back the Federals and then slip away into the night. His rag-tag Confederate army would fight again at Bentonville on March 19. Sherman, who reported 682 casualties among his troops at Averasboro, wrote the next day that Slocum's "Twentieth Corps struck the first line, turned it handsomely and used the Charleston brigade up completely, killing about 40 and gathering about 35 wounded and 100 well prisoners, capturing 3 guns, but on advancing farther encountered the larger line, which they did not carry, but was abandoned at night." The Civil War was about to come to an end.[12]

---

12 Mark L. Bradley, *Last Stand in the Carolinas: The Battle of Bentonville* (Campbell, CA, 1996), 114-118, 123-126, 132-133; *OR* 47/2-871; Gadsden King, "Civil War Remanences."

1865 Photographs of the Abandoned Castle

Unlike many of the defenses around Charleston, it appears that the evacuating Confederates made little effort to disable or destroy either the ordnance or facilities at Castle Pinckney on February 17, 1865. As such, these photographs provide a unique look at a Confederate fort undamaged by war and ready to defend the Charleston Harbor.

The tall sloped earthen sand and sodded walls that encased much of Castle Pinckney can be seen in this circa 1865 photograph of its western wall. In the closing years of the Civil War, Confederates used enslaved labor to build these earthen walls, thereby transforming the obsolete brick castle into a modern and dangerous earthen barbette battery with a 7-inch double-banded Brooke gun and three 10-inch Columbiads. Hidden under the sloped earthen walls are the Castle's iconic whitewashed brick walls and its casemate gun embrasures. Only a row of chimney tops that belonged to the barracks are recognizable from the old fort. The two earthen mounds on top of the structure are transverse's built to protect the large cannons and their gun crews. There is a faint silhouette of a man standing atop the parapet between the two mounds. Atop the right transverse is a tall wooden signal and watch tower. A smaller chimney appears to the right of the chimney row, and this pipe provided ventilation to the new bombproof. To the right of the Castle are wooden support buildings – a guard house, carpenters' shop, blacksmiths shop and a hospital. In the center of the photograph, behind the remains of a wooden wharf, is a small building near the waterline that was probably used as a latrine by the garrison. *Matthew Locke*

Lowering the Stainless Banner: 1864–1865

This 1865 glass negative published by E. and H. T. Anthony shows the interior of Castle Pinckney looking to the southwest, with James Island observable behind the masts of the ships at anchor in the harbor. In the foreground is a 10-inch Columbiad mounted on its center pintle barbette carriage. Stamped into its trunnion is the date 1862, and recent archeological excavations and research have tentatively identified this Confederate-made cannon as gun #1687. There is a protective patch covering the gun's vent hole located at the top and to the rear of the gun. Below the breech of the large gun are the cranks first invented by Joseph Yates in 1862. Behind the gun are the two protective dirt traverses, with the base of a signal and watch tower on top of the closer traverse. The wooden staircase leads from the rampart to the parade ground. Protruding from the dirt wall just past the base of the stairs is a square ventilation shaft leading into an underground magazine; to the right of that, covered by vertical boards, is one of the two entrances to the magazine. On the rampart under the flagpole are two stacked piles of cannon balls (10-inch hollow spherical case shot), each ball weighing 100 pounds.

Between the two small staircases that lead to a landing by the flagpole is a stack of shells for the 7-inch Double-banded Brooke Rifle identifiable by the square headed bolt that secured the sabot to the shell. To the right of these Brooke shells are neatly stacked wooden ordnance boxes and crates. At the top of the stairs is a limber chest placed inside a cut-out recess at the base of the traverse. Directly to the right of the limber chest are two stands of 10-inch grape shot, as well as a stacked pile of 10-inch canister. Resting up against this stack is a four-handled cradle that would have been used to carry the 10-inch canister and Brooke shells to their respective guns. Each 10-inch canister round held 72 individual 2-inch round iron shot, that when fired turned the Columbiad into a giant shotgun. The rear of the second 10-inch Columbiad is also visible in this photograph. This Confederate-cast gun has a distinctive mushroom cascabel and rachet elevations sockets. To the right of the gun is a wall of gabions, which were cylindrical wicker containers filled with earth and used to strengthen the position. *Library of Congress*

Published by E. and H. T. Anthony, this 1865 glass negative of the interior of Castle Pinckney was taken from underneath the piazza of the barracks to the right of the sally port. A wooden plank staircase leads from the small open parade ground to the ramparts. On a raised platform to the right of the base of the staircase is a pile of 10-inch strapped solid shot while to its left are two rows of 10-inch canister laying down with their top plates facing the photographer. Barely visible behind them are upturned 10-inch strapped shot. Behind the wooden planks that rest against the sodded earth is the entrance to a tunnel that led to casemate 9 (the Castle's former ordnance storeroom). To the left of the tunnel entrance are a stacked pile of 10-inch spherical shells, with several of their fuse holes exposed. The normal practice would be to point the ball downward to prevent water from entering the cavity in the shell. At the top of the stairs, one can see the breech (rear) of a 7-inch double-banded Brooke Rifle that is mounted on barbette carriage. As with the Columbiads (previous photo), the Brooke Rifle and carriage appear to be undamaged, even to the point of having its elevation spindle running through the cascabel. Left of the Brooke is the breech of another 10-inch Columbiad mounted on a barbette carriage, its mushroom cascabel showing its distinctive rachet elevation sockets and the triangular elevating apparatus with another stacked pile of 10-inch strapped solid shot to its left. *Library of Congress*

Chapter 12

American Bastille
1865–1875

> "Now Sir," added the Colonel, "I have a little hotel where men of your stamp are boarded. Orderly!" The orderly came into the room.
> "Orderly, take my friend, Mr. Monahan, to Castle Pinckney under guard."[1]

The fall of the blockade-running ports of Charleston and Wilmington brought great excitement to Northern politicians eager to see these long sought after prizes. In March 1865, a Congressional delegation left New York on the steamship *Fulton* stopping at Hilton Head by way of Fort Monroe.

The group included eleven Republican senators, congressmen, and Lincoln's former secretary of war, Simon Cameron. Many of these senators, such as Benjamin Wade and John Sherman of Ohio, would return to Washington and become important players in Reconstruction politics. Senators James Grimes of Iowa and Lyman Trumbull of Illinois would be among the six senators who broke ranks with their fellow Republicans and voted in 1868 against the impeachment of President Andrew Johnson. Together with family members, friends, and servants, the 61-person delegation arrived at Brown's Wharf on the morning of March 20. Waiting carriages took them on a tour of war-torn Charleston. In the afternoon, they boarded two boats for an excursion around the harbor, including stops at Fort Sumter, Castle Pinckney, and Fort Moultrie. Their notable hosts were Adm. Dahlgren of the Navy, on the steamer USS *W. W. Coit*, and Gen. Gillmore of the Army, who brought his dispatch steamer *Diamond*, along with his general staff and a band.[2]

---

1 *Boston Recorder*, April 28, 1865.

2 "Distinguished Visitors," *Charleston* [SC] *Daily Courier*, Mar. 21, 1865, 2.

On April 14, 1865, now Bvt. Maj. Gen. Anderson, under an overcast sky, raised the Stars and Stripes above Fort Sumter precisely four years to the day after he had lowered the national flag in the initial bombardment that had started the Civil War. Northern dignitaries and soldiers had been ferried across the harbor to witness the historic ceremony. Hundreds of newly freed African Americans watched the proceedings from the deck of Robert Smalls's *Planter*. Framed around this exuberant celebration was the surrender of the Army of Northern Virginia at Appomattox Court House on April 9 and the assassination of Abraham Lincoln on the evening of April 14. Northern reporters who came for the ceremony wrote about the desolation of a ravaged Charleston, now triumphantly nicknamed "Gillmore's Town," and described an unrecognizable Castle Pinckney as a "pile of white sand, with a few chimneys sticking up inside." The *Brooklyn Daily Eagle* correspondent noted that the pavements on many of the city streets were missing, having been taken up by the Confederates and used to strengthen Castle Pinckney and Fort Ripley.[3]

After the fall of Charleston, Castle Pinckney was occupied on February 17, 1865, by the 21st USCI (U.S. Colored Infantry) and briefly used by Union authorities as a prison for captured Confederate soldiers. By the summer of 1865, however, Castle Pinckney had been designated as a military prison. Many Union soldiers trying to keep order in the Palmetto State in the aftermath of the war were late enlistments, and many were formerly enslaved people. Discipline within the ranks in the Department of South Carolina had become a problem in 1865, with alleged cases of mutiny, rape, desertion, and even murder. On April 23, 1865, Mrs. Elizabeth M. Ravenel wrote from Charleston to her aunt Rosa Pringle in Society Hill, South Carolina, passing on rumors from her sister Maria Middleton. Elizabeth reported that a "plot" among the "Negro soldiery" had been broken up, resulting in large-scale executions—23 at Castle Pinckney, 17 at the Charleston jail, and a large number on James Island. Official records never mention this aborted plot that culminated in mass executions. Ms. Ravenel's account is probably a case of hearsay gossip playing on people's worst fears.[4]

Records show that Pvt. Grant of Company H, 21st USCI was convicted of killing one of his fellow soldiers and was executed at Castle Pinckney on June 23. The firing squad was made up of soldiers from the 21st USCI and the 127th New York Volunteers, with last rites given to a resigned Grant by a Catholic priest. August saw four military prisoners sent to Castle Pinckney, and in September,

---

3 Robert Rosen, *Confederate Charleston*, 150-153; "From Charleston," *New York Tribune*, Apr. 20, 1865, 1; "Charleston by Daylight," *Brooklyn* [NY] *Daily Eagle*, Apr. 21, 1865, 4.

4 SCHS, Letter, Mrs. E. M. Ravenel to Mrs. Rosa M. Pringle, Apr. 23, 1865.

Castle Pinckney was used during Reconstruction as a prison for both civilians and soldiers. This photograph is believed to have been taken in April 1865 by J. D. Reading of Savannah and shows prisoners relaxing in the interior of the Castle. A USCI sentry walks the parapet by the flagpole. *Library of Congress*

eight soldiers, members of the 21st USCI, 26th USCI, or the 128th USCI, were sentenced to jail terms distributed between Sing Sing, New York, and Castle Pinckney. In October, Pvt. Orange Page of the 35th USCI and three privates from the 6th Infantry were sent to the Castle.[5]

A second group of prisoners held at Castle Pinckney were civilians convicted by military commissions of crimes ranging from theft to murder. With the state under martial law and local courts not in operation, it was left to the military to adjudicate justice. For example, former slaves Bill and Jack were convicted by the military court in September of breaking in and stealing furniture from the plantation home of Dr. Huger in the Parish of St. John's Berkeley. They were sent to Castle Pinckney to serve a sentence of hard labor.

With the Charleston Harbor reopened to all commerce, the lighthouses at Castle Pinckney and Fort Sumter needed to be rebuilt. By March 1866, the Castle

---

5 "Military Execution," *Charleston* [SC] *Daily Courier*, Jun. 24, 1865, 2; "General Orders No. 97," *Charleston* [SC] *Daily Courier*, Sep. 19, 1865, 2; "Headquarters Military District of Charleston," *Charleston* [SC] *Daily Courier*, Oct. 20, 1865, 2; "General Orders, No. 50," *Charleston* [SC] *Daily Courier*, Oct. 23, 1865, 1.

had a new yellow-painted lighthouse standing 36 ft. high, or 41 ft. above sea level, with a red light projected by a sixth order Fresnel lens. This lighthouse would function until December 1878, when the new Fort Ripley Lighthouse replaced it. With the war over, the sand that had been packed by the Confederate laborers against the old brick walls was beginning to recede. Castle Pinckney looked like a crowded compound with four wooden buildings—a hospital, a carpenter's shop, a guardhouse, and a blacksmith's shop—standing outside the sally port.[6]

In September 1865, Maj. Gen. Sickles arrived in Charleston as the newly appointed military commander of South Carolina with the duty of "reconstructing" the war-torn state. Sickles was a former New York politician and a controversial general who had lost his right leg at the battle of Gettysburg. The 46-year-old Democrat was a political ally of the new president Andrew Johnson. "Devil Dan" Sickles would have to do his best to reconcile the competing interests of former Confederates, widows, freedmen, pro-Union Southerners, and the eyes of judgmental newspaper journalists and Washington politicians. Sickles set up his headquarters in the former brick mansion of Thomas Hamlin White at 33 Charlotte Street, which was two blocks east of the Union barracks in the former Citadel. At the start of 1866, he had 352 officers and 7,056 Federal troops to help restore a semblance of order, as well as the cooperation of the gifted Provisional Governor James Orr. By the end of the year, Sickles's force had been reduced to 2,700 men. In a state with such competing interests, control of local and state governments became a tenuous and violent affair.[7]

Monthly garrison returns for Castle Pinckney are broken out for September 1865 through December 1866. In September, the Castle was garrisoned by Company A, 33rd USCI under Capt. Niles G. Parker. There were 76 soldiers in all, with Parker being the only commissioned officer. The October report notes that Ordnance Sgt. James Skillin returned to his post at the Castle on October 11, 1865. Skillin had been the post's ordnance sergeant when three Charleston militia companies seized the Castle on December 27, 1860. He had survived the war, re-enlisting for a sixth time at the Rome Arsenal in New York in 1864. His daughter Katie had, in 1863, married Capt. William Harn of the 3rd New York Independent Battery. Harn had been a young sergeant present at the 1861 surrender of Fort

---

6 "Stealing," *Charleston* [SC] *Daily Courier*, Sep. 25, 1865, 4; "General Order number 27, Department of the South," *Savannah* [GA] *Daily Herald*, Mar. 26, 1865, 5; "Office of Lighthouse Inspector," *Charleston* [SC] *Daily Courier*, Mar. 7, 1865, 2; "Marine Journal," *Boston* [MA] *Daily Advertiser*, May 25, 1866.

7 Thomas Keneally, *American Scoundrel: The Life of the Notorious Civil War General Dan Sickles* (New York, 2002), 319-320, 325.

Major General Daniel Sickles used Castle Pinckney as a prison for both civilians and soldiers when he commanded the Military District for North and South Carolina during Reconstruction. This photograph is attributed to the Mathew Brady Sudio.

National Portrait Gallery

Sumter. From 1870 to 1875, Harn and Skillin would run the Morris Island Lighthouse together.[8]

There are three documented escapes from Castle Pinckney during the Reconstruction years, with the first leading to court martial proceedings against Capt. Parker. The 39-year-old Massachusetts native was charged with neglect of duty for allowing a prisoner to escape in February 1866 and, more importantly, for not being present at his post when the escape occurred. Ordnance Sgt. Skillin and two sergeants from the 33rd USCI served as witnesses to the charges. Parker argued that he had been in ill health and excused from duty by the attending physician at the post. He further claimed that his regiment was preparing to be mustered out and had turned in their weapons. With this in mind, he had "taken extra precautions under the circumstances to provide for the safety of the prisoners under my charge." Parker won his case and was "honorably acquitted" and then discharged from the army. The former captain chose to remain in South Carolina, becoming active in Reconstruction politics and being elected the state treasurer in 1868.[9]

In February 1866, Company D, 35th USCI assumed control of Castle Pinckney. It was a short posting as the next month Company K, 128th USCI under 1st Lt. James H. Van Vort, a native of Fishkill, New York, moved into the

---

8 RMP, Castle Pinckney, 1865-1866; Re-enlistments of James Skillin, Feb. 27, 1864, New York City, Mar. 11, 1867, Charleston, SC, Register of Enlistments in the U.S. Army, 1798-1914, NARA, M233.

9 Letter, N. G. Parker to M. N. Rice, Feb. 14, 1866, Military service records of Captain Niles Gardner Parker, 33rd United States Colored Infantry, NARA, RG 94, roll 42.

Captain Niles Parker commanded Castle Pinckney in 1866. He was court martialed for allowing a prisoner to escape. Ordnance Sgt. Skillin testified against Niles. After his discharge, Niles was elected state treasurer of South Carolina. In 1877, he was charged with corruption and theft dating back to his time in office. *Baxter B. Fite, III*

Castle. The ten companies of the 128th, under the overall command of Col. H. Danielson, were spread out between the Charleston jail, Sullivan's Island, Fort Sumter, and Castle Pinckney. The 6th United States Infantry, regulars under Col. Henry Clitz, was garrisoned at the Citadel by Marion Square. On October 1, 1866, Companies of C and E, 37th USCI were sent from Forts Creswell and Fisher in North Carolina to reinforce Sickles in Charleston. They were assigned to the three forts of Moultrie, Sumter, and Castle Pinckney. Capt. Alonzo Clark Rembaugh, age 27, set up his battalion headquarters at Castle Pinckney. Rembaugh would go on to medical school in 1873 and become a prominent Philadelphia physician. The December post report also lists the name of eight privates who had previously deserted the 6th and 8th Infantry and were now prisoners at Castle Pinckney.[10]

In September 1866, a military court convicted Pvt. James Clark of Company G, 128th USCI for his involvement in the *Idea* Mutiny, which had taken place on Folly Island that summer. Made up of former enslaved men from Lowcountry plantations, the 128th had been formed only days before Lee's surrender at Appomattox, and, despite their military inexperience, these soldiers in blue were being counted on to police South Carolina through Reconstruction. Living in canvas tents on Folly Island, the soldier's boredom seemed to be immediately broken by the arrival of the steamer *Idea*. The men of Company G headed for the pier hoping there would be a party on the ship's deck that night. Their white officer, the newly arrived 1st Lt. Lester Hall, raced across the beach to shepherd the soldiers back to camp. Hall's shouted orders were ignored by the soldiers in

---

10 RMP, Charleston Harbor, 1866, M617, roll 191.

his new company and the situation quickly deteriorated to the point that Hall pulled his revolver and arrested Pvt. Nelson Hicks. This did not end matters, and that evening, a confrontation in the street of the camp ensued between Lt. Hall and his enlisted men, who had loaded and bayoneted their rifles. A running gunfight followed, with Hall killing one soldier and wounding two others. The next morning, Hall was again confronted, this time by Pvt. James Clark yelling for justice. Shots were fired, and Hall escaped down the beach. After an eight-day court martial in Charleston, Clark was sentenced to hang from the gallows at Castle Pinckney at 10:00 a.m. on September 28. The execution was delayed until November 1 and then put off indefinitely. Clark's fate is not recorded in the military records, which have significant gaps in this period of American history.[11]

A grisly murder followed by a scandalous trial has always captured the attention of newspaper readers in America. In 1866, the curious legal proceedings revolving around the notorious Brown's Ferry Murders captivated the nation. On the evening of October 8, 1865, three soldiers of the 1st Battalion of Maine Volunteers were murdered at Brown's Ferry on the headwaters of the Savannah River, some 30 miles south of Greenville. The soldiers were guarding 15 bales of cotton seized by officers of the Treasury Department, and suspicion immediately fell on the owners of the cotton. Arrested and sent to Columbia were Francis Gaines Stowers of Hart County, Georgia, James Crawford Keys and his son Robert, and Elisha Byrum, all from Anderson County, South Carolina. The four men were arrested and sent to Columbia, where they were held in jail for several weeks before being brought before a military commission at the Citadel in Charleston. The trial lasted for two long months, with the testimony of the ferry operator and black neighbors living near the ferry considered critical. The admission of accounts from former enslaved people surprised observers of the proceedings, as blacks testifying against whites had been deemed inadmissible in antebellum courtrooms. The defendants had the financial wherewithal to hire two superb lawyers, Armistead Burt, and Gen. James Conner. The second month of the tribunal was spent listening to 25 prominent South Carolinians, including Gov. James Orr, testify to the upstanding character of Francis Stowers and James Crawford Keys.

On April 22, 1866, the commission, made up of five officers and headed by Maj. Gen. Charles Devon, a former Massachusetts lawyer, found the four defendants guilty on all counts and sentenced them to death by hanging at Castle Pinckney at 10:00 a.m. on April 27. Gen. Sickles publicly announced the tribunal's

---

11 "Private James Clark," *The United States Army and Navy Journal and Gazette of the Regular and Volunteer Forces* (New York, 1863-1898), 48 vol., 4:86; Jonathan Lande, "Mutiny in the Army," *The Civil War Monitor* (Spring 2019), 9:54-65.

verdict but commuted the sentence of the two younger men, both Confederate veterans, to life in the penitentiary of Concord, New Hampshire. Sickles hoped the guilty older men would be hanging in the shadows of the gallows long before any public outcry could be generated. The four prisoners were immediately sent to Castle Pinckney.[12]

On April 25, President Johnson, who was immediately besieged by Southern petitions, sent a reprieve by telegraph to Charleston, leaving the four Southerners at Castle Pinckney to await further legal clarification of their fate. On May 7, the Charleston correspondent for Augusta's *Daily Constitutionalist*, writing under the pen name SIGMA, managed to interview the men in their cells at the Castle. Though the men had chains on their hands and feet, they had no complaints about their island captors and thought their situation improved from the city jail. They stated that their rooms were much cleaner and better ventilated, and the food was better. Above all, they were out of solitary confinement and could again converse with one another.[13]

On June 30, attorneys Burt and Conner filed an application to Judge George Bryan of the U.S. Court of the District of South Carolina, arguing that, with a now functioning federal court, this case should never have been tried before a military commission. The lawyers for the defendants were basing their application on a recently decided case that had been heard before the U.S. Supreme Court. In Ex parte Milligan, the nation's highest court ruled that trying civilians before a military tribunal was unconstitutional when civil courts were in operation. Judge Bryan agreed and issued a writ of *habeas corpus* demanding that Gen. Sickles produce the said prisoners to his courtroom or be in contempt of the federal court. Sickles refused and turned away the marshal of the court, arguing it was a matter for the president to decide.

As tensions between two federal branches mounted, President Johnson, on July 23, ordered Sickles to send the prisoners by steamer to Fort Jefferson in the Dry Tortugas, some 70 miles south of Key West, where they were to serve their life sentences. Because of its extreme isolation, Fort Jefferson had been used throughout the Civil War to hold hundreds of Union soldiers accused of mutinous conduct or desertion. By 1866, only a few dozen military and political prisoners were still held at the fort, but their number included Dr. Samuel Alexander Mudd, who had set the broken left fibula of Lincoln's assassin John Wilkes Booth, and the colorful British soldier of fortune George St. Leger Grenfell, who had been arrested

---

12 Mell Glenn, *The Story of a Sensational Trial* (Greenville, 1965), 53, 59, 73-76, 81-83; "The Anderson Prisoners," *Atlanta* [GA] *Weekly-Atlanta Intelligencer*, Aug. 8, 1866, 8.

13 "Our Charleston Correspondence," *Daily* [GA] *Constitutionalist*, May 9, 1866, 2.

for his ambitious plot to free the Confederate prisoners held in Chicago's Camp Douglas. The four convicted Brown's Ferry murderers had spent three months at Castle Pinckney, but their time in the Caribbean brick fortress known for its barbaric treatment of prisoners proved to be less than two weeks as, on August 6, they were transported north to Fort Delaware. This change of prison venues seems to have been the work of William Henry Trescot of Charleston and Orville Hickman Browning, soon to become Johnson's secretary of the interior. Once in Delaware, the four prisoners were brought before Judge Willard Hall of the U.S. District Court for the State of Delaware, who ruled that their trial by a military commission was "unconstitutional and irregular" and freed the four men. They returned home to a hero's welcome in November 1866.[14]

Hoping to raise money to rebuild the Catholic orphan asylum of Charleston, Bishop Patrick Lynch arrived hat in hand in New York City in April 1866. His cause was quickly adopted by the Union War Prisoners' Association, whose members remembered that Lynch had regularly visited the Northern prisoners at Castle Pinckney in 1861 and provided them with money and necessities. Proceeds from an evening lecture by the celebrity defense attorney James T. Brady at the Cooper Union Hall were to be passed on to a grateful Lynch. Brady, ironically, had in 1857 successfully defended Dan Sickles, then a New York congressman, for the murder of Philip Barton Key in Lafayette Park across from the White House. The handsome Key had been romancing Sickles's attractive young wife, Teresa. The Prisoner's Association gathered at the Metropolitan Hotel on July 25 to present Bishop Lynch with $1,235. In accepting the financial gift presented to him by Gen. James MacIvor, the Irish Lynch remarked, "If, gentlemen, you were in a little trouble when first I formed your acquaintance, I am in a great deal of trouble now, but you have come to my aid, and I thank you from the bottom of my heart."[15]

In December 1866, a congressional committee was formed to investigate the reprieve, transfer, and discharge of the four Brown's Ferry defendants. The proceedings were partly an attempt to embarrass President Johnson and Secretary of War Edwin Stanton. Sickles would be among six department commanders who took the witness stand. These generals painted a picture of rampant lawlessness throughout the South that only martial law could resolve. On March 2, 1867, the Military Reconstruction Act was passed by a Radical-majority Congress over

---

14 "The Anderson Prisoners," *Atlanta* [GA] *Weekly-Atlanta Intelligencer*, Aug. 8, 1866, 8; MPR, Fort Jefferson, Tortugas, Sep. 1866; "Keys, Stowers, & Byrum," *Anderson* [SC] *Intelligencer*, Nov. 29, 1866, 3; Michael Garlock, *Cathedrals of War: Florida's Coastal Forts* (Palm Beach, 2022), 116-117; "Reconstruction," *Semi-Weekly* [NY] *Tribune*, Dec. 7, 1866, 1.

15 "Presentation to Bishop Lynch, of Charleston S.C.," *The* [NY] *Irish-American*, Jul. 7, 1866, 2.

the veto of President Johnson. Gen. Sickles would command one of five military districts, the 2nd District of North and South Carolina, at his sole discretion until new state constitutions could be written and passed, the 14th Amendment ratified by the state, and the right to vote guaranteed for black male citizens. After the ratification of the 1868 constitution and the election of a Reconstruction assembly, the presence of the U.S. Army in South Carolina was reduced to 881 troops.[16]

Military tribunals for the 2nd Military District took place in Charleston every few months. Typically, a half dozen soldiers were brought up on various charges that ranged from drunkenness on duty, disobedience of orders, to desertion. Sentences typically included a loss of pay and confinement at hard labor, often at Castle Pinckney. For example, on May 20, 1867, 6th Infantry Pvt. Hugh McQuire was found guilty of being drunk on duty at the Citadel and abandoning Post 1 and going to bed. McQuire was sentenced to three months of hard labor at the Castle. Five days later, the tribunal ordered 12 soldiers from the 6th and 8th Infantry imprisoned at Castle Pinckney to be transferred to Fort Macon, North Carolina.[17]

In the summer of 1867, Castle Pinckney was garrisoned by a company from the 40th USCI under Capt. William Welsh. Recruited from the Baltimore and Washington, D.C. area, the 40th was one of six all-Colored Army regiments created by the 39th Congress in 1866. The white officers included the 32-year-old Welsh, who had been a schoolteacher in Mount Vernon, Ohio, before the Civil War. He joined the 4th Ohio Infantry and, in February 1864, became a captain of Company K, 19th USCI. At the battle of the Crater near Petersburg on July 30, 1864, half of the men in the 19th became casualties. Welsh's hearing was permanently impaired that day from exploding shells. While at Castle Pinckney, Capt. Welsh had a large ledger book created to record the prisoners under his care. August 1867 was the first month listed in Welsh's detailed ledger (see Appendix 17). It shows there were 50 prisoners at the Castle, mostly Federal soldiers of both races, there for desertion, misconduct, larceny, and other offenses. Welsh also kept a separate ledger book for commissary supplies purchased for his Company F. Those pages from 1867 and 1868 reveal that his soldiers garrisoned at the Castle had a bountiful supply of food, which included rice, beets, string beans, fish,

---

16 Mell Glenn, *The Story of a Sensational Trial*, 86-88; Walter Edgar, *South Carolina: A History* (Columbia, 1998), 397.

17 General Orders, No. 26, U.S. Court Martial proceedings, 2nd Military District, May 22, 1867, General Orders, No. 27, Prisoner transfer from Castle Pinckney to Fort Macon, May 27, 1867, Freedmen's Bureau Records, 1865-1878, M843, 3-4.

potatoes, coffee, tea, onions, beef, pork, butter, cabbage, turnips, raisins, codfish, apples, pears, oysters, and lobster.[18]

On February 11, 1867, 21-year-old Pvt. Charles Askie of Company C, 37th USCI was confined to Castle Pinckney, awaiting trial for manslaughter. The 37th consisted of former slaves living around Plymouth, North Carolina, and the regiment included 11 Askie men from Bertie County. A month earlier, 43-year-old George Askie, also a private in Company C, had accidentally drowned near Fort Sumter. He was with a detachment of soldiers loading timbers at Fort Sumter to be taken to Castle Pinckney, and the rough water caused the timbers to shift, knocking Askie off the boat. The 37th was mustered out of service on February 11, 1867, the same day that Charles Askie was sent to Castle Pinckney. While there are no further military records on the fate of Charles Askie, he does appear in the 1880 Federal Census as a farmer living in Bertie County, North Carolina.[19]

On October 21, 1867, the *Charleston Daily News* reported that Tristram Braddy of Little Rock, South Carolina, had been released from Castle Pinckney after two months of confinement. Braddy told the local reporter that there were about 45 prisoners at the Castle, "confined upon every species of charges or crimes." Because much of this federal military justice was done in secrecy, the American public did not know who had been confined there, how they were being treated, whether they benefited from legal counsel, or how long they were to be held. As the final arbitrator of these cases, Sickles was criticized for his "bayonet rule" over the state of South Carolina. Southern newspapers began referring to Sickles as a biblical "Satrap" with tyrannical powers. Johnson did not like that Sickles was issuing general orders across his two-state district that, among other things, imposed a moratorium on imprisonment and foreclosure of debt without first clearing his orders with the president. Ultimately, it was the continued jousting between Sickles's military rule and members of the state and federal judiciary that led to Sickles dismissal on August 10, 1867, to be replaced by Gen. Edward Canby.[20]

---

18 Robert McDonald, "Formation of the Buffalo Soldiers, 1866," www.BlackPast.org., Jan. 23, 2021; Kyle Nappi, "Retracing Hallowed Grounds from the Battle of the Crater," posted at Muster, the website of the *Journal of the Civil War Era*, www.journalofthecivilwarera.org, Aug. 3, 2021; William Welsh, *Record of Prisoners, Castle Pinckney, Charleston Harbour, Commanded by Captain W. Welsh, 40th Infantry*, Aug. 1867 to Aug. 1868, NARA, RG 393; William Welsh papers, RHC-89, Grand Valley State University Special Collections and University Archives. The all-Colored Army Regiments created by the federal government in 1866 were the 9th and 10th Colored Cavalry Regiments and the 38th, 39th, 40th, and 41st Colored Infantry Regiments.

19 Charles Askie Military Service Records, Colored Troops 36th-40th Infantry, NARA, RG 94, M1993; 1880 Federal Census for Bertie County, NC, NARA, RG 29, roll 953, 228A; "37th U.S. Colored Troops," Civil War Plymouth Pilgrims Descendant Society, cwppds.org.

20 "Local Matters," *Charleston* [SC] *Daily News*, Oct. 21, 1867, 3; "Second Military District: Change of Commanders," *New York Times*, Sep. 9, 1867, 3; Thomas Keneally, *American Scoundrel*, 333.

In April 1868, "S.D." a special *New York World* correspondent, wrote about his Charleston forts tour. Castle Pinckney, he reported, "is kept in good repair, garrisoned by a company of negro troops, and used as a place of confinement for those who become unlovely in the eyes of military power." By June 1868, the Charleston District was garrisoned by companies from the 8th, 12th, and 40th U.S. Infantry. Castle Pinckney was held by Company D, 40th USCI under Capt. George Choisy. Choisy replaced William Welsh in April but continued maintaining the prisoner ledger until August 1868. It appears that sometime between late 1868 and early 1869, the garrison at Castle Pinckney was removed, and the prison closed. It would never be an active military post again. In the 1870s, the U.S. army kept a light touch on Charleston with only two companies, roughly 200 men, barracked at the Citadel. Forts Moultrie, Pinckney, and Sumter were each watched over by an ordnance sergeant.[21]

James Skillin finished his career as the ordnance sergeant and lighthouse keeper at the Castle, though he nearly lost his life to a belligerent soldier serving as his assistant in August 1869. According to various newspaper accounts, Pvt. Johnson returned to the Castle from the city at noon in an intoxicated state. Skillin refused his request to return to the city, and Johnson refused Skillin's orders to resume work around the fort. The private declared his intention to kill Skillin and raced up the stairs to the armory to secure a rifle. Skillin followed but was met at the top of the stairs with Johnson holding a loaded rifle. The 48-year-old ordnance sergeant was shot at close range, with the bullet cutting off the forefinger of the raised left hand and then hitting the left breast and exiting through the shattered shoulder blade. While Skillin's wife attended him, Johnson, who had realized the gravity of what he had done, took a small boat to the city and brought back a Dr. Bailey. A detachment from the Citadel arrived and arrested Johnson without incident. Military doctors viewed the severe wound with alarm believing it was fatal or, at the very least, that the arm would have to be amputated.

Neither outcome came to pass, and James Skillin, the long-time watchman of Castle Pinckney, pulled through. He would be unsuccessful in his attempt later that year to gain an appointment as a lieutenant despite his status as a "disabled person," but he did begin receiving a military pension in 1875 as an "invalid." James Skillin spent his final years back in his home state of Maine, while his son-in-law William Harn, a Fort Sumter veteran, became the lightkeeper at St. Augustine. Harn's wife Katherine, who witnessed the 1860 seizure of Castle Pinckney by South Carolina

---

21 "South Carolina. In the City by the Sea," *The* [NY] *World*, Apr. 11, 1868, 1.; RMP, Charleston garrison, Jan. 1871—Apr. 1879; "Battey Leave of Absence, Special Order No. 153," Jul. 6, 1868, Letters Received by the Adjutant General, 1861-1870, NARA, M619.

A ca. 1875 photo by Jesse A. Bolles shows the interior of Castle Pinckney after it had been abandoned by the federal garrison. The earthen embankments were beginning to deteriorate.
University of South Carolina

militia, survived her husband and for a short time in 1889 was appointed second assistant lightkeeper at that Florida post.[22]

---

22 "Shooting Affray at Castle Pinckney," *Charleston* [SC] *Courier*, Aug. 2, 1869, 1; Letter, Skillin to Townsend, Nov. 18, 1869, Letters Received by Commission Branch, 1863-1870, RG 94, M1064, roll 449; Skillin pension, US Civil War Pensions Index, 1861-1900, NARA, RG 15, T289.

Chapter 13

Lighthouse Depot
1876–1916

Donald Cameron was the son of Lincoln's secretary of war, Simon Cameron, and would, in 1876, assume the same cabinet position under President Ulysses S. Grant. As an efficient administrator, the younger Cameron saw no purpose in keeping Castle Pinckney as part of the War Department.

On November 15, 1876, Cameron dismissed the ordnance sergeant and ordered all military ordnances be removed from the post, writing, "as there will remain but four obsolete guns, only valuable as scrap iron, and as the work is not at present needed as one of the defenses of the harbor it can be turned over temporarily to the custody of the Treasury Department." Two years later, at the request of the secretary of treasury, Castle Pinckney was transferred to the control of the Lighthouse Service for use as a supply depot.

As one of the first agencies created by the national government, the Lighthouse Service had complete responsibility for constructing and maintaining all lighthouses, beacons, buoys, and public piers along the coast of the United States. Over time, hundreds of lighthouses were built and set into operation along the East Coast and the Gulf of Mexico. By 1840, kerosene was replacing whale oil as the fuel of choice, and the adoption of the Fresnel lens (pronounced "Freh-nell"), which used prisms mounted at precisely engineered angles to cast the light radiating from the illuminant in a brilliant narrow beam, allowed sailors to determine their position despite being several miles out to sea. In the post-Civil War years, a strong professional esprit de corps developed among the navy-blue uniformed personnel of this national Lighthouse Service. Gaining employment with the Service was considered a secure and plum civil service posting.

For administrative purposes, the Lighthouse Board, which oversaw the Lighthouse Service, divided the coastline into districts, each with its own defined area of geographic responsibility. The 6th District ran from New River Inlet, North Carolina south to Cape Canaveral, Florida, and, by 1881, serviced 56 lighthouses, each with its respective keeper. Charleston seemed the ideal location for the district's headquarters and as a supply station to service the numerous lighthouses, beacons, and buoys that fell along their 700 miles of coastline. The central supply depot for each district was a beehive of activity as clerks kept records of supplies issued and acquired, and mechanics repaired buoys and other needed equipment. The district lampist was a master mechanic responsible for the maintenance of all of the district's lamps, lenses, and clockwork. He was frequently away on "house calls" to various lighthouses.[1]

To make the dilapidated Castle Pinckney into a practical supply depot, the Lighthouse Board spent significant sums of taxpayer money. The Gale of 1874, described as "short, sharp, and decisive" by the *News and Courier*, had battered the wharves and ships along East Bay Street, and the hurricane also swept away Castle Pinckney's Civil War-era wharf. In 1878, Maj. Peter Hains, the engineer for the 6th District, requested proposals to build a new wooden wharf at Castle Pinckney that would be 120 ft. long and 48 ft. wide. The following year an appropriation of $10,000 was made to establish a complete depot at Shute's Folly. Several buildings were constructed, including a large storehouse and a home for the resident depot keeper. The low-lying nature of Shute's Folly was not ideal for a depot and its muddy topography forced the creation of a system of wooden platforms with riprap stone protection to allow the workers to move between the wharf and the various buildings.[2]

The old brick Castle structure sat beside this new construction and remained abandoned. An 1879 sketch by William Martin Aiken shows the barracks chimneys still in place and a dark sloping bank of dirt obscuring at least one of the Castle walls. 1st Lt. Thomas N. Bailey of the Corps of Engineers wrote in an 1884 inspection tour that the old Castle was "in a dilapidated condition; the walls having settled and cracked." He added that the roofs of the magazine had fallen in,

---

1 Letter, Secretary of War Cameron to the Secretary of Treasury, Nov. 15, 1876, Records of the U.S. Coast Guard, Light House Service, NARA, RG 26, box 168; Douglas Peterson, *U.S. Lighthouse Service Tenders 1840-1939* (Annapolis, 2000), XV. The duties of the various lighthouse keepers never ended as the lighthouse lens had to be polished, the windows scrubbed clean, metal cans filled with fuel carried up the narrow stairs, the lamp wicks trimmed, soot cleaned from glass chimneys, and the clockwork that turned the lens had to be rewound every four hours.

2 "To Wharf Builders," *Charleston* [SC] *News & Courier*, Nov. 22, 1879, 2; "Notice to Mariners," *Savannah* [GA] *Morning News*, Oct. 31, 1878, 7; *Annual Report of the Light-House Board to the Secretary of Treasury* (Washington, D.C., 1852-1910), 1878: 45, 1882:41. Hereafter cited as ARLHB.

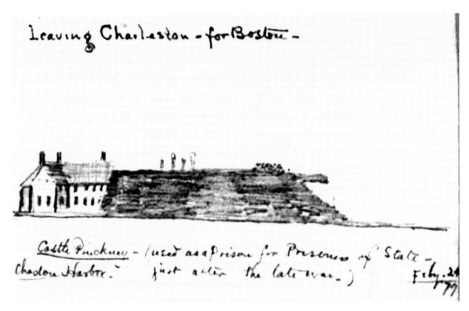

An 1879 pencil sketch of Castle Pinckney drawn by Charleston-born architect William Martin Aiken. A dark sloping bank of dirt still covered at least one of the Castle walls. *Lowcountry Digital Library & College of Charleston Libraries*

the gun carriages had rotted away, and the gun tubes were half-buried in the sand. The barracks, he observed, were a "dangerous wreck." In 1891, a reporter for the *News and Courier* noted that, "The crooked walls and the broken-down barracks in the interior are the result of cyclones, earthquake and time's decay, rather than the work of man [during the Civil War]."[3]

In 1875, the Lighthouse Board proposed building a screw-pile lighthouse on the Middle Ground of the Charleston Harbor in 9 ft. of water some 500 ft. southeast of the foundation of old Fort Ripley. A screw-pile lighthouse was designed to be lightweight and relatively inexpensive to build. A yellow wooden tower would sit atop iron, stilt-like legs. The iron legs were shaped like corkscrews so they could be turned into the sandy bottom of the harbor and lock into place. The new lighthouse, which was operational in December 1878, was built where the Folly Island and main shipping channels separated, and it replaced a smaller beacon that stood at the end of Castle Pinckney's long wharf. The Fort Ripley

---

3 James Percival Petit, "Out of Oblivion: Castle Pinckney," *Sandlapper Magazine* (Jul. 1969), 75; "News from the Castle," *Charleston* [SC] *News & Courier*, Jan. 25, 1891, 2; SCHM, Roger W. Young, "Castle Pinckney, Silent Sentinel of Charleston Harbor," Apr. 1938, 62.

Shoal Light Station, with its fixed red light of the 6th degree, was built at the cost of $20,000 and stayed in operation until 1932.⁴

The 6th District was fortunate to have the resourceful and charismatic James Wilfred Whiteley, a native son of England, serve as the resident depot keeper at Castle Pinckney from 1880 until his death in 1907. Responsible for all the government stores kept on the island, he was also a shipbuilder and able resource for determining how all ongoing repairs across the district should proceed. James and his wife Annie raised ten Whiteley children on Shute's Folly during these years. Middle son Pinckney Lamberton Whiteley was born there in 1886, named for both his birthplace and Lighthouse Inspector Benjamin Lamberton. Annie Whiteley was the daughter of Capt. Henry Brown, who commanded the USLHT *Alanthus* for the Lighthouse Service. It was probably with the help of Brown that James Whiteley secured his job overseeing the depot. The Whiteley children attended school in the city by sailing across the harbor in a cat-rigged bateau named "Pinckney," and the family attended church on Sundays at St. Michael's. Capt. Whiteley also kept a paternal eye on the harbor, where he and his family members were said to have rescued some 35 boaters and sailors over the course of nearly three decades.⁵

In 1882, the 6th District received a sparkling new inspection tender christened the USLHT *Wisteria*. She was placed under the command of the 52-year-old Capt. Brown, a Union Navy veteran and native Norwegian. It was a tradition in the Lighthouse Service that their tender ships were given botanical names indigenous to the area they were to be assigned. These specialized ships were called tenders because they "tended" to the needs of the scattered posts and navigation buoys of the Lighthouse Service. The *Wisteria* flew the triangular Lighthouse Service flag and was responsible for rebuilding and repairing river beacons, attending to the buoys, making inspections, and delivering supplies to the numerous lighthouses and lightboats. This 167-foot-long tender had been built for $55,000 and was propelled by side paddle wheels powered by a 'lobster-back" coal-burning steam boiler. Her iron hull was painted black, and its gray wooden decks supported a wooden superstructure that was painted white.

Based at Castle Pinckney, the *Wisteria* was a busy ship. In 1891 alone, her crew painted 362 buoys, patched 39 buoys, repaired 137 buoy chains, recovered

---

4 John Hairr, *A History of South Carolina Lighthouses* (Charleston, 2014), 135, 138, 144.

5 Department of Interior, *Official Register of the United States, Containing a list of Officers and Employees in the Civil, Military, and Naval Service* (Washington, DC, 1861-1905), 1881: 213-214, 220-221, 229-230; 1900 U.S. Federal Census for Moultrieville, Charleston, South Carolina; roll: 1521; 8.

The colorful Captain James Whiteley ran the Castle Pinckney Supply Depot from 1880 until his death in 1907. He and his wife, Annie Brown Whiteley, raised ten children on Shute's Folly.
Whitely Family Papers

11 buoys found adrift, and did 64 days of work at the Charleston Depot on Shute's Folly. The inspector of the district, Commander James Green, was required to visit the 182 lighthouses and post-lights in his territory quarterly, and the *Wisteria* carried him, as well as rations, coal, and supplies for the keeper, to his appointed stops. In 1891, Capt. Brown's ship, with a crew of six officers and 16 men, traveled 12,223 miles and burned 610 tons of coal. In December 1896, the "excellently appointed" ship would also have the honor of taking President Grover Cleveland to and from Georgetown down the Winyah Bay to the South Island plantation home of former Confederate Gen. Edward Porter Alexander. There, the 275-pound chief executive and sportsman had the opportunity to do some mallard hunting. The USLHT *Wisteria* served the Lighthouse Service in Charleston until 1907, when both Brown and Whiteley died from natural causes.[6]

In the early 1880s, the Castle Pinckney wharf suffered from teredo shipworms eating way at the pier supports. In response, yellow zinc sheathing was put around the piles, and 20 fender piles were driven along the sides of the wharf to give it further support. Ten thousand feet of decking was also replaced. Much of these repair efforts came to naught when the cyclone of August 25, 1885, damaged large segments of the wharf and tore the tin off the roof of the storehouse. This furious hurricane also stripped the roof off St. Michael's Church and destroyed most of the Cooper River wharves. A Norwegian bark and an Italian brig were both driven ashore at Shute's Folly. Repair efforts on the wharf commenced immediately with

---

6 Douglas Peterson, *United States Lighthouse Service Tenders, 1840-1939*, 27, 51; USLHT *Wisteria* Clipping File, NARA, RG 26, Box 27, NC-63, Entry 13-PDF; ARLHB, 1891:105; "The President's Luck," *The Birmingham News*, Dec. 17, 1896, 7.

An 1882 photograph of the iron side-wheel USLHT *Wisteria*. The lighthouse tender, under Captain Henry Brown, operated from Castle Pinckney until 1907. *United States Lighthouse Society*

42 piles driven into the sand, sheathed in no. 13 zinc, and then most of the decking was replaced with 3" board. Unfortunately, the shipworms would plague the wharf through the 1890s.[7]

There was no rest for the weary as the great Charleston Earthquake struck a year later, on August 31, 1886, killing 60 people and damaging or destroying more than 1,000 brick buildings. According to the *1886 Annual Lighthouse Report*, the janitor of the District Six headquarters, which was in the basement of the Exchange Building, was killed under the falling walls during the earthquake. Whiteley and Brown responded to the emergency by giving shelter to the homeless on both the *Wisteria* and on the island. With people fearful of sleeping in their homes at night, Brown resorted to constructing temporary tents on the wharf made from old sails and awnings.

On August 22, 1888, a bateau carrying three men and a boy capsized in rough seas. Their plight was observed from the Castle Pinckney wharf by Annie Whiteley, the wife of the depot keeper. Despite gale winds coming across the harbor from the

7 ARLHB, 1883:59, 1887:63.

The USLHT *Wisteria* operated from Castle Pinckney from 1882 until 1907. In this 1896 photograph, Captain Henry Brown and his officers look down from the bridge to a busy working deck. President Grover Cleveland spent a night on the ship in 1896. *The Whitely Family*

southwest, 13-year-old Maud King, Annie's daughter from her first marriage, and her sister-in-law, Mary Whiteley, did not hesitate but quickly lowered the small station boat into the angry water. The two young ladies reached the beleaguered men just as they were coming to the end of their endurance. The successful rescue gained the attention of the *Charleston News & Courier*, and soon the story was repeated in newspapers across the nation. Even two decades later, newspapers recounted Maud's story among those of women who had fought "storm and surf" to save lives. On March 11, 1889, a ceremony took place at the Charleston Customs House honoring the two brave young ladies who lived on Shute's Folly. In a ceremony presided over by Mayor Bryan in a packed courtroom, silver medals for lifesaving were presented to Maud and Mary by Commander R. D. Hitchcock of the 6th District. A fine yacht under construction in Charleston was immediately named the Maud King, in honor of the "Heroine of Castle Pinckney."[8]

The Great Sea Islands Hurricane of August 26 and 27, 1893, completely wrecked the Charleston Lighthouse Depot. The storm tore apart the storehouse

---

8 "They Saved Three Lives," *Charleston* [SC] *News & Courier*, Mar. 12, 1889, 8; "Women Who Proved Their Heroism in the Face of Death," *Washington Times*, Jul. 20, 1902, 2.

This 1892 sketch of the busy Castle Pinckney wharf appeared in *Harper's Weekly*. *Harper's Weekly*

and "lay open its contents to the action of the wind and the seas, and to scatter its stores in every direction and for long distances." Boats stored on the high ground behind the Castle were swept away, and great anchors weighing more than 4,000 pounds "were flung about the place like so much timber." The waves reached the Whiteley dwelling house, forcing Capt. Whiteley, his wife, and their ten children to seek shelter from the fury of the tempest on the leeward side of the Castle. Though waves occasionally broke over the family, even the smallest children came through without a whimper. Not surprisingly, the long wooden wharf at Castle Pinckney was rendered unusable. Inspector M. R. S. MacKenzie and Engineer Eric Bergland, the two highest-ranking officers in the 6th District, filled a joint report following the storm lamenting the fact that "there was a great demand made upon the depot for stores and supplies at the very time that its defects and weakness had deprived the district of its reserves." This Great Islands Hurricane of 1893 also washed away the Fort Sumter lighthouse, which had stood on a berm outside of the remains of the old brick fort. For the next two decades, ships entering the tricky Charleston Harbor entrance at night used a light from atop the steeple of St. Philip's Church to gain their bearings.

Capt. Bergland and Commander MacKenzie believed that Castle Pinckney was too exposed to hurricanes to be a viable location for a supply depot over the long term. "The lesson taught by all this," they wrote Washington, "is that our depots should be so built as to be able to resist the greatest storms, and so located as to permit the construction of solid buildings on firm foundations." They recommended that the supply depot at Castle Pinckney not be repaired but

Photograph of Maud King and her stepbrother Henry Whiteley taken around 1890. Maud was dubbed the "Heroine of Castle Pinckney" for her bravery in the 1888 rescue of three drowning men. Ten years later, Henry would gain attention for his discovery of human remains that were washed ashore on Shute's Folly. *The Whitely Family*

that the funds be used to purchase a more protected and proper site. They estimated that a new depot with twin docks built on an iron substructure would cost $110,300. Two years later, the estimate had been whittled down to $35,000.

In December 1894, Depot Keeper James Whiteley repulsed two raids of "whiskey constables" who believed that large amounts of contraband liquor were stored inside the Castle. In the morning, three South Carolina constables arrived at the wharf demanding the right to search the island. Whiteley replied that they were free, like any visitors, to walk about, but they could not open any boxes or packages unless they could produce a federal warrant, as Castle Pinckney belonged to a federal agency. Unable to do so, the three men returned to the city, but only after gaining permission to fish from the wharf the following Sunday. In the evening, Chief Constable Fant brought six constables with him but was refused the privilege of landing. Whiteley told an angry Fant that "he might have a thousand gallons, but that made no difference, that they could not land, as it was after sundown." The agents were welcome to return at the next sunrise. In the end, no contraband liquor was ever found at Castle Pinckney.[9]

The entrance to Charleston Harbor was dramatically changed in 1895 with the construction of stone mole jetties stretching seaward from Sullivan's Island and from Morris Island. These two lines of stone created a new channel so that ships could sail directly into the Atlantic Ocean rather than using pilots to find a crossing over the shifting sand bars. By funneling the tides through this newly created narrow gorge, U.S. engineers had increased the speed of the currents, thereby

---

9 "May Become a Casus Belli," *Charleston News* [SC] *and Courier*, Dec. 13, 1894, 12.

A 1900 photograph of small boats kept near the walls of Castle Pinckney. Depot keeper James Whiteley and his large family sought refuge here during the Great Sea Islands Hurricane of 1893. *Lowcountry Digital Library and the Museum of Charleston*

pushing the river sand away from the channel and off to the sides. Unfortunately, this change in the sweep of the tides has eroded much of Morris Island, washing away the remains of Battery Wagner and leaving the Morris Island Lighthouse no longer on dry land.[10]

On August 26, 1898, 19-year-old Henry "Bunty" Whiteley, the eldest son of James and Annie Whiteley, came across a human skull and a scattering of bones that had washed ashore on Shute's Folly. While most of the flesh had been torn away by crabs and fish, three clues to the possible identity of the skeleton were found along the water line: a torn regulation army jacket, a pair of trousers with a gold Elgin pattern watch in one of the pockets, and a foot with the shoe still attached. Stamped inside the shoe was J. McGowan. U.S.Q.D.M.B., 1888-1889. Determining who this deceased young soldier was, and how he came to meet his end, was of great interest to the newspapers and citizenry of Charleston for the next few weeks. Speculation centered on the five regiments of volunteers—the 2nd and 3rd Wisconsin, the 16th Pennsylvania, the 6th Illinois, and the 6th Massachusetts Regiments—who passed through Charleston that August on their

---

10 "Harbor's Main Channel Will Be Changed," *Charleston* [SC] *News & Courier*, Apr. 20, 1955, 1.

way to the fighting in Cuba and Puerto Rico. Unfortunately, no identification was ever made, and the remains were buried in the city's potter field.[11]

In the spring of 1897, Col. A. C. Kaufman, a banker, broker, and philanthropist from Charleston, made national headlines by aggressively campaigning for the transformation of Castle Pinckney into a sanitarium for aged and disabled Union veterans. A facility for 1,000 men would be dedicated to the memory of Maj. Anderson, the hero of Fort Sumter. Col. Kaufman told newspapers nationwide that the design for the new building would favor the Palace of the Doges in Venice. As the chief of the Vanderbilt Benevolent Association, Kaufman brought a delegation to the national Capitol and presented a petition to "Pitchfork Ben" Tillman. The South Carolina Senator agreed to sponsor the bill in the Senate, but he advised the petitioners to gain as many endorsements as possible, particularly that of the fraternal GAR—The Grand Army of the Republic. In August, the Union veterans at their national encampment in Buffalo voted unanimously to endorse the enterprise. Methodist Bishop John P. Newman, twice chaplain of the U.S. Senate, was another strong advocate for a Yankee sanitarium in the South, chiefly Charleston, the "City by the Sea." The South Carolina legislature followed suit on February 10, 1899, passing an act that deeded to the federal government the rest of Shute's Folly to build the sanitarium. Three weeks later, Tillman's bill with an appropriation of $100,000 for the project easily passed the Senate and was sent to the House Committee on Military Affairs. There it seemed to stall.

Having just fought a war with the nation of Spain over Cuba, Secretary of War Elihu Root did not want to see his military budget diluted by Civil War memorials. Hearing in September 1899 that the Lighthouse Board could not find an affordable site in Charleston for a new supply depot, Root endorsed a plan from the Treasury Department to build the depot on the Castle Pinckney site. Root was politically shrewd enough to write Miles Benjamin McSweeney, the governor of South Carolina, asking if the citizens of the Palmetto State had any "historical associations" to Castle Pinckney which would lead to their objection in the demolition of the Castle to make way for the new island buoy station.[12]

On October 10, 1899, Governor McSweeney held a contentious hearing in Columbia. Maj. George Edwards, president of the Charleston Chamber of Commerce, and Col. W. B. Wilson, president of the Merchant's Exchange

---

11 A modern-day check of the incomplete unit rosters from this period failed to produce a match; "A soldier's Skeleton," *Charleston* [SC] *News & Courier*, Aug. 27, 1898, 8; "A 'Missing' Soldier," *Charleston* [SC] *News & Courier*, Aug. 30, 1898, 4.

12 "The Harbor Sanitarium," *Evening* [SC] *Post*, Oct. 2, 1899, 2; "The Harbor Sanitarium," *Evening* [SC] *Post*, Oct. 17, 1898, 8; "A Home for Federal Veterans," *Augusta* [GA] *Chronicle*, Nov. 24, 1897, 6; "Secretary Root's Tact," *New York Times*, Oct. 1, 1899, 19.

Bank, advocated for a new buoy station on Castle Pinckney. Campaigning for the sanitarium was Col. Kaufman and his attorney William Parker. Edwards and Wilson argued that the soldier's home was a "very doubtful project at best." At the same time, the $150,000 proposed to be spent on the lighthouse supply base was a needed infusion for the Charleston economy. They argued that if the governor objected to the lighthouse project, it would be built in Jacksonville, Savannah, or some other point. Why not put the sanitarium in a different place in the Charleston vicinity? Kaufman rose to say that the proposed soldier's home and Castle Pinckney were forever linked. It was the "place of places." Their success in the U.S. Senate had hinged on two points: Castle Pinckney was an extremely healthy place but also an isolated place. The old soldiers would be removed "from bar rooms and other temptations." Dr. Edward H. Kellers, a prominent Charleston physician who had been a Confederate surgeon stationed at Castle Pinckney for eight months during the war, had been quoted a year earlier saying, "I can conceive of no healthier spot than Castle Pinckney Island. In fact, can conceive of none. The climate is perfect." It was the Lighthouse Board that needed to look harder for a suitable site near Charleston.

Known for his political "horse sense," Governor McSweeney perceived there was no consensus and wrote Secretary Root that a restored buoy station at Castle Pinckney was a local matter that "largely concerns the city of Charleston." He returned the decision to Washington, writing that Root was welcome to consult the mayor and city council of a divided Charleston. Seeing no real objection, Root considered the matter settled and ordered Maj. E. H. Ruffner to begin planning the new buoy station on Castle Pinckney. Col. Kaufman's dream of creating the Anderson Sanitarium had abruptly ended.[13]

The new blueprints for the Lighthouse Supply Station were innovative in that they recommended constructing the necessary buildings atop the old fort itself as a means of staying above the August and September hurricanes. After gaining permission from the War Department, construction got underway in 1900 and was finished, at a cost of $175,000, by the end of 1901. The fort's brick walls were reduced to 13 feet above the high tide mark, the sally port and embrasures were sealed with brick, and the fort's interior filled with 700 cubic yards of sand and mud. The earth was dredged from shoals in the vicinity and deposited on the wharf, where it was transferred to small railroad cars on a three-foot gauge track that ran from the wharf up and over the Castle walls. Once the 12,195 square ft.

---

13 "A Home for Federal Veterans," *Augusta* [SC] *Chronicle*, Nov. 24, 1897, 6; "Fate of Castle Pinckney," *Charleston* [SC] *News and Courier*, Oct. 11, 1899, 2; "Castle Pinckney Site," *Evening* [SC] *Post*, Oct. 30, 1899, 3.

A 1901 photograph showing the interior of Castle Pinckney shortly after a contractor had filled and leveled the interior space. Four buildings would be constructed atop this elevated platform.

National Archives

of raised level ground was established, a large storehouse, an oil house, an engine house, and a new two-story dwelling house for the keeper, James Whiteley, were constructed, all with solid brick walls. A new wharf, with piers made from stone and iron, was built that extended out to the channel and was two feet higher than the old one. Finally, the basement of the Exchange Building at the end of Broad Street was converted into offices for the district inspector and the working lamp shop. A year later, a new submarine cable for a telephone line was run between Charleston and Castle Pinckney.[14]

By 1902, the 6th District had three ships based at Castle Pinckney. Besides the large *Wisteria*, there was the USLHT *Pharos*, an old but reliable wooden schooner, and two relatively new naphtha-powered boats, the 33-ton *Water Lily* and the

14 ARLHB, 1900:115, 1903:68; "New Lighthouse Supply Station," *Evening* [SC] *Post*, Sep. 1, 1900, 4.

A 1902 photograph of the newly completed Depot for the 6th Lighthouse District. The lighthouse keeper's house was impressively large and featured indoor plumbing. It did not settle correctly and was torn down and replaced in 1907. *National Archives*

19-ton *Snow Drop*. At 1:00 a.m. on June 5, 1902, two faithful dogs began barking at the sight of a fire that had broken out in the oil house atop Castle Pinckney. An explosion of the 15,000 gallons of stored kerosene oil might have destroyed the entire station, but a heroic Capt. Whiteley entered the oil house by himself with a fire extinguisher. Soon cans of oil and turpentine were being thrown out of the building and away from the flames. The entire Whiteley clan, six children in all, including Maud King, now a bookkeeper for the Lighthouse Service, joined the battle and extinguished the fire after a two-hour fight.

On June 8, the *Charleston News and Courier* did an Expose entitled "Whiteley's Little Realm." The reporter was given a complete tour of the new facility that held 15,000 gallons of illuminating oil, 20,000 pounds of rope, and 4,000 gallons of paint "kept here at all times ready for immediate delivery." In the evening sunset, the visitor sat on the airy, broad second-floor piazza of the new keeper's cottage, admiring the picturesque view, and appreciating the "dreamy sort of stillness in the air." Across from him sat Whiteley, smoking a cigar in his big steamer chair. "You see," said the Englishman with a smile, "I have my own little kingdom and I am, in a measure, monarch of all I survey."[15]

Capt. Whiteley died in 1907, probably from cancer, and was replaced by Capt. Iver Larson, who had been a capable officer on the USLHT *Wisteria* for 16 years.

15 ARLHB, 1902,:145-147; "Captain Jim Whiteley Dies in Baltimore," *Evening* [SC] *Post*, May 21, 1907, 1; "Castle Pinckney," *The Wilmington* [NC] *Messenger*, Jun. 13, 1902, 1.

The 6th District underwent several changes beginning in 1907 under the energetic leadership of Commander Hugh Rodman. The largest was the conversion of the kerosene oil burning lamps in the various lighthouses to acetylene gas. A new tender named the *Cypress* was built in Norfolk and replaced the aging *Wisteria*. At Castle Pinckney, the keeper's house, that had been built in 1900, was torn down and replaced by a wooden bungalow with eight rooms and broad galleries on all sides. The 1900 house had never settled correctly, and the large cracks in its brick walls gave the Federal reservation an unsightly appearance. The abandoned buildings at marsh level were also torn down.[16]

In December 1910, Savannah sent a petition to Washington, D.C., requesting that the headquarters for the 6th District of the Lighthouse Service be moved to their city. The Georgians argued that Savannah was more centrally located in the district and offered "fine accommodations" for the lighthouse department and a supply base within the city limits. Castle Pinckney was criticized in the petition as being too difficult for ships to reach during low tide. Brunswick, Georgia, soon threw their hat in the ring as a candidate for the supply depot. In January 1912, after consulting with South Carolina Rep. George Swinton Legaré, the secretary of the treasury forwarded to Congress an appropriation request for $125,000 to build a new depot for the 6th District on the peninsula of Charleston. The appropriation was passed on October 22, 1913, and the site eventually selected was Chisolm's Rice Mill at the end of Tradd Street on the Ashley River. The 6.8-acre site would hold both the supply depot, district offices, and a new wharf, some 520 feet in length and built in three sections, that would allow the two tenders in the district, the *Cypress* and *Mangrove*, as well as the smaller District ships to all tie up at the same time. The old dock at Castle Pinckney was returned to the War Department on January 8, 1917, after occupancy by the Lighthouse Service for nearly 39 years.[17]

The present-day Ashley River Coast Guard Station at the end of Tradd Street in Charleston served as the supply depot for the Lighthouse Service from 1916 to 1939, when President Franklin Roosevelt placed the Service under the command of the United States Coast Guard. On the grounds of this modest base are several

---

16 "Improvements for our Light Houses," *Evening* [SC] *Post*, Nov. 23, 1907, 1; "May Use Acetyline Gas: Light House Department Contemplates Great Changes," *Charleston* [SC] *News & Courier*, Dec. 4, 1907, 6.

17 "Savannah Seeks Headquarters," *Charleston* [SC] *News & Courier*, Dec. 10, 1910, 10; "To Move Light House Depot," *Charleston* [SC] *News & Courier*, Jan. 9, 1912, 10; "Government Soon to Begin Work at Chisolm's Mill," *Charleston* [SC] *News & Courier*, Mar. 15, 1914, 11; *Annual report of the Commissioner of Lighthouses to the Secretary of Commerce and Labor for the fiscal year ended 1915* (Washington, D.C., 1916), 166.

monuments, including two mounted beacons, one red, and one green. They are tributes to the men who had repaired the navigational aids in Charleston since 1880. A little-known fact is that Capt. Henry Brown invented the first true bell buoy in Charleston in 1852 when he was a young lieutenant in the Lighthouse Service. The clanging sound from the buoy bells has often been the only warning mariners lost in the fog that dangerous conditions lay ahead. The Charleston Iron Works cast this first bell buoy, with Brown's design incorporating a 300-pound bell under which a cannon ball rolled around on a grooved plate. As the buoy was moved by the swells of the sea, the cannonball moved about, striking the sides of the bell.[18]

18 Walking Tour Brochure, Charleston Coast Guard Station, 2017; Thomas Tag, "Fog Bells by Thomas Tag," United States Lighthouse Society webpage, uslhs.org/node/1722.

Chapter 14

Holding the Hot Potato
1916–2011

On October 15, 1924, President Calvin Coolidge honored Castle Pinckney, along with the Statue of Liberty and Forts Pulaski, Marion, and Matanzas, by designating them as National Monuments. His proclamation was based on an act passed by Congress in 1906, and his action brought the number of National Monuments to 35.

This designation would only translate into modest federal funding for Castle Pinckney. In fact, the designation as a National Monument was withdrawn from Castle Pinckney in 1956 with the statement that the fort "was never an important link in the system of coastal fortifications." In the eyes of the National Park Service, the Castle had never come under hostile fire and therefore lacked "historical significance." In short, it was not in the same tier of national memory as Forts Moultrie and Sumter.[1]

After the Lighthouse Service left Castle Pinckney in 1916, the post was assumed by the U.S. Army Corps of Engineers and used as a warehouse and supply base. It was a neglected spot with a small day shift and a night watchman living in the office building, which had been converted into a small apartment. In 1919, the engineers built a two-story quarter boat by the wharf of the Castle. This strange-looking houseboat was painted yellow and would often be seen anchored near the Castle in the years to come. The boat provided acceptable quarters for up to 24 men employed by the department to do surveying projects. In 1929, the dilapidated

---

1 "A National Monument," *Charleston* [SC] *Evening Post*, Dec. 11, 1924, 10; "To Improve Monument," *Charleston* [SC] *News & Courier*, Oct. 19, 1927, 5.

A 1924 photograph of the U.S. Corps of Engineer Supply Depot at Castle Pinckney taken by an Army Air Force plane. *National Archives*

wharf was torn down and replaced by a creosoted timber pier measuring 100 ft. long and 30 ft. wide, and a quantity of riprap was deposited along the base of the seawall.[2]

Chief Edward M. Musgrove, a long-time employee of the Engineer Department, oversaw operations at the Castle through both the Great Depression and World War II. He was an experienced dredger and career public servant. In the summer of 1929, Edward P. McClellan, Inspector of the U.S. District Engineers, gained permission to move his family into the unoccupied lightkeeper's house atop Castle Pinckney. For the next six years, McClellan commuted by boat to his office in the Customs Building while his three children did the same going to public school on the Charleston peninsula. His son, E. P. McClellan, was so taken by his experience of growing up on a harbor island that he wrote a delightful book about his childhood memories. Published in 1998 and illustrated by Bill Smith, *The Ghosts of Castle Pinckney* describe this rambunctious boy's encounters with nature, his rides down the "dummy line" railroad to the wharf, and other unsupervised adventures. In all, a time that E. P. McClellan would describe as being "proximal to heaven."[3]

In the early 1930s, the different historical societies of Charleston, among them the Hibernian Society and the St. Andrew's Society, organized a memorial association under J. C. Dillingham to build a towering statue to Gen. William Moultrie and the defenders of the fort on Sullivan's Island. They intended to locate the memorial atop Castle Pinckney and, in the vein of the Statue of Liberty, have a grand welcoming landmark for Charleston Harbor. Any chance of success with this undertaking to mark the first victory in the War of Independence was dashed by the Great Depression, but it was a signal that many schemes and plans for the use of Castle Pinckney would be forthcoming in the next 75 years.

---

2 "Odd Residence Attracts Notice, *Evening* [SC] *Post*, Sep. 11, 1919, 10; "New Pier Constructed," *Charleston* [SC] *News & Courier*, Dec. 3, 1929, 2.

3 "Musgrove, 37 years With Government, in Group Honored," *Charleston* [SC] *News & Courier*, Mar. 15, 1944, 3; E. P. McClellan, Jr., *The Ghosts of Castle Pinckney* (Charleston, 1998), iv, 15.

In 1933, the national government transferred the ownership of Castle Pinckney and its 3.5 acres from the Department of the Army to the Interior Department. This did not immediately change the day-to-day use of the fort as it continued as a working supply base for the U.S. Army Engineers. In 1935, studies were commenced by the National Park Service to determine the feasibility of doing one large-scale restoration project at either Fort Johnson, Fort Moultrie, or Castle Pinckney. There was precedent for this, as the NPS had just completed restoration projects at Jamestown and Yorktown. Fort Sumter, at the time, was not an option as it remained part of the Department of the Army.[4]

By 1938 it was clear that the National Park Service was actively questioning the value of the Castle as a National Monument, especially one that was inaccessible to visitors. Herbert Kahler, the region's superintendent, wrote the head of the National Park Service that "it is believed that the area does not have sufficient historical value to warrant its classification as a National Monument." Khaler recommended that nothing be done to develop the site but to wait until the War Department was willing to relinquish their control of Fort Sumter.

In 1940 and 1941, South Carolina city, state, and federal politicians advocated for constructing an anchorage area in the Charleston Harbor for Navy cruisers, destroyers, and submarines. The Navy endorsed the idea of a site between Castle Pinckney and Fort Moultrie, but as a "low priority" project. Congressman Mendel Rivers pushed a 1.8-million-dollar appropriation for dredging the area through the committee on rivers and harbors. The appropriation for dredging even managed to pass the House of Representatives before losing momentum as the war ended. A T2-SE-A1 oil tanker named the *Castle Pinckney* did participate in World War II. Launched in late 1944 from Portland, Oregon, the tanker served in the Pacific Ocean theater before being purchased by Standard Oil and being renamed the *ESSO Everett*.[5]

In 1947, the Interior Department approached the Army about trading Castle Pinckney for Fort Sumter. NPS historian Dr. Charles Porter would write that year, "Castle Pinckney never had enough on the ball historically for us to make anything of it, but with Fort Sumter we can really do something worthwhile." Fort Sumter was made a National Monument the following year and transferred to the National Park Service. It was not until 1951 before Congress passed a bill transferring title

---

4 "Citadel Cadets to Hear Fulmer," *Evening* [SC] *Post*, Oct. 28, 1932, 6; "U.S. May Restore One of 3 Historic Charleston Sites," *Charleston* [SC] *News & Courier*, Jun. 24, 1935, 1.

5 "Engineer to Scan Navy Base Plans," *Charleston* [SC] *News & Courier*, Mar. 12, 1940, 14; "Committee Approves Anchorage," *Evening* [SC] *Post*, Apr. 30, 1941, 1; Auke Visser's Famous T-Tankers Pages, www.aukevisser.nl/t2tanker/.

of Castle Pinckney to the secretary of the army. Unwanted by the military, efforts began immediately to dispose of the old island fortress. South Carolina Senator Burnet Maybank inquired whether the City of Charleston, Charleston County, or the State of South Carolina wanted the 3.5-acre property. Only the City of Charleston expressed a mild interest in acquiring the surplus property, but there was little follow-up.[6]

On May 11, 1954, a small ceremony took place on the wharf of Castle Pinckney, formally transferring the old fort from the Army Corps of Engineers back to the National Park Service. Like the military, the NPS had little desire to keep this "red-headed step-child" and planned to dispose of it once the National Monument designation was removed. Rep. Mendel Rivers' bill, H.R. 3042, which abolished Castle Pinckney's status, worked its way through the 82nd Congress and was signed by President Eisenhower in March 1956.[7]

In 1955, Col. Clyde Zeigler, the district engineer for the Corps of Engineers, announced plans for a major realignment of Charleston's main shipping channel. Where ships had traditionally made a "dogleg" near Fort Johnson and sailed up the Cooper River with the city on its port side (left) and Castle Pinckney on its starboard side (right), the new 35-foot-deep channel would run between Mount Pleasant and Castle Pinckney along the old Hog Island Channel. Completed a year later, the new channel ran 22 miles in a nearly straight direction up the Cooper River from the harbor entrance to Goose Creek. Over the next fifty years, this channel realignment and subsequent channel deepening projects would dramatically erode the marsh island of Shute's Folly. In 1997, the Corps of Engineers reported that the island of Shute's Folly had shrunk from 224 acres to 41 acres. Marshland to the north and east of the Castle had been swept away by the channel current, and by 1999 waves were lapping the outer walls of Castle Pinckney itself. That year, the Corps and Ports Authority paid $256,935 to build a 260-foot breakwater of granite riprap to protect the structure from further erosion. The breakwater along the southeastern side of Shute's Folly is 40 ft. wide at its base and seven ft. wide at its top.[8]

6 "South's Share in Fort's History to be Stressed," *Evening* [SC] *Post*, Jul. 24, 1947, 16; Henrietta Means, "Interior Department's Offer to Give Castle Pinckney to Army Brings 'No, Thank You', *Charleston* [SC] *News & Courier*, Jun. 10, 1952, 18; "Maybank Seeks Transfer of Castle Pinckney," *Evening* [SC] *Post*, Jun. 17, 1952, 3.

7 Belvin Horres, "U.S. Park Service Takers Custody of Castle Pinckney," *Evening* [SC] *Post*, May 12, 1954, 5; H.R. 3042: An Act to abolish the Castle Pinckney Monument and to transfer the jurisdiction of the lands therein contained to the Secretary of the Army.

8 "Harbor's Main Channel Will Be Changed," *Charleston* [SC] *News & Courier*, Apr. 20, 1955, 1; Lynne Langley, "Fortification of Castle Pinckney Goal of Corps of Engineers, SPA," *Charleston* [SC]

Holding the Hot Potato: 1916–2011

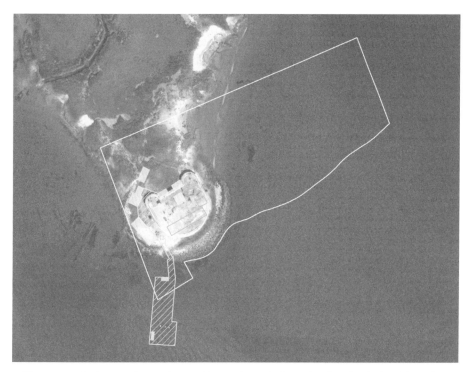

The rectangular box on this modern ariel view shows the boundary line for the land deeded to the Federal government from South Carolina in 1805. Most of this land has been washed away since the main harbor shipping channel was re-aligned in 1956. *John Fisher*

In 1956, the 100-room Castle Pinckney Inn opened on Cannon Street near the Ashley River Bridge. The motor court's spacious lobby featured a mural of Castle Pinckney painted by a prominent local artist, Maurice John Lenhardt. It was not long before several proposals were made that same year to acquire the Castle Pinckney island site. The mayor of Charleston, William Morrison, wanted to turn the old fortification into a sewage disposal plant, while the South Carolina Ports Authority wanted the spot as a dredge spoil area. One official wanted Castle Pinckney as an immigration station, and Capt. Chester Taylor wished to establish a nautical school atop the Castle. The winner would be the Ports Authority which purchased the 3.5 acres from the General Services Administration for $12,000. The March 4, 1958 deed transfer ceremony took place at the Castle with the assistance of a Citadel color guard. Authority Chairman Cotesworth Pinckney

---

Post & Courier, Sep. 2, 1997, 5; Tony Bartleme, "Erosion Threat," *Charleston* [SC] *Post & Courier*, Jul. 13, 1999, B1.

Means, a direct descendant of Gen. Thomas Pinckney, announced that the marsh area would be used as a dredge spoil area for silt and mud pumped from the harbor channel. At the same time, he proposed that the fortress be excavated, restored, and turned into a state park and museum.[9]

A Castle Pinckney Restoration Group was soon established to work with Chairman Means. Chairman of the Charleston Museum Milby Burton headed the committee. The summer of 1958 saw underbrush and trees removed from the parapets and test borings made to determine how much sand and dirt would need to be excavated from the fort's interior. By 1961, however, Chairman Means made it clear that no funding was available to restore Castle Pinckney. Burton's committee was disbanded a year later, and the restoration plans were abandoned. In 1964, the Ports Authority was rebuffed in their attempt to give the Castle Pinckney property back to the National Park Service. Left with few options, the Ports Authority transferred the title in trust on October 30, 1964, to the South Carolina Shrine Organization. Two temples, the Omar Temple of Charleston and the Hejaz Temple of Greenville, would oversee a new feasibility project. One year later, the Shriners returned the property to the Ports Authority after determining that any restoration project would be "impractical."[10]

Abandoned and virtually ignored, the various wooden buildings around and atop Castle Pinckney sat empty from 1933 until 1967. The shallow waters around the Castle remained popular with local fishermen seeking Seatrout, Red Drum, Black Seabass, and Jack Crevelle. The curious among them were often seen poking around the old buildings. Two days before Christmas 1967, a fire swept through the old 1906 caretaker's house atop the Castle. Aided by a 30-mile-per-hour wind, the fire faced little opposition from crews sent from the Charleston Fire Department and the Coast Guard. Their attention focused on keeping the fire from spreading to the nearby warehouse. No investigation of the cause of the fire was ever performed.

On April 23, 1968, the board of the Ports Authority agreed to transfer the title of Castle Pinckney to the Fort Sumter Camp 1269 of the Sons of Confederate Veterans. Camp commander Daniel Ravenel reported that the Charleston

---

9 "Formal Opening Set for Giant Motel," *Charleston* [SC] *News & Courier*, Aug. 27, 1956, 8; "Taylor Asks City to Withdraw Claim to Castle Pinckney," *Charleston* [SC] *News & Courier*, Apr. 17, 1956, 10; Tom Perry, "Deed to Castle Pinckney Goes to the Port Authority," *Charleston* [SC] *News & Courier*, Mar. 5, 1958, 12. The Bee Street Garage on the MUSC Campus is where the Castle Pinckney Inn once stood.

10 Coyte White, "Historic Fort May Be Restored," *Charleston* [SC] *News & Courier*, Feb. 1, 1961, 11; "Castle Pinckney Restoration Plans Apparently Halted," *Evening* [SC] *Post*, Jun. 22, 1962, 12; "Deeded in Trust to Shrine Group," *Evening* [SC] *Post*, Oct. 30, 1964, 1; "Shrine Temples Drop Plans For Castle Pinckney Fort," *Charleston* [SC] *News & Courier*, Oct. 28, 1965, 13.

camp's goal was to establish a monument and museum in the Castle in time for the Tricentennial Celebration in 1970. James Percival Petit, the adjutant of the camp and a respected historian, wrote one of the better articles on the history of Castle Pinckney in the July 1969 edition of the *Sandlapper* magazine. Petit described Castle Pinckney as "the only remaining castle-type fortress in America capable of practical restoration." On April 12, 1969, with Mayor Palmer Galliard in attendance, the SCV camp performed a dedication ceremony on the 108th anniversary of the firing on Fort Sumter "to all persons who have defended the city in time of war." It was the first time in more than a century that the Confederate flag had flown above Castle Pinckney, and the strains of "Dixie" once again echoed within the walls of the fortification.[11]

An enthusiastic Fort Sumter SCV Camp launched fundraising drives, cleaned up the site, and tore down the dilapidated warehouse atop the Castle. After filing a detailed application, the camp, with the assistance of the South Carolina Department of Archives and History, was able, in August 1970, to place Castle Pinckney on the National Register of Historic Places. Their application described a restoration program divided into seven phases. Unfortunately, the heritage group found their ambitions to be a tall order, and a lack of funds chronically hampered their efforts. Excitement was generated when Project Director James A. Turner unearthed a 10-inch Columbiad in September 1969. By March 1975, however, J. Percival Petit, now the camp commander, and Lt. Commander Vic Brandt III reported that their modest treasury was exhausted, and that no prominent donor had stepped forward to move the restoration project forward. In 1976, a $10,000 grant from the American Revolution Bicentennial Commission did allow for some masonry wall repairs and removing portions of the delipidated pier.[12]

In 1977, a $15,000 grant from the Coastal Plains Commission allowed the SCV to hire Wilbur Smith Associates of Columbia to do a feasibility study on the restoration and future use of Castle Pinckney. Another grant gave the University of South Carolina Institute of Archeology funds to conduct studies on the condition of the Castle walls. Frank Inabinet, the consultant in charge of the feasibility study, submitted his 100-page report to Vic Brandt and the SCV Camp in February

---

11 "No Investigation of Fire at Castle Pinckney Likely," *Charleston* [SC] *Post & Courier*, Dec. 24, 1957, 15; "Sons of Confederate Veterans to Acquire Castle Pinckney," *Charleston* [SC] *Post & Courier*, Apr. 24, 1968, 15; James P. Petit & James A. Turner, "Out of Oblivion: Castle Pinckney," *Sandlapper* (July 1969), vol. 2, 7:66; Belvin Horres, "Fort Consecrated to Our Defenders," *Evening* [SC] *Post*, Apr. 12, 1969, 11.

12 National Register of Historic Places Nomination form for Castle Pinckney filed on Jul. 16, 1970; Barbara Williams, "Delegation Okays School Bill," Charleston [SC] *Post & Courier*, Mar. 25, 1975, 11.

1978. Inabinet believed that the first improvements, such as building a fishing pier with a bait & tackle shop, should be designed, and built to generate future revenue that could be used for historic preservation. The site would also require a self-contained utility system and a new concrete dock for ferry boats to pull up to. He warned that permits from different government agencies would be a significant challenge. Inabinet presented several concept ideas that would add a marina, restaurant, general store, museum, and a sandy beach area to the property. The first five years of his plan would require a capital investment of $265,500. In 1984, the Sons of Confederate Veterans, realizing their ambitions exceeded their capabilities, quietly gave Castle Pinckney back to the South Carolina Ports Authority, but not before the City of Charleston had requested and been given 300 or so loose bricks from the site to repair and replace those on the sidewalk in downtown Washington Park.[13]

Over the next 20 years, there would be turmoil at the South Carolina Ports Authority over finding a historical association or government entity that would assume responsibility for restoring Castle Pinckney. In 2006, Robert Behre, a reporter at the *Post & Courier*, wrote, "While humans are having a hard time figuring out just what to do with Castle Pinckney, another species seems to have things all figured out." Castle Pinckney had become home to more than 200 brown pelican nests. According to state biologists, the pelicans had, somewhere between 1999 and 2003, begun moving their nests from the marsh to the fort itself. Their continued presence leaves an undeniably powerful odor and makes human visits to the Castle problematic during the breeding season from March to October.

In June 2011, the board of the State Ports Authority agreed to transfer ownership of the Castle Pinckney property to the Sons of Confederate Veterans Camp 1269 for, symbolically enough, a framed Confederate ten-dollar bill. There was now renewed hope for the old fort.[14]

---

13 Jack Leland, "Castle Pinckney Studied," *Evening* [SC] *Post*, Jun. 15, 1977, 1; Frank Inabinet, Castle Pinckney *Restoration: A Development Program*, submitted by Wilbur Smith & Associates for the Fort Sumter SCV Camp, Feb. 1978.

14 Robert Behre, "A Castle for the Birds," Charleston [SC] *Post & Courier*, Dec. 18, 2006, B1; David Slade, "New Hope for Old Fort," Charleston [SC] *Post & Courier*, Jun. 22, 2011, B7.

Castle Pinckney was in an overgrown state when it was sold by the South Carolina Ports Authority to the Fort Sumter Camp of the Sons of Confederate Veterans in 2011. *John Diskes*

Epilogue

The preservation of Castle Pinckney remains a daunting task. For the last eight decades, the fortification has sat ignored, a forgotten monument to the past, with most of its secrets long forgotten. Since 2012, the stewardship of Castle Pinckney has again rested with the Fort Sumter Sons of Confederate Veterans Camp 1269. In January 2013, the camp established The Castle Pinckney Historical Preservation Society (www.castlepinckney.org), a dedicated 501c3 non-profit foundation focused on the ongoing maintenance and care of Castle Pinckney, as well as raising funds for its long-term preservation. Charlestonian Robert Mikell has been the president of the Society since its inception.[1]

The first order of business has been removing trash and cutting back the dense foliage that has grown atop the Castle. Folk tales that the old remains were infested with rats and poisonous snakes proved to be surprisingly true. With the flat top of the old ruin largely cleared, a large 35 ft. flagpole was erected close to where the Castle's original flagpole once stood. Flags of historical significance and national symbolism, including those of the United States, South Carolina, and the Confederate States of America, are now raised at different times of the year over the Castle. The rich maritime history of Charleston and visits to the city by important dignitaries have also led to the flying of the national flags of Ireland, France, England, Israel, and Ukraine.

---

1 The Castle Pinckney Historic Preservation Society has tax-exempt status with the Internal Revenue Service, and contributions are therefore deductible from federal income taxes.

Citadel cadets flying "Big Red" over Castle Pinckney in 2019. Behind Shute's Folly is the Arthur Ravenel, Jr. Bridge and the USS *Yorktown* aircraft carrier. *Cliff Roberts*

There has been speculation that Civil War cannons and military ordnance are still buried in the dirt that engineers used to fill the Castle's interior parade ground in 1900. The muzzle of one 10-inch Columbiad was exposed to visitors in the 1960s. Its barrel casting number #1687 shows it to have been cast at the Tredegar Foundry in Richmond in November 1862. Another rumor from the 1980s was that the gun had been stolen on a flatbed barge in the dead of night. This always seemed extremely unlikely as the barrel of this giant cannon weighs 13,365 pounds. It is likely that the four heavy guns that protected the fort in 1865 remain buried in the dirt, while it is probable that the ordnance in the magazine was removed before the 1900 renovation took place.

Castle Pinckney is an archeological time capsule in the harbor of one of North America's most historic cities. As such, the Society approached the South Carolina Institute for Archeology and Anthropology (SCIAA) for assistance and guidance as work began to excavate and clear the site. In March 2019, John Fisher, a state archeologist, and former U.S. combat engineer, made the first of more than a dozen visits to the Castle. Often accompanied by students and volunteers from the Fort Sumter Camp, his controlled digs have proved fruitful. On a sunny afternoon in February 2020, a six-foot probe hit iron, and a test trench revealed the curved surface of a gun barrel. A second 10-inch Columbiad had been found to the excitement of all present. This cannon, with casting number #1676, was made at the Tredegar

Identified as barrel #1676 and affectionately referred to today as "Abigail," this Tredegar Foundry 10-inch Columbiad rests next to one of the Castle's pintle mount blocks which anchored a 24-pdr. cannon. *Matthew Locke*

Foundry in October 1862. Near the second gun were two massive granite pintle mount blocks, which in 1860-61 would have allowed the wooden barbette carriages that mounted the 24-pounders to pivot, and traverse left to right. The pintle and carriage would have had a combined weight of over 8,000 pounds.

John Fisher has a place in his soul for Castle Pinckney, a sentiment shared by many of us who have walked its ramparts. Over the course of many digs, his teams have uncovered hundreds of artifacts dating from the lighthouse depot years or even decades earlier. Among the finds are a brass 1832 U.S. military jacket button, a small civilian button, bottles of brightly colored paint, pieces of cut pig bone, domestic crockery, glassware, and complete beer bottles. Glass marbles that children played with were found near where the kitchen of the second house would have stood. Near the foundation of the second house, two solid shot cannon balls were uncovered, perhaps found by the McClellan children when they lived on the island.

In the summer of 2019, the first international excavation of Castle Pinckney began. In conjunction with the SCIAA and with the assistance and blessing of the Castle Pinckney Preservation Society, students and teachers from the University College of London undertook a three-week excavation of sections of the fort's interior. Their goals were to create a series of test pits, determine what was left of the barracks, stabilize and expand the ground that is surrounding both of the identified cannons, as well as record the remaining brick architecture that made up the Castle's rampart on which the barbette battery would have stood. Significant work was done, and the results were encouraging. However, as with almost every excavation done at the Castle, each question answered presents a set of new questions. Sadly, the COVID-19 Pandemic delayed the return of the

A drone photograph taken at the end of a two-week excavation in 2022. Clearly visible are the 1901 foundations of the storage warehouse and oil house. Next to the Castle walls are the remains of the six ft. thick brick reinforcement wall built in the 1850s to further protect the ordnance storerooms from artillery shelling. Water damage to the brickwork of the 1811 circular wall is evident. *Jason Parker*

British archeology students, led by Senior Archeologist Giles Dawkes, until the summer of 2022.

In early 2021, 24-hour security cameras were mounted at the Castle to provide security and monitor the once-endangered Eastern Brown Pelicans during their nesting season. The cameras are powered by both a solar panel and a turning wind generator. With a wingspan of between six and eight ft. and weighing between seven and ten lbs., the Eastern Brown Pelican is the only variety of pelican in the world that is not white. Their nests typically hold two or three white eggs, and the mating adult pair share incubation duties for roughly 28 days. The pelican nests cover much of the interior of the Castle or are scattered among the low scrubby bushes outside the brick walls.

One recently accomplished task has been the construction of a security gate in front of the Castle's sally port. This could not be done until the area around the sally port had been fully excavated and the entrance to the fortress fully exposed for the first time in a hundred years. The handsome entrance has beautifully carved brownstone rock pillars on either side of the gate. This brownstone also decorated much of the top level of the Castle and the numerous embrasures. The archeologists also discovered a carved granite flood sill at the bottom of the sally port designed

Archeologist John Fisher excavating the sally port entrance in 2022. The excavation revealed a tapered granite flood sill installed before 1860 across the bottom of the sally port to serve as a barrier against tidal flooding. *Matthew Locke*

to prevent a tidal surge from flooding through the main gate. This feature also explained why the Castle's main gates opened outwards, unlike the inward-facing gates of most fortifications.

At present, there are two ongoing priorities. The first is to ensure safe access to the site, and the second is to reinforce the structural integrity of the Castle itself. There is presently no wharf for boats to tie up to, so the archeological work undertaken to date has been restricted largely to what can be transported to the island in small flat-bottomed boats. Equipment must then be carried through the mud and over granite boulders by hand. The Society has recently secured a permit to construct a permanent dock by the Castle. Access to the site will remain restricted to approved visitors.

The second major challenge has dire consequences if left unaddressed. In short, it is increasingly apparent that the harbor is steadily consuming Shute's Folly and that the Castle, at its southern tip, is slowly sinking or subsiding into the pluff mud. What was, in the mid-1700s, an island of over 220 acres has now been reduced to little less than 25 acres, and much of what remains is swampy tidal marsh with little ground that remains dry at low tide. The brick foundation of the Castle rests on hundreds of wooden piles sunk vertically into the soft earth at the time of its 19th-century construction. While not a perfect solution, the piles maintained the Castle's structural integrity, through time and tides, until 1862, when Confederates placed heavy sandbags around the scarp wall to defend against rifled enemy artillery. By 1863, the brick walls were cracking and sinking from this added weight. Confederate authorities had new pilings driven into the earth around the perimeter of the Castle so that heavier guns could be mounted on the parapet and tons of earth and sand could be shipped in and placed on either side of the old brick walls. In 1901, tons of dirt, sand, building material, and concrete was brought in to build a flat surface along the top of the Castle. This added weight has only exacerbated the subsistence issue. Finally, the almost continuous dredging of the Hog Island Channel, now to a depth of 52 ft. at low tide, is eroding the island and undermining the Castle's brick foundation. Comparing historical photographs with what is exposed today reveals that the brick walls have sunk as much as three feet in some places. This is in addition to the significant vertical cracks, noticeable swelling, and displacement of brickwork that is evident everywhere, but especially around the Castle's eastern bastion and eastern wall, which face the Hog Island Channel.

Despite these significant challenges, the Castle Pinckney Historical Preservation Society is determined that this site, with 220 years of Southern history, a fortification that once held Charleston by the bridal, and one that saw the first military action of what would become the American Civil War, will not be abandoned, nor forgotten. The story told in these pages should again let Castle Pinckney take its rightful place alongside its sister forts of Moultrie, Johnson, and Sumter as the sentinels of Charleston's historical legacy.

Appendix 1

Patriotic Toasts Given at the Naming Ceremony at Fort Pinckney, September 27, 1798

The following are the patriotic toasts that were drank amidst the cheers of the Company, which dispersed early in the evening, highly pleased with the construction of the Fort, and the polite attention of the Engineer (George Izard). Taken from the *Newport Mercury*, October 30, 1798.

1. Fort Pinckney
2. The President of the United States
3. The Commander in Chief of the armies of the United States
4. Major-general Pinckney
5. The officers and soldiers of the American army.
6. The American navy.
7. The People—May they never forget their rights, and always remember their duties.
8. To the memory of those who have fallen in defense of the liberties and independence of our country.
9. The Congress of the United States.
10. Agriculture and Commerce.
11. The Nations in friendship with America.
12. Confusion to the foreign and domestic enemies of America.
13. The fair sex.
14. General (Justice John) Marshall
15. Our ministers abroad.
16. A speedy and lasting peace to all the world.

Appendix 2

1814 Resolution Written from Castle Pinckney in Consequence of the Restoration of Capt. Gill by President James Madison and Signed by Col. William Drayton and Other Officers of the Army

Castle Pinckney, Charleston   1 April 1814

To: Colonel Walback, Adjutant General

Sir, Enclosed I have the honor to transmit you a copy of resolutions entered into by the Officers of the Army in the harbour of Charleston.

With the greatest respect I have the honor to be, Sir, Your most obedient servant,

Jacob Warley, Lieutenant, 2nd Regiment of Artillery

Charleston Harbour   28 February 1814

The undersigned Officers of the United States Army having learned with much surprise that Captain Robert M. Gill of the 2nd Regiment of Artillery who had been dismissed from the Service on charges of "practicing an imposition, for cowardice, & generally for conduct unbecoming of an Officer and a Gentleman" has been returned to his former rank in the Army. And being strongly imbued with the idea that after the solemn decision of the Court composed of men of Honor and unimpeachable Integrity upon a full and impartial hearing, and that decision so entered by the Commanding General, There can be no doubt of the truth of the allegations, Do Resolve:

1st That they will have no personal intercourse with Captain Gill beyond the strict line of their duty and that they do not conceive him to be entitled to the Privileges and Respect due to a Gentleman and a Man of Honor.

2nd That a copy of these Resolutions be transmitted to each post in the Harbour of Charleston and to other military Posts in the Sixth District and to the Adjutant General's office at Washington City.

Drayton, William, Col., 18th Reg. of Inf.; Forney, Dell, Maj., 2nd Arty.; Campbell, James, Maj., 43rd Inf.; Boudlow, Jacob, Capt., 2nd Arty.; Donoho, Sanders, Capt., 2nd Arty.; Padget W. G., 18th Inf.; Dent, James, Judge Advocate 6th District; Smith, William, Ensign, 18th Inf.; James, J. Hamilton, Capt., 8th Inf.; Brown, Lowndes, Lt., 2nd Arty.; Johnson, R. Post, Lt., 18th Inf.; Warley, Felix B., Capt., 8th Inf.; Stevens, Joseph L., Hospital Surg.; Champlin, S., Arty.; McBane, Robert, Lt., 18th Inf.; Blount, John G., Capt., 18th Inf.; Smith, J. L., 2nd Lt., Engineers; Grimke, J., Acting Surg., 18th Inf; Taylor, William, Capt., 18th Inf.; Butler, George, Capt., 18th Inf.; Soukett, John H., Hospital Surgeon; Dearing, James H., Lt., 2nd Arty.; Taylor, George, Ensign, 18th Inf.: Tisdale, William, Lt., 18th Inf.; Taylor, H. P., Capt., 18th Inf.; Cowen, William James, Lt., 2nd Arty.; Wathens, J., Lt., 18th Inf.; Aiken, Thomas, Hospital Surg., 6th District; Warley, Jacob, Lt., 2nd Arty.; Sharpe, Edwin, Lt., 2nd Arty.; Elfie, Thomas, Lt., 1st Arty.; Niel, Adrian, Lt., 2nd Arty.

Appendix 3

Clothing Received at Castle Pinckney, November 5. 1832, from Maj. G. Bender, Quartermaster

In the private collection of author Cliff Roberts

(4) Four Sergeants Coats, (2) Two Corporals Coats, (2) Two Musicians Coats, (30) Thirty Privates Coats, (4) Four Sergeants Cotton Overalls; (4) Four sergeant cotton Shirts; (10) Ten Leather Stocks, (20) Twenty Shakos & Letters, (80) Eighty Pairs. Stockings, (90) Ninity Pairs Socks, (15) Fifteen Haversacks, (30) Thirty Trousers, (80) Eighty Gray Wool Overalls, (20) Twenty Frocks, (2) Two Axes, (70) Seventy Flannel Shirts, (80) Eighty Privates Cotton Overalls, (20) Twenty Privates cotton Jackets, (80) Eighty Privates cotton   Shirts, (40) Forty Gray Jackets, (25) Twenty Five Blankets, (20) Twenty Great Coats, (80) Eighty Pairs Shoes, (10) Ten Knapsacks, (40) Forty Bands, (40) Forty Pompoms, (15) Fifteen Caps & Covers, (15) Fifteen Plates, (20) Twenty Cockades, (80) Eighty Pairs Land Bootees.

Signed for by H Saunders, Captain of Artillery

Appendix 4

An 1834 "Memorial" Petition of the Officers of Castle Pinckney Requesting a Transfer from Charleston at the Conclusion of the Nullification Crisis

July 8, 1833   To Major General Alexander Macomb commanding the army.

The memorial of the officers of the army, stationed in the harbour of Charleston S. C., respectfully presents, that, the undersigned served in the said harbour during the past winter and are now exceedingly disagreeably situated in regard to the citizens of Charleston.

A number of the undersigned were on this station at the commencement of the unpleasant excitement consequent upon the measures of South Carolina, for nullifying the laws of congress and shared in the difficult and delicate, though necessary duty of preparation for resisting the refractory state, and in consequence of their integrity to the government they have the honor to serve, they are looked upon with jealousy and distrust.—

From report, the citizens of Charleston, have hitherto been [complimented] for their civilities to the military; but now convinced as they are of the determined adherence of the officers on this station to the constitution and the principles of the General Government, we are ruined and treated as unworthy strangers and it has been intimated to one of the undersigned from respectable authority, that the dominant party have it in contemplation to apply to the executive for the removal of all those who have thus become obnoxious to their dislike.—

The undersigned having served faithfully during the late painful excitement arduous preparation for resisting their discontented fellow citizens, and knowing, that the very fact of their willingness to oppose nullification, secession or rebellion, has shut them out from all intercourse and forever closed the door of that good— fellowship which ought to exist between the citizens and the military throughout the country, respectfully entertain the opinion that the General-In-Chief, will agree with them, that it is but admirable on their part to wish anxiously to be withdrawn from this harbour and give place to others who have not incurred in the discharge of their duty the distrust and dislike of the South Carolinians.—

The undersigned would finally, respectfully suggest for the consideration of the General-in-Chief, whether, in addition to its being ardently desired by themselves, the measure would not be sanctioned by the policy of the government.

Saunders, Henry, Capt., Co. A, Artillery
Mallory, H.S., Lt., Co. H, 1st Regiment Artillery
Bailey, Jno., Lt., 1st Regiment Artillery
Williamson, John, Lt., 1st Regiment Artillery
Hawkins, H.S., Asst. Surgeon.
Heiskell, H. L., Surgeon
Turner, George W., Lt., 1st Regiment
Ammen, Jacob, Lt., 1st Regiment Artillery

Appendix 5

Field & Staff Officers of the 1st Rifles, South Carolina Militia (1860-1861)

Published in the *Charleston Mercury*, April 22, 1861

Pettigrew, J. J., Col.; Branch, J. L., Lt. Col.; Capers, Elison, Maj.; Barker, T. G., Adjt.; Hanckel, A. S., QM.; Perkins, R. G., QM Sgt.; Young, L. G., Cmsy.; Gregg, B., Cmsy. Sgt.

MEDICAL STAFF
Trescot, G. E., M.D., Surg.; Ogier, T. L., Jr., M.D., Asst. Surg.

COMPANY OFFICERS.

Washington Light Infantry:
Simonton, C. H., Capt.; Wilkie, Oct., 1st Lt.; Lloyd, E. W., 2nd Lt.; Carson, J. M., 3rd Lt.;

German Riflemen:
Small, Jacob, Capt.; Young, H. Ed., 1st Lt.; Lengnick, A., 2nd Lt.; Mensing, H., 3rd Lt.;

Moultrie Guard:
Palmer. B. W., Capt.; Barnwell, —., 1st Lt.; Flagg, C. E. B., 2nd Lt.; Stoney, W. E., 3rd Lt.;

Palmetto Riflemen:
Melchers, A., Capt.; Issertel, R., 1st Lt.; Schuckmann, P., 2nd Lt.; Cohen, A. D., 3rd Lt.;

Carolina Light Infantry:
Pinckney, B. G., Capt.; Chambers, Jno., 1st Lt.; Lee, Hudson, 2nd Lt.; Munroe, Jno., 3rd Lt.;

Meagher Guard:
McCrady, Ed., Jr., Capt.; Heyward, W. N., 1st Lt.; Parker, P. P., 2nd Lt.; McCarthy, John, 3rd Lt.;

Zouave Cadets:
Chichester, C. E., Capt.; Gilchrist R. C., 1st Lt.; White, E. John, 2nd Lt.; Walpole, B. M., 3rd Lt.

Appendix 6

1858 Returns of Officers and Privates in the Meagher Guard

In the McCrady Family Papers, South Carolina Historical Society

13 OFFICERS

Daly, Edward, Capt.; Lowndes, James, 1st Lt.;Parker, O.P., 2nd Lt.; O'Connor, Barthol, 1st Sgt.; Murphy, John E., 2nd Sgt.; Hargrave, John, 3rd Sgt.; Baker, William, 4th Sgt.; Furlong, John, 1st Cpl.; Cleary, Maurice, 2nd Cpl.; Sheridan, Thomas, 3rd Cpl.; Beatty, Joseph, 4th Cpl.; O'Grady Michael, 5th Cpl.; Kilroy, Michael, 6th Cpl.

51 PRIVATES

Barry, Daniel; Barry, Robert; Birmingham, John; Cannon, Patrick; Carr, John; Cleary, Patrick; Clinton, James; Collins, Michael; Conroy, John; Cummins, William; Delaney, James; Deveran, William; Dunne, Michael; Fitzgerald, Stephen; Foley, William; Graham, James; Hartigan, Thomas; Harvey, James; Harvey, Michael; Hennesy, Thomas; Irwin, Christopher; Kennedy, James; Kilhooley, Patrick; Longheran, M.Y.; Malone, Philip; McCaffer, John; McCarroll, Henry; McCarthy, John; McCarthy, Timothy; McDonnell, Thomas; McGrath, Michael; McLoughlin, Patrick; Morris, Richard; Murray, Thomas; Nolan, James; O'Brien, William; O'Donnell, Micheal; O'Keeffe, Patrick; O'Roarke, John; Pierce, Matthew; Powers, Daniel; Ryan, Edward; Ryan, Michael; Sheridan, John; Smith, John; Staunton, Michael; Walsh, John; Walsh, Patrick; Weldon, Patrick; White, David

Appendix 7

Roster of the Washington Light Infantry (WLI)

Listed below is the Roll Call of the WLI on July 4, 1860, and who, according to the unit's records, were still on the active member roster in January 1861. Columns list name, militia rank, date of joining the WLI, and subsequent Confederate service. Octavius Wilkes commanded Company A of the WLI and Edward Lloyd commanded Company B. Company C of the WLI was a militia/local defense company organized independently of the Confederate and state military authorities to assist in the defense of the city in times of emergency and comprised of men unfit or exempted from regular military service.

OFFICERS

Name	Rank	Date	Service
Simonton, Charles H.	Capt.	18 Jan 1850	Co. A, WLI, 25th S. C. V.
Wilkie, Octavius	1st Lt.	22 May 1846	Co. B, WLI, 25th S. C. V.
Lloyd, Edward W.	2nd Lt.	30 Jun 1846	Co. B, WLI, 25th S. C. V.
Carson, James M.	3rd Lt.	30 Apr 1851	Co. A, WLI, 25th S. C. V.
Robb, James Jr.	Orderly Sgt.	16 Apr 1849	Co. A, B, WLI, 25th S. C. V.
Blum, Robert A.	2nd Sgt.	29 Apr 1851	Co. B. WLI, 25th S. C. V.
Courtney, Wm. A.	3rd Sgt.	29 Apr 1851	General and Staff Officer C. S. A.
Schulte, J. Hermann	4th Sgt.	29 Apr 1851	Co. B, WLI 25th S. C. V.
Evans, Benjamin F.	5th Sgt.	22 Nov 1852	
Olney, Hiram B.	1st Cpl.	22 Nov 1855	Co. A, WLI, 25th S. C. V.
Ravenel, Danl., Jr.,	2nd Cpl.	22 Aug 1856	Capt. Parkers Co. (Marion Art'y)
Greer, William R.	3rd Cpl.	10 Feb 1857	Co. B, WLI, 25th S. C. V.
Finley, William W.	4th Cpl.	20 Aug 1856	Co. A, WLI, 25th S. C. V.
Marsh, David C.	5th Cpl.	4 Jan 1855	Co. A, WLI, 25th S. C. V.
DeTreville, R.	6th Cpl.	21 Feb 1859	Co. C, 1st SC Infantry

PRIVATES

Artman, John	5 Jul 1841	Martins Co. 3rd Regt State Troops
Ancrum, James Hasell, Jr.	21 Jun 1860	Co. A, Hamptons Legion
Burger, Samuel J.	23 Jun 1848	Co. B. WLI 25th S. C. V.
Branch, John L.	3 Jul 1858	
Bird, Charlton H.	16 Feb 1857	Co. C. WLI***
Bomar, J. Edward	20 Apr 1858	Co. B. WLI, 25th S. C. V.
Brodie, Thomas F.	6 Feb 1854	Co. C. WLI
Bacot, Pierre	21 Feb 1859	Co. K, C, 1st SC Infantry
Barbot, Julian	21 Feb 1860	Co. A. WLI, 25th S. C. V.
Bomar, Robert A/H	21 Jun 1860	Co. A. Hampton Legion
Brown, J. B.	12 Jul 1852	
Browne, Samuel N.	18 Jun 1860	Co. B. WLI, 25th S. C. V.
Brantley, Beverly B.	22 Jun 1860	Co. A. Hampton Legion
Black, C. T.	1 Jul 1860	Co. B. WLI, 25th S. C. V.
Calder, Alexander, Jr.	18 Jun 1837	Co. C. WLI
Calder, James, Jr.	6 May 1845	Co. A, WLI, 25th S. C. V.
Conner, George D.	22 Aug. 1856	Co. A, WLI, 25th S. C. V.
Cuyler, E. P.	28 Jun 1853	
Cantwell, P. Henry	3 May 1858	Co. B, WLI, 25th S. C. V.
Carroll, Edward	6 Jun 1856	Co. B, 2nd SC Art'y
Cudworth, E. N.	22 Jun 1847	Co. C. 17th Batt'n SC Cavalry
Copes, Frederick	30 Apr 1860	Co. B, WLI, 25th S. C. V.
Copes, Joel	21 Feb 1859	Co. A, Hampton Legion
Cotchett, W. Dana	Feb 1860	Co. A, WLI, 25th S. C. V.
Cudworth, Alfred	22 Jun 1860	Co. A, B, WLI, 25th S. C. V.
Chichester, Charles E.	18 Jun 1860	Capt. Gilchrists Co, SC Art'y
Douglass, Campbell, Jr.	30 Sep 1845	Co. A, WLI, 25th S. C. V.
Dawson, Joseph	2 Jul 1846	Co. C. WLI
DeTreville, Edward W.	21 Feb 1859	Co. B, WLI, 25th S. C. V.
Dickinson, James H.	15 Mar 1859	Co. A, WLI, 25th S. C. V.
Dotterer, Wm. A.	17 Apr 1860	Co. A, WLI, 25th S. C. V.
Darby, E. H.	16 Jun 1860	Co. L. 1st SC Infantry
Dibble, S. W.	30 Jun 1852	Co. A, WLI, 25th S. C. V.
Estill, Alex D.	14 Jan 1858	Capt. Estills Co., SC Local Defense
Esnard, C. L.	16 Jun 1860	
Ferrall, John J.	22 Aug 1848	Co. C. WLI
Fraser, J. B.	20 Jun 1857	
Finley, William C.	30 Apr 1860	Co. C. WLI
Folker, Octavius F.	Feb 1843	Co. A. WLI, 25th S. C. V.
Farrar, Charles D.	15 Jun 1860	Co. C. WLI
Gregg, William, Jr.	9 Feb 1860	Co. K, 19th SC Infantry
Gyles, F. A.	3 Apr 1860	Co. A, 25th SC Infantry
Gardner, John H.	19 Jun 1860	Co. A, Hampton Legion
Greer, Henry I.	9 Feb 1860	Co. B, WLI, 25th S. C. V.

Appendix 7: Roster of the Washington Light Infantry (WLI) 213

Gale, R. W.	25 Apr 1853	Co. B, WLI, 25th S. C. V.
Goodrich, George C.	15 Jun 1860	Co. C, WLI
Graham, G. C.	15 Jun 1860	Co. L, 1st SC (McCreary's) Infantry
Gardner, J. S.	(Not Known)	
Harper, F. M.	30 May 1855	Co. A, WLI, 25th S. C. V.
Hatch, Melville S.	6 Jun 1857	Signal Corps, C. S. A.
Herriot, W. J.	9 Mar 1849	Co. C. WLI
Hayne, Isaac	21 Feb 1859	Capt. Parkers Co. (Marion Art'y)
Honour, Fred H.	1 Feb 1856	Co. A, WLI, 25th S. C. V.
Happoldt, A. M.	18 Jun 1860	Co. C. WLI
Houston, John Henry	22 Nov 1856	Co. B, WLI, 25th S. C. V.
Howell, Lamar S.	30 Jun 1860	Co. C. WLI
Jones, Paul	22 May 1833	Co. C. WLI
Jones, J. Walker	22 Nov 1855	Co. A, WLI, 25th S. C. V.
Jenkins, C.J.	3 Jul 1860	
Johnson, Charles H.	29 Apr 1851	Co. B, WLI, 25th S. C. V.
Johnson, James E.	4 Apr 1859	
Kiddell, George	22 Aug 1851	Co. C. WLI
Kinsey, George F.	29 Jun 1847	Co. C. WLI
Kingman, John W.	18 Jan 1850	Co. A. WLI, 25th S. C. V.
Klinck, Theodore K.	28 Jan 1859	Co. A, Hampton Legion
Lovegreen, Lawrence B.	26 May 1849	Co. B, WLI, 25th S. C. V.
Lowndes, T. Pinckney	7 Jan 1858	Capt. Parkers Co. (Marion Art'y)
Legnick, Alfred	28 Jan 1859	Capt. Melchers' Co. (German Art'y)
Lanneau, Fleetwood, Jr.	7 Feb 1859	Co. B, WLI, 25th S. C. V.
Lambert, Walter	2 Apr 1849	Co. A. WLI, 25th S. C. V.
McQueen, Donald, Sr.	4 July 1835	
Marsh, James G.	28 Jan 1853	Co. B, WLI, 25th S. C. V.
McDowell, J. England	6 Feb 1857	
McDowell, R. H., Jr.	13 Feb 1858	Co. B, WLI, 25th S. C. V.
McDowell, Arthur	30 Jun 1860	
McLeod, H. A.	29 Mar 1858	
Mathews, Christopher	4 Apr 1859	Co. B, WLI, 25th S. C. V.
Mulkie, Thomas D.	3 Jul 1858	Co. A, Hampton Legion
Masterman, Edward T.	28 Jan 1859	Co. A. Hampton Legion
Muckenfuss, W. M.	20 Mar 1860	Co. A. WLI, 25th S. C. V.
Morris, W. R.	15 Jun 1860	
Mitchell, Frazer G.	29 Jun 1860	Brooks Lt. Art'y
Norton, J. H.	6 Jun 1856	Co. C, WLI
O'Sullivan, Thomas F.	11 Mar 1857	Co. A, WLI, 25th S. C. V.
Owens, William C.	21 Jun 1860	Co. A, WLI, 25th S. C. V.
Paxton, W. Y.	22 Nov 1845	Co. C, WLI
Prince, S. H.	6 Jun 1856	
Pennal, Robert E.	10 May 1852	Co. A, WLI, 25th S. C. V.
Prince, J. H.	6 Jun 1856	Co. C, WLI

Passaliague, L.L.	2 Jul 1856	
Porter, W. H.	28 Jun 1858	
Phelps, Francis L.	22 Jun 1846	Co. C. WLI
Phelps, George L.	15 Jun 1860	Co. A, Hampton Legion
Phelps, John B.	18 Jun 1860	Co. A, WLI, 25th S. C. V.
Parry, J.D.	17 Apr 1860	Co. G, 7th SC Cavalry
Reid, Andrew, Sr.	3 Jul 1846	
Reid, Andrew, Jr.	2 Jul 1855	Co. C, 17th Batt'n SC Cavalry
Rodgers, Thomas L., Jr.	11 Jan 1859	Co. C. WLI
Rhett, Burnette S., M.D.	21 Feb 1860	
Rivers, Winfield M.	10 Dec 1847	Co. C. WLI
Rowland, C. Elliott	20 Feb 1857	Co. A, WLI, 25th S. C. V.
Ross, James A.	21 Feb 1859	Co. A, WLI, 25th S. C. V.
Ryan, Thomas C.	15 Jun 1860	Capt. J. T. Kanapaux's Co., SC Art'y
Ryan, James L.	15 Jun 1860	Co. C. WLI
Spencer, G. W.	17 Jun 1847	Co. C. WLI
Simmons, J. A.	15 Oct 1850	
Schreiner, John H., Jr.	22 Aug 1854	Co. C. WLI
Steadman, W. K.	16 Jun 1860	Co. G, 7th SC Cavalry
Small, John J.	28 Jan 1859	Co. D, 5th SC Cavalry
Salinas, F. E.	10 Feb 1860	Co. A, 23rd SC Infantry
Simons, James S.	17 Apr 1860	1st Reg't Rifles (Branch's) SC Militia
Sparnick, Henry. Jr.	15 Nov 1859	
Stocker, J. D.	23 Aug 1852	Co. B, WLI, 25th S. C. V.
Salas, Francis P.	22 Aug 1858	Co. C. WLI
Smith, J. Ralph	16 Mar 1846	
Smith, W. Walton	20 Jul 1847	Co. C. WLI
Trout, Thomas B.	26 Jun 1846	Gen. & Staff
Thouron, J. A.	27 Jan 1841	Co. C. WLI
Thouron, J. E.	11 Dec 1856	16th Regt. SC Militia. Jones Co.
Teague, J. N.	16 Jun 1860	Co. C, 1st SC Art'y.
Taft, Robert M.	2 Jul 1857	Co. B, WLI, 25th S. C. V.
Trumbo, A. S.	18 Jun 1860	Co. B, WLI, 25th S. C. V.
Warren, Benjamin W.	30 May 1841	
Williams, H. H., Jr.	2 Jul 1856	Co. B, WLI, 25th S. C. V.
Whitmore, William	3 Apr 1860	Co. A, Hampton Legion
Woodbury, Stratford B.	22 Jun 1860	Co. B, WLI 25th S. C. V.
Young, J. Kershaw	22 Jun 1860	Capt. Jeter's Company, SC Lt. Art'y.

Appendix 8

A Newspaper Description of Castle Pinckney That Appeared in Many 1860 and 1861 Newspapers. This appeared in the *Yorkville Enquirer* on January 3, 1861.

Castle Pinckney is a small work, situated on the southern extremity of "Shutes Folly Island," between Hog and Folly Channels. Though in itself not a very considerable military work, yet from its position, commanding as it does the whole line of the eastern wharves it becomes of the utmost importance for it to be held by the state authorities. It is in fact, the immediate outwork of the city, useful to annoy an invading fleet should it pass the outer forts, and to render their landing difficult, if not impossible. In its plan it presents to the south a semi-circular face, the eastern and western faces are formed by the line of the rampart following the direction of the of the tangent to the circular arc at its extremity, and for a distance of twenty yards; the north side is plain; at both the northeastern and north western angles are semi-circular bastions, the outer extremities of the arcs being tangent respectively to the eastern and western sides of the fort.

There are two rows of guns—the lower being in casemates [bombproof], the embrasures for which are about seven feet above low water mark, and the upper being barbette. The height of the rampart is twenty and the width thirty-two feet. The width of the outer wall and parapet is six feet, the depth of the casemate is twenty feet, height ten; the diameter [east and west] of the castle is one hundred and seventy feet. The entrance is on the northern side, on either side of which are the officers and privates' quarters, mess room, &c. The ascent to the barbette is made on the northeastern and northwestern corners of the terre-parade-plein. In the center of the latter is the furnace for heating shot.

Around the foot of the scarp wall is a breakwater about twelve feet in width, horizontally, which has its western side extended in a tangent direction to the north to form the landing. The landing is protected by the fire of several guns sweeping its length.

Appendix 9

Confederate Signal System Conceived by Castle Pinckney Commander Col. James Johnston Pettigrew and Used to Communicate Among Harbor Forts for the Duration of the War

Charleston [S.C.] Dec 31st 1860

To His Excellency, F. W. Pickens, Governor of South Carolina,

Sir; - Under instruction from Col J. J. Pettigrew Commanding Castle Pinckney, I beg leave to submit the following proposition for a code of signals to be established in the Harbor for the purpose, of communicating with the several posts in said Harbor, and with the city.

1st Between Castle Pinckney, and the City.

a. In the day time.

If three flags, placed in the following order, the one above the other [numbering from above] Red, Black and White, be set from the flag staff, it will indicate that a large force is approaching, and that assistance is wanted.

If a single red flag to be set, it will indicate that a force is threatening an attack and if a black flag is added—, that we can meet it.

b. In the night time.

Three lanterns, shown on the west bastion on the same line with each other, two red and one white, will indicate the approach of an overwhelming force.

One Red lantern-, that an attack is threatened.

One red and one white—, that we can meet it.

2nd For the Harbor.

Three rockets in rapid succession (say ten seconds interval) will indicate the approach of a large force-, send assistance—.

One rocket will indicate a threat of attack—, —prepare to assist.

The rockets should be of the largest size, should in bursting omit color balls of fire, the colors in every instance to be the same in every rocket.

Appendix 10

Record of the Baltimore Volunteers Who Enlisted in the Army of the Confederate States of America at Castle Pinckney Between March 25, 1861 and April 6, 1861

Name	Country/City/State	Age	Occupation
Adams, James			
Affelder, William	Germany	18 years	Clerk
Albert, William	Baltimore County, MD	19 years	Gasfitter
Asplin, John			
Bailey (Bealey), Henry	Germany	19 years	Confectioner
Bailey, Thomas Charles	Monroe County, NY	23 years	Papermaker
Baker, Francis	Georgetown, D.C.	21 years	Confectioner
Biddle, Richard F.	Baltimore, MD	28 years	Iron Molder
Boyle, Dennis	Baltimore, MD	21 years	Framer
Boyle, Michael	Baltimore, MD	19 years	Farmer
Brady, Edward J.	Ireland–County Mayo	19 years	Shoemaker

Appendix 10: Record of the Baltimore Volunteers

Name	Origin	Age	Occupation
Christian, Eance (Jans)	Denmark	27 years	Laborer
Clark, John	Baltimore, MD	28 years	Bricklayer
Cloud, John Lenard	Baltimore, MD	23 years	Seaman
Crate, Frederick Thos.	Baltimore, MD	21 years	Carpenter
Crawlord (Crawford), William	Philadelphia, PA	21 years	Blacksmith
Dedrick, Hammond	Green County, NY	30 years	Seaman
Delahunty, Thomas	Ireland	25 years	Soldier
Donnelly (Donley), Charles	Baltimore, MD	24 years	Framer
Eaton, Joseph	Baltimore, MD	22 years	Laborer
Eff, John	York County, PA	21 years	Wheelwright
Ellis, Edward	Baltimore, MD	29 years	Bricklayer
Farr, Peter	Ireland	35 years	Machinist
Finnigan, Patrick	Ireland	22 years 6 mos.	Hostler
Flannagan, Michael	Ireland–County Galway	23 years	Laborer
Foster, Peter	Philadelphia, PA	21 years	Laborer
Golden, Wisley	Albany County, NY	19 years	Ship smith
Hall, Isaac	Hanover County, VA	25 years	Bricklayer
Hammill, Joseph A.	Baltimore, MD	22 years	Tinman
Hart, Samuel	New York, NY	35 years	Butcher
Hennessey, John William	Ireland, County Queens	22 years	Stone Cutter
Hilbert, George	Baltimore, MD	21 years, 10 mos.	Ropemaker
Hill, Henry	Elkton, MD	29 years	Shoemaker
Hobbs, William H.	Baltimore, MD	19 years	Plasterer
Jones, James W.			
Kelbaugh, Henderson	Baltimore, MD	25 years	Trunk Maker
Kelly, Edward F.	Baltimore, MD	20 years	Carpenter
Lang, Henry	Germany	24 years	Barkeeper
Lannes, John H.	Baltimore, MD	24 years	Shoemaker
Leason, Frederick (Patrick)	Denmark		Laborer
Leatherbury, George W.	Somerset, MD	23 years	Sailor
Lemmon, Charles B.	Seneca, OH	24 years	Sailor
Long, John	Baltimore, MD	21 years	Barkeeper
Lonnorgan (Lonnorgen), Lewis	New York, NY	17 years, 5 mos.	Clerk
Lynch, Daniel		32 years	
Lyons, William	Ireland	25 years	Laborer
Marty, Gabriel	Switzerland	21 years	Confectioner
Massey, Oliver	Baltimore, MD	21 years, 6 mos.	Tinner
McCarthy, Timothy J.	Ireland–County Cork	33 years	Silversmith
McCaull, John A.	Harpers Ferry, VA	20 years	Shoemaker
McGregor, James	Baltimore, MD	28 years	Shoemaker
McLaughlin, Thomas	Baltimore, MD	20 years	Ship Carpenter
McLee, Charles W.	Baltimore, MD	21 years	Carpenter
McNeir, William T.	Anne Arundel County, MD	26 years	Carpenter
Moffitt, William	Cecil County, MD	29 years	Molder
Moog, George	France	45 years	Baker

Moore, Thomas Henry	Upper Canada	25 years	Laborer
Mullany, Patrick	Ireland	22 years	Laborer
Murgotten, Charles	Baltimore, MD	18 years	Bar-Keeper
Murty, Joseph	Ireland–County Lowe	20 years	Gasfitter
Naid, James	Baltimore, MD	30 years	Blacksmith
Newman, Morris	St Louis, MO	30 years	Soldier
Nichols, William L.	Orange County, NC	25 years	Clerk
O'Connell, David Joseph	Baltimore, MD	20 years	Huckster
O'Connell, Edward	Ireland	23 years	Laborer
O'Riordion, Timothy I.	Ireland–County Limerick	24 years	Gardener
Owings, William Henry	Baltimore, MD	22 years	Laborer
Quinn, Thomas Franklin	Baltimore, MD	21 years, 6 mos.	Type Founder
Robinson, William	Ireland	23 years	Coachman
Rodley, Edward S.	Baltimore, MD	21 years, 7 mos.	Butcher
Schulter, John	Baltimore, MD	19 years	Tinner
Seward, George W.	Baltimore, MD	18 years	Carpenter
Sheckells, Richard H.	Baltimore, MD	19 years, 6 mos.	Clerk
Sheehan (Sheon), Michael H.	Ireland–County Limerick	19 years	Gasfitter
Smith, Charles	New York City, NY	21 years, 3 mos.	Baker
Smith, John	Ireland–County Kings	22 years	Workman
Smith, Edgar Thos	Baltimore, MD	21 years, 10 mos.	Ambrotypist
Sturgis, McDougald	Columbus, GA	21 years	Tanner
Terry, Edward A.	Paris–France	19 years	Sailor
Thompson, Andrew	Edinburgh–Scotland	24 years	Sailor
Torrington, John	Baltimore, MD	19 years	Woodturner
Tucker, Charles W.	Baltimore, MD	21 years	Carpenter
Walker, James	Portsmouth, VA	24 years	Farmer
Wallis, James	London City – England	27 years	Farmer
Warnick, John F.	Charlestown, VA	25 years	Property Owner
Westenberger, John Randolph	Baltimore, MD	24 years, 2 mos.	Machinist
Westfall, George	Baltimore, MD	23 years	Carpenter
Wheatley, Joseph	England – Great Britain	26 years	Barber
Weidmer, John Peter	Switzerland	22 Years	Chairmaker
Williams, George W.	Baltimore, MD	22 years	Laborer
Wills, John R.	Baltimore County, MD	20 years, 6 mos.	Tinner
Wills, Henry O.	Washington, D.C.	25 years	Bookkeeper
Wilson, George Washington	Baltimore, MD	24 years	Seaman
Wilson, George	Baltimore, MD	23 years	Ship smith
Wilson, John	Baltimore, MD	22 years	Bookbinder
Worth, Frank A.	Baltimore, MD	20 years	Carpenter
Worth, John A.	Baltimore, MD	24 years, 8 mos.	Bookkeeper

Place of birth according to the enlistment document: Age

Germany	3	Maryland	46	16-20	22	
Switzerland	2	Virginia	4	21-25	53	

England	2	Georgia	1	26-30	13
Scotland	1	Missouri	1	31-35	4
France	2	Pennsylvania	3	36-40	0
Ireland	15	New York	6	41-45	1
Canada	1	District of Columbia	2	46-50	0
Denmark	2	Ohio	1	Unknown	4
Unknown	4	North Carolina	1		
Total:	32 (33%)	Total:	65 (67%)	Grand Total	97

Appendix 11

1861 Castle Pinckney Armaments Inventory

"Inventory of ordnance and ordnance stores taken by Capt. Charles H. Simonton as agent for the Confederate States of America and William G. Eason as agent of the state of South Carolina at Castle Pinckney in Charleston Harbour."

Class No 1—Ordnance

7 24-pdr Iron Garrison Guns; 2 42-pdr Iron Garrison Guns

Class No 2—Artillery Carriages

3 24-pdr Casemate Carriages Complete; 1 24-pdr Barbette Carriage Complete; 2 42-pdr Casemate Carriages Complete; 1 24-pdr Barbette Carriage S.C.; 1 32-pdr Barbette Carriage Complete U.S.; 1 24-pdr Barbette Carriage Complete U.S.; 1 8-inch Barbette Carriage, 2 1-inch Marsilly Carriage, S.C., 2 24-pdr Siege Carriages. Old with New wheels S.C.—Drawn by the state; 1 8-inch bore Chassis on Centre Pivot S.C.; 2 Centre Pintle Blocks S.C.; 4 42-pdr Chassis; 1 24-pdr Chassis; 1 Travelling Forge. Drawn by Capt. Calhoun; 3 Caisson Boxes. Drawn by Capt. Calhoun.

Clap No 3—Artillery Equipment & Implements

23 Wood maneuvering Handspikes; 20 Linstock; 6 Port Fire Sticks; 2 Tompions for 32-pdr; 2 Port Fire Cases damaged; 9 Quoins; 5 Primer Wires; 3 Gun Gimblets; 2 Globe Lanterns; 2 Port Fire Shears; 1 Gunners Pouch; 2 Tube Pouches; 4 Pass Boxes; 13 Iron roller Handspikes; 5 Powder measures; 6 Poder Measure Copper cups; 2 Fuse Mallets; 2 Wood Fuse Setters; 1 Budge Barrel; 1 Iron Crowbar; 5 Sponge Head & Staves for 24-pdr; 4 sponge & staves 8-inch; 2 Worms; 2 ladles 24-pdr; 5 Rammers 24 pdr; 4 Rammer Heads for Shell.

Clap No 4—Cannon Balls

2,177 24-pdr Solid Shot; 1,629 42-pdr solid shot; 1,903 8-inch solid shot; 104 1X inch solid shot; 75 12-pdr solid shot; 301 24-pdr Shell; 108 24-pdr Spherical Case; 208 8-inch Columbiad Shell; 69 8-inch Howitzer Shell; 1,348 10-inch Mortar Shell; 23 10-inch mortar shell Loaded; 1 1Xin Dahlgren shell loaded; 22 8-inch shell loaded, 88 8-inch shell loaded S&S; 77 12-pdr Shot S&S;

191 24-pdr Stands Grape; 32 42-pdr Cannister; 6 8-inch Cannister; 52 24-pdr Grommet Wads; 68 42-pdr Grommet wads; 81 24-pdr grommet wads, 48 42pdr grommet wads.

Clap No 10—3 Wrenches for Gun Carriages; 8 Casemate Pintles; 2 Casemate Tongues; 2 Casemate Elevating Screws; 1 Hot Shot Grate; 1 Copper Auger; 1 Cannon Scraper.

Appendix 12

List of Union Prisoners of War Confined in Castle Pinckney, Charleston, South Carolina, October 17, 1861

This list appeared in the November 24, 1861, *New York Atlas* newspaper and was taken from a letter submitted by Alfred Alcock of the 11th New York Infantry

OFFICER BARRACKS

Wilcox, Orlando B, Col. 1st Mich.; Woodruff, W. E., Col. 2nd Ky.; Corcoran, Michael, Col. 69th N.Y.; Neff, G. W., Lt. Col. 2nd Ky.; Potter, John D., Maj. 38th N.Y.; Austin, Geo, Capt. 2nd Ky.; Fish, R. A., Capt. 32nd N.Y.; Drew, J. D, Capt. 2nd Vt.; Withington, William H., Capt. 1st Mich.; Farrish, J. A., Capt. 79th N.Y.; Griffin, M., Capt. 8th N.Y.; Gordon, L., Capt. 11th Mass.; Shurtleff, G. W., Capt. 7th Ohio; Jenkins, E. W., Capt. Naval Brigade; Sprague, J. W., Capt. 7th Ohio; Dempsey, J. W., Lt., 2nd N.Y.; Waiter, G. W., Lt. 1st Conn.; Gordon, D. S., Lt. 2nd Dragoons; Underhill, A. H., Lt. 11th N.Y.; Ford Kent, J., Lt. 3rd Inf.; Califf, G. W., Lt. 11th Mass.; Fay, W., Lt. 25th N.Y.; Wilcox, A. T., Lt. 7th Ohio; Hamblin, Thos., Lt. 38th N.Y.; Connolly, E., Lt. 69th N.Y.; Stone, L. H. Dr., U.S. Army; McGregor, J. Dr., 3rd Conn.; Gray, Chas. Dr., US Army; Griswold, S. Dr., 38th N.Y.; Eddy, H., Chaplin 2nd Conn.; Dodge, G. W., Chaplin 11th N.Y.; Worcester, F. E., Chaplin 71st N.Y.; Cooper, Chaplin N.H.

CASEMATE NUMBER 1
"Hotel De Zouave"

Alcock, A., 11th N.Y.; Ferguson, John, 11th N.Y.; Perrin, H. L., 11th N.Y.; Hopkins, J., 11th N.Y.; Terwilliger, A., 11th N.Y.; Imms, W., 11th N.Y.; Weir, J. J., 11th N.Y.; Lemmon, A. J., 11th N.Y.; Butler, J. T., 11th N.Y.; Lyons, Edward, 11th N.Y.; Carmody, A. F., 11th N.Y.; McArthur, A., 11th N.Y.; Thos. Carroll, 11th N.Y.; Sandell, E. C., 11th N.Y.; Stevenson, W. M., 11th N.Y.; Smith, W., Engine 18; Stevenson, W., 11th N.Y.

CASEMATE NUMBER 2

Reed, E. A., 11th N.Y.; Ennis, J., 79th N.Y.; McCartney, S. 79th N.Y.; Reynolds, J., 79th N.Y.; Roylance, J., 79th N.Y.; Pollock, R., 79th N.Y.; Haig, J., 79th N.Y.; McCut, D., 79th N.Y.; Huley, Jos., 79th N.Y.; Gray, M., 79th N.Y.; Davis, A. W., 79th N.Y.

CASEMATE NUMBER 3

Drewery, G. W., 1st Mich.; De Boise, —, 1st Mich.; Taylor, J. H., 11th N.Y.; Porter, Noah, (dead) 1st Mich.; Walker, R., 1st Mich.; Gregg, J., 1st Mich.; Smalls, J. D., 1st Mich.; Haskell, J., 5th Maine; Harvey, C. C., 1st Mich.; Brown, F., 5th Maine; Goldsmith, G., 1st Mich.; Brant, A., 5th Maine.

CASEMATE NUMBER 4

Blanchard, H., 1st Mich.; Newell, W. B., 1st Mich.; Haynes, J., 1st Mich.; Pomeroy, T. E., 1st Mich.; Johnson, W., 1st Mich.; Ranser, J., 1st Mich.; Lancy, J., 1st Mich.; Satuanous, F., 1st Mich.; Marx, W. J., 1st Mich.; Schmartman, T., 1st Mich.; Moore, C. B., 1st Mich.

CASEMATE NUMBER 5

Arndt, J., 1st Mich.; Ingersoll, J., 1st Mich.; Bailey, G., 1st Mich.; Moran, M., 1st Mich.; Bolio, F. T., 1st Mich.; Maetzke, W., 1st Mich.; Ewers, Chas., 1st Mich.; Rease, F. D., 1st Mich.; Edwards, A. M., 1st Mich.; Phillips, O. S., 1st Mich.; Farrar, N. M., 1st Mich.; Reynolds, W. L., 1st Mich.; Fleming, N. H., 1st Mich.; Stewart, G. C., 1st Mich.; Kelly, J., 1st Mich.

CASEMATE NUMBER 6

Craig, A., 1st Mich.; Stitz, J., 1st Mich.; Worts, S. H., 1st Mich.; Russell, A. N., 1st Mich.; Whitcomb, C. B., 1st Mich.; Trask, J. N., 1st Mich.; Brink, H., 1st Mich.; Barker, J. N., 1st Mich.; Starkweather, J. H., 1st Mich.; Archer, Jno., 1st Mich.; Wiseman, G., 1st Mich.; Trim, C. S., 1st Mich.; Baker, G. W., 1st Mich.; Cross, E., 1st Mich.; Baker, M., 1st Mich. Calm, C. H., 1st Mich.; Tuttle, J. G., 1st Mich.

CASEMATE NUMBER 7
"Music Hall, 444 Broadway"

Barry, Thomas, 11th N.Y.; O'Brien, Thomas, 11th N.Y.; Bragdon, W. W., 11th N.Y.; Scott, J., 79th N.Y.; Conly, P., 11th N.Y.; Dale, W., 79th N.Y.; Logan, J. F., 11th N.Y.; Hyland, J., 79th N.Y.; Taylor, J. F., 11th N.Y.; McCormick, T., 79th N.Y.; Vanness, E., 11th N.Y.; McGregor, A., 79th N.Y.; McGeehan, Thos., 11th N.Y.; Thomas, T., 79th N.Y.; Van Hosen, L., 11th N.Y.; Brisdy, R., 79th N.Y.; Stewart, R., 79th N.Y.

CASEMATE NUMBER 8

Sutherland, R., 79th N.Y.; Kennedy, J. G., 79th N.Y.; Collins, J., 79th N.Y.; Ware, C. S., 79th N.Y.; Muir, J., 79th N.Y.; Tryon, D. S., 79th N.Y.; Craddock, A., 79th N.Y.; Beaumont, J., 79th N.Y.; Graham, J., 79th. N.Y.; Bishop, Edward, 79th N.Y.; McNeil, C., 79th N.Y.; Scott, J., 79th N.Y.; McKim, R., 79th N.Y.; Wherry, R., 79th N.Y.; Russell, D., 79th N.Y.; Everett, R., 79th N.Y.; Armstrong, Thos., 79th N.Y.

Appendix 13

Muster Roll of the Charleston Zouave Cadets, February 7, 1862

The Charleston Zouave Cadets garrisoned Castle Pinckney from September 1861 to March 1862. This roll was transcribed by Dibble/Welsh in 1904 and has been augmented by an undated muster roll compiled by A.W. Riecke. Where the name or rank information differs, the variation has been placed in parentheses. The February 7, 1862 muster roll is in the Confederate Museum at Market Hall, Charleston.

OFFICERS

Chichester, Charles E., Capt.; Gilchrist, Robert C., 1st Lt.; White, E. John, 2nd Lt.; Walpole, Benjamin M., 3rd Lt.; Welch, William A., Orderly Sgt.; Harvey, Wilson Q. (G.), 2nd Sgt.; White, Samuel A., 3rd Sgt.; Whitney, Henry F., 4th Sgt.; Witte, Arnice (Armin) F., 1st Cpl. (Color Sgt.); Melvin, B. F., 1st Cpl.; Quintin, William, 2nd Cpl.; Ramspeck, George A., 3rd Cpl.; Orace (Grace), James J., 4th Cpl.

PRIVATES

Auld, Donald J.; Baker, Fred G.; Baker, George S.; Bennett, H.; Dwight-Billings, A.; Boyce, J. H.; Burke, Joseph F.; Brown, S. Chatburn; Blake, Edward W.; Belle (Bell), Eugene B.; Buckheit (Buchheit), Phillip; Bee, William F.; Cannody; Clacius, Felix; Champline (Champlin) Edward A.; Chapman; Castles, A. (H.); Cox, George R.; Cox, Benjamin F.; Deveraux, W.; Dibble, Virgil C.; Donnelly, L. James; Donnelly, S. J. ; Diefenbach, John C.; Eason, John R.; Forbes, John T.; Fischer, Felix; Forley (Torley), Charles B.; Fox, Frank; Fosberry, F.; Frey, Joseph J. B.; Gregory, Oliver F.; Goldsmith, M. M.; Hahenieht, John D.; Hepp, Frank C.; Hughes, William L.; Hughes, Frank P.; Hill, John R.; Jennings, William E; Jagen (Jager), Adolph J.; Keegan, Thomas; Lanener, John; Loyen (Loyer), Theodore P.; Livingston; Lyons, Thomas J.; La Coste, Chas.; Leathe, John M.; Lactenberger, Louis; Le Queux, William; Quinn, M.; Quintin J.; McQuine (McGuire), William Q. (G.); McBride, Patrick V. ; Meaghen (Meagher), Thomas; Miller, John; Mustand (Mustard), David; Moore, M.; McKay, John L. (S.); Nelson, William A.; O'Mara, John; O'Mara, W.; Miller, E. North; O'Farrell, Patrick W.; Olsen, Charles M.; Ostendorff, J Henry; Pemberton, William W.; Pernal (Pennal), Alexander E.; Quinlivans (Quinlivan), Michael; Riecke, Anthony W.; Riecke, George; Ryan, Thomas; Robertson, John F.; Shepherd, George; Sahlmann (Sahlman), Luden (Luder); Sheardon (Shearson), Louis; Skerritt, John; Smith (Smyth), John; Smith, P.; Stoll, A. E.; Taverner, John H.; Todd, William H.; Thompson, J. A. (H.); Von Dohlen, Conrad A.; Webber; Whitridge, Alonzo C.; Whitridge, George R.; Whitridge, H.; Welch, Edgar A. (H.); Milles (Willis), John A. (H.); Wood, William A. (H.).

Fit for duty on the February 7, 1862 muster roll were four officers, seven sergeants and corporals, and 42 privates. Two musicians (John & illegible) and two boat hands (Moses & illegible) are also noted on the February muster roll. Numerous notations on this roll offer additional information about individual members of the Zouave Cadets:

Appendix 13: Muster Roll of the Charleston Zouave Cadets

Whiting, H. F.	Promoted from Cpl. to Sgt.	Dec. 10 61
Whitbridge, G. R.	Promoted from Pvt. to Sgt.	Dec. 10 61
Whitbridge, G.R.	Vol in CEC Co	Jan. 18 62
Melvin, B. F.	Vol in CEC Co	Jan. 18 62
Quintin, W.	Vol in CEC Co	Jan. 18 62
Dibble, V. C	Resigned	Jan. 1 62
Leathe, J.	Vol in CEC Co	Jan. 18 62
Whitbridge, A.	Vol in CEC Co	Jan. 18 62
Welch, E. A.	Vol in Marion Rifles	Mar. 3 61
Quintin J.	Resigned	Dec. 3 61
Burke, J.	Resigned	Dec. 3 61
Billings	Work in County	Oct. 23 61
Champlain, Ed	Resigned	Dec. 3 61
Donnally	Work in County	Oct. 1 61
Forbes, J.	Resigned	Dec. 3 61
Fosberry, F.	Resigned	Dec. 3 61
Hepp, F.	Resigned	Dec. 3 61
Keegan J.	Resigned	Dec. 3 61
Moore, W.	Example	Dec. 3 61
Quinn, M.	Discharged	Dec. 3 61
Ryan, D.	Example	Mar. 28 61
Sahlmann, L.	Resigned	Dec. 3 61
Smith, P.	Example	Mar. 24 61
Von Dohlen, C. A.	Resigned	Dec. 3 61

Appendix 14

Roster of 1st Regiment South Carolina Artillery Officers, June 12, 1863 (with remarks added in 1865)

The 1st South Carolina Artillery garrisoned the various Confederate forts and posts in the Charleston Harbor for most of the Civil War. Found in the papers of Thomas Middleton, Middleton Family Papers, South Carolina Historical Society. The roster lists the rank, name, residence, & remarks for each officer.

Rhett, Alfred, Col.	Charleston	Captured at Averasboro, NC Mar. 15 65
Yates, Joseph A., Lt. Col.	Charleston	
Blanding, Ormsby, Maj.	Sumter District	Severely wounded at Averasboro, NC Mar. 16 65
King, J. Gadsden, Capt.	Charleston	Company F
Peronneau, W. H., Capt.	Charleston	Company G; Retired Oct. 64

Harleston, Francis H., Capt.	Charleston	Company D; Killed at Bombardment of Fort Sumter Nov. 24 63
Fleming, D. G., Capt.	Columbia	Company B; Promoted to Colonel of 22nd SCV. Killed by mine at Petersburg, VA Aug. 64
Mitchell, J. C., Capt.	Ireland	Company I; Killed at Bombardment of Fort Sumter, Jul. 20 64
C. W. Parker, Capt.	Charleston	Company C
Macbeth, J. Ravenel, Capt.	Charleston	Company E; Captured on Morris Island, Jul. 10 63. Exchanged Nov. 64. Severely wounded and captured at Averasboro, NC Mar. 16 65
Blake, Francis D., Capt.	Charleston	Company A; Captured Mar. 20 65
Lesesne, Henry R., Capt.	Charleston	Company H; Killed at Averasboro, NC Mar. 16 65
Gaillard, Alfred S., Capt.	Fairfield District	Company K; Severely wounded and captured at Battle of Bentonville, NC Mar. 19 65
King, MacMillan, 1st Lt.	Charleston	Promoted vice Harleston deceased. Wounded at Bentonville, NC Mar. 19 65
Rhett, Julius M., 1st Lt.	Charleston	Promoted vice Fleming resigned. Wounded at Averasboro, NC Mar. 16 65
Inglesby, Charles, 1st Lt.	Charleston	Promoted vice Mitchell deceased.
Pringle, Jas. R., 1st Lt.	Charleston	Promoted vice Peronneau retired.
Irwin, W. E., 1st Lt.	York District	Severely wounded at Battery Wagner. Retired.
Alston, J. J. P., 1st Lt.	Charleston	Died Oct 63.
Lowndes, Edward, 1st Lt.	Charleston	
Kemper, Kosciusko, 1st Lt.	Alexandria, VA	
Simpkins, W. S., 1st Lt.	Beaufort	
Boylston, S. Cortes, 1st Lt.	Charleston	Regimental adjutant.
Waties, Thomas Davis, 1st Lt.	Charleston	Wounded at assault on Battery Wagner, Jul. 18 63. Retired.
Haynesworth, George E. 1st Lt.	Sumter	
Ravenel, Elias Prioleau, 1st Lt.	Charleston	Died Jun. 1863
Bee, John S., 1st Lt.	Charleston	Killed on Morris Island, Jul. 10 63
Frost, Henry. W., 1st Lt.	Charleston	Captured near Fayetteville, NC Mar. 10 63
Dargan, T. George, 1st Lt.	Darlington	Wounded at Averasboro, NC Mar. 16 65
Middleton, John, 1st Lt.	Charleston	
Fickling, Eldred S., 1st Lt.	Beauford	Wounded at Averasboro, NC Mar. 16 65
Johnson, W. H., 1st Lt.	Beauford	
Jones, Iredell, 2nd Lt.	York District	Promoted vice Ravenel deceased. AAHC staff Rhett Brigade.
LaBorde, Oscar M., 2nd Lt.	Columbia	Promoted vice Bee deceased. Killed at Averasboro Mar. 16 65

Heyward, J. Guerard, 2nd Lt.	Charleston	Promoted vice Alston deceased. Captured on Morris Island Jul. 10 63. POW Johnson Island.
Grimball, William M., 2nd Lt.	Charleston	Promoted vice Irwin retired. Died Aug. 64.
Simkins, Eldred I., 2nd Lt.	Beauford	Promoted vice King promoted.
Middleton, Thomas A., 2nd Lt.	Charleston	Promoted vice Rhett promoted. Captured near Bentonville, NC Mar. 20 65.
Colcock, William F. Jr., 2nd Lt.	Charleston	Promoted vice Grimball deceased.
De Saussure, Henry W., 2nd Lt.	Charleston	Promoted vice Pringle promoted.
Stuart, Henry M., 2nd Lt.	Beauford	Promoted vice Waties retired. Killed at Averasboro, NC Mar. 16 65

Appointments:

Durgan, I. Furman	Darlington	
DeLornie, Thos. M.	Sumter	Wounded at Bentonville Mar. 19 65.
Reynolds, James C.	Wash., D.C.	Wounded at Bentonville Mar. 19 65.
Huger, Cleland K., Jr.	Charleston	Died Mar. 64
Harleston, John	Charleston	Captured near Bentonville Mar. 20 65.
Dubose, Robert M.	Winnsboro	
Cooper, Robert L.	Sumter	
Robertson, Jas. L.	Charleston	Wounded at Bentonville, Mar. 19 65.

Appendix 15

1st South Carolina Artillery Companies that Served at Castle Pinckney

The 1st Artillery Regiment was reorganized and placed into Confederate service on March 25, 1862, from companies and men of the 1st Artillery Battalion of South Carolina, that had, a year earlier, participated in the bombardment of Fort Sumter. The heavy artillery regiment would eventually consist of ten companies serving at various locations around the harbor including Forts Sumter & Johnson, Batteries Gregg & Wagner, as well Castle Pinckney and Fort Ripley. Between February 1862 and February 17, 1865 available records show that Castle Pinckney and Fort Ripley were garrisoned by four companies of the 1st South Carolina Artillery Regiment.

Roster of Company E, 1st South Carolina Artillery

Company E was posted at Castle Pinckney from Feb/Mar 1862 to May/June 1862, and again from May 1864 to June 1864. Elements of the company were also posted at Fort Ripley from Mar 1864 to April/May 1864.

Alston, John Julius P.; Aniss (Annis), Charles L. (D.); Appleton, William; Baker, J. E.; Baker, W. (William) J. (T.); Band (Brand), John; Bandon; Bannon (Bennon), Patrick; Barnes, Michael; Beales,

Joseph; Bee, John S.; Bell, Robert C.; Bennoit (Bonnoitt), James (John) E.; Berger (Burger), George H.; Bethea, E. S.; Bishop, Warren; Black, J. M. (W.); Blanding, Ormsby; Boggs, T. (Thomas) G.; Braggeman (Bruggemann), D. (W.) W. (D.); Brannon, Hugh; Brannon, John; Brannon (Brennon) (Brennan), Pat (Patrick); Brian (Bryan), John; Brock, W. O.; Broderick, Michael; Broome, Isaac; Brown, John; Brown (Browner) (Browne), Thomas (T.) E.; Brownlee, J. F.; Bryan, John; Bryan, John; Burgess, W. J.; Burke, Daniel; Burke, James; Burns, James; Burns, Samuel; Byrne, John; Callaghan (Callahan), Thomas; Carraway, J. A. (J.) M.; Carroll, James; Carroll, Jesse; Carver (Carwin), J. (John) Wise (W.); Castleman, P. J.; Chandler, William A.; Chapman, J. W.; Child, William; Clark, P.C.; Clune, Richard A.; Coker, J. M.; Coker, W. D.; Coleman, Austin; Coleman, W. J.; Collins, Calvin; Cook, William; Cooper, R. (Robt) L.; Coward, W. L.; Cranford, W. B.; Cullen, Daniel; Darcey (Darcy), Patrick; Davis, Charles; Davis, H. F.; Davis, William; Deal, J. A.; Dean, James; Dennis, J. A. (N.); Dennis, W. W.; Desmond, Humphrey; Detell (Detels) (Ditell); Devine (Divine), Martin (Norton); Dietriech, Adam; Doherty (Dougherty), Barney; Donlan (Donlin) (Donlon), Peter; Doody (Duddy), William; Doran, John; Doran, Thomas; Dowdle, T. S.; Duboise (Dubose), B. L.; Elbrooke (Ellerbrook), William; Engal (Engle), Frederick; Evans, Harrison; Fahay (Fahey), Thomas; Fenton (Finton), John (J) (Joseph); Ferguson, William; Fitzgerald, Michael; Flin (Flynn), John (T.) Thomas; Flynn, Thomas; Foley (Folley) (Foly), James; Forrest, G. W.; Fox, Thomas; Galloway, Thomas; Garman (Gorman), Mike; Garvin, W. T.; Gibbons, J. W.; Gillespie (Gillespy), James; Glenn (Glynn), Thomas; Golden, William; Good, J. W.; Grady, W. L.; Graham, John; Green, J. M.; Grimball, William H.; Hafner, Andrew; Hagan (Hagin), John; Hailey (Hailley) (Haily), Jerry (Jeremiah); Haillard (Hillard) (Hilliard), Con (Cornelius); Haimes (Haines) (Hames), William; Hamrick, H. (Henry) M. (N.) (W.); Harrison, Thomas W.; Harrison, C.S. 2nd; Hawkins, Joseph B.; Hayes, J. H. Hayes, Michael; Heins (Hines), Edward (Eibe) (E.) (F.) (Frederick); Henricks (Hendrix), W. K. (R.); Hewitt, Thomas; Hipp, J. L.; Houck, R. H.; Howard, James; Huger, C. K.; Hynch, Thomas; Johnson, Benjamin; Johnson, J. H.; Keele (Keels), B. A.; Keels, L. J.; Kelly, John; Kelly, Michael; Kemper, Kosciusko; Kenney, Michael; King, John; Kisler, J. A.; Larry, Larry; Lavender, Robert; Lee, James; Lesesne, H. D. (R.); Lovett, J. J. (John) (T.); Lynch, John; Maguire (McGuire), John; Maloney, Joseph, Maroney (Mulrooney), Barnard (Barney); Marshall, William; Martin; McCall, S. S.; McClure, T. H.; McConnell, Louis, McElveen, J. M.; McElveen, T. (S.) Sparks; McGuire, Dudley P.; McIntosh, H. L.; McKee, Robert; O. Mealy (O'Meally) (O'Mealy), Alex (Alexander); Middleton, Thomas A.; Mitchell, John; Mitchell, Thomas; Mitchell, William; Mowry, James; Moye, W. R.; Murphy, Dennis; Murphy, John; Murphy, William (L.); Nealon (Neeland), Roger; Nelson, J. L.; Newman (Nueman), Lewis (Louis); Nicholl (Nicolas) (Nicolls), J. W.; Norton, Daniel; Norton, Patrick; O'Bryan (O'Bryne), Patrick; O'Bryan (O'Bryne), Patrick; O'Neal (O'Neil), William; O'Toole, Edward; Oliver, Martin; Parnell (Pownall) (Pownell), (John) William (W.); Pate, Nicholas; Philips, Thomas F.; Pierce, Isaac; Pitts, Aaron; Player, F. M.; Player, J. W.; Pope, Elijah; Posey, J. U.; Powell, Joseph; Price, John; Pringle, James Reid; Quirk, Thomas; Rabbit (Rabit), Patrick; Ralford, Charles; Reely (Reilly) (Reily) (Riley), Malacy (Malachi) (Malachy) (Malichie) (Malichy); Revell, George W.; Rhodes, N. (W.) E.; Robertson, Hewstom (Houston); Rodgers, J. D.; Rodgers, W. (William) T.; Rush, A. W.; Ruan, James; Schaill, William; Schnaars (Sneers), Martin; Seaglar, H. H.; Serritt (Suret), Francis; Shay (Shea) (Shey), Patrick; Shyrock, James T.; Smalls, Paul; Smith, F. H.; Smith, John; Smith, Joseph; Stepp, William; Stewart (Stuart), G. W.; Strother, Allen B.; Sullivan, Jerry; Sullivan, John; Sullivan, John; Sullivan, J. (T.); Thompson, James; Tierman (Tiernan) (Feirman), Miles; Trainer, William; Trotter, Rueben; Walsh (Welch), D. (David) H.; Walters, Moses; Welch, James; Welch, R. J. (L.); Welch, Thomas W. (William) I. (T.); West, George E.; White, John;

Appendix 15: 1st South Carolina Artillery Companies 227

White, Mathew; White, Thomas; Williams, Ambrose; Williams, John; Wilson, James; Wilson, John; Wonamaker, J. A.; Wood, Jefferson; Yarborough, J. A.; Yates, Joseph A.

Roster of Company F, 1st South Carolina Artillery

Company F garrisoned Castle Pinckney between May 1864 and February 17th 1865

Abadie, A.; Adcock, John W.; Anderson, Charles; Arthur, David S.; Austin, Thomas; Avant, M.; Bailey, I. G.; Baker, William; Barefield, John; Barrett, John (William); Barton, A. B.; Beckham, B. (Bolivar) S. (S.) William Best; Betts, Orville; Bishop, W. D.; Boney, R. W.; Booke (Buck), William; Bowers, John; Boylston, S. (Samuel) Cordes; Brangan, Alexander; Brock, James; Bronson (Brunson), William (A.); Brown, Alexander; Browning, Hamilton; Browning, J. B. (F.); Bryson, James C.; Burch, Hilliard; Burns (Byrnes), John; Cahill, Patrick; Campbell, A. (Archibald); Cannon, John; Cantrell; (Cantrill), Mark; Carroll, James; Carroll, Wilson; Carter, John; Carty, W. P.; Carver (Carwin), J. (John) Wise (W.); Cathcart, G. W.; Chapman, M. (N.) D.; Cherry, Thomas; Christopher, Marada B.; Clancy, Daniel; Clater (Clator) (Clayton), John; Coleman, Thomas F.; Coleman (Colman), William (W.) R.; Connelly (Connolly), Thomas; Conner, Morris; Connor (Connors) (O'Connor), Patrick; Cooper, James C.; Cooper, W. (William) F.; Cooper, William J. (T.); Costello, John; Costello, Patrick; Couhig, Thomas J.; Cross, Josias O. W.; Darlington, Ed.; Davis, Thomas; Davis, William; De Hart (Dehart), B. D.; Dickerson (Dickinson), Lewis; Dickerson (Dickinson), Mike (M.); Donaher (Donahu) (Doniher) (Donougher), Thomas; Donegan, John; Donlan, Peter; Downs, John; Duffy, John; Dumphries, William; Dunnigan, John; Durham (Dunn) (Derum), Benjamin (Berry) (B.) (D.); Easterling, John A. (E.); Eldridge, William; Ellison, H. A.; Erwin, Hodson (Woodson) H.; Erwin, W. (William) T. (Y.); Fahay (Fahy), Michael; Fitzgerald, Thomas; Fletcher, Croton (J.); Floyd, Roland; Foley, James; Forester (Forrester) (Foster), William; Fougerat, A. (Julius) T. (A.); Fullum (Fulmer), Lin (Levi); Garrett, William T.; Garvin, Emanuel; Geese (Geise) (Giese), Charles; Geiger (Gieger), G. J.; Gibbon (Gibbons), Patrick D.; Gidney, J.; Gidney, W. A.; Gillispie, James D.; Graham, William R.; Grant, Joseph (Thomas); Green, George; Green, Henry; Grove, Rueben H.; Hambright (Hamright), L. (Phillip); Hamilton, A. G. (J.) (T.); Harris, Marion; Harris, W. J. (William); Harris, William C.; Hassey. Patrick; Hayes, Michael; Hearsay (Hersey) (Hersay), George R. (K.); Hessie, Michael; Hollywood, Thomas; Holmes, William G.; Howell, W. P.; Hughes, William; Humphries, William; Irvin (Irwin), Joseph H.; Jefferson, Thomas; Jennings, S. (Silas) W.; Johnson, John F.; Johnson. John (Johnathan); Jones, Thomas W.; Kadey, Mark; Keller, James L.; Kelly, George; Kelly, John; Kelly, Thomas; Kennady, Elmore (E.); Kennady, Jasper (J.); King, John Gadsden; King, McMillan; Lacy, Michael; Lee, Dixon; Littlefield, Willis; Loveridge, Frederick; Luder, David; Macomson (Maconeson), J. (John) F. (M.); Madden (Maddin), John; Madray, George W.; Madray, James; Malden (Mauldin), Irving (Irvin); Manning, Edward (John) (A.); Marsh, John L. (T.); Martin, J. E. A.; Maugra, John; Mayer (Myer) (Myers), John (J.) H.; Mayers (Myers), Charles; William A. McCall, William A.; McClemmons (McClimans), John P.; McClure, Arthur R.; McGlenchy, Michael; McHugh, John; McKinney (McKennie) (McKenny), Julius; McLean, John; McQuinn, John; Merritt, James M.; Merritt, Richard; Meyers, J. N.; Middleton, John; Middleton, Thomas A.; Mignot, Paul; Miles, John A.; Miller, Charles H.; Miller (Mullar), Frederick; Moore, James T.; Moore, John; Moore, M. S.; Neely, Thomas; Nicoll (Nicol) (Nicolls) (Nichol) (Nichols), William (Wm) (W.); Numan, S. P.; O'Brien, Hugh; O'Neill, Daniel; O'Neill, Owen; Odae, John; Ottolingue, Isreal; Pain (Payne), Isaac (W.); Pain (Payne), Richard; Parnell (Pownall) (Pownell), (John) William; Patrick, Emanuel, M.; Patrick, J. (John) B.; Patrick, Lawrence M.; Patrick, William D.; Payne, William;

Peeler, D. (David) L. (S.); Persel, (Purcell), Michael (M.); Phillips, James (Jas) (J.) A.; Phillips, T. P.; Prater, F. M (N.); Preston; Rhodes, Amon; Richey, George W.; Richey, James R.; Richie (Ritchie), John; Rhett, J. (Jullius) M. L.; Ritter, John (T.) F.; Robert, P.; Roberts, W. J. C.; Robertson, Abraham; Robertson, Henry C.; Robertson, Stephen A.; Rutledge, B. (R.) S.; Ryan, E. (Edward) E. (C.); Ryan, Patrick; Ryan, Peter; Sarratt, G. B.; Sawyer, George; Saxon, J. A.; Shaw, William; Sherdan, John; Sheriff, A. (Alfred); Sheriff, Exodus; Simmins (Simons), William; Smith, F. (H.) A.; Smith, George W.; Smith, W. (William) B.; Sord, Henry A.; Stall (Stoll), (John) (T.); Stanton, H. A.; Stegall (Stigall), John; Stegall (Stigall), Sidney; Stephenson (Stevenson), Samual; Subber (Suber) (Suhet), J. (James) A.; Sullivan, Dennis; Sullivan, Timothy; Syzemore, Benjamin; Taylor, Morgan; Thornton, Geo. (George); Tidwell, M. (W.) R.; Tigue, Abraham; Timmons, Randelson (R.) M.; Titworth, Elbert; Tully (Tulley), John (Jno) F. (T.) Turner, H. (W.) P. (Perry); Tyler, W. W.; Upton, Tobias; Vincent (Vinsett), John (Johnson); Wade, M. D.; Walker, James; Walker, M. C.; Wallace, Lewis W.; Walsh, Henry; Weaver, Adam; West, Joel; Weyman, Charles; White, J. H.; White, James B.; Whitehead, J. (James) L. (S.); Wood, Henry; Wood, Joseph W.; Woodward, J. B.; Wynne, Hiram R.

Roster of Company G, 1st South Carolina Artillery

Company G garrisoned Castle Pinckney between May 1863 and October 1863

Allen, Alfred; Alston, John Julius P.; Amadei (Amadia) Antonio; Anderson, Moses; Andrews, George; Andrews, Marvel; Ansley, Andrew; Arnold, James B.; Ashford, Dennis H.; Axson (Axson) John M.; Axon, Lewis S.; Bates, Aaron; Bee, John S.; Bell, John; Bennett, Samuel; Benton, John; Blackstock, Nehemiah; Blackwell, William; Bligh, Michael; Boyle, Terrence (Terence); Brabham, J. Nathaniel; Brien (Bryan) (Bryant) John; Broom, Marcus; Brown, Gilbert; Brown, Isom; Brown, William; Bunch, James; Burns, John H. P.; Carrol, John; Carver, Allen; Chandler, Aaron; Chandler, Moses; Coffer, Jesse B.; Collins, Calvin; Collins, J. B.; Corcoran, Thomas; Corcoran, William; Cornett, John; Cornett, William; Crawford, (David) D. (W.); Crawford, Peter C.; Daniel (Dannial); Daniels (Dannials) (Danials), John; Davis, Addison A. (S.); Derrick, James E.; Desmond (Dismond), Humphrey; Dudley, Joseph; Dupree, Josiah (Josias) (G.); Durham (Derum), Benjamin (Berry) (B.) (D.); Durham, Richard (W.); Edwards, Daniel (Dannial) J.; Edwards, Garner D.; Edwards, John L.; England, Ephraim (Epheream) (E.); Ford, Elias; Forrester, Eli; Friday, Thomas; Frost, Henry (W.) W. (H.); Funderburk, Jeremiah; Gardner, John L.; Gillespie, John; Goodson, Vardra M.; Gray, William A.; Green, George; Green, John; Griffin, Horatio; Gueary (Guerny) (Guerry), John G. (J.); Gunter, D. (David) J.; Haines (Hains) (Hayne), Robert R.; Hall, Samuel; Henderson, Charles J.; Henery (Henry), Joseph G.; Hill, Charles D.; Hill, Felix G.; Holland, Joshua; Holley, John; Hudson (Hutson), Thomas J.; Hutson, Calvert P.; Jackson, Daniel K.; Jackson, Edward; Jackson, Morgan; Jackson,Thomas (Rufus); Jennings, William T.; Johnson (Johnston), George W.; Johnson, Richard; Johnson, Waddy; Keith, John A.; Kelly, Michael; King, James H. (W.); Kitsinger, Stephen (S.) (E.); Knight, Hamilton; Knight, Reddick; Lallis (Lolis) (Lollas) (Lollis), Griff; Lankford, Dennis; Lankford, Martin. V. (Van) B.; Lankford, Wales S.; Lawless, Michael; Leach, Hosea; Lollis, William T.; Lovelace, John; Lymes (Lyne) (Lynes), J. (Jesse) C.; Mahoney, John; Mann, John (T.); Maree (Mauree) (Merce), Abraham; McCall, William J. P.; McCallister, Jesse A.; McClure, David; McClure, James (M.); McClure, Jasper (W.); McClure, Leander; McCoy, David; McCoy, James; McCoy, William A.; McCrackin (McCracken), William; McCullum, James; McElhenny, J. P.; McFederidge, Austin; McGill, Andrew Jr.; Mickle (Mickler) (Micklon), Nicholas; Miller, Joel D. (Joseph); Moody, John; Morris, James H. (W.); Morris, Thomas J.; Mulkie (Mulky), William; Nealy (Neely), Hezekiah

Appendix 15: 1st South Carolina Artillery Companies

M.; Parrish, Booker A.; Patterson, D G. (Greenberry); Patton, John; Peebles, George W.; Pelfvey, Woodson; Peronneau, William (W.) H.; Price, James; Ravenel (Ravanel), E. (Elias) P. (Prioleau); Raxter, Charles C.; Redmond, Morgan; Reynolds, James C.; Rice, William R.; Rider (Ryder), George; Robertson, David; Robertson (Robinson) (Robson), Frank (Francis) (M.); Robinson (Robison), James (Joseph) G. (J.); Rodgers (Rogers), W. (William) T.; Roony, Thomas; Saercey (Searcey) (Sercy), John A. (H.); Sanders, (Saunders), Charles; Scoggins, James; Shope, William G.; Simkins, Eldred J.; Smith, William B.; Spencer, William; Stone, Robert; Stoublefield (Stubblefield), Calvin; Stoublefield (Stubblefield), Francis; Stoublefield (Stubblefield), Henry; Stoublefield (Stubblefield), Hiram K.; Stoublefield (Stubblefield), Lemuel; Stoublefield (Stroublefield) (Stubblefield), William; Swaney, Albert M.; Swaney (Sweaney), Henry E.; Swaney (Sweany) (Sweeney), James; Swaney (Sweany) (Sweeney), John M.; Swaney (Sweany) (Sweeney), Laborin D.; Swaney (Sweany) (Sweeney) Merritt R. (W.); Swaney (Sweany) (Sweeney), Richard H.; Sweeny, C. (Calvin); Thomson, Jesse S.; Thompson, John (S.); Tinsley (Tinzler), Charles (C.); Tinsley, Thomas J.; Troy, Thomas J.; Turner, R. (Robert) F. (T.); Turner, Waddy; Wesley, H. M.; Whitesides, J. T.; Wilson, Mathew; Winningham, James; Winningham, Joshua; Woods, Henry; Woods, Woods

Roster of Company H, 1st South Carolina Artillery

Company H garrisoned Castle Pinckney between May 1862 and May 1863 and from November 1863 to May 1864.

Addis, William; Agin, Michael; Allen, Martin; Armstrong, William; Baldwin, James A.; Barrett, David; Baxley, Archy; Bell, Henry (K.); Bellows, Warren (William); Birt, G (Gillespie) E.; Blackburn, Alexander; Blackwell, Andrew J.; Blocker, John R.; Bocock, John T.; Bonham, Henry; Bottoms (Bottones), Reuben (R.) P. (H.); Bowen, Elijah M.; Bradley, Stephen; Brice, James; Brown, James (1st); Brown, James (2nd); Brown, John; Brown, John; Buck, William; Birch, Thomas C.; Burrell, George H. (W.); Burrell, James; Burton, Joseph; Byman, Andrew (A.) J.; Byman, James C.; Cain, Darling; Campbell, John A.; Canning, Stephen; Cantrell, Andrew P.; Carleton, Thomas; Carson, Henry; Carter, Andrew; Carter, John H.; Caskey, John D.; Cilvanis (Cylvanus) (Silvates), Joseph; Clancey, Phillip; Clark, William H.; Clemson, (John) Calhoun (C.); Cochran, George W.; Cochran (Corcoran), James (J.) T. (F.) (T.); Cochran, John R.; Cockran, Daniel; Connor, John; Cosgrove, James; Couch, Benjamin F.; Couch, Smith; Coward, (Cowerd), Isaac (Jason); Coward, Thomas J.; Crausbee, Archy; Crawford, James (J.) M.; Crawford, John (T.); Curtis, John; Dagle, Peter; Dagle, Thomas; Dargan, F. (T.) G. (George); Darnell, William; Davis, Elias; Davis, (W.) Warren (R.) R. (A.) (B.) (W.); Dean, Henry; Delahoe (Delehoe) (Delihoe), Francis; Dellingham (Dillingham), James (M.); Dent, George William (W.) (B.) (G.) (W.); Dillon, John; Doughty, Peter; Duffey (Duffy), Michael; Dunn, James; Durant, William; Eaton, Humphrey; Eller, George C.; Eller, James L.; Eller, John (Joseph) M.; Eller, Samuel J.; Ellett (Elliott), John (J.) P (E.); Erwin, William (W.) E.; Falbert, Adolphe; Farley, Henry (H.) (S.) S. (H.); Ferguson, Gideon (G.); Ferguson, Joseph; Finity, Thomas; Flynn, Patric (Patrick); Fowler, William A.; Fox, John; Fox, William; Fradey (Frady), General W.; Fradey (Frady), Thomas J (G.); Frady (Fradey), Henry; Frady, Marcus (M.) (L.); Gandy (Gaudy), William H.; Garlin, Daniel P.; Garrett, John; Garrett, William; Gee, Charles L.; Gee, Isaac; Gee, John Henery; Gee, Walter D. (H.) (L.); Givens, John; Gormese (Gormise), Felix; Granger, William; Green, William L.; Gregory, William; Gunter, Elsey (E.) (Ely); Halcomb (Holcomb), Bennett (Bennet) (G.) (J.); Haley, H.; Hall, Abner M.; Hayes, Thomas; Head, Francis (F.) M.; Herman (Hermon), Joseph; Hermon, John; Hester, Decatur; Hicks, John (A.); Hill, Thomas D.; Holcomb,

(Holcombe), Rueben P.; Holcomb, Thomas J.; Hooper, Enos; Hooper, Isaac M. (Mac); Hooper, James; Hooper, William; Hugh (Hughes) Hughs), John; Hughes, Nathan D. (H.); Hughes, (Hughs), Thomas (James) J.; Hews, (Hughes) (Hugh) (Hughs), William (W.) J. (G.); Hyde, Walter H. (G.) (J.); Icailt (Icault), Theodore; Jeddyn (Jeddyon) (Jedyon) (Judson), Dennis (Denis); Jenkins, John; Jimpliss, Toristorio; Johnson, Allen (A.) (R.); Johnson, George; Johnson, Henry G.; Johnson, Lindsey M. (D.) (L.); Johnson, Martin; Johnston, Jonathan; Jones, John B.; Jones, Robert; Jordan, Elijah; Jordan (Jourdon), John E.; Kell, Andrew J.; Kell, Leonard M.; Kell, Robert B.; King, Henry; Lail (Laile), James; Langston, Elijah; Langtry, James W.; Larpentuer, Amend B.; Lesesne, H. (Henry) D. (R.); Llewllyn, William; Lawson Love, Eli (Elias); Loveless (Lovelace) (Lovlace), John; Lowndes, Edward (E.); Magowan, Frank; Mallen (Mallin) (Mallon), Edward; Markee (Markay), Patrick); Marsengill, (Mesingale) (Massinger), Finney (F.) (Fenny) (Henry); Marshall, Frank; Maxwell, Joseph; McAteer, John; McCall, William J. P.; McCloud, Charles; McCormick, Charles; McCrary (McGeary), James; McGowan (McGowin) (McGowen) (Magowan), Frank (Frances) (Francis); McHugh, Francis; McKenna (McKenney) (McKenne) (McKennan) (McKane), Patrick; McMinn, John; Melton (Milton), James (F.); Middleton, E. (Edwin) B.; Milan, William; Miller, John; Mims, Bud; Moncier, John; Mongo (Mungo), George (G.) F.; Monin, James C.; Monios, Antonio; Montague, Paul; Morris, George; Murphy, Patrick; Murphy, William (L.); Murphy, William; Murray (Murry), William; Meyers, John; Nedow, Benjamin; Newton, Edwin; Nichols (Nickles), William, R.; Nickles, James; Nichol, John; Norris, James T.; Northcutt, William; O'Keefe (O'Keeffe), Michael J. (I.); O'Mally (O'Mealy), Martin; Ohmsted (Olmsted), George; Olivet, Edwin A.; Ordon (Orton), Newton G.; Oulter (Outlan) (Outler), Stephen; Owens, E. (Elijah) M.; Page, Thomas; Painter, Barney; Payne, Greene; Phillips, Dawson; Picklesimer (Picklesimon), Abraham; Pitman, Stephen; Prince, Joseph A.; Prueitt, Willis; Ratigan (Rattigan), Peter; Reynolds, James C.; Reynolds, Martin; Rhodes, John; Rhodes, Jonathan; Roach, William; Rosenberg, Charles; Ruple, Joseph H.; Ryan, John; Sanderson (Saunderson), Henry; Schoaltz (Schultz), William (Wilhelm); Schollick, John; Shaffer, Theodore (Thomas); Shirley, Berryman; Shope, John R.; Simpson, William; Sinclair (St. Clair), William; Sinnet (Sinnott), John; Sissom, (Sisum) (Sisson), D. (David) (James) O.; Sisum, George W. H. Smith, Abraham; Smith, Cheny (Cheney); Smith, Frederick; Smith, Hammond (Harmon) (Hammon); Smith, James; Smith, John; Speed, John; Spencer, Henry (Patrick); Spencer, James O.; Starksberger, William; Starnes (Starns), John F.; Steward (Stewart) (Stuart), W. (William) M.; Stolte, George; Straney (Streeney), Patrick; Tanner, John; Tanner, Robert A.;Tassaro (Tchario) (Tessierro) (Tisharo), Benjamin; Teem (Teems), Peter M.; Thomas, George W.; Thomas, Tullius; Thurston, James M. (W.); Tropolet (Tropolett) (Torapolet), R. (Robert); Turner, R. A.; Wallace, Frederick; Waters (Wortes), John; Waters, Nathan; Welborne, Aaron; Welborne (Welbourne), John; Welbourne, Wiley C.; Wetherford, William; Whitmire, John W.; Wiggens, Stephen; Wilburn, A.; Wilkens, Jacob P.; Williams, Austin C.; Williams, John; Wilson, Francis; Wilson, James M. (W.); Wright, Charles; Wright, George; Yaw, Edward

Appendix 16

List of Prisoners from the 54th Massachusetts Confined at Castle Pinckney

Those captured on James Island were examined and interviewed on July 18, 1863 by Confederate staff officer William Henry Trescot. Those captured at Battery Wagner were interviewed by Trescott on July 20th. From Bonham file, Letters Received by the Confederate Adjutant and Inspector General, 1861-1865.

Name	Age	Described	Captured	Hometown
Jeffries, Alvis	38	Free negro	James Island on 16th	Cleveland, OH
Council, George	40	Virginia slave	James Island on 16th	Philadelphia, PA
Smith, Enos	30	Free negro	James Island on 16th	Pennsylvania
Blikes, Lemuel	16	Free negro	James Island on 16th	Reedsville, MA
Caldwell James		Free negro	James Island on 16th	Battle Creek, MI
Worthington, Henry		Meztico	James Island on 16th	Defiance, Ohio
Harrison, William	35	Negro slave	James Island on 16th	Ralls County, MO
Wallace, Fred F.	21	Light negro	James Island on 16th	Chicago, IL
Williams, Olmstead	36	Light mulatto	James Island on 16th	Detroit, MI
Williams, Oscar		Negro slave	James Island on 16th	Carroll County, MD
Proctor, Joseph		Free negro	James Island on 16th	Williamsport MD
Kirk, Henry		Mulatto slave	James Island on 16th	Marion County, MO
Dickerson, Wesley		Negro slave	James Island on 16th	Ralls County, MO
Leatherman, John		Free negro	James Island on 16th	Jackson County, MD
Taylor, Willie	16	Free negro	Battery Wagner on 18th	Mount Healthy, OH
Woods, Stuart		Free mulatto	Battery Wagner on 18th	Carlisle, PA
Hill, William F.		Free negro	Battery Wagner on 18th	Boston, MA
Green, Alfred			Battery Wagner on 18th	Boston, MA
Anderson, Solomon E.		Free negro	Battery Wagner on 18th	Pennsylvania
Allen, James		Free negro	Battery Wagner on 18th	Dayton, OH

Appendix 17

Record of Prisoners Confined at Military Prison Castle Pinckney, Charleston Harbor; Commanded by Capt. Walsh, 40th U.S. Infantry, for the month of August 1867

From the ledger book Record of Prisoners, Castle Pinckney, Charleston Harbour, Commanded by Captain W. Welsh, 40th Infantry, Aug. 1867 to Aug. 1868 now held at the National Archives

Prisoner	Residence	Age	Color	Height	Nativity	Offense	Sentence
Fisher, George W.	5th Cavalry	22	White	5'5"	German	Desertion	1 Year
Singleton, Kit	St. Helena	25	Black	5'9"	SC	Murder	
Kelly, Michael	6th Infantry	21	White	5'5"	Ireland	Misconduct	6 Months
Carney, John	8th Infantry	23	White	5'4"	Ireland	Misconduct	6 Months
Boyst, Richard	5th Cavalry	21	White	5'8"	NY	Desertion	6 Months
Donnelly, John	5th Cavalry	19	White	5'5"	DC	Misconduct	6 Months
Manning, Daniel	6th Infantry	21	White	5'8"	Ireland	Misconduct	6 Months
Right, Simeon	40th Infantry	20	Black	5'6"	TN	Misconduct	1 Year
Watson, John	40th Infantry	22	Black	5'10"	GA	Desertion	6 Months
Garrison, James	Darlington	41	White	6'1"	NC	Assault	2 Year
Brown, Julius	40th Infantry	21	Black	5'7"	Canada	Mutiny	6 Months
Wright, James	40th Infantry	27	Black	5'9"	GA	Unknown	
Jones, John	Edgefield	23	White	5'8"	SC	Theft	
McGuire, Hugh	6th Infantry	20	White	5'8"	NJ	Drunk	3 Months
Jennings, Bill	Augusta	25	White	5'8"	Ireland	Outlaw	
Smith, James W.	40th Infantry	23	Black	5'6"	SC	Asleep	3 Months
Washington, Char	Charleston	26	Black	5'7"	SC		
Simmons, Richard	40th Infantry	23	Black	5'8"	SC	Asleep	3 Months
Dauris, Joseph	6th Infantry	25	White	5'7"	England	Desertion	1 Year
Reilley, John	6th Infantry	26	White	5'7"	Ireland	Desertion	6 Months
Hooks, Charles E.	Litchfield, CT	23	White	5'7"	CT	Larceny	
Leeble, Samuel	Sumter	32	White		Swiss	Assault	
Hassett, Daniel	6th Infantry	21	White	6'1"	PA	Misconduct	3 Months
Eagle, Richard	29th Infantry	22	White	5'10"	Ireland	Desertion	6 Months
Howard, Angel	6th Infantry	19	White	5'9"	ME		
Horan, James	16th Infantry	19	White	5'10"	NY		
Garigan, James	6th Infantry	21	White	5'8"	NJ	Desertion	6 Months
Farrell, Joseph	6th Infantry	19	White	5'6"	NY	Misconduct	6 Months
Heleck, William	6th Infantry	25	White	5'7"	Germany		
Frenchild, Fred	6th Infantry	24	White	5'7"	Germany		
Lewis, George	6th Infantry	21	White	5'9"	GA	Desertion	6 Months
Williams, Peter	Edisto Island	22	Black	5'10"	SC	Burglary	6 Months

Prisoner	Residence	Age	Color	Height	Nativity	Offense	Sentence
Chambers, Hewitt	Edgefield	24	Black	5'8"	SC	Murder	
Smith, Thomas	5th Cavalry	23	White	5'8"	Ireland	Desertion	
Dolama, Dominico	5th Cavalry	49	White	5'9"	Italy	Desertion	
Brown, William	5th Cavalry	27	White	5'9"	DC	Desertion	
Daily, Owen	Columbia	28	White	5'8"	Ireland	Assault	6 Months
Radcliff, Charles	Columbia	20	White	5'8"	SC	Assault	6 Months
Polson, George	Darlington	28	White	5'10"	SC	Larceny	
Bryant, Edward	6th Infantry	24	White	5'2"	NY	Desertion	6 Months
Lapelle, Joseph	6th Infantry	29	White	5'6"	SC	Neglect	2 Months
Dodds, Michael	29th Infantry	29	White	5'5"	Ireland		
Wright, William	6th Infantry	21	White	5'8"	NY		
O'Sullivan, Patrick	6th Infantry	18	White	5'9"	Ireland	Desertion	
Donlin, John	6th Infantry	22	White	5'9"	Ireland	Desertion	
Heyward, Josiah	Charleston	26	Black		SC		
Collins, Edward	Marion	29	White	6'0"	SC	Murder	
Braddy, James T.	Marion	39	White	6'1"	SC		
Hooker, Joseph	29th Infantry	36	White	6'0"	TN	Misconduct	6 Months
Nichols, Robert	29th Infantry	21	White	6'0"	Ireland	Desertion	

Record of Prisoners Confined at Military Prison Castle Pinckney, Charleston Harbor. Commanded by Capt. Walsh, 40th U.S. Infantry, for the month of March 1868

Prisoner	Residence	Age	Color	Height	Nativity	Offense	Sentence
Right, Simeon	40th Infantry	20	Black	5'6"	TN	Misconduct	1 Year
Meleck, William	6th Infantry	25	White	5'6"	Germany	Desertion	6 Months
O'Sullivan, Patrick	6th Infantry	19	White	5'9"	Ireland	Desertion	
Collins, Edward	Marion	29	White	6'0"	SC	Murder	
Lappee, William	16th Infantry	40	White	5'6"	Germany	Desertion	6 Months
Keith, James A.	Greenville	40	White	6'0"	SC	Murder	
McCord, John	Richmond	22	Mulatt	5'4"	GA	Burglary	9 Years
McCord, Henry	Richmond	20	Mulatt	5'6"	GA	Burglary	9 Years
Howle, Henry	Richmond	23	Black	5'5"	GA	Burglary	9 Years
Chamberlain, Cal	Richmond	24	Black	5'8"	GA	Burglary	9 Years
White, William	6th Infantry	21	White	5'8"	NY	Desertion	
Higgins, Thomas	8th Infantry	25	White	5'7"	PA	Desertion	2.5 Years
Gales, Jeremiah	40th Infantry	21	Black	5'9"	PA	Desertion	
Brady, Charles	8th Infantry	22	White	5'6"	NC	Desertion	2.5 Years
Hussey, Charles	8th infantry	19	White	5'6"	ME	Desertion	2 Years
Gales, William	40th Infantry	27	Black	5'8"	NC	Asleep	3 Months
Winston, Wil	40th Infantry	21	Black	5'1"	VA	Asleep	3 Months
Kelly, Michael	6th Infantry	21	White	5'5"	Ireland	Rape	5 Years
Donohoe, John	6th Infantry	33	White	5'6"	Ireland	Rape	5 Years
Carpenter, Mar	Charleston	22	Malutt	5'6"	TX	Larceny	6 Months
Works, John A.	5th Cavalry	19	White	5'4"	IL	Desertion	5 Months
Barton, Austin	Fredericksburg	26	Black	5'9"	VA	Larceny	5 Years

Young, Young	40th Infantry	19	Mulatt	5'6"	MD	Desertion	1 Year
Graham, Graham	8th Infantry		White			Desertion	
Piper, Charles	8th Infantry		White			Desertion	
Hogan, Jason	Ordnance		White			Mutiny	3 Months
Green, Henry	Ordnance		White			Mutiny	3 Months
Brown, Julius	40th Infantry		Black				
Winfield, James	40th Infantry		Mulatt			Larceny	
Grace, Joseph	40th Infantry						
Perry, Oliver	Edgefield	21	White		SC	Murder	
Hamilton, Char	Edgefield	21	White		AL	Murder	
Hare, Solomon	40th Infantry		Black			Murder	
Wilson, Isiah	40th Infantry		Black			Murder	

Appendix 18

1895 Memoir of Jane E. Chichester

A Lady's Experience Inside the Forts in Charleston Harbor: During the War was privately published in pamphlet form in 1895. Jane E. Chichester (1835-1914) was the wife of artillery Capt. Charles E. Chichester.

As it was my great fortune to spend some time in both Castle Pinckney and Battery Wagner, while the war was raging, it may prove interesting to recall some incidents with those visits.

CASTLE PINCKNEY

After the First Battle of Manassas in Virginia, in July, 1861, a number of Federal prisoners captured on that occasion, were sent to different places South for safe keeping. The detachment sent to Charleston, consisting of about 30 officers and 100 privates, was confined in Castle Pinckney which had been hastily fitted up for their reception, by putting floors and bunks in the casemates with heavy doors to close and lock at night, for the privates, and fitting up the eastern half of the officer's quarters for the officers.

The castle is built in a semi-circular form, with a curtain or straight wall on the North side, in the centre of which is the sally-port or entrance to the parade ground, around which the casemates are built. In the centre of the parade a hot shot furnace stood. Around this building, grates were built for the different messes to cook their food. These were protected from the weather by a shed roof. My Husband's company, "The Charleston Zouave Cadets," were detailed by the order of Gen. Ripley to garrison the castle and guard the prisoners.

The latter made themselves as comfortable as possible; each was occupied by a certain number, who gave fancy names to them, thus for instance, one was called, "No1 Hotel de Zouave," as it contained a number of men belonging to a New York Zouave Regiment. Another was called "No7 Music Hall, 444 Broadway." Each mess was required to keep their casemate, cooking utensils, bedding, etc., in perfect order, ready for daily inspection by the Officer of the Day. A certain number were also detailed each morning to do general police duty for that day, sweeping off the parade ground, washing down the drains, and attending to all sanitary duties, so as to preserve the health of all those in the Fort.

Some of the prisoners did not relish this work of sweeping and cleaning every day. One man [Tuttle] in particular refused to take his tour of duty when his turn came, and continuing obstinate even after my husband had reasoned with him and explained to him the necessity of the work, saying, "that he had rather starve to death than obey the order," he was finally put in the "Dungeon," as it was called—one of the casemates prepared for such emergencies, and given bread and water three times a day. After holding out a day or two and eating nothing, he finally came to terms, begging to be released, and promising to do his full share of policing whenever his turn came, which promise he faithfully kept. The other prisoners saw the justice of the requirements and acknowledged the same by doing their duty promptly and cheerfully. Of course, the officers were exempt from such duties.

As prisoners, it was necessary to keep them under the strictest surveillance and discipline, still they were well fed and cared for, and experienced none of the trials and hardships endured by other prisoners later in the war. Within the last few years, my husband received a very kind message from one of the officers through the Rev. Mr. Grant of the Circular Church, and it was gratifying to know that he frankly acknowledged that although they were subjected to the most rigid discipline, yet it was always tempered with the strictest justice. Many of the prisoners passed their time in carving trinkets and other articles in wood and bone. One of them made pretty napkin rings out of the round bones of the beef.

When the Federal blockading fleet outside the bar, but in plain view of the castle, was largely increased, it was thought to remove the prisoners into the interior of the State, lest and attempt be made to rescue them, or that signals might be secretly exchanged between them. This idea was strengthened, somewhat by finding a powerful pair of opera glasses in a box sent to one of the officers, and which Gen. Ripley refused to have delivered to him. We have often wished since the war to return them to their owner, but have never been able to learn his whereabouts.

EQUIPPING THE FORT

My husband with his command was ordered to remain in the Castle after the prisoners were removed, and superintended the alterations required to be made to change it from a prison to a thoroughly equipped military post. The floors, bunks, doors, etc., were all torn out of the casemates and heavy guns were mounted in each. Guns were also mounted above, to point over the parapet of the fort.

It was at this period that I spent some time at the castle. On our first arrival, I with my maid, occupied the small frame building outside the fort, which you can see distinctly as you pass on the ferry-boat to and from Sullivan's Island. It was formerly the hospital, but we occupied it until the officer's quarters inside the fort could be put in a habitable condition.

IN THE FORT

We soon moved into the fort and occupied the quarters assigned to the Commandant of the Post. These were on the East side of the Fort, in the second story. One room was the office, or

Headquarters, another was the dining room for the commissioned officer's mess, and the third our bedroom. The non-commissioned officers and privates occupied the western end as their quarters. Downstairs were the kitchen, dining room, guard room and other apartments.

GARRISON LIFE

It might be supposed that life in a fort would be uneventful and tedious, but such is by no means the case. A soldier's duties like a sailor's, are never done; or, rather there is no idle time. At daylight, the garrison would be roused up by the drum and fife playing "Reveille," which meant, that the men must rise, dress, and fall in line to answer to roll call. At sunrise a gun was fired and the garrison flag run up. After roll call the men would return to their quarters, roll up their mattresses and bedding in perfect order, and stand by their bunks at "attention" while the officer of the day passed along inspecting them closely, and woe to the man who did not have them put away neatly and properly.

Next came "Breakfast call" when the men would fall in and be marched by the non-commissioned officers to their places at the table in the mess hall. The breakfast usually consisted of fried bacon, corn bread, molasses and a tin cup full of steaming hot coffee – with sugar but without milk, as condensed milk was not known then. This was followed by Guard-mounting, which always attracted the attention of the officers and men. A commissioned officer was officer of the day, designated by wearing his sash across his shoulder and breast, and a sergeant or corporal and a sufficient number of men to furnish guards for the different "posts" where sentinels were stationed constituted the new guard for the ensuing 24 hours, receiving those, who had served for the past 24. After the new guard was stationed' and had taken up their quarters in the guard room, the old guard were marched to the edge of the marsh to fire the loads out of their muskets. They were then free from all duties for the day, and could sleep or spend time as they pleased. If they desired, they could obtain written leave of absence to go over to the city.

Then came "police duty," to clean up the fort and put everything in perfect order. The post boat which had gone over to the city, returned about this time bringing the mail, dispatches and the fresh meat for the day. On certain days the Surgeon came over and the sick men, if any, responded to the "Doctor's call" and received the necessary medical attention. The rest of the morning was spent drilling the men in artillery and infantry tactics until half an hours before "Dinner call," which was always promptly responded to. The afternoon was given to recruit and squad drill and other duties that would daily arrive.

Dress parade in the evening was the event of the day. At this time orders were read, guard for the next day announced, and other matters attended to. At sundown, another gun was fired, and the garrison flag hauled down, carefully folded up and put in its place. The followed supper, after which the men were at liberty until bedtime, which was signaled by "Tattoo" when they were expected to retire to their beds and be there when the officer of the day passed through the quarters. "Taps" followed meaning "all lights out" in the men's quarters. In the evening, a half hour before "Tattoo" a few taps of the drum were given inviting all who wished to repair to Headquarters and join in family worship, and the larger portion of the company always responded. We had no Moody and Sankey Hymn books then, but sang the good old time hymns and tunes, there being a number of fine singers among the officers and men.

The services consisted of singing, reading a portion of the scripture, with the occasional remarks and prayer. A number of those men who afterwards became Ministers, Elders, Deacons, Stewarts, Wardens, Vestrymen and private members of churches, have stated that their religious impressions date from those services. On Sunday morning, a most rigid inspection was made of everything in the fort, after which the men were at leisure for the rest of the day. Usually there would be religious services, either by some minister invited over from the city, or by the officers, and the evenings spent in singing hymns.

MY LAST VISIT TO THE CASTLE

I had often recalled with pleasure my experience in the Castle and wished I could revisit the old fort. This wish was gratified when about eight or ten years ago, my husband who had become a Seaman's Chaplin, and I were invited by Capt. Anderson, of the "Pharoo," to spend the day with them on their vessel which was going out that day as far as the bar. We stopped some time at Castle Pinckney to deliver some timber, thus giving us an opportunity to go ashore and visit the castle again. We found many changes on the outside. The Light-house Department of the US Government had made it the storing place for all the Light Stations along the coast. Expensive wharves had been constructed, and large store houses erected. The storekeeper, Capt. Whiteley, and his family lived in the house we had formerly occupied. It was his sister and daughter who subsequently performed an act of bravery worthy of a Grace Darling, by springing into a small boat and rowing out to the rescue of two drowning men, and bringing them safely to shore, for which heroic act they were presented by the governor with silver medals.

My husband and I wandered inside of the fort to see how it looked. Everything betokened decay and desolation. The wooden portions of the gun carriages had long since rotted away, and the guns were lying where that had fallen, some of them almost entirely covered and hidden away under the accumulation of years of sand, grass and weeds. All signs of life had disappeared, and all the garrison we saw was a cow, a hog and a goat, and as they seemed to resent being disturbed, we turned and left them in supreme command and possession of the old fort.

Bibliography

Newspapers

Anderson Intelligencer (SC)
Age (Philadelphia)
American Mercury (Hartford)
American Presbyterian (Philadelphia)
Atlanta Weekly-Atlanta Intelligencer
Augusta Chronicle
The Autauga Citizen (Prattville)
Boston Daily Advertiser
Brooklyn Daily Eagle
Burlington Free Press
Carolina Gazette
Charleston Daily Courier
Charleston Daily News
Charleston Mercury
Charleston Post and Courier
Centinel of Freedom (Newark)
Cincinnati Daily Commercial
City Gazette (Charleston)
Cleveland Plain Dealer
Columbian Register (New Haven)
Connecticut Gazette
Corsicana Daily Sun (Texas)
The Cross and Baptist Journal (Cincinnati)
Daily Constitutionalist (Augusta)

Daily National Intelligencer (Washington, D.C.)
The Daily Union (Washington, D.C.)
Delaware Gazette & State Journal
The Georgia Chronicle and Gazette of the State (Augusta)
The Irish-American (New York)
Jackson Citizen (Michigan)
Lancaster Daily Intelligencer
Lowell Daily Citizen and News
The Merchants' Magazine and Commercial Review
Milledgeville Georgia Journal
New Bedford Mercury
New Haven Palladium
New York Atlas
New York Herald
New York Times
New York Tribune
Newport Mercury
Niles' Weekly Register (Baltimore)
Norwich Packet
Ohio Statesman (Columbus)
Philadelphia Inquirer
Philadelphia Press
The Port Royal New South
Savannah Daily Herald
The Savannah Georgian
South Carolina Gazette (Charleston)
Southern Confederacy (Atlanta)
The Statesman (Yonkers)
The Tri-Weekly Chronicle (Augusta)
The United States Army and Navy Journal and Gazette of the Regular and Volunteer Forces
The Wilmington Messenger (Delaware)
The World (New York)

Manuscripts & Collections

Bentley Historical Library, University of Michigan
    Reminiscences of James Gilmore Tuttle, 1901.

Charleston Library Society, Charleston, South Carolina
    Frank Inabinet, "Castle Pinckney Restoration: A Development Program," 1978.

The Charleston Museum Archives, Charleston, South Carolina
    1861 Letter from Pettigrew to Mitchell

City of Charleston Archives, Charleston, South Carolina
    Records of the Surveyors of the City of Charleston, 1817-1916

Bibliography

Connecticut Historical Society, Hartford, Connecticut
  Eddy Papers
Confederate Museum at Market Hall, Archives, Charleston, South Carolina
  Chichester letters
Cornell University Library, Ithaca, New York
  Buell Collection, American State Papers
Georgia Department of Archives & History, Morrow, Georgia
  Civil War Remanences of Gadsden King, J. Gadsden King Papers
Harvard Business School, Baker Library Special Collections, Cambridge, Massachusetts
  Henry W. Griswold Papers
House Divided: The Civil War Research Engine at Dickinson College, Carlisle, Pennsylvania
  The Retaliatory Act, Confederate Congress, May 1, 1863
Grand Valley State University Special Collections, Allendale, Michigan
  William Welsh Papers, 1855-1908
Missouri Historical Society Library, St. Louis, Missouri
  Thomas Butler Gunn Diaries, 1818-1902
National Archives, Washington, D.C.
  RG 77: Cartographic and Architectural Records
  RG 94: Records of the Adjutant General's Office, 1780's-1917
  RG 94: Register of Enlistments in the US Army, 1798-1914, volumes 49 & 50
  RG 94: Monthly Returns from the 1st & 2nd Artillery Regiments, 1831-1840, Returns from Regular Army Non-Infantry Regiments, 1821-1916. M727
  RG 94: Letters Received by the Office of the Adjutant General, 1805-1821. M566
  RG 94: Letters Received by the Office of the Adjutant General, 1822-1860. M567
  RG 94: Letters Received by the Office of the Adjutant General, 1861-1870, M619
  RG 94: Returns from U.S. Military Posts, Returns from Charleston Harbor, 1812-1852, M617
  RG 95: Records of the Office of the Quartermaster General
  RG 109: Civil War Service Records - Confederate soldiers from South Carolina. M267
  RG 393: Record of Prisoners, Castle Pinckney, Charleston Harbour, Commanded by Captain W. Welsh, 40th Infantry, Aug 1867 to Aug 1868.
  US Court Martial proceedings, 2nd Military District, Freedmen's Bureau Records, M843
Rubenstein Library at Duke University, Special Collections
  Guard Report, 1864, Castle Pinckney, Charleston, Confederate States of America Collection
South Carolina Historical Society Archives, Charleston, South Carolina
  Jane Chichester, *A Lady's Experiences Inside the Forts of Charleston During the War*, pamphlet.
  Confederate Ordnance Bureau Records, 1860-61.
  Letter from Mrs. E.M. Ravenel to Mrs. Rosa M. Pringle
  Letter from Samuel W. Dibble to Miss Harriet Williams, Jan. 8, 1860.
  Edward B. Middleton Papers, 1842-1913
  Anthony W. Riecke Papers, 1879-1899
  James Simons Military Papers, 1860-1862

University of Michigan, William Clements Library, Ann Arbor, Michigan
 James Moncrieff Papers

University of Michigan, Bentley Historical Library, University of Michigan,
 James Gilmore Tuttle, *Reminiscences*, 1901

University of South Carolina Library, University Libraries, Columbia, South Carolina
 Charles Cotesworth Pinckney letters
 Records of Confederate States of America, Army, Corps. Of Engineers
 Henry David Ravenel, Private Journal 1863-1865

Washington and Lee University Special Collections and Archives, Lexington, Virginia
 David Flavel Jamison Papers

Wilson Library at the University of North Carolina, Special Collections
 Diary of Dr. Charles Carroll Gray
 William Lowndes papers, 1754-1941

Private Collections
 1832 Original requisition from Captain William Saunders, Castle Pinckney
 1863 Letter home from Lt. W.H. Grimball, Fort Ripley

Government Publications

American State Papers: Documents, Legislative and Executive, of the Congress of the United States, 1789-1819, Military Affairs, vol. 3, Washington, Gales & Seaton, 1832.

American State Papers: Documents, Legislative and Executive, of the Congress of the United States, 1832-1836, Military Affairs, vol. 5, Washington, Gales & Seaton, 1860.

Annual Report of the Light-House Board to the Secretary of Treasury for the Fiscal Year Ending June 30, 1893, 1896, 1897, 1900, 1903. Washington, D.C., Government Printing Office, 1893, 1896,1897, 1900, 1903.

The Army Register of the United States. Philadelphia, 1813.

Board of Officers, *Instruction for Heavy Artillery*. Washington, D.C., Government Printing Office, 1863.

Pierce, Franklin, *Message from the President of the United States to the Two Houses of Congress at the Commencement of the First Session of the 34th Congress, Part Two*. Washington, D.C., Beverley Tucker, 1855.

Reports and Selections of the General Assembly of the State of South Carolina at the Regular Session Commencing January 9, 1900. Columbia, Bryan Printing, 1900.

United States Naval War Records Office. *Official Records of the Union and Confederate Navies in the War of the Rebellion*, 30 volumes. Washington, D.C., 1894-1922.

United States War Department. *The War of the Rebellion: A Compilation of the Official Records of the Union and Confederate Armies*, 128 volumes. Washington, D.C., 1880-1901. Cited as *OR*.

Published Primary Sources

Beard, Thomas, *The Papers of Captain Thomas J. Baird, Third Regiment of Artillery, 1813 to 1828*. Philadelphia, 1848.

Brown, George M., *Ponce de Leon and Florida War Record*. St. Augustine, G.M. Brown, 1902.

Bruce, Henry, *Memoirs of Peter Henry Bruce Esq*. Dublin, J. & R. Byrn, 1783.

Calhoun, John C., *The Papers of John C. Calhoun*, edited by Robert Lee Meriwether & William Edwin Hemphill, Columbia, University of South Carolina Press, 1959, volume 12.

Conrad, August, *Schatten Und Lichtblicke Aus Dem Amerikanischen Leben Wahrend Des Secessions-Krieges*. Hanover, Germany, 1879. Reprinted in 2011 by the British Library, Historical Print Editions.

Davis, Jefferson, *The Papers of Jefferson Davis*, 1853-1855, edited by Lynda L. Crist and Mary S. Dix. Baton Rouge, Louisiana State University Press, 1985, volume 5.

Denison, Frederick, *Shot and Shell: The Third Rhode Island Heavy Artillery Regiment in the Rebellion, 1861-1865*. Providence, Third R.I.H. Art. Vet. Association, 1879.

Doubleday, Abner, *Reminiscences of Fort Sumter and Fort Moultrie in 1860-61*. New York, Harper & Brothers, 1876.

Emilio, Luis F., *History of the Fifty-Fourth Regiment of Massachusetts Volunteer Infantry, 1863-1865*. Boston, Boston Book Company, 1894.

Fox, Gustavus, "Confidential Correspondence of Gustavus Vasa Fox, Assistant Secretary of the Navy, 1861-1865," edited by Robert Means Thompson & Richard Wainwright, *Publications of the Naval Historical Society*, Volume 9, 1920.

"Fragments of War History Relating to the Coast Defense of South Carolina, 1861-'65, *Southern Historical Society Papers*, edited by Rev. J. William Jones, volume 26.

Harris, W.A., *The Record of Fort Sumter From Its Occupation by Major Anderson, to Its Reduction by South Carolina Troops, During the Administration of Governor Pickens*. Columbia, South Carolinian Job Printing Office, 1862.

Hassler, William W., *One of Lee's Best Men: The Civil War Letters of General William Dorsey Pender*. Chapel Hill, University of North Carolina Press, 1965.

Laurens, Henry, *The Papers of Henry Laurens*, edited by George Rogers, David Chesnutt, & Peggy Clark. Columbia, University of South Carolina Press, 1980, volume 8.

Lincoln, Abraham, *The Collected Works of Abraham Lincoln*, edited by Roy Basler. New Brunswick, N.J., 1953–55, vol. 6.

Magrath, *Speech of the Hon. A. G. Magrath, The Irish Volunteers: Memorial Meeting and Military Ball, Oct-Nov 1877*. Charleston, News & Courier Book and Job Presses, 1878.

Mott, Smith B., *The campaigns of the Fifty-second regiment, Pennsylvania volunteer infantry, first known as "The Luzerne regiment."* Philadelphia, J.P. Lippincott, 1911.

Phelps, W. Chris, *Charlestonians in War: The Charleston Battalion*. Gretna, Pelican Publishing, 2004.

Porter, Anthony Toomer, *Led on! Step by step, scenes from clerical, military, educational, and plantation life in the South, 1828-1898*. New York, G.P. Putnam, 1898.

Porter, John B., "On the Climate and Salubrity of Fort Moultrie and Sullivan's Island, Charleston Harbour, S. C., with Incidental Remarks on the Yellow Fever of the City of Charleston" *The American Journal of the Medical Sciences*. Philadelphia, Blanchard & Lea, July 1854.

Ruffin, Edmund, *The Diary of Edmund Ruffin*, edited by William Kauffman Scarborough. Baton Rouge, Louisiana State University Press, 1972.

Scott, Robert Garth, *Forgotten Valor; The Memoirs, Journals, & Civil War Letters of Orlando B. Willcox*. Kent, Kent State University Press, 1999.

Seigler, Robert S., *South Carolina's Military Organizations During the War Between the States*. Charleston, History Press, 2008, volume 4.

Shurtleff, W., "A Year with the Rebels," *Itinerary of the Seventh Ohio volunteer infantry, 1861-1864, with roster, portraits and biographies*. Edited by Lawrence Wilson. New York, Neale Publishing, 1907.

Simms, William Gilmore, *The Letters of William Gilmore Simms*. Columbia, University of South Carolina Press, vol. 4, 1955.

Simms, William Gilmore, *The Pen as Sword: Simms and the Beginning of the War—Rediscovered Writings from 1861*. Columbia, University of South Carolina Press, 2007.

Totten, Joseph, *Report of General J.G. Totten on the Subject of National Defenses*. Washington, A. Boyd Hamilton, 1851.

Washington, George, *The Diaries of George Washington*, edited by Donald Jackson and Dorothy Twohig. Charlottesville, University of Virginia Press, 1979, vol. 6.

Wilson, Lawrence, *Itinerary of the Seventh Ohio volunteer infantry, 1861-1864, with roster, portraits and biographies*. New York, Neale Publishing, 1907.

Published Secondary Sources

Edwin C. Bearss, *The First Two Fort Moultries: A Structural History*, Fort Sumter National Monument, Office of Archaeology and Historic Preservation, 1968.

Bell, Jack, "Robert P. Parrott's Checkered History," *The Artilleryman Magazine*, Winter 2022.

Bennett, Chet, *Resolute Rebel: General Roswell S. Ripley*. Columbia, University of South Carolina, 2017.

Bennett, Cuskaden & Smith B. Mott, *The campaigns of the Fifty-second regiment, Pennsylvania volunteer infantry, first known as "The Luzerne regiment."* Philadelphia, J.P. Lippincott, 1911.

Bonds, John B., "Opening the Bar: First Dredging at Charleston, 1853-1859," *The South Carolina Historical Magazine*, July 1997, Vol. 98.

Bristoll, William Merrick, "Escape from Charleston." *American Heritage*, April 1975, volume 26.

Bradley, Mark L., *Last Stand in the Carolinas: The Battle of Bentonville*. Campbell, CA, Savas Woodbury Publishers, 1996.

Bibliography

Capers, Walter B., *The Soldier-Bishop Ellison Capers*. New York, Neale Publishing, 1912.

Chaffin, Tom, *The H.L. Hunley: The Secret Hope of the Confederacy*. New York, Hill & Wang, 2008.

Chambers, Herbert O., *And Were the Glory of Their Times*. Wilmington, Broadfoot Publishing, 2014. Artillery volume of the South Carolina Regimental-Roster Set.

Corcoran, Michael, *The Captivity of General Corcoran*. Philadelphia, Barclay & Co., 1862.

Courteney, William A., *The Centennial of Incorporation, 1883*. Charleston, News & Courier Presses, 1884.

Crawford, Samuel, *The History of Fort Sumter: An Inside History of the Affairs of 1860 and 1861, and the Events which brought on the Rebellion*. New York, Francis Harper, 1896.

DeSaussure, Charlton & Izard, George, "Memoirs of General George Izard, 1825" *South Carolina Historical Magazine*, Jan. 1977, vol. 78, no. 1.

Detzer, David, *Allegiance: Fort Sumter, Charleston, and the Beginning of the Civil War*. New York, Harcourt, 2001.

Dougherty, Kevin, *Military Leadership Lessons of the Charleston Campaign, 1861-1865*. Jefferson, NC, McFarland & Company, 2014.

Walter Edgar, Walter, *South Carolina: A History*. Columbia, University of South Carolina Press, 1998.

Egan, Timothy, *The Immortal Irishman: The Irish Revolutionary Who Became an American Hero*. Boston, Houghton Mifflin Harcourt, 2016.

Eisenhower, John, *Agent of Destiny: The Life and Times of General Winfield Scott*. New York, The Free Press, 1997.

Elmore, Tom, *The Flags That Flew Over Castle Pinckney: Research, Analysis, Findings, and Recommendations*, 2013.

Emerson, Eric & Karen Stokes, *Days of Destruction: Augustine Thomas Smythe*. Columbia, University of South Carolina Press, 2017.

Field, Ron, *American Civil War Confederate Army*. London, Brasseys UK, 1998.

Foote, Lorien, "A Confederate Concession," *The Civil War Monitor*, Winter 2021.

Garlock, Michael, *Cathedrals of War: Florida's Coastal Forts*. Palm Beach, Pineapple Press, 2022.

Glenn, Mell, *The Story of a Sensational Trial*. Greenville, Keys Publishing, 1965.

Grenan, Shaun, *We Have Them On Our Own Ground: Zouaves at Gettysburg*. Gettysburg, Shaun Grenan, 2021.

Hairr, John, *A History of South Carolina Lighthouses*. Charleston, History Press, 2014.

Hamer, Philip May, *The Secession Movement in South Carolina, 1847-1852*. Allentown, H. Ray Haas & Co., 1918.

David Heisser, David & White, Stephen, *Patrick N. Lynch 1817-1882: Third Catholic Bishop of Charleston*. Columbia, The University of South Carolina Press, 2015.

Hendrix, Patrick, *A History of Fort Sumter: Building a Civil War Landmark*. Charleston, The History Press, 2014.

Heyward, Dubose, *Peter Ashley*. New York, Farrar & Rinehart, 1932.

Hicks, Brian & Schuyler Kropf, *Raising the Hunley*. New York, Random House, 2002.

Howe, Daniel Walker, *What Hath God Wrought; The Transformation of America, 1815-1848*. New York, Oxford University Press, 2007.

Janney, Caroline E., *Ends of War: The Unfinished Fight of Lee's Army after Appomattox*. Chapel Hill, University of North Carolina Press, 2021.

Jones, Robert Alston, *Charleston's Germans*. Milwaukee, Robert A. Jones, 2021.

Johnson, John, *The Defense of Charleston Harbor Including Fort Sumter and the Adjacent Islands*. Charleston, Walker, Evans & Cogswell, 1890.

Keneally, Thomas, *American Scoundrel: The Life of the Notorious Civil War General Dan Sickles*. New York, Doubleday, 2002.

King, Alvy, *Louis T. Wigfall: Southern Fire-eater*. Baton Rouge, Louisiana State University Press, 1970.

Lande, Jonathan, "Mutiny in the Army," *The Civil War Monitor*. Spring 2019, vol. 9.

Lane, Carl, *A Nation Wholly Free: The Elimination of the National Debt in the Age of Jackson*. Yardley, Westholme Publishing, 2014.

Long, Grahame, *Dueling in Charleston: Violence Refined in the Holy City*. Charleston, History Press, 2012.

McCleskey, Turk, *The Road to Black Ned's Forge: A Story of Race, Sex, and Trade on the Colonial American Frontier*. Charlottesville, University of Virginia Press, 2014.

McGregor, Jeremiah S., *Life and Deeds of Dr. John McGregor*. Foster, Press of Fry Brothers, 1886.

McQuarrie, Gary, "William Waud: 'Special Artist' for Leslie's and Harper's," *Civil War Navy*, Winter 2020.

Melton, Jack W., *The Half-Shell Book: Civil War Artillery Projectiles*. Charleston, Historical Publications, LLC, 2018.

Petit, James & Turner, James, "Out of Oblivion: Castle Pinckney," *Sandlapper*, July 1969.

Pickenpaugh, Roger, *Captives in Blue: The Civil War Prisons of the Confederacy*. Tuscaloosa, University of Alabama Press, 2013.

Pohanka, Brian C., "Fort Wagner and the 54th Massachusetts Volunteer Infantry," *American Civil War Magazine*, September 1991.

Ravenel, Beatrice St. Julien, *Architects of Charleston*. Charleston, Charleston Art Association, 1945.

Ripley, Warren, *Artillery and Ammunition of the Civil War*. New York, Van Nostrand Reinhold Company, 1970.

Rosen, Robert N., *Confederate Charleston: An Illustrated History of the City and the People During the Civil War*. Columbia, University of South Carolina Press, 1994.

Smith, Henry, "Hog Island and Shute's Folly," *South Carolina Historical Magazine*, April 1918.

Smith, William Roy, *South Carolina as a royal province, 1719-1776*. New York, MacMillan Company, 1903.

Stanton, Robert Livingston, *The Church and the Rebellion Against the Government of the United States*. New York, Derby & Miller, 1864.

Starr, Louis Morris, *Bohemian Brigade; Civil War Newsmen in Action*. New York, Knopf, 1954.

Stephenson, N.W., "Southern Nationalism in South Carolina in 1851," *The American Historical Review*, Jan. 1931, vol 36.

Strarobin, Paul, *Madness Rules the Hour*. New York, PublicAffairsBooks, 2017.

Thompson, Michael D., *Working on the Dock of the Bay: Labor and Enterprise in an Antebellum Southern Port*. Columbia, University of South Carolina Press, 2015.

Tidball, Eugene C., *"No Disgrace to My Country:" The Life of John C. Tidball*. Kent, Kent State University Press, 2002.

Weaver, John R., *A Legacy in Brick and Stone: American Coastal Defense Forts of the Third System, 1816-1867*. McLean, VA, Redoubt Press, 2018.

Weinhart, Richard P., *The Confederate Regular Army*. Shippensburg, PA, White Mane Publishing Company, 1991.

Williams, Donald M., *Shamrocks and Pluff Mudd: A Glimpse of the Irish in the Southern City of Charleston, South Carolina*. Charleston, Donald M. Williams, 2005.

Wilson, Clyde, *Carolina Cavalier: The Life and Mind of James Johnston Pettigrew*. Athens, University of Georgia Press, 1990.

Wise, Stephen, *Gate of Hell: Campaign for Charleston Harbor, 1863*. Columbia, University of South Carolina Press, 1994.

Theses & Dissertations

Lewis, Kenneth & William Langhorne, William, *Castle Pinckney: An Architectural Assessment with Recommendations*, Research Manuscript, University of South Carolina Commons, 1978.

Wade, Arthur, *Artillerists and Engineers: The Beginnings of American Seacoast Fortifications, 1794-1815*, A Doctor's Dissertation submitted at Kansas State University, 1977.

Weirick, David, *Castle Pinckney: Past, Present, Future*, A Thesis Presented to the Graduate Schools of Clemson University and the College of Charleston, May 2012.

Websites

1781 Letter from Nathaniel Greene to George Washington, Founders Online, National Archives, https://founders.archives.gov/documents/Washington/99-01-02-06607

1794 Letter from Henry Knox, Papers of the War Department 1784-1800, https://wardepartmentpapers.org/s/home/item/46380.

1799 Letter from Staats Morris to Alexander Hamilton, Hamilton Papers, Founders Online, National Archives, https://founders.archives.gov/documents/Hamilton/02-01-02-0526.

1807 Letter from Henry Dearborn to William Linnard, The Sol Feinstone Collection of the American Revolution, American Philosophical Society. https://diglib.amphilsoc.org/islandora/object/text:326029/.

1832 Letters between Joel Poinsett & Andrew Jackson, The Papers of Andrew Jackson, Rotunda, the digital imprint of the University of Virginia Press, Charlottesville. https://rotunda.upress.virginia.edu/founders/JKSN-01-10-02-0367

Butler, Nic, War of 1812 Fortifications in Urban Charleston, 5 Sep 2014, Walled City Task Force, https://walledcitytaskforce.org/category/fortifications/page/4/.

Butler, Nic, "The Hard: Colonial Charleston's Forgotten Maritime Center," Charleston Time Machine, Charleston County Public Library, posted May 5, 2023. https://www.ccpl.org/charleston-time-machine/the-Hard-colonial-charlestons-forgotten-maritime-center.

"Fog Bells by Thomas Tag," United States Lighthouse Society webpage, https://uslhs.org/fog-bells.

McDonald, Robert, "Formation of the Buffalo Soldiers, 1866," Jan 23, 2021, www.BlackPast.org.

Nappi, Kyle, "Retracing Hallowed Grounds from the Battle of the Crater," Aug 3, 2021, www.journalofthecivilwarera.org.

National Park Service, "The Echo," https://www.nps.gov/articles/the-echo.htm. Posted 11 July 2020.

Nohrden, Neil F., "Captain Carsten Nohrden's Sword," 2013, Charleston Museum website, https://www.charlestonmuseum.org/news-events/captain-carsten-nohrdens-sword/

Auke Visser's Famous T - Tankers Pages, https://www.aukevisser.nl/t2tanker/index.htm.

Register of the Navy for the year 1818, 15th Congress, Naval History and Heritage Command, www.navy.history.mil/research/library/online-reading-room/.

"Battery A, 2nd U.S. Artillery," Wikipedia, https://en.wikipedia.org/w/index.php?title=Battery_A,_2nd_U.S._Artillery&oldid=1000229516

Index

Accommodation Wharf, 61
Adams, James H., 58
Adams, John Quincy, 25
Adger's Wharf, 140-141
Aiken, William Martin, 176, *sketch* of, 177
Aiken, William, 49
Alcock, Alfred O'Neil, xvii, 90-93, 95-97, 137, quote, 90-93, 95-97, 137
Alexander, Edward Porter, 140, 179
Alice (blockade runner), 132
Alston, John Julius Pringle, xvii, 135
Amelia (brig), 41
American Journal of the Medical Sciences, 46
American Revolution, 6, 18, 78, 197
Anderson Samuel S., 47
Anderson, Edward Clifford, 132
Anderson, Robert: background of, 62; opinion of Castle Pinckney, 56; leadership of, 54, 55, 56, 57, 58, 59, 60, 62, 63, 64, 65, 70, 162, 185, 186; quote, 56
Arezano, Pedro, 9
Armistead, Addison Bowles, xvii, 18-19
Armistead, Lewis Addison, 19
Army of Northern Virginia, 82, 119, 162
Ashley River, 63, 189, 195
Askie, Charles, 171
Askie, George, 171
Audubon, Mary Eliza Bachman, 27

Augusta Chronicle, 11
Averasboro, battle of, 157

Bailey, Thomas N., 176-177, quote, 176
Baltimore, Maryland, 16, 45, 55, 81-83, 86, 170
Baltimore American, 82
Bankhead, James, 21, 44
Barnard, Samuel, 28
Barnwell, Robert W., 58
Barnwell, William, 86
Barrineau, R. H., 145
Battery Beauregard, 73, 123, 126
Battery Bee, 73, 126, 129, 144
Battery Glover, 126
Battery Gregg, 131, 135, 144, 149
Battery Marshall, 73
Battery Ramsey, 126
Battery Wagner (Fort Wagner): battle of, 130-132; description of, 130-131; destruction of, 184; disposition of wounded, 131-132; service at, 115, 119, 135, 144, 149; siege of, 134-135
Beauregard, Pierre Gustave Toutant: xvii, background of, 77-78; leadership of, 80-86, 89, 123-124, 129, 133-134, 139-142, 144, 147, 152; *image*, 129; quote, 123
Behre, Robert, 198, quote, 198
Bennett, Augustus G., 154, 156

Bentonville, battle of, 157
Bergland, Eric, 182
Bethany Cemetery, Charleston, 76
Blanding, Ormsby DeSaussure, xvii, 80
blockade running, 118, 161
Boag, Theodore Gaillard, xviii, 91, 95, 97, 104-105
Bolles, Jesse A., 173
Bonham, Milledge, 133-134
Booth, John Wilkes, 168
Boston Herald, 139
Bowman, Alexander Hamilton, 38
Braddy, Tristram, 171
Brady, James T., 169
Brady, Mathew, 96, 100, 106, 127, 165
Bragg, Braxton, 81
Branch, John L., 90
Brandt, Vic III., 197
Brewerton, Henry, 29
Brink, Henry, 96-97
Bristoll, William Merrick, 84, quote, 84
Brooke Rifled Gun (cannon), 145, 152, 155, 158-160
Brooke, John Mercer, 152
Brooklyn Daily Eagle, 162
Brooks, Thomas Benton, 140
Brown, Henry, xviii, 178-181, 190
Brown's Ferry Murders, 167, 169
Browning, Orville Hickman, 169
Bruce, Peter Henry, 2
Bryan, George, 168
Buchanan, James, 50, 56-58, 63-64, 130, quote, 64
Buell, Don Carlos, 57
Burroughs, John, 150
Burt, Armistead, 167-168
Burton, Milby, 196
Butler, Pierce, 8
Butler, William, 123
Byrum, Elisha, 167

Calcius, Clemens, 93
Calcius, Felix, 93
Caldwell, Charles Henry, xviii, 20
Calhoun, John C., 18, 25-26, 28, 34 *image*, 26, quote, 26
Cameron, Donald, 175
Cameron, Simon, 161, 175
Camp Douglas, Chicago, 169

Canby, Edward, 171
Capers, Ellison, xviii, 58-60, 65
Carlyle, William, 71
Carroll, Francis Fishburne, xviii, 139
Carroll, Loius, 139
Cass, Lewis, 28
Castle Clinton, 13, 22, *image*, 14
Castle Pinckney: 54th Mass prisoners, 128-133, 231; Baltimore volunteers, 82-84, 86, 216-217; Bull Run Prisoners, 92-102, 169, 220-221; Confederate seizure of, 60-63; construction & repair of, 15-17, 32, 48-49, 57, 73, 92, 137-138, 142-145, 151-152; depot for Lighthouse Service, 175-180, 186-189; description of, 16-17, 30, 53, 71, 115, 162, 164; *diagram* of, 33, 143, 155, 156; experimental weapons, 76-77, 138-139; Federal bombardment of, 138, 144, 149-151; *images* of, 27, 28, 45, 62, 75, 158-160, 163, 173, 184, 188, 199, 204; importance of, 28, 30, 43-44, 49, 56, 59-60, 62, 74, 83, 114; inspection of, 21-22, 29, 73, 76, 80; garrison of, 44, 46, 65, 71, 79, 120, 128, 135, 144-145, 149, 164; lighthouse of, 48, 164; ordnance of, 18, 21, 35, 44, 64, 86-87, 123, 142, 146, 152; Reconstruction prison, 162, 167, 170-171, 231-234; Secession Crisis of 1832-33, 26-35
Castle Pinckney (tanker), 193
Castle Pinckney Brotherhood, 98-99
Castle Pinckney Historical Preservation Society (CPHPS), 201, 203, 205-206
Castle Pinckney Inn, 195
Castle Williams, 13, 15, *image*, 14
Catlin, George, 38
Cecile (steamer), 92
Cevor, Charles, C., 140
Chapman, Conrad Wise, 99
Charleston: 1833 fire, 32-33; 1861 fire, 104; city council, 41-42; Confederate evacuation, 153, 156-157; Federal bombardment of, 134, 138, 150, 153; Federal presence, 21; Yellow fever outbreaks, 42
Charleston (steamboat), 38
Charleston City Jail, 50, 91, 162, 166, 168; 1861 fire, 104-105; Bull Run prisoners, 96, 98, 101-105; 54th Mass prisoners, 131-134
Charleston Courier, 20, 34, 50, 59, 64-65, 72, 83, 86, 132, 150

Charleston Daily Courier, 77-78, 82
Charleston Daily News, 171
Charleston Gas Light Company, 140
Charleston Harbor: change channel, 183-184, 194; defense of, 22, 66, 125-127, 144; dredging of, 48-49; *image* 34; forts, 38, 58, 96, 113, 120, 123, 128, 150; lighthouses, 163-164; map of, ix; treacherous conditions of, 23, 178-180; yellow fever, 41-42
Charleston Mercury, 44, 50, 54, 65-66, 75, 77, 91, 101, 114, 133, 149
Charleston News & Courier, 176, 181, 188
Charleston Post & Courier, 198
Charleston Railroad, 113
Charleston Tri-Weekly Courier, 129
Charlestown: *map*, 3, colonial, 3-6
Chichester, Charles Edward: xviii, 91-93, 100-102, 104, 106, 114-116, 119, *image*, 111, 115, quote, 100, 119
Chichester, Jane Elizabeth Chamberlain: xviii, 114-116, *image*, 116; quote, 115; memoir of, 234-237
Childs, Frederick Lynn, xix, 82-83
Chisholm, Alexander Robert, 139, quote, 139
cholera, 41
Choisy, George Louis, xix, 172
Churchill, Sylvester, 45
Circles of Fire, 125-127, 144
Circular Church, 35, 104
Citadel Green, 60, 63, 79
Citadel, College, 60, 72, 79, 93, 145, 156, 164, 166-167, 170, 172, 195, 202
City Gazette, 20
Clark, James, 166-167
Clay, Henry, 26, 34
Cleveland, Grover, 179, 181
Clinton, Henry, 5
Clitz, Henry, 166
Coates, W. S., 145
Cole's Island, 86, 121-122
College of Charleston, 61
Collins, John, 53-54
Colquitt, Alfred, 128
Columbia, South Carolina, 98, 105, 153-154, 167, 185, 197
Columbia Times, 29
Columbiad (cannon), 116, 124, 142, 144-147, 150, 152, 155-156, 158-160, 197, 202, *image*, 203

Compromise of 1850, 43
Confederate Museum at Market Hall (Museum at Market Hall), 101
Confederate Naval Ordnance Works, Selma, 152
Confederate Regular Army, 81-82
Confederate Regular: Army: Artillery: *Lee's Company*, 86; *Winder's Company*, 86
Confederate Relic Room and Military Museum, Columbia, 153-154
Confederate Second National (flag), 128, 153-154, *image*, 154
Confederate States of America, 77, 80, 86-87, 99, 114, 201
Connecticut Troops: Infantry: *2nd*, 96; *3rd*, 102, 105; *6th*, 131; *7th*, 131
Conner, James, 167-168
Conrad, August, 93, 114
Cook, George Smith, xix, 94, 106, *image*, 107
Coolidge, Calvin, 191
Cooper River, 2, 3, 5, 22, 41-42, 61, 81, 121, 141, 154, 179, 194
Cooper, Samuel, 56, 64, 82
Cooper Union Hall, New York, 169
Corcoran, Michael, xix, 95-99, 102-105, *image*, 96, quote, 98, 105
Cosmopolitan (hospital ship), 132
Courtenay, William Ashmead, 66, image, 67
Crafts, William, 10
Craven, John, 132
Crawford, Wylie, 73, quote, 73
CSS *Charleston*, 156
CSS *Indian Chief*, 141
CSS *Palmetto State*, 142
Cullum, George Washington, xix, 48-49
Cumming's Point, 72-73, 80-81, 135
Cuskaden, Samuel, 154-156, quote, 156

Dahlgren, John, 127, 131, 161
Dahlgren gun, 126-127, 146
Daily Constitutionalist, 168
Danielson, H., 166
Davis, Jefferson C., 57
Davis, Jefferson F., 49, 77, 80, 90, 99, 113, 120, 123, 133, 153
Davis, W. W. H., 142, 145, quote, 142, 145
Dawkes, Giles, 204
Dawson, John L., 46
Dawson, John, 132

De Saussure, Wilmot, 63
Dearborn, Henry, 15
Democratic 1860 Convention, 54
Denison, Frederic, 138, 150, quote, 150
Department of the South, (U.S.), 132, 150, 152
Department of South Carolina, Georgia, & Florida, 113, 123, 153
Devon, Charles, 167
Diamond (steamer), 161
Diamond, John, 10, 15
Dibble, Samuel, W., 72
Dillingham, J. C., 192
Dixon, George, E, 141
Dodge, G. W., 99
Doubleday, Abner, 55-59, 63
Dougherty, Kevin, 113, quote, 113
Douglas, Frederick, 133
Drayton, John, 17
Drew, John T., 93, 99, 102-103, quote, 93, 99, 102-103
Du Pont, Samuel Francis, 101, 122, 126-127
Dueling, 20-21

E. & H. T. Anthony, 159-160
Eason & Brothers, 147
Eason, James M., 48
Eastern Brown Pelican, 198, 204
Echo (trading ship), 49-51
Echols, William Holding, xix, 137, 143
Eddy Hiram, 96, 99, quote, 96
Edward's Tobacco Warehouse, 90, 98
Edwards, George, 185-186
Eisenhower, Dwight D., 194
Eisenhower, John S. D., 34
Elbridge, Gerry, 1
Eliason, William Alexander, xix, 32-33
Ely, Alfred, 98, 103
Emancipation Proclamation, 133
Enchantress (privateer), 103
Engle, J. L., 21
Ennis, John W., 92, 95, 101
Erving, John, 44
Erwin, Ephriam A. S., 123
ESSO Everett, (tanker), 193
Etowah, 121-122
Eustis, Abraham, 38
Eustis, William, 17
Evans, Nathan "Shanks", 89

Farley, Henry Saxon, xx, 120-121, 128, 144
Farley, Jacob, 19
Federal Arsenal, Charleston, 44, 63, 66
Ferguson, S. W., 83
Feilden, Henry. W., 149
Fillmore, Millard, 43
First Bull Run (1st Manassas), battle of, 89-90, 96-98, 100, 103-104, 133, 137
First System (coastal fortifications), 10
Fisher John, 202-203, image, 205
Floating Battery, 81, 83
Floyd, John B., 54, 56, 57, 63, quote, 63
Folly Island, 41, 121, 128, 166, 177
Foote, Henry, 44
Forney, Jacob Munroe, xx, 19
Fort Armistead, 26
Fort Capron, 43
Fort Delaware, 157, 169
Fort Jackson, 22
Fort Jefferson, 168
Fort Johnson, 2, 4, 7-9, 11, 14-15, 17-19, 21, 31, 37, 41, 73, 78, 84, 116, 121-122, 125-126, 140-141, 149, 193-194, 206
Fort Lafayette, 91-92
Fort Lamar, 122
Fort Macon, 22, 170
Fort Mechanic, 9
Fort Mellon, 39
Fort Monroe (Fortress Monroe), 22, 30, 44, 105, 161
Fort Moultrie, 7-9, 11, 18, 20-21, 29, 30-31, 37, 43-44, 54-55, 72-73, 84
Fort Palmetto, 86
Fort Pemberton, 123
Fort Pinckney, 7-11, 15-16, 207, *map* of, 10
Fort Pulaski, 22, 128, 191
Fort Putnam, 144, 150
Fort Ripley: construction of, 121-124, 126; description of, 8; Federal capture of, 155-156; garrisoning of, 124, 128, 144; ordnance of, 124, 138, 144, 152
Fort Ripley Lighthouse, 164, 177-178
Fort Sumter: ix, 155, 162, 197; Confederate bombardment of, 80, 83-85, 106; construction of, 22, 37; Federal bombardment of, 134, 151; Federal naval attack, 126; garrisoning of, 128; national park designation, 193
Fort Sumter SCV Camp 1269, 196-197, 201

Fort Trumbull, 35
Fort Walker Flag: 77-78, *image*, 78
Fort Winyah, 18
Foster, John Gray, xx, 49, 55-59, 63-64 74, 80, 152, quote, 64
Fox, Gustavus Vasa, 83, 122
France, 1, 8, 9, 12, 201
Frank Leslie's Illustrated Newspaper, 59, 75, 85
Frazer's Wharf, 152
Frost, Henry Rutledge, 130
Fulton (steamship), 161

Gadsden, Christopher, 9
Gaillard, Palmer, 197
Gaines, Edmund Pendleton, 21
Gallatin, Albert, 12
Gates, William, 37
Gazelle (balloon), 140
General Clinch (steamer), 50, 58, 63
General Moultrie (dredger), 48-49
Georgetown, South Carolina, 18, 113, 179
Georgia Troops: Artillery: *Chatham Artillery,* 140
Gerry, Elbridge, 1
Gettysburg, battle of, 19, 82, 130, 164
Gibbes, Mary Augusta, 94
Gibbes, Robert Wilcot, 65
Gibbes, Wade Hampton, 65
Gibbs, George, 90
Gilchrist, Robert Cogdell: xx, 92-95, 119, *image*, 111
Gill, Robert M., xx, 19-20, 207-208
Gillmore, Quincy, 128, 131, 134, 138, 161-162, quote, 134
Gooding, James Henry, 142
Gordon, James, 16
Gordon, John, xx, 1, 13, 16
Gorgas, Josiah, 147
Gowan, John, 22-23
Grand Army of the Republic, 185
Grant, S. Ulysses, 175
Gray, Charles Carroll, xx, 105
Great Britain, 12, 13, 20
Great Sea Islands Hurricane, 181-182
Greeley, Horace, 85, 132
Green, E. C., 93
Green, James, 179
Greene, Nathaniel, 5, quote, 5
Gregg, Maxey, 87

Grenada, 102
Grenfell, George St. Leger, 168
Grimball, William Heyward, xxi, 135, quote, 135
Grimball's Landing, battle of, 128
Grimes, James, 161
Griswold, Henry William, xxi, 35-36
Griswold, S. Dr., 97, 103
Gruver, William H., 145
Gunn, Thomas Butler, 71-72, 85, quote, 72, 85

Hagood, Johnson, 122, 129
Haig, James, 100-101
Hains, Peter, 176
Hains, Robert, 137
Hall, James, 132
Hall, Lester, 166-167
Hall, Willard, 169
Halleck, Henry, 153
Hamilton, Alexander, 9, 15
Hamilton, Daniel Heyward, 50
Hamilton, James, 31
Hanckel, Allen, 71
Hancock, John, 4
Hangman's Point, 3-5
Hanover, Germany, 93
Hanson, Weightman Kay, 38-39
Happoldt, J. M., 23
Hardee, William J., 81, 153, 157
Hardy, Charles, 134
Harn William, 164-165, 172
Harney, William, 39
Harper's Weekly, 59, 62, 85, 182
Harris, David Bullock, xxi, 137, 140
Hart, Samuel, 82
Haslett, Robert E., 82
Hayne, J. W., 134
Hayne, Robert, 29
Hayne, Theodore Brevard, xxi, 86
Hays, William, 43
Heileman, Julius, 26, 28
Heiskell, Henry Lee, 30
Hennessy, John A., xxi, 155-156
Heyward, Dubose, 83-84, quote, 84
Hibernian Hall, 61
Hibernian Society, 192
Hicks, Nelson, 167
Hilton Head, South Carolina, 77-78, 113, 122, 132, 152, 161

Hitchcock, R. D., 181
HMS *Leopold*, 12
Hog Island, 2
Hog Island Channel, 2, 29, 125, 194, 206
Holmes, Robert Little, xxi, 69, 71-72
Hovey, Walter, 75
Huger, Francis, 9
Hume, William Jr., xxi, 144-145
Humphries, Frederick, 63
Hunley, H. L. (submarine), 139-141
Hunley, Horace, 141
Hunter, David, 122, 128
Hurd, Samuel D., 104-105
Hutchinson, Thomas Leger, 43, 49

I'On, Jacob Bond, xxi, 18-20
Idea (steamer), 166
Idea Mutiny, 166-167
Illinois troops: Infantry: *6th*, 184
Inabinet, Frank, 197-198
Ingelsby, Charles, 120, 138, 144
Institute Hall (Secession Hall), 54, 58, 104, 118
Isabel (steamship), 118
Interior Department, 193
Izard, George, xxi, *image*, 8
Izard, Ralph, 8-9

Jackson, Andrew, 20, 25- 26, 29, 31-32, 34, quote, 29
James Island, South Carolina, 114, 121-123, 128, 129-130, 138, 140, 159, 162
Jamison, David Flavel, xxii, 73, 76
Jefferson, Thomas, 11-12
Jeffries, Alvis, 130
Jeffries, Walter, 134
John A. Moore (steamer), 101
John Adams (corvette), 17
John Fraser & Company, 118
Johnson, Andrew, 161, 164, 168-171
Johnson, Jonathan, xxii, 150
Johnson, Robert, 125
Johnston, Albert Sidney, 81
Jordan Thomas, 140

Kahler, Herbert, 193, quote, 193
Kaufman, Abraham Charles, xxii, 185-186
Kellers, Edward H. Dr., 186
Kelly, Edward, 82
Key, Phillip Barton, 169
Keys, James Crawford, xxii, 167

Keys, Robert, 167
Kiawah Island, 121
Kiddell's Wharf, 23
King, Edna Maud, xxii, 181, 188, *image*, 183
King, John Gadsden, xxii, 65, 73, 76, 78, 149, 151, 153-154, 157, quote, 154, 157
Kirk, John O., 21
Knox, Henry, 1, 8
Koppel, Hugo, 61

Lamar, Thomas, 122
Lamberton, Benjamin, 178
Larson, Iver, 188
Laurens, Henry, 4
Laurens, James, 4
Lavin, Robert, 34
Lazaretto (Quarantine Hospital), 41-43, 49
Lebby, Nathan, 48
Lebby, Robert Dr., 41-42
Lee, Francis Dickinson, xxii, 139
Lee, Robert Edward, xxii, 81, 113, 115, 118, 120-122, 146, 166, quote, 120
Lee, Stephen Dill, xxiii, 86
Lee, Thomas, 30
Legare, George Swinton, 189
Lehman, George, 27
Lenhardt, Maurice John, 195
Lesemann, Johann Diedrich, 79
Lesesne, Henry Russell, xxiii, 144-146, 149, 157
Lighthouse Inlet, 128
Lighthouse Supply Depot, 175-176, 178-180, 182, 185-189, *images*, 182, 187, 188
Lincoln, Abraham, 54-55, 77, 80, 87, 90-91, 104, 133-134, 161-162, 168, 175
Lincoln, Benjamin, 5
Linnard, William, 15
London Illustrated News, 72
Long, Grahame, 21
Longacre, James Barton, 26
Lord, S. Jr., 79
Louisiana Troops: Infantry: *Jeff Davis Louisiana Battalion*, 90, *Madison Guard*, 90
Louisiana Wayside Hospital, Charleston, 128, 150
Lowd, Allen, 26
Lowndes, Rawlins, 3
Lowndes, Thomas Pinckney, xxiii, 54, 64-65, 71, 74, 127, 150, 154, quote, 54, 64-65, 71, 74, 150

Index

Lynch, Patrick Neeson, xxiii, 65, 99, 132, 169; *image*, 100, quote, 169

MacBeth, Charles, 156
MacKenzie, M.R.S., 182
MacIvor, James, 169
Macomb, Alexander: xxiii, 15-18, 28, 34; *image*, 16, quote, 28
Madison, James, 19-20
Maffitt's Channel, 49
Magnolia Cemetery, 97, 150
Magnolia Parade Ground, 58
Maine Troops: Infantry: *1st Battalion*, 167; *2nd*, 104
Market Street Wharf, 43
Marsh Island, 2-3, 194
Marshall, John, 1
Martello Tower, 13-15
Massachusetts Historical Society, 78
Massachusetts Troops: Infantry: *6th*, 184; *54th*, 128-134, 142
Maybank, Burnet, 194
Maynadier, William, 64
McClane (cutter), 34
McClellan, Edward P., 192
McCrady, Edward, 134
McCrady, Edward, Jr., xxiii, 60-61, 79, quote, 79
McCrady, John, xxiv, 61-62
McDowell, Irvin, 89
McGowan, J., 184
McGrath, Andrew, 153, quote, 153
McGregor, John Dr., 102
McHenry, James, 11
McQuire, Hugh, 170
McSweeney, Miles Benjamin, 185-186
Meade, Richard Kidder Jr., xxiv, 56-57, 60, 62-63
Meagher, Thomas Francis, 61, 87, 98
Means, Cotesworth Pinckney, 196
Medical College of South Carolina, 130
Merchant's Exchange Bank, 185
Mexican War, 38, 43, 45-46, 48, 60, 97
Michel, Francis, 35
Michigan Troops: Infantry: *1st*, 90-91, 96-97, 104; *4th*, 92, 100
Middle Ground, 121-122, 125, 137-138, 177
Middleton, Edward Barnwell, xxiv, 145, 147-149

Middleton, Maria, 162
Middleton, Thomas, 151, 154
Mikell, Robert, 201
Miles, William, Porcher, 114, 135
Minerva (brig), 10
Mintzing, Jacob Frederick, 75
Mississippi Troops: Infantry: *Mississippi Rifles*, 90, *Natchez Rifles*, 90
Mitchell, Nelson, 69-70, 134
Moncrieff, James, 5-6
Moncrieff's Battery, 5
Monroe, James, xxiv, 20-22, *image*, 22
Montalembert, Marquis de, 13
Montgomery, Alabama, 77, 80-82
Moog, George, 82
Morris Island, 42, 72-73, 75-76, 79-80, 83, 85, 93, 126-128, 130-131, 134-135, 137-139, 142, 145, 150-152, 154, 165, 183-184
Morris Island Lighthouse, 165, 184
Morrison, William, 195
Morse, Adolphus E., 140
Moultrie, William, 7-9, 192
Moultrieville Jail, 35
Mount Pleasant, South Carolina, 2, 21, 156, 194
Mudd, Samuel Alexander, 168
Mulcaster, Frederick George, 4
Munro, John, 47
Murdoch, Robert, 85
Murphy, James, 46
Museum at Market Hall (Confederate Museum at Market Hall), 101-102, 115-116, 129
Musgrove, Edward M., 192

Nance, William, 129
National Park Service, 191, 193-194, 196
Negro Seaman Law, 48
New Bedford Mercury, 142
New Orleans, Louisiana, 12, 20, 25, 41, 48, 98, 106, 122
New York Atlas, 91, 96
New York City, New York, 1, 11, 41, 48, 97, 161, 169
New York Evening Post, 72
New York Express, 83
New York Harbor, 13, 15, 22, 83, 91
New York Herald, 91, 134, 137-138
New York Times, 97, 104
New York Tribune, 85, 132

New York Troops: Artillery: *3rd*, 164; Infantry: *11th*, 90; *38th*, 97, 103; *69th*, 90, 98; *79th*, 90, 92, 95, 100; *127th*, 162
New York World, 172
Newman John, P., 185
Niagara (steamer), 50
Nina (steamer), 58, 61, 63
Nohrden, Carsten, xxiv, 76, 79
Northeastern Railroad Station, 90
Nullification Crisis, 25-26, 31, 33-35, 74-75

Oberlin College, 99
Ohio Troops: Infantry: *4th*, 170; *7th*, 91
Orr, James L., 58, 164, 167
Osceola, 38
Osiris (steamer), 71

Page, Orange, 163
Parker, Charles, 43
Parker, Isaac, 23
Parker, Niles Gardner, xxiv, 164-165, quote, 165, *image*, 166
Parker, William, 186
Patrick, M. A., 26-27
Pemberton, John C., 120-123
Pender, William Dorsey, 82
Pennsylvania Troops: Infantry: *16th*, 184; *52nd*, 154-155; *104th*, 142, 145
Peronneau, William Henry, xxiv, 128-130, 138, 144
Perrault, Paul Hyacinthe, 8
Perrin, Harry, 97
Petersburg Railroad, 90
Petigru, James Louis, 60, 94
Petit, James Percival, 197
Pettigrew, James Johnston, xxiv, 54, 58-63, 65-66, 69-72, 74-75, 86, 215-216, *image*, 55
Pettigrew, William, 97
Philadelphia Press, 146
Pickens, Francis Wilkinson, xxv, 57-60, 63, 69-70, 73, 80, 120, 123 quote, 70, 80
Pickering, Timothy, 10
Pierce, Franklin, 48
Pinckney, B. G., 60
Pinckney, Charles Cotesworth, xxv, 1, 5, 11, 17, 20, *image*, 7
Pinckney, Thomas, xxv, 8, 11, 19, 196
Planter (steamship), 121-122, 162
Platt, Charles, 47

Poinsett, Joel Roberts, xxv, 29, 31, *sketch*, 31, quote, 29, 31
Polly (brig), 16
Polony, Jean Louis, 9
Port Royal, South Carolina, 113, 150
Porter, Anthony Toomer Rev., xxv, 59, 65, quote, 59, 65
Porter, Charles, 193, quote, 193
Porter, Giles, 38
Porter, John B., xxv, 46-47
Porter, Noah, 96
Poussin, Guillaume Tell, 22
Pringle, James Reid, xxv, 128, 151
Pringle, Rosa, 162

Randolph, George W., 122
Ravenel Daniel, 196
Ravenel, Elizabeth M., 164, quote, 164
Ravenel, Henry William, 153, quote, 153
Read, Jacob, 15
Reading, J. D., 163
Rebellion Road, 2
Relyea, C. J., 121
Rembaugh, Alonzo Clark, 166
Reynolds, Frank, 65
Rhett, Alfred Moore, xxvi, 128, 141, 151, 154, 156-157
Rhett, Robert Barnwell Jr., 44, 54
Rhett's Point, 2
Rhode Island Troops: Artillery: *3rd*, 138, 150, 155
Richmond, Virginia, 90, 98, 103, 105-106, 113, 119-120, 122, 129, 134, 140, 146-147, 152-153, 202
Richmond Examiner, 90
Richmond Prison Association, 98
Riecke, Anthony Wilhelm, xxvi, 93, 114-115, 117-119, *image*, 117, quote, 93, 114-115, 118-119
Ringgold, Samuel, 33
Ripley, James W., 31
Ripley, Roswell Sabine, xxvi, 73, 85, 103, 113-116, 123, 125-127, 141, *image*, 127, quotes, 125-126
Rivers, Mendel, 193-194
Rodman, Hugh, 189
Rogers, William, 4
Roland, John Frederick, 46
Romain (brig), 11

Index

Rome Arsenal, New York, 164
Roosevelt, Franklin D., 189
Root, Elihu, 185-186
Rosen, Robert, 118, 151
Rubenstein Library, Duke University, 151
Ruffin, Edmund, xxvi, 73, 80, quote, 73, 80
Ruffner, E.H., 186
Rutledge, Edward, 9-10

Salisbury, North Carolina, 98, 105
Sallie, 102
Salmon, Matthew, 10
Sandlapper (magazine), 197
Saunders, Henry, xxvi, 26-27, 29-32, 34-35, quote, 26, 27, 34-35
Savannah, Georgia, 84, 113, 120, 128, 140, 142, 153, 163, 186, 189
Savannah Railroad, 113
Scanlan, Charles, 114
Schimmelfennig, Alexander, 151-152
Scott, Robert, 97
Scott, Winfield, xxvi, 28, 30-32, 34, 83, 117, quote, 31
Seabrooks, Whitemarsh, 43
Secession Crisis of 1832-33, 26-34,
Secession Crisis of 1850-51, 43-44
Secessionville, battle of, 122
Second System (coastal fortifications), 11, 13
Seminole Indian chiefs (Cloud, Coahajo, Micanopy, Osceola), 38
Seminole War, 38, 45, 54
Seven Days, battle of, 140
Shanaghy, Michael, 46
Sharpe, Edwin, 19-20
Shaw, Robert Gould, 128, 130-131
Sherman, John, 161
Sherman, Thomas, 101
Sherman, William T., 43, 152-153, 157, quote, 152
Shurtleff, Giles W., 91, 97, 99
Shute, Joseph, 2-3
Shute's Folly: defense of, 5, 15, 29, 38; description of, 2, 4, 5, 8, 42, 92, 101, 121-122, 184-185; *image*, 195; meaning of folly, 2-3; pirates, 3-4; shrinking, 5, 194, 205-206; *map*, 5; storm damage, 23, 176, 181-182
Sickles, Daniel Edgar, xxvi, 164, 166-171, *image*, 165
Silkenat, David, 89

Simms, William Gilmore, 114
Simons, James, 63, 69-70
Simonton, Charles, 60, 79
Sixth Lighthouse District, 176, 178, 181-182, 187-189
Skillin, James (Skillen), xxvii, 54, 56, 60-63, 164-165, 172, quote, 62
Skillin, Katherine (Katie), 63, 164, 172
Slocum, Henry, 157
Smalls, Robert, 121-122, 162
Smith, Bill, 192
Smythe, Augustine Thomas, 142, 144, quote, 142, 144
Snow Drop, 188
Sol Legare Island, battle of, 128
Sons of Confederate Veterans, 196, 198
South Carolina Historical Society, 78, 145, *image*, 78, 117
South Carolina Institute for Archeology and Anthropology (SCIAA), 202
South Carolina Troops: Artillery Units: *1st (Rhett's Regiment)*, 119-120, 124, 135, 137, 145, 149, 154, 156-157, 223-230; *1st Battalion*, 119; *15th (Lucas Battalion)*, 86; *Gist Guard Heavy Artillery*, 119; Cavalry Units: *5th*, 145; Infantry Units: *1st*, 87; *25th*, 145; *27th*, 145; *Charleston Battalion*, 134; *Hampton Legion*, 119; Militia Units: *1st Regiment Artillery*, 63; *1st Regiment Rifles*, 54, 58, 60, 71, 86, 90, 93; *4th Brigade*, 60; *Beauregard Light Infantry*, 90; *Cadet Riflemen*, 35, 63; *Carolina Light Infantry*, 60, 65, 69, 71, 75, 90; *Charleston City Guard*, 102; *Charleston Light Dragoons*, 54, 91; *Charleston Riflemen*, 54; *Charleston Zouave Cadets*, 90-95, 101-101, 104-106, 108-111, 114-119, 222-223; *Emerald Light Infantry*, 87, 114, 118; *German Artillery*, 63, 75-76, 79; *German Fusiliers*, 54, 79; *German Hussars*, 91; *German Riflemen*, 79, 90; *Jamison Rifles*, 90; *Jasper Greens*, 54, 87; *Lafayette Artillery*, 63; *Marion Artillery*, 63, 65, 71, 76, 78-79, 85, 145, 149; *Meagher Guards*, 54, 60-61, 65, 71, 75, 79, 87, 114, 118, 210-211; *Montgomery Guards*, 54, 87; *Moultrie Guard*, 90; *Palmetto Guards*, 54, 63; *Palmetto Riflemen*, 79, 90; *Sumter Guard*, 35; *Union Light Infantry*, 33; *Vigilant Rifles*, 54; *Washington Artillery*, 63; *Washington Light*

Infantry, 33, 54, 60-66, 71, 75, 79, 90, 211-212, *image*, 67
South Carolina Ordinance of Secession, 58
South Carolina Ports Authority, 194-196, 198-199
South Carolina 1860 Secession Convention, 58, 119
South Carolina Shrine Organization, 196
Spann, John R., 18
Spooner, William, 150
St. Andrew's Hall, 58, 104
St. Augustine, 4, 38-39, 172
St. Matthew's Church, 75
St. Michael's Church, 1, 178-179
St. Philip's Church, 182
Stanton, Edwin, 133, 169
Star of the West (steamer), 72-73, 93
Stegall, John., 151
Stono Inlet, 121
Stono River, 86, 114, 121, 128
Stowers, Francis Gaines, 167
Straton, James, 35
Stribling, Francis, 18
Strong, George, C., 131
Sullivan's Island, 19, 30, 44, 55, 71, 73, 79-81, 101, 118, 123, 126-127, 129-130, 138, 141, 166, 183
Sumner, Charles, 133
Swartwout, Henry, 44-45

Taliaferro, William Booth, 131
Tariff of Abominations, 25
Taylor, Chester, 195
Taylor, George, 6
Taylor, James, 20
Terry, Alfred, 128
The Ghosts of Castle Pinckney, 192
The Statesman, 156
Third system (coastal fortifications), 22, 37
Thomas Swan (steamer), 82
Thomas, George H., 43
Tickler (fishing smack), 41
Tidball, John Caldwell, xxvii, 44, 46-47
Tillman, Ben, 185
Torch (torpedo boat), 139
Townsend, Edward, 49-50
Trapier, James Heyward, xxvii, 38, *image*, 39
Tredegar Iron Works, 146, 152, 202, *image*, 203

Trenholm, George, Alfred, 118
Trescot, William Henry, 130-131, 169
Treville, Robert De, xxvii
Trumbull, Lyman, 161
Turner, James A., 197
Turner, W. P., 151
Tuttle, James Gilmore, xxvii, 92, 97, 99-101, 105, quote, 92, 97, 105
Two Friends (schooner), 4
Tyler, John, 32

Union War Prisoners Association, 99, 169, image, 99
U.S. Coast Guard, 189, 196
U.S. Corps of Engineer Supply Depot, 191-194, *image*, 192
U.S. Custom House, 11, 29, 63, 73, 181
U.S. Troops: Artillery Battalions: *1st*, 21; Artillery Regiments: *1st*, 26, 37, 54; *2nd*, 9, 18-19, 26, 44; *3rd*, 35, 44; Cavalry Units: *1st Dragoons*, 82; Colored Infantry: *19th*, 170; *21st*, 154, 162-163; *26th*, 163; *33rd*, 165; *35th*, 163-165; *37th*, 166, 171; *40th*, 170; *128th*, 163, 165-166; Infantry: *6th*, 163, 166, 170; *7th*, 38-39; *8th*, 166, 172; *9th*, 86; *12th*, 172; *18th*, 19; *40th*, 172; *43rd*, 19
U.S. Lighthouse Service: 175-179, 188-191
U.S. War Department, 1, 9-10, 38-39, 54, 86, 154, 175, 186, 189, 193
USLHT *Pharos*, 187
USLHT *Alanthus*, 178
USLHT *Cypress*, 189
USLHT *Mangrove*, 189
USLHT *Wisteria*, 178-181, 187-189, *image*s, 180, 181
USS *Chesapeake*, 12
USS *Dolphin*, 49
USS *Experiment*, 30
USS *Housatonic*, 141
USS *Keokuk*, 126-127
USS *Lynx*, 20
USS *Mahopac*, 156
USS *Natchez*, 30
USS *New Ironside*, 126
USS *Onward*, 122
USS *Passaic*, 126
USS *Prometheus*, 20
USS *W. W. Coit*, 161
USS *Weehawken*, 127

University College London (UCL), 203
University of South Carolina, Institute of Archeology, 197

Valentine Museum, Richmond, 106
Van Vort, James H., 165
Vanderlyn, John, 22
Vermont Troops: Infantry: *2nd*, 93
Verplanck, Guilian, 32
Vias, Robert, 35
Vicksburg, battle of, 123, 130

Wade, Benjamin, 161
Wagener, John Andreas, xxvii, 75-79, quote, 76, *image*, 76, 78
Walker, Leroy Pope, 77, 81-82
Walker, William S., 142
Walpole, B. M., 111
Walters William T., 82
War of 1812, 17-18, 45, 59, 146
Warren Lasch Conservation Center, North Charleston, 141
Washington, George: birthday observance, 33, 80; Charleston visit, 5-8; president, 1, 8; Revolutionary War, 5, 62
Washington, J. McPherson, 78-79
Washington, William, 9, 78
Water Lily, 187
Waud, Alfred, 85
Waud, William: xxvii, 85, *sketch*, 75
Welsh, William, xxvii, 170, 172
West Point Military Academy, 38, 43-48, 65, 73, 77, 82, 120

Wheeler, Joseph, 157
White, Edward Brickell, xxviii, 10, 70, 73-74, quote, 74
White, Edwin J., 118
White, E. John, 108, 111
White, Thomas Hamlin, 164
Whiteley, Annie Brown, 178-180, 184
Whiteley, Henry "Bunty," 184, *image*, 183
Whiteley, James Wilfred, xxviii, 178, 182-183, 187-188, *image*, 179
Whiteley, Mary, 181
Whiteley, Pinckney Lamberton, 178
Wigfall, Louis T., 81-83
Wilbur Smith Associates, 197
Wiley, Thomas, 94
Willcox, Orlando Bolivar, xxviii, 91, 95-97, 99, 103-104, quote, 95, 103
Williams, Jonathan, 13-16
Wills, Henry O., 82
Wilson, John Lyde, 21
Wilson, W. B., 185
Winchester Republican, 30
Winder, Charles, S., 86
Wisconsin Troops: Infantry: *2nd*, 184; *3rd*, 184
Wise, Stephen, 130
Withington, William Herbert, xxviii, 100, 104

Yates, Joseph Atkinson, xxviii, 119-120, 159
Yellow Fever, 9, 35, 39, 41-43, 46-47, 49

Zeigler, Clyde, 194
Zouave uniform, 94

About the Authors

W. Clifford Roberts, Jr. (left) is a retired businessman and educator and co-author of *Atlanta's Fighting 42nd: Joseph Johnston's "Old Guard"* (2020). Cliff was raised outside of Washington, D.C. He has a BA in Southern History from Vanderbilt University (1981) and an MBA from Emory University (1983). Cliff is an active board member of several historical, preservation, and genealogical associations. He lives with his wife Vicki and their dog Hashbrown in downtown Charleston.

Matthew Locke (right) was born and educated in London where he worked as an Executive Officer in the British Civil Service. As a passionate student of the Civil War and living historian, he visited Charleston in 1999, fell in love with the city, and became fascinated with Castle Pinckney. He moved to South Carolina in 2001 and began researching the history of the Castle and Shute's Folly Island. In 2021, he was appointed as a Guardian of Castle Pinckney and works there with archaeologists, historians, and conservationists. Matthew, his wife Jacqueline, and daughter Abigail live just outside of Charleston.